WATCHDOG: A HISTORY OF THE CANADIAN PROVOST CORPS

ANDREW R. RITCHIE

Watchdog

A HISTORY OF THE CANADIAN PROVOST CORPS

THE CANADIAN PROVOST CORPS ASSOCIATION

Copyright © 1995 by Andrew R. Ritchie

ISBN 0-9699647-0-6

Printed by University of Toronto Press Incorporated

Design: William Rueter

Canadian Cataloguing in Publication Data

Ritchie, Andrew R.
  Watchdog : a history of the Canadian Provost Corps

  ISBN 0-9699647-0-6

  1. Canada. Canadian Army. Canadian Provost Corps – History.
  2. Canada – Armed forces – Military police – History.
  I. Canadian Provost Corps Association. II. Title.

UB825.C3R57 1995   355.1′3323′0971   C95-931515-2

The Canadian Provost Corps Association
P.O. Box 62007
Burlington, Ontario
L7R 4K2

Contents

Foreword   vii
Acknowledgements   xi

1 The First Provost   3
2 The Corps is Born   15
3 Early Days in the United Kingdom   23
4 Bumper, Tiger and Spartan   43
5 The Dieppe Raid   50
6 Sicily, Italy and Goldflake   56
7 Northwest Europe, June 1944–October 1945   64
8 The Reichwald, Hochwald, Groningen and Victory   92
9 Repatriation   105
10 The War in Canada   113
11 The Interim Force   130
12 Absentees and Deserters   137
13 Beginning The Resurrection   144
14 Provost in the Militia   155
15 Korea   165
16 NATO   192
17 Towards Professionalism   202
18 Lonely Postings   221
19 Brotherhood and Badges   235
20 A Few Good Men   256

References and Notes   290
Appendices   307

Foreword

Watchdog is more than a compilation of historical data concerning the Canadian Provost Corps. It is, primarily, a story of challenge and achievement told through the personal experience of people who were there. Sometimes the challenge was easily met; at other times it was extremely difficult, requiring courage, imagination, conviction and improvisation. Thus, it is a story about people in war and peace since, at all times, the accomplishment of the task depended on the dedication and emergent leadership of the individual Provost person who made a profound impact on the high standards achieved by the Canadian Provost Corps.

The author, Colonel Andrew Ritchie, served with the Provost Corps throughout the greater part of its existence and experienced, firsthand, the growing pains of an organization new to the Canadian Army. He has captured the essence of the early problems when the Corps was learning its trade and step-by-step, with the side use of personal experiences of then serving members, takes the reader through the gradual development of the skills and professionalism of the men of the Corps to the point when it was required to put its organization and training to the test by the exacting standards of actual operations.

If the ultimate test of the professionalism of a Corps is its ability to adjust and adapt to the everchanging conditions of employment in war and peace, then the performance of the various units of the Canadian Provost Corps, from its creation in 1940 until its formal dissolution in 1968, was outstanding. As the Canadian Army, and its involvement in World War II, developed so did the Canadian Provost Corps grow in expanded responsibilities, stature and numbers. This was not by accident! From the very outset careful attention was paid to selection and training of Provost, augmented by a solid nucleus of trained men from the Royal Canadian

Mounted Police, permanent force and militia. The resultant professionalism displayed by Provost units, primarily in traffic control, made them indispensable to Commanders who did not hesitate to assign them additional roles as situations developed, in such aspects as PWs, stragglers and refugees. To quote Field Marshal Montgomery (1945): "The Battle of Normandy, and subsequent battles, would never have been won but for the work and cooperation of Provost on the traffic routes." It was not surprising, therefore, that the Canadian Provost Corps was the only 'new' Corps added to the military establishment after World War II. Gratefully, Andy Ritchie includes the entire 'minutes' of a conference held in 1949 which, in my opinion, established the firm foundation for the postwar Provost Corps, and is indicative of the farsightedness of the senior officers of the Corps at the time. Thereafter, wherever the Canadian Army served on NATO or United Nations operations the Provost Corps was included. At home it assumed full police responsibilities at NDHQ and all Army camps until absorbed by the Security Branch, in the unified Canadian Forces, in 1968.

The style of this history combines historical data with a free flowing narrative, which makes for an interesting and easy read. Worldwide and purely Canadian historical events are outlined, followed by the manner in which these historical milestones impacted on the Canadian Army and, ultimately, shaped the Canadian Provost Corps. His use of several anecdotal narratives gives *Watchdog* a human dimension and dispels the tendency of any historical writing to become a somewhat dull dissertation of facts. It is also clear that a conscious effort has been made throughout this book to promote a better understanding of the ordinary Canadian soldiers and the problems they faced in day-to-day military life, in and out of battle.

I cannot imagine anyone more suited to write this history than Andy Ritchie. It is a story that needed to be told, and it is admirable that it has been done by a devoted Provost who was in a position to know because he lived through it all from July 1940 as a private until his retirement in September 1967 as a colonel. In fact, Andy Ritchie was the last Provost Marshal (Army) and the first Director of Security in the unified Canadian Forces. It should be noted that he has elected to not to include himself in the Chapter *A Few Good Men* nor, for example, has he identified himself in the book where he was Commanding Officer, 13 Provost Company during Normandy operations described in Chapter 7. As for his qualifications under *A Few Good Men*, suffice to say that after 27 years of military service, Andy Ritchie still continues his active involvement with former Provost Corps members and the Security Branch through their respective associations. Following retirement from the Canadian Army he continued to serve as a volunteer in several local and national organizations, including 15 years in St. John Ambulance (Ontario) where he became one of five Area Commissioners. As a volunteer Probation and Parole Officer in Metropolitan Toronto he was actively involved in liaison between the courts and various offenders for another 7 years, and he still actively supports such worthy institutions as the Canadian War Museum, the Conference of Defence Association Institute and the Royal Canadian Military Institute. He was the first patron of the Canadian Security Officers Association and served as the Colonel Commandant of the Canadian Provost Corps Association for 8 years, until 1990. To top off the commitment of this outstanding serviceman and Provost to his Corps, for the past several years he has been researching and writing this book.

In conclusion, *Watchdog* fills an important gap in the published history of the Canadian Army detailing, as it does, in a personal way the origin, the people, the challenges and achievements of a Corps which occupied a place in the military establishment for 28 years but which no longer exists today - The Canadian Provost Corps. This book is required reading for all former Provost members for, like I, you will relive memories and become aware of events and aspects of your Corps which you did not know previously. For military historians, and others, it will serve as a most useful reference about a Corps which existed only 28 years but whose impact on the current Security Branch is still being felt some 25 years later because of the selection standards, training, motivation and dedication of its members of Provost background.

Brigadier General Walter J. Dabros, CD

Acknowledgements

Given the enormous volume of historical writing on the varied activities of the Canadian Army in two world wars, as well the turbulent post-nuclear era, it is surprising that almost nothing has been recorded on the organization and work of the Canadian Provost Corps and its predecessor, the Canadian Corps of Military Police. This book is an attempt to redress this omission. It traces some of the salient features of the provost service of the Canadian Army up to the Unification of the Navy, Army and Air Force on 1 February 1968.

The Corps of Military Police and the Canadian Provost Corps of the Canadian Army were forerunners of the current Security Branch of the Canadian Armed Forces. I was a little surprised, and greatly encouraged, to find there was no serious shortage of research material, although personal knowledge of persons and events greatly assisted in locating information. As a necessary prelude to the activities of the Corps it was necessary to establish the general settings of the Canadian Army during the period covered. The major source for these events was the four volumes of the Official History of the Canadian Army by our illustrious historian Colonel Charles P Stacey, and his accomplice Lieutenant Colonel G W L Nicholson. The splendid work of contemporary historian Desmond Morton, *A Military History of Canada*, provided much relevant information, as did several wartime regimental histories such as *Dileas* (*48th Highlanders*) by Kim Beattie, and *Warpath* (*Algonquin Regiment*) by George Cassidy. My personal *Staff Officer's Notebook*, which I carefully prepared during my time as a student at the Canadian Army Staff College in Kingston (1951) was a most useful reference for much staff data on the Canadian Army of that era. A great deal of highly relevant information was gleaned from a personal, almost complete, set of Canadian Army Journals from 1954 to 1965.

The information of a purely Corps nature came from a variety of sources, all authentic and for the most part non-contradictory, thus enhancing their credibility and easing the burden of verification. Sources included material from the National Archives in Ottawa, such as war diaries, provost reports and orders-in-council. A detailed *Résuméd History of the Canadian Provost Corps*, prepared by Colonel P A Puize as of 31 August 1943, was a fountain of information for the Corps' early years. My personal books and papers, gathered over a fifty year period, justified their storage space by making it possible to write, with much assurance, on a variety of events. I carried out personal or telephone interviews with over thirty former Corps members relative to matters where each had a special knowledge. Perhaps the single most important contribution came from a number of personal, anecdotal narratives provided, in response to my written request, by forty former Corps members. These short but poignant vignettes worked wonders in relieving the monotonous recital of bare, historical facts. Equally important, this generous support from my colleagues did much to bolster my sometimes flagging motivation to complete this venture. Like myself none of these contributors are names known in most households, nevertheless it is entirely fitting that they be listed here. They are well known to myself and to each other, and richly deserve mention.

A W (Alan) Abrams, Zurich, Ontario
H M (Howie) Baker, Beaconfield, Quebec
E (Sid) Batty, Surrey, British Columbia
A S (Art) Bird, Victoria, British Columbia
G (George) Blyth, Colborne, Ontario
R F (Reg) Bornor, Barrie, Ontario
A G (Sandy) Cameron, Toronto, Ontario
W E R (Ray) Chambers, Thamesford, Ontario
E (Chris) Christensen, East York, Ontario
W J (Walter) Dabros, Kingston, Ontario
J A (John) Dowsett, Kingston, Ontario
J S (Jack) Dunn, Ottawa, Ontario
G (George) Elliott, Kingston, Ontario
J V (Jim) Findlay, Agincourt, Ontario
M L (Marcel) Fortier, Gloucester, Ontario
W (Walter) Gatehouse, Penetanguishene, Ontario
A (André) Gauthier, Orleans, Ontario
R T (Bob) Grogan, Nepean, Ontario
O (Orval) Hanna, Burnt River, Ontario

B S (Burt) Hebert, Gabriola Island, British Columbia
L N (Lorne) Henderson, Nepean, Ontario
R J H (Reg) High, Courtenay, British Columbia
J (Jim) Hooper, Ottawa, Ontario
J D (Jim) Lumsden, Nepean, Ontario
A E (Tony) Macaskill, Halifax, Nova Scotia
H (Howie) Mansfield, Gloucester, Ontario
M A (Moe) Martin, Toronto, Ontario
J L (Laurie) Paulhus, Nepean, Ontario
W J (Bill) Patterson, Calgary, Alberta
T J (Tom) Quirk, Vancouver, British Columbia
A B (Robbie) Robertson, Victoria, British Columbia
G (Gary) Roncetti, Port Perry, Ontario
A J (Tony) Scotti, Sebastian, Florida
A H (Sam) Stevenson, North Delta, British Columbia
S W (Syd) Sweeting, Mississauga, Ontario
R G (Bob) Thomas, Burlington, Ontario
D (Don) Tresham, Ottawa, Ontario
J (Jim) Walsh, Westmount, Cape Breton, Nova Scotia
G (George) Wilkinson, Victoria, British Columbia
A E (Earl) Wilson, Victoria, British Columbia

At the very least *Watchdog* should serve as a start-point for any future historian who may, in the fullness of time, wish to extend and expand on this original record. Finally, I am much indebted to my son Ian, a writer and published author, for his careful review of the initial manuscript and providing a list of valuable comments and suggestions. Any errors or omissions are solely my own.

A.R.R.

WATCHDOG: A HISTORY OF THE CANADIAN PROVOST CORPS

1

The First Provost

This is the story of an organization that was hastily formed by Army headquarters in Ottawa during the early months of World War II. It was named the Canadian Provost Corps and its function was to provide police service for the Canadian Army at home and abroad. Apart from the Canadian Military Police Corps (CMPC), which functioned from 1917 to 1920 in World War I, this was a new addition to Canada's military establishment. It was launched without benefit of cadre, without any doctrine, equipment or precise role. There was no guideline for establishments, standards or training. It had no tradition to fall back on nor did it have any of the trappings so cherished by the older NPAM regiments and corps such as badges, buttons, guidons, marches, bands or former heroes and special people. Its very newness was, perhaps, its only advantage since it had no skeletons to hide or unpleasantness to ignore.

While new to the Canadian Army there had been a police or provost service in some of the earliest armies of the world. History clearly records the presence of this element as far back as the Roman army at the time of Augustus Caesar[1] 27BC–14AD. The Praetorian Guard was an elite force which varied in size between three and ten cohorts[2]. It was stationed in Rome with the task of suppressing riots and insurrections and protecting the Emperor. Augustus decided this body of troops was too large and unwieldy to be effective for his personal protection. He wanted a smaller, loyal and handpicked group so he formed a special inner corps which he named "Speculatore", the first provost. Michael Grant, in his Army of the Caesars, states[3]; "These legionary Speculatores continued to exist during the empire, being especially employed for the carrying of urgent despatches and, in addition, for military police functions of various kinds". The Speculatore were privileged above the ordinary legionnaire in various ways such as twelve years mandatory service instead of twenty, and pay of 375 denarii per month versus 225. They also received a cash gratuity on discharge of 5000 denarii as opposed to 3000 for a regular. Marcus Antonius honoured his Speculatore by the issue of a coin with the words "Cohortus Speculatorum" on the obverse side. The reverse shows three standards, ornamented by wreaths, on the prow of a ship. A high honour indeed.

The word "provost" came into general use in the British army in the early fourteenth century. It is derived from the old English word "prafast" or the French "profost", in turn from the medieval Latin term "propositus praeponera" meaning "placed before". Thus a literal translation is "one in authority" from "prae" before, and "ponera" to place.

Edward III had a Provost Marshal in his army at Crecy, in 1346. Historians have recorded many references to the existence of provost in the British and French armies from the fourteenth century onward. If the King required provost to enforce discipline in an army raised by baronial levy among under privileged peasants, the reasons for a lack of discipline is not hard to find. Although brave and stalwart in battle, the soldiers need for food, health and basic necessities was almost totally ignored. Food was obtained by foraging off the countryside and local inhabitants; looting was a means of supplementing the meagre pay and when wounded or ill they had to depend on a comrade for aid and comfort. A more sinister and common cause of undisciplined conduct was the provision and availability of alcoholic drink, in copious quantities. The neglect of the common soldier and the disparities between their lot and the privileged nobles and knights is described by the early French historian, Jean Froissart[4]:

The King and his rich lords were followed by carts laden with tents, pavilions, mills, and forges to grind their corn and make shoes for their horses, and everything of that sort which might be wanting. But the common soldier made use of what provisions they could get.

Charles I in the decade preceding the civil war in England, 1642–51, issued one of several regulations for the organization and duties of provost in the military. One such proclamation states[5]:

The provost must have a horse allowed him and some soldiers to assist him and all the rest commanded to obey and assist, or else the Service will suffer; for he is but one man and must correct many and therefore he cannot be beloved.

And he must be riding from one garrison to another to see the soldiers do no outrage nor scathe the country.

The First Provost

A lack of discipline in Wellington's army during the Peninsula War is illustrated by the following description of the rape, pillage and murder carried out by the victorious British troops following the capture of the fortress at Badajoz (Spain) in April 1812[6], at the cost of huge casualties:

What scenes of horror did I witness there. They can never be effaced from my memory. There was no safety for the women even in the churches; and any who interfered or resisted were sure to get shot. Every house presented a scene of plunder, debauchery and bloodshed, committed with wanton cruelty on the defenceless inhabitants by our soldiery. All of this from what had been, twelve short hours previously, a well-organized, brave, disciplined and obedient British army.

We can only guess what caused these excesses following victory in battle. Wellington had a Provost Marshal (and provost men) who was under orders to: "execute any men he may find in the act of plunder. This being so, one must assume that all ranks were also well aware of this severe penalty, yet it had no apparent deterrent affect. In any event, the Provost Marshal and his provost assistants of this era were not only empowered to arrest persons found committing offences, but it was also their duty to judge guilt or innocence, to pronounce and finally carry out the sentence[7]. No wonder he could not be beloved.

Colonel R Coulin in his *Historique et Traditiones de la Gendarmerie Nationale* traces the Police Militaire of the French army back to the early fourteenth century. The early marechausse were mounted cavalry trained to carry out police duties in wartime. In 1536 this organization was also tasked with carrying out some security and police services for the civilian population. In 1791, the marechausse were succeeded, in fact absorbed, by the Gendarmerie Nationale which has been in continuous existence to this day. This proud Force participated in most of France's wars[8] at home and abroad, including the battles of Holdschoote (near Dunkirk) 1793, Villodrigo (Spain) 1812, Taquin (Algeria) 1843, Sebastopol 1855 and Indochina 1945–1954. In addition to their military police functions they now police the smaller towns and highways in all of France. That they have long held a position of importance in the Army is illustrated by an extract of a letter sent by Napoleon to one of his Marshals, during the long march of the Imperial Army to invade Russia[9]: "My cousin, you inform me that there are 520 policemen in the Army. This number is sufficient but they are wrongly distributed. I do not understand why policemen should be employed to guard baggage. A military policeman is not a rider. He is a policeman who must be assigned a position." Regrettably, the misuse of military policemen on mundane tasks has continued to be a vexing problem for those primarily responsible for the discharge of authorized military police duties.

The foregoing narration touches on the origin of military police in early European armies. There are two or three conclusions. Most obvious is the uncertainty that large bodies of troops will continue to behave in a disciplined manner when living, moving and fighting on foreign soil. Secondly, the behaviour of any army closely reflects the prevailing social standards of its country. Finally, the employment of a well-trained, disciplined police and security corps may be one of the few options left to senior commanders to ensure a consistent and uniform system of law and order whether at home stations, in a foreign land or during battle.

The World War I Story

At the outset of what we now call World War I, the Canadian military contained absolutely nothing that even remotely resembled a military police element. In fact it contained very little of any element required by a country which was about to wage all out war, in a foreign land, against a formidable foe. On 4 August 1914 the small Permanent force consisted of two cavalry regiments, two batteries of field artillery, an infantry regiment, the Royal Canadian Regiment (RCR) and a few service support troops such as engineers, signals, supply and transport, ordnance and medical corps. The bulk of the non-permanent militia was contained in some sixty-five battalion-size units comprising cavalry (the armoured corps not yet formed), artillery and infantry. All were under strength and few had any equipment. In what must be considered a miracle, the Canadian people produced in the next four years a fighting force of 628,000[10] men. Of this number 60,000 were killed in battle.

During the first years of the War the small Regimental Police (RPs) section of infantry regiments was the only police element of the army. Their main task seems to have been supervising defaulters, clearing canteens at closing time and guarding soldiers under arrest in guardrooms. They were "badged" as members of their regiments and were selected on the basis of good conduct and reliability. Their policing responsibilities only applied to members of the regiment. This situation prevailed until October 1917 when the Canadian Military Police Corps was authorized by General Orders 93 and 94 issued by the Minister of Militia and Defence. Privy Council Order 722 of 22 March 1918, which was promulgated to the Army by CEF Routine Order 486 of 25 April 1918, conferred corps status on the military police detachments under the designation "Canadian Military Police Corps". This action was instrumental in coordinating military police activity at home and abroad. It resulted in a marked improvement in the dress, deportment and general discipline of the troops throughout Canada. These orders set out in some detail, the organization, command and establishment of this new Corps. The strength was to be 30 officers, 13 warrant officers class 2, 11 quarter-master sergeants, 14 sergeant clerks, 100 sergeants, 100 corporals and 582 lance-corporals for a total 850 all ranks. It was specifically directed that the majority, at least two-thirds of the personnel, were to be transferred from officers and soldiers of good character who had been or were still serving at the Front. A Provost Marshal with the rank of Colonel was authorized along with a Deputy Assistant Adjutant General (DAAG) in the rank of Lieutenant Colonel. Assistant Provost Marshals (Majors), Deputy Assistant Provost Marshals (Majors) and/or Deputy Assistant Provost Marshals (Captains), were provided on a scale of one each for the eleven military District headquarters across Canada[11]. It was further directed that 34 members were to be mounted and receive an additional 20 cents per diem pay, presumably as recompense for the extra duties of caring for the 34 mounts which were also authorized on the establishments. It is not known if the special "perks" given to his Speculatore by Augustus Caesar were used as a guideline in forming this military police organization. Coincident or otherwise, the General Order stipulated that 25 percent of the Corporals could be made Acting Sergeants without pay, and 50 percent of the Lance Corporals could be Acting Corporals, again without pay. There were no privates.

A Canadian Expeditionary Force (CEF) Routine Order of April 1918 (six months after the issue of GO 93/94) re-emphasized that only the best type of man was to be recommended for transfer to the CMPC, and that no transfer would be finalized until a one month probation period had expired, and the candidate was accepted by the CMPC.

Colonel Gilbert Godson Godson[12], DSO DCM was appointed Provost Marshal, Dominion of Canada on 4 December 1917. As a Company Commander with No 16 Battalion CEF he was severely wounded, twice mentioned-in-despatches, and awarded the Distinguished Service Order (DSO) and the Distinguished Conduct Medal (DCM). It seems most fitting that Canada's first ever Provost Marshal should so clearly possess those qualities prescribed for all ranks of the Military Police Corps in respect to service, character and experience. He was given very precise direction and powers with regard to his duties. He could issue orders to assistant Provost Marshals (under the command of General Officers Commanding) on technical matters involving police work; order an Assistant Provost Marshal to effect the arrest of any officer or soldier when sufficient evidence was available and visit and inspect *without* previous notification.

In a further move to improve the efficiency of this new Corps the CMPC School was formed at Ottawa, on 1 June 1918. Courses of three weeks duration were conducted for Military Policemen until it closed on 11 March 1919. This necessary part of the CMPC was commanded by an Assistant Provost Marshal with the rank of Major whose name, regrettably, we do not know.

Early in 1918, an APM and a detachment of CMPC personnel was established in New York City. This contingent reported to Colonel Godson Godson and shared responsibility with an already established British Military Police detachment for dealing with wayward Canadian servicemen, mainly deserters, in the Northeast region of the United States. Records indicate that it dealt with 958 cases up to 1 November 1918 when it was withdrawn and disbanded.

It is necessary to return to the overall political and military situation in order to find the reason for the belated action to form a military police element for the Forces. The overall military build up in Canada had proceeded at a rapid pace from a standing start. The defence budget had risen to $11 million by 1914. Large training camps had been established at Petawawa (1905), Valcartier (1914) and Borden. The Permanent Force strength in early 1914 was 3,110 with another 74,000 in the Militia (NPAM) across Canada.

Initially there was no problem filling the ranks of the Canadian Expeditionary Force (CEF) with eager volunteers. However, with the addition of a further 170 infantry battalions[13], together with cavalry, artillery and combat support units as well as the Navy and the Air Force, a serious manpower crisis soon emerged. Canada's population of 8 million simply could not supply manpower to staff an expanding military establishment now suffering staggering casualties[14], to say nothing about the demands of agriculture and a rapidly growing war industry.

After much political anguish, the Government of Robert Borden enacted the Military Service Act in December, 1917. This law basically stated that single men from twenty to thirty-four years must register and be liable for military service, unless exempted. The following excerpt from Desmond Morton's book, *A Military History of Canada*, tells us something about the aftermath of this Act.

It was not a brilliant success. Pressed for compromises and for the full protection of individual rights, Meighen's law said more about exemptions and appeals than service. Boards of Selection, in which government and opposition were equally represented, nominated 1,239 local tribunals. Their decisions could be questioned by 195 appeal courts and by a central appeal judge, Lyman Duff of the Supreme Court of Canada. Potential conscripts and their lawyers could find grounds for exemption ranging from family hardship to conscientious objection. When the first class (single men from twenty to thirty-four years of age) was notified, 280,510 of the 404,395 filed for exemption.

Further statements quoted from this well researched source are equally relevant.

In Quebec, local boards granted almost blanket exemption to French speaking applicants but, according to Duff's recollection, "they applied conscription against the English speaking minority of Quebec with a rigor unparalleled.

On January 3, when the first conscripts were ordered to report, barely twenty thousand appeared. Many who had failed to win exemptions simply disappeared. The small federal police forces, the Dominion Police in the East and the Royal Canadian Mounted Police in the West, had the thankless job of tracking them down. In Quebec a clash seemed inevitable. It came on Easter weekend in Quebec City. Military police seized a young man with no papers. Furious crowds attacked the Military Service Registry and tossed records into the snow. Then they roamed the streets, smashing windows of English owned businesses. Ottawa despatched General Tessard and the only available troops, seven hundred soldiers, from Toronto. At night on Easter Monday, a few soldiers, trapped in a square and pelted with ice and snow, opened fire. Four civilians were killed; many were injured. The violence shook everyone. The riots stopped.

No wonder the Prime Minister of Canada was most reluctant to invoke similar legislation some twenty two years later.

The Dominion Police had been organized in Ottawa earlier in response to the need for a force to perform ever-increasing police and security duties. it was a civil force with a total strength of about 780 in late 1917. On 31 May 1918, under Privy Council Order 754, this force was transferred from the Justice Department to the Department of Militia and Defence and placed under control of the Provost Marshal. It was designated as the "Civil Branch" of the CMPC with the primary task of assisting in the apprehension of absentees and defaulters under the Military Service Act.

The following statistics give some idea of the size and effort of the Canadian Corps of Military Police from June 1917 to November 1918:

CMPC strength in Canada	1853	(includes 300 cavalry to assist in MSA enforcement)
CMPC Civil Branch (Dominion Police)	969	
CMPC Overseas	484	
CMPC N.Y. City (estimated)	50	
Total	3356	

Apprehensions carried out under Military Service Act	19,824
Apprehended – failing to report	9,454
Arrests other than Military Service Act	12,915
Arrests for desertion	2,304

The Coolie Repatriation

In September 1919, nearly a year following the November 1918 armistice, there was an event which seems to have been ignored by historians. It centres on the employment of a large number of Chinese coolies in the British Expeditionary Force in France on pioneer or basic engineering tasks. They were used to dig trenches, construct earthworks, repair roads and related labour intensive jobs in a static field army. Records are not completely reliable however it is estimated there were about 100,000 of these coolies in France at the end of the War. The British government decided to return them to China which led to an agreement between the two governments whereby Canada would provide a military unit to process and handle them from their arrival by sea at Halifax, across Canada by rail to Vancouver. They would then be embarked in ships for seaports in China.

A Special Guard unit of the CMPC was formed in September 1919 for this task. It had a strength of 542 all ranks with a further detachment of 50 located at a Transit Camp at Williams Head, B C This work entailed long hours of train guard and escort duty between Halifax and Vancouver with little or no time off between trips. The fact that the majority of these labourers had no desire to return to their homeland greatly increased the degree of vigilance to be exercised by these military policemen. It was a continuous round of head counts, unloading, supervision of train boarding, feeding, exercise, day and night shifts, de-training, more head counts and supervision of embarkation at Vancouver. Incomplete records account for 48,276 moved across Canada between September 1919 and April

1920, however it is believed the true figure is closer to 70,000. This unit was composed entirely of men who had overseas experience in World War 1. It was reported that their dress, discipline and deportment was "second to none". The Special Guard was disbanded on 30 June, 1920 and the Canadian Military Police Corps ceased to exist.

With all the privilege of hindsight it is quite easy to question some aspects of the short-lived CMPC organization, and comment on others. It appears that they were not given any special powers of arrest but relied on their ranks, as superior officers, to effect an arrest. Why else would the appointment of so many LANCE ranks be made? The estimate of total numbers required must have been an educated guess since there was no precedent. Finally, it seems obvious that the formation of a military police corps so late in the war was due to about equal parts of military need, and the political necessity caused, in large measure, by the conscription issue. The most positive aspect must surely be the good judgement used in staffing the Corps with reliable, disciplined and experienced soldiers from units of the Canadian Expeditionary force.

The RCMP

Canada's first national police force was organized in 1873 to meet an urgent need for the introduction of law and order in the vast, empty prairie lands lying between Manitoba and the Rockies, North of the forty-ninth parallel. Reports reaching John A MacDonald in Ottawa told of ever increasing lawlessness in the form of wholesale murder, horse-stealing, drunken brawling and Indian fights. American wolfers[15], whiskey traders and an assortment of US Army deserters, smugglers, gamblers and whiskey-runners supplied the Indians with incredibly bad booze[16], in return for horses, furs or buffalo robes. In order to correct this situation and restore control to this vast territory, the Government enacted legislation forming the North West Mounted Police[17], a decision which was to have a profound influence on "peace, order and good government" in Canada from that day onward.

This Force was to be patterned after a cavalry unit and was to consist of 550 mounted police under control of a Commissioner[18] and Superintendents who were also to be appointed ex-officio justices of the peace. The epic story of the hardships endured by these early lawmen and their superb work in restoring and maintaining the rule of law in Canada, is well known to most Canadians. Perhaps what is not common knowledge is their contribution to Canada's military effort during the past century.

In 1885 the NWMP fought in the Riel Rebellion as a cavalry unit, suffering four killed in action, another four dying of wounds and eleven badly wounded. During the Boer War 1899–1902, a total of 30 officers and 260 men served in different cavalry units of the Canadian Army[19]. The RNWMP provided a cavalry squadron in World War I which served in France and Flanders. A further RNWMP squadron served in Russia with the Canadian Siberian Expeditionary Force 1918–19.

Given the background of military service in Canada's armed forces it is no surprise that Commissioner S T Wood, in a letter dated 13 September 1939, recommended authority be granted to form a provost company from RCMP volunteers[20]. This matter was referred by the Minister of Justice to the Minister of National Defence who readily approved the offer. The unit, to be designated 1 Provost Company (RCMP), was to serve with the 1st Canadian Infantry Division, then being mobilized, for service in the Canadian Active Service Force (CASF). Some of the agreed conditions of service[21] for the RCMP personnel were:

- volunteers must be no older than age 45 years;
- meet physical fitness standards of CASF soldiers;
- DND to be responsible for pay and allowances on the scale authorized for CASF military personnel, as well as all costs incurred during the mobilization period;
- authorized Canadian Army uniforms, kit and accoutrement to be worn;
- RCMP badges to be worn, also a police service brassard (arm band) with the letters "RCMP";
- volunteering implies agreement to serve outside Canada;
- applicants to be medically examined in the Military District where they apply;
- the mobilization period to end 1 November 1939, the Force to provide 120 men for this company as well as casualty replacements;
- all equipment, rations and supplies to be the responsibility of DND.

General Order 1074 of 30 September, issued by DND, authorized this unit. The concentration at "N" Division in Ottawa was completed by mid-October. They arrived in RCMP dress and were billeted and rationed in various quarters, including a drafty metal Quonset hut, formerly an aircraft hangar. Training was started immediately on motorcycle riding, traffic control point duty, map using and the army style of close order drill which varied somewhat from that in vogue at the RCMP Depot in Regina. The war establishment of a Provost Company was the same as its counterpart in the

British Army. It comprised a headquarters section of 3 officers, an RSM, CQMS and nine other ranks, plus six sections each of 1 sergeant, 2 corporals and 13 lance corporals, for a total of 116 all ranks. Inspector W R Day was appointed Officer Commanding with the rank of Captain while another senior RCMP NCO, George Ball, was to be the first Regimental Sergeant Major (RSM). Additional officers and NCOs were selected for the remaining establishment vacancies. Army uniforms and personal kit were issued in early December. On 9 December the Company arrived in Halifax and immediately boarded the H M S Aquatania which sailed on 10 December arriving at Gourock, on the Clyde, on 17 December 1939. That this unit was formed from individuals serving across Canada, concentrated in Ottawa, trained, outfitted then moved overseas in the space of less than three months was, by any standard, a remarkable achievement.

The Company, along with several other units of 1 Division, was stationed in Aldershot. Their ancient barracks was built during the Peninsular War in the days of Wellington's army. Badajoz barrack was allocated to these newly arrived "police soldiers" and was to be their home until mid-June 1940. We now go to a diary kept by a member[22] of the unit.

In Aldershot we engaged in various forms of elementary training which included map reading, etc. On 22 May 1940, the first draft of reinforcements numbering 17 arrived. On 23 May 1940 the Canadian First Division was ordered to move in convoy under the direction of No 1 Provost Company to Dover, England. Six members were chosen to be General McNaughton's personal body guard on the inspection of the evacuation of troops from Dunkirk. On 11 June 1940, the day after Italy had declared War, the first Canadian Division once more took the road, this time for Plymouth where units went aboard the French Liner "Ville D'Algier" on 13 June, 1940, and put to sea. We arrived in Brest, France noon 14 June 1940. Advanced inland about 5 miles. France had fallen. Were successful in getting aboard an old British freighter "Cyclops" which carried us back to Plymouth. Took up First Line Defence in the southern portion of England. On 6 September 1940, the Canadian Provost Corps Depot was formed[23]. Seventeen men were transferred to the Depot as instructors. The third draft of reinforcements[24] (survivors from the ship "Nerissa") arrived. The first casualty was Constable C J Johnstone who lost his life on the "Nerissa". During the interval between arrival from France and the present day[25], the Company has been pursuing the regular duties of control during troop manoeuvres and other police duties.

This brings the Company up to mid-June 1940 at which time the Canadian Provost Corps came into existence. Henceforth these RCMP originals would be progressively integrated into the many Corps units, as well as with the headquarters of field formations, ie Army, Corps and Divisions. While they retained their identity as members of their famous Force, they were in large measure the pathfinders of the "Canadian Provost Corps" in the turbulent days of WWII.

2

The Corps is Born

The preceding pages deal with the military police of some early armies in a variety of historical setting. During the course of research it was a pleasant surprise to discover there was no particular scarcity of historical data on that subject. What was surprising is the fact that our contemporary historians have totally ignored the Canadian Provost Corps. Perhaps the most pointed example of this omission is that not one mention of the Corps is to be found in the official history of the Canadian army, Six Years of War by C P Stacey. Appendix "J" of this reference does, however, explain in a small print footnote that the Provost Corps came under the Camp Commandant, NDHQ. It is therefore resolved to redress this oversight by recording some of the salient features of the Corps, a task made more onerous by the passage of time.

The basic fighting formation of the Canadian Army in World War II was the DIVISION. The Division was regarded as the smallest single grouping of fighting arms and support services, under a single commander, that could operate on its own in battle for an extended period. There were two kinds, infantry and armoured. An infantry divisions' basic fighting element was three "brigades" each of three infantry battalions, together with the necessary command (headquarters), control (communications) and "service support[26]" elements. The "Armoured" (tank) division had two brigades, one armoured and one infantry, each of three regiments/battalions. In addition to the considerable numbers of Home War Establishment (HWE) troops required for recruiting, training, administrative and security duties. Canada produced and maintained overseas three infantry and two armoured divisions. An additional two "Independent" armoured brigades, each of three tank regiments and service elements was also part of the order of battle.

The ultimate size of the CASF upon reaching its full development was an Army of two corps with three infantry and two armoured divisions plus two Independent armoured brigades. There was, of necessity, a large number of training, supply, communications, maintenance and security troops required in both Canada and overseas to provide the basic infrastructure for the field formations.

In order to understand the role of provost in a theatre of war it is necessary to have some knowledge of the way the Army is organized for battle. The accompanying table (Table 1) will provide some idea of the structure, size and shape of an infantry division for battle. In practice it functioned like a well-honed team in which every unit fully understood and played its part.

Privy Council Order 67/3030 dated 15 June 1940 authorized the Canadian Provost Corps, as part of the Canadian Active Service Force (CASF). It did not detail the organization of units, but it did define the manpower ceiling and established a Provost Marshal[27]. The organization tables or war establishments for most Canadian Army field units were patterned after the British Army and the Provost Corps was no exception. Those for the base units in Canada and United Kingdom were referred to as Home War Establishments (HWE) where the shape and size depended on local requirements.

The overall responsibility for organizing the field units of the Canadian Provost Corps rested with the General Officers Commanding the Division and his staff, however most of the detailed work was done by theofficer selected as the Assistant Provost Marshal (APM). The HWE units were the responsibility of the Provost Marshal and the District staffs. The following account of some of his personal experiences was provided by then Lieutenant Howard M Baker[28] of Montreal. His narrative sheds a good deal of light on the mobilization process and it also gives some long overdue acclaim to Colonel Phillip Auguste Puize, the officer appointed Provost Marshal in June 1940.

I had the privilege, and pleasure, of knowing Colonel Puize for many years before the start of World War II in connection with many police associations and organizations. In those years, he had been Director of the Quebec Provincial Police and also Director of St Vincent de Paul Penitentiary. I respected him as a competent peace officer and administrator who controlled his commands with an "iron fist", but never in a harsh manner. Socially, it was always a pleasure to be in his company as he had a dry sense of humour which belied his normally rather austere physical appearance.

TABLE 1
A Canadian Army Infantry Division – 1945

Headquarters and units	Total all ranks	Vehicles W–Wheels T–Tracks	Remarks
HQ infantry	832	165 W	Includes senior staff Officers and heads of the Arms and Services. The HQ functions in two groups: Main and Rear. The totals also include signal, tpt, defence, medical, pay, postal, provost & chaplain elements.
Arms Infantry division signal regt (RCCS)	438	120 W	This unit provided wireless, line and DR service for all HQ and units. It operates highly decentralized.
Reconnaisance (HQ & 4 sqns) (RCAC)	1,030	125 W 95 T	The eyes and ears of the division.
Field artillery (Towed) (RCA) (3 Regiments in a division)	2,190 (730)	447 W 27 T (149 W) (9 T) (24 x 105 mm guns)	The figure in brackets are totals for each of *three* regiments.
Anti-tank regiment (Artillery) (RCA)	800	164 W 20 T (24 Towed	A Regiments HQ and four batteries. Total of 48 × 17 Pdr A-TK guns. 24 SP Guns)
Light anti-aircraft regiment (RCA)	898	223 W	Three batteries of 18 guns each. Total 54 × 40mm guns.
Engineers (RCE) Field park Squadron (1) Field squadon (3)	258 828 (276)	74 153 (51)	Includes a bridge troop carrying Bailey bridge equipment. Main duties: road repair, bridging, minefield clearance, water supply.
HQ infantry brigade (3 per Division)	669 (223)	192 (64)	Includes section of locating battery, defence Pl. Signal – Troop and LAD (repair unit).

TABLE 1 (*Concluded*)

Headquarters and units	Total all ranks	Vehicles W–Wheels T–Tracks	Remarks
Infantry battalion (RCIC) (3 per brigade or 9 in a division)	8,550 (950)	972 (108)	Incls: 360 Bren carriers 664 Lt machine guns 216 A Tk projectiles 234 2″ mortars 54 3″ mortars 54 6 Pdr A Tk guns
Machine gun battalion (RCIC)	764	195	Includes three machine gun companies plus one heavy mortar company.
Services Division column RCASC (Command located at Divison HQ [Rear])	1,281	409	Organized into 4 Transport Companies. Tasks: supplies POL, ammunition, rations, Tpts troops.
Field ambulance (RCAMC) (3 per Division)	693 (231)	135 (45)	Establishes AID Posts, initial treatment of casualties, evacuates wounded to field hospital.
Field dressing station (RCAMC)	122	21	Surgery and transfusions.
Ordnance field park (RCOC)	228	84	Includes a mobile laundry and bath unit. Main tasks: provision of general stores and clothing.
Infantry workshop (RCEME) (3 per Division)	570 (190)	168 (56)	Recovery and repair of guns, equipment and vehicles. The Light Aid Detachments are attached to major units.
Division provost company (CProC)	124	26 W 42 M/C	Role and organization described elsewhere.
Total	20,075	3,857	

At the start of World War II, I was in the Montreal Police Department in charge of the Traffic Engineering Bureau. For the first few months of the war I worked with Colonel Bovey on some local counter intelligence work. This consisted mainly in tracing down "fifth columnists" who were a bit of a nuisance, and turning them over to the RCMP. Sometime in 1940, Colonel Piuze was given the task of organizing the Canadian Provost Corps by the authorities in Ottawa in view of his outstanding military career both during, and after World War I. So, I was very pleased when HQ, MD4 told me Colonel Piuze had suggested I be asked to organize a Provost Corps Company and a Military Detention Barracks for that District.

Naturally, I accepted, got a "Leave of Absence" from the Police Department, said "Good-bye" to Colonel Bovey, enlisted, started my organizational work in one large room at District Depot No 4, and after work, spent my evenings hopping around from armoury to armoury, and various other military installations, for all sorts of instruction and training in order to qualify me for my Commission as an "Officer and a Gentleman".

His final accolade came when he recommended me to General Page to be his DAPM in the 4th Canadian Infantry Division he was forming. I wanted to get overseas, so gladly accepted his invitation when it was proffered, and joined the division in Debert in November 1941. I treasure a letter Colonel Piuze wrote me when I left Military District No 4. He thanked me profusely for the work I had done, but I know I would never have "made the grade" without his understanding, knowledge and assistance.

Howie Baker's account illustrates the remarkable speed of the mobilization process. Here we have, in the space of nine months, a division already overseas, another (2 Cdn Inf Div) nearly ready, literally hundreds of new headquarters, depots, temporary buildings, recruiting centres and new units being formed. The challenging process of turning civilians into soldiers cannot be better exemplified than by Howard Baker's situation whereby he was busy forming a HWE provost company and a detention barracks while still qualifying as a second lieutenant. The Provost Marshal, meanwhile, was repeating this scenario in each of the eleven Military Districts across Canada, as well as assisting with the organizing of the provost units required by field formations.

The system used to recruit the officers and men for Canadian Provost Corps units was simple. As units were authorized, each of the MDs was given a quota of men to recruit, the total to equal the WE strength. Recruits were posted to the new unit where the selected officer commanding (OC) organized the requisite ranks, equipment, training and duties. Quite easy if you say it fast. Incidentally, this system accounts for the fact that most of the field provost units were made up of men from almost every Province. This had a beneficial affect on the spirit and morale of the unit as each man was called upon repeatedly by his peers to defend his status as a "lumberjack", "herring-choker", "cattle-puncher", "stubble-jumper", "stump-puller", or "city-slicker". This good natured camaraderie assisted materially in the development of a brotherhood and corps spirit which was to last for years to come. HWE provost units were manned much the same except that the initial quotas were probably made up from men residing in the same province or region. This was sensible, having regard to easing the break-up of family life for married persons.

The complete list of Provost units and headquarters is listed on Table 2. It shows the formation with which they were affiliated, the location or theatre, and the title and designation of each. Footnotes to this table provide further details as to their size and role.

TABLE 2
World War II Formations and Affiliated C Pro C Units at Maximum Strength – 31 December 1945

SERIAL	FORMATION	THEATRE/LOCATION	C PRO C UNIT
	FIELD		
1	*Cdn Inf Div	UK, Sicily, Italy, NWE	1 Provost Coy (RCMP)
2	*Cdn Inf Div	UK, (Dieppe), NWE	2 Provost Coy
3	*Cdn Inf Div	UK, NWE, (D-Day)	4 Provost Coy
4	*Cdn Armd Div	UK, NWE	8 Provost Coy
5	*Cdn Armd Div	UK, Italy, NWE	5 Provost Coy
6	1 Cdn Armd Bde	UK, Italy, NWE	Brigade Pro Section
7	2 Cdn Armd Bde	UK, NWE	Brigade Pro Section
8	*Cdn Corps *(HQ & Corps Tps)	UK, Italy, NWE	3 Pro Coy (8 Secs) 1 L of C Pro Coy 1 Cdn Fd Punishment Camp
9	*Cdn Corps *(HQ & Corps Tps)	UK, NWE	13 Pro Coy (8 Secs)
10	Cdn Sec GHQ & L of C Tps	UK, NWE	2 L of C Pro Coy
11	*First Cdn Army and Army Tps	UK, NWE	11 Pro Coy (8 Secs) 7 Pro Coy S I U Section 2 Cdn Fd Punishment Camp 1 Cdn Army POW cage (Sep 44 - July 45)

TABLE 2 (*Continued*)

SERIAL	FORMATION	THEATRE/LOCATION	C PRO C UNIT
	BASE (UK)		
12	*CMHQ (London)	UK	6 Pro Coy (Det in Scotland) SIU Section 1 Cdn Detention Barracks (Headley)
13	*HQ & Rft Units (England)	UK	4 Cdn Detention Barracks (Reading) 9 Pro Coy & 14 & 17 Coys C Pro C Depot (Aldershot)
	MILITARY DISTRICTS (CANADA)		
14	*MD 1 Ont	London	
15	*MD 2 Ont (Camp Borden)	Toronto	A total of 18 provost companies numbered from 30 through 48 were formed during the periods viz: 1940-9, 1941-5, 1942-3, 1944-1. The total strength of all companies was 38 officers and 2,242 other ranks
16	*MD 3 Ont (Petawawa)	Kingston	
17	*MD 4 PQ	Montreal	
18	*MD 5 PQ	Quebec City	
19	*MD 6 NS	Halifax	
20	*MD 7 NB	Saint John	
21	*MD 10 Man	Winnipeg	
22	*MD 11 BC	Victoria	
23	*MD 12 Sask	Regina	
24	*MD 13 Alta	Calgary	
25	Newfoundland	St John's	No 18 Pro Coy
26	*Pacific Command	Vancouver	10 Provost Company (Field WE)
27	Training and Reinforcements	Camp Borden	A-32 C Pro C Training Centre
28	Military Detention Barracks	Canada 28 MDBs	From 60 through 88 less Nos. 82 & 85

THE CANADIAN PROVOST CORPS REACHED A MAXIMUM AUTHORIZED STRENGTH OF 6,120 IN SEPTEMBER 1945

(a) Asterisk * denotes Canadian Provost Corps staff representation. The Provost Marshal in Ottawa was the senior appointment with rank of Colonel. Deputy Provost Marshals (DPMs) were located at Canadian Military HQs (CMHQ) and HQs, First Canadian Army, with Lieutenant Colonel rank. Five of the eleven Deputy Assistant Provost Marshals (DAPMs) at HQs Military Districts were also lieutenant colonels. The Assistant Provost Marshals (APMs) at the HQs of 1 and 2 Canadian Corps and all of the Divisions were Majors as were the DAPMs in MD's 1, 3, 5, 6, 7, 12 and 13. Canadian Provost Corps units were commanded by either a major or captain.

(b) Serials 8, 9 and 11. These Companies had eight sections. The divisional companies had six sections, each of 1 sergeant, 2 corporals and 13 lance corporals.

TABLE 2 (*Concluded*)

(c) Serial 12. The DPM CMHQ was located here. No 6 Provost Company had the onerous task of policing the City of London. It was formed in the United Kingdom in late 1940 and reached a strength of 318 all ranks. It provided detachments in Scotland and one or two other locations in the United Kingdom.

(d) Serial 12. No 1 Canadian Detention Barracks was a large detention facility located at Headley Downs, near Grayshott, Sussex. It was commanded by an officer of lieutenant colonel rank.

(e) Serial 13. No 14 and 17 Provost Companies were formed in the United Kingdom (Aldershot) during 1945 and 46 for provost duties in connection with the repatriation of Canadian troops to Canada. No 9 Provost Company was formed in the United Kingdom later in 1940 for duty with the Base and Reinforcement units in Southern England.

(f) Serials 14 through 24. By the end of the War there were eighteen provost companies in Canada, with a total authorized strength of 3,025 all ranks. There were Detachments at sixty-nine locations across Canada.

(g) Serial 26. HQ Pacific Command was established in Vancouver and served by No 10 Provost Company, a field WE. It commanded the operation in the Aleutian Islands during 1943, and was later given the task of planning the organization of 6 Canadian Division (Pacific Force) which was to be formed of volunteers from NWE, after the cessation of fighting. No 16 Provost Company, largely a paper unit, was listed on the Order of Battle but was made redundant by the defeat of the Japanese, August 1945. However it must be noted that a number of Canadian Provost Corps officers and men had volunteered and some were actually moved to Vancouver.

(h) Serial 27. A-32 Canadian Provost Corps Training Centre operated in Camp Borden from November 1942 to May 1946. It had a staff of seventeen officers and 148 other ranks. It trained 950 reinforcements for field units; 905 for units in Canada and 42 officers of lieutenant rank.

(i) Serial 28. A total of 28 Military Detention Barracks operated in Canada. Twenty-five of these were still functioning as late as August 1945. The total Canadian Provost Corps strength was 537 all ranks. The total cell capacity was 1,962. The smallest, located at Terrace, B C, had 16 cells. The largest, No 86 in Camp Borden, had 200 cells. The total Canadian Provost Corps strength of MDBs was 20 officers and 517 men.

3

Early Days in the United Kingdom

Getting Organized

One of the early priorities of Army Headquarters was to set up a command structure to deal with the progressive build up of Canadian troops in the United Kingdom. The main headquarters and the first to be organized was Canadian Military Headquarters (CMHQ) in London. It was responsible for liaison with British authorities as well as the promulgation of policy on a wide range of matters related to Canadian formations and units. Headquarters Canadian Reinforcement Units (HQCRU) was a secondary element responsible for holding, training and allocating reinforcements arriving from Canada. It reported to CMHQ. The Canadian Divisions and Corps in the United Kingdom were allotted an operational role of defence in the southern counties bordering the English Channel. Notwithstanding this preoccupation, a high priority was given to individual, unit and formation training by GOCs. A quick glance at Tables 1 and 2 should help clarify the situation that pertained for most of the war years.

It is now time to talk about this individual called a "provost". What was his background, where did he come from and what did he do? What was the environment in which he worked? It seems the general characteristics of a good provost had not changed since Colonel Godson Godson's day. He must still be physically fit and strong, of good character, disciplined, alert, trustworthy and possess a good knowledge of his trade. By a stroke of good luck the Corps received men who were exactly what it needed. The need for trained police, schooled in the law and its application, was met by the infusion of RCMP and a good percentage of well trained policemen from various civil police forces. The "stiffening" element required for all around smartness in dress and deportment was filled by a goodly number of PF and NPAM soldiers; persons like Grey, Tosdevin, Whittington and Secord come to mind. Following a general appeal a large number of well-trained and disciplined men transferred to Canadian Provost Corps from various field units and reinforcement pools. Finally, those men who enlisted into the Corps at recruiting depots in Canada were well motivated and of good appearance and character. Taken together, this varied manpower gave Canadian Provost Corps units a good nucleus on which to build.

Field companies, and to a lesser extent base companies, were organized with a headquarters section and six (or eight) sections. The provost section was the workhorse of every field company throughout WWII. The section sergeant was the leader in every sense of the word. He had two corporals and twelve lance-corporals, which gave him two sub-sections of seven each. Last, but by no means least, he had another lance-corporal who functioned as driver of the section truck, quartermaster, storeman, mailman, barber and most important of all: THE SECTION COOK. He had no official job description and received no special training, however he was a master at improvisation and an expert "scrounger" who possessed the morals of a bandit and the manners of a diplomat. It was largely due to his efforts that a Provost Section was able to exist in a detached situation for lengthy periods. In other words, the provost section was self-contained and it was this flexibility, more than anything else, which enabled a field provost company to operate independently under diverse and often difficult circumstances. The section, at least initially, was issued with a variety of mostly useless traffic control equipment such as paraffin lanterns, enamelled roadsigns, alpha stencil sets, paint and camouflage nets. It did, however, have some sensible cooking utensils and a burner.

A provost section, in fact each member, had to be mobile in order to do his job. Apart from a HQ truck (30 cwt) and another (15 cwt) in each section, a high degree of mobility was achieved by issuing everyone with a motorcycle[29]. At one stage, in early 1943, an armoured division company had 96 Harleys. The down side to the MC was the toll it took on life and limb during the days in England while riding on narrow, unmarked roads and lanes, and in blackouts. The resulting casualties to man and machine were somewhat decreased, but never eliminated, by the introduction of jeeps to replace some motorcycles, commencing in 1943.

Corporal A.E. Wilson[30] of "A" Section, No 5 Provost Company, 5 Canadian Armoured Division tells us about one particularly tragic event.

Following the deployment of the 5th Armoured Division overseas to Aldershot and its environs in Southern England in November 1941, traffic control tasks became one of No 5 Provost Company's main operational training commitments. For Canadian vehicle drivers generally driving conditions in the United Kingdom were very different to those experienced in Canada. They had to become accustomed to driving on the left hand side of the road. The roads, including highways, were narrower and more winding, with one-lane bridges and intersection roundabouts; and due to invasion possibilities all route and directional signs had been removed. These conditions and the inexperience of many drivers, combined with youthful recklessness, led to many accidents and vehicle convoy movement problems. For small, independent convoy manoeuvres the Provost employed mobile traffic control methods in use at that time. This involved a pointsman mounted on a motorcycle regulating traffic at cross-roads and, when the last vehicle passed, he then accelerated to the head of the column (leap frog) until required to repeat the procedure.

On 6 May 1942 a Section of No 5 Provost Company was engaged in providing mobile traffic control for a vehicle convoy training manoeuvre. The route selected passed through the villages of Farnborough and Fleet, and continued in a northwest direction on a paved secondary road. A railway also passed through Fleet, over which the route crossed on a narrow bridge at a right angle. The approach to the bridge was at a 45 degree angle, sloping sharply upwards to the centre of the bridge and falling sharply downwards past the centre, providing clearance for the railway steam engine's smoke stack. The Provost pointsman assigned to the intersection prior to the bridge (about 500 meters) waved the last vehicle of the convoy through and mounted his motorcycle to rejoin the head of the convoy. He didn't make it. He apparently accelerated to a high speed to the centre of the bridge ignoring a 15 mph speed limit sign, and became airborne, cleared a one meter high guard rail and crashed through the roof of a second storey building situated alongside the railway. He evidently died instantly from a fractured neck and a ruptured spinal cord, and the motorcycle coming to a rest on the centre of a double bed.

Mention should be made of the items of personal kit and equipment issued to every member of a field unit. The standard battle dress, boots and headdress was worn, with cloth shoulder titles "Canadian Provost Corps" sewn on the upper sleeve of the tunic. The cap badge was worn over a scarlet cloth patch. Other distinguishing items included an armband with the word "PROVOST" or "MP" embroidered in large letters. Eventually the white web belt[31] and shoulder strap was taken into wear, as was the distinctive PROVOST lettering on the MC crash helmet. The issue sidearm[32] was carried, fully loaded, in a holster on the left hip. A square, box-type flashlight which clipped on the web belt was issued but discontinued, probably because batteries were seldom available. A variety of rain wear in the form of capes and leggings was issued for use when operating a MC in rainy weather. None of this was overly popular. For that matter neither was the rain. Finally, he carried a police notebook[33] in his upper tunic pocket.

Learning The Trade

Training has always been a basic function of command in any army. While techniques and methods change, the sequence of training for battle has always been conducted in three stages: individual training, unit training and formation training. There were problems in achieving a uniform standard of training in Canadian Provost Corps units. With the ever present knowledge of hindsight it seems clear there were two main reasons for this. Most, not all but most, senior commanders placed unfair emphasis on the training of "ARMS" units as opposed to "SERVICE" units. Whereas the arms (infantry, artillery and armour) could devote their full-time and all resources to training, the service support units were expected to perform their normal function within the formation as well as training each member on the basics of soldiering and the special requirements demanded by his Corps. The vast difference in the extent of knowledge already possessed by men of varying backgrounds has been mentioned. For example, the civil policeman was well grounded in general police work, the former NPAM soldier understood organization and could perform the routine of a military unit, and the transfers from other units were well trained soldiers. The new Provost recruits, particularly in the hastily formed early divisions, received very little basic training. It was not uncommon for a provost to find himself on patrol, escort or traffic control duty within a few days of enlistment, with or without the benefit of an experienced partner. Ideally there should have been a central training unit where everyone coming to the Corps could be trained to a specified level in the special-to-corps subjects. However A-32 Canadian Provost Corps Training Centre was not formed until November 1942, and these were not ideal times.

The first training establishment (mentioned in John Primrose's diary) was the Canadian Provost Corps depot formed in Aldershot during September 1940. Its designation as a "depot" belied its task which was to train the "transferees" from other corps in provost subjects such as: motorcycle riding, military law, report writing, (time, date, place, I was, I saw, I did), traffic control at intersections (point duty), map using, police procedure ("never take a trim pair of ankles down a back alley for a "twopenny" upright"), PT and close order drill. This course lasted for six weeks and was, perhaps, best remembered by the candidates for two things: its intensity and the enthusiasm of the RCMP instructional staff[34].

Another feature of this course was an inspection visit by the newly appointed Provost Marshal at CMHQ in London. Colonel A D Cameron, was a WWI veteran who rose to Captain rank with the Lord Strathcona Horse, a cavalry regiment. At the start of WWII he was serving in the Gold Coast Police[35] (now Ghana) in West Africa as one of four Assistant Commissioners. This was a well organized and efficient force and all officers who had military training, and there were quite a number, were allowed to rejoin the Army. The fact that he and Major General P J Montague[36] had been "saddle-mates" in WWI undoubtedly was a factor in A D Cameron's selection for this important post. In any event he would arrive, following the usual vigorous session of pressing, shining and polishing, to inspect a class of about thirty aspiring Canadian Provost Corps hopefuls. He had a sharp eye, a soldierly bearing and much police and military experience. He was also a shrewd judge of men and a strict, but fair disciplinarian. He will be remembered for asking searching questions such as: "Why do you want to be a provost?" and "Do you think you are good enough to make others be good?" Passing this inspection and obtaining a reasonable grading from the Instructional Staff assured the plebe of admission to the corps. He was then permitted to wear the Canadian Provost Corps badge and shoulder titles. The Provost depot moved from Badajoz to Maida Barracks in October 1941 where it became the Canadian Provost Corps Holding and Reinforcement unit, under CRU HQ, for the remainder of the War. This small but very important unit continued to have a "refresher" training capability. It had an establishment of 3 officers and 18 other ranks.

The term "special to corps subjects" mentioned above should be explained. This was the basic skills and knowledge required by members of a Provost Company that would enable them to perform their duties with some degree of efficiency. First he must possess a sense of responsibility, a degree of intelligence, be well disciplined, trustworthy and of good character. It was his duty to present a neat appearance and set an example in dress and deportment, and he must be physically fit for combat. While a fool proof screening[37] process had not yet been invented, nevertheless by close observation and supervision a fair measure of success was achieved in meeting these demanding standards. Captain Howard Baker had this to say about his experiences when organizing No 8 Provost Company:

In November 1941, I vacated my appointment as DAPM of Military District No 4, reverted to the rank of Captain, and headed for Debert Military Camp to take up a new appointment as DAPM of 4th Infantry Division[38]. On arrival there, I found that No 8 Canadian Provost Company had already been formed, and immediately found I had a problem on my hands.

As happened in so many similar cases, when a new Unit was being formed, the various Military Districts across Canada were allotted a quota of soldiers to supply in order to bring the Unit up to Establishment. Unfortunately, as was often the case, some of the Districts found this a good opportunity to get rid of both Officers and Other Ranks they considered "undesirable" for a variety of reasons. As a result, poor old No 8 Company was staffed by three rather elderly Officers, two of whom were World War I veterans, and the third a very retiring individual. Even physically, many of the other Ranks left a lot to be desired.

After discussion with the Divisional Adjutant-General, arrangements were made to have everyone in the Company undergo a searching medical examination. The results were shocking, and about forty Provosts were immediately returned to the Military Districts they came from. Ottawa appreciated the problem when it was explained to them, and new quotas were again demanded from some of the Districts.

Unfortunately, some Districts again tried to get rid of their "misfits:. In one case, a draft of ten men from one district were all found to be medically and physically unfit for service in an Overseas Infantry Division, and were all returned to that District. In some cases, some of the men returned to Districts were listed "For Immediate Discharge". To cut a long story short we went through approximately one hundred and twenty five "draftees" before we managed to get the forty replacements we needed to bring the Company up to strength. Similar problems were encountered in regard to suitable replacements for the Officers, and this problem was only finally settled satisfactorily after we got Overseas.

Regardless of where, when or how he received it, the provost in a field formation had to be trained, as an essential minimum, in the following subjects:

- Point duty – As a "pointman" he must, by clear signals, regulate the flow of traffic through an intersection;
- Vehicles – Ride and maintain a motorcycle as well as operate a jeep or small truck;
- Map using – Be able to relate the detail on an Ordnance Survey map to the ground, measure distance, follow a route and determine elevations;
- Police procedures – Possess a fair knowledge of military law and local rules of conduct applicable to soldiers. Must know his powers and responsibility for an arrest, maintenance of a police notebook, presenting evidence in written and/or oral form;

- Army organization – must have a fair knowledge of the units and headquarters in the formation, including types, locations and approximate numbers; know and recognize Army ranks.

So far this discourse on training has focussed on several negative aspects and may have created an impression that little or no training was carried out in Provost Companies. In fact each unit had an ongoing programme which ultimately produced a well trained provost. One did not hear the term "on-the-job-training" but in fact this was exactly what happened.

They learned by doing the job under the supervision of an NCO or in the company of an experienced hand. If he had never ridden a motorcycle, the sergeant or section corporal would teach him on some back road or common. Likewise, a rookie would be paired with an old hand for his first few patrols. More formal training on matters such as military law and organization was conducted, on a section basis, at regular intervals. He was instructed on the fundamentals of "point duty" by a section NCO and practiced under supervision till judged ready to work on his own. The degree of proficiency being displayed by a pointman on duty created much banter and good natured rivalry between the members of different companies.

A unique feature of life in the Canadian Provost Corps was the low level of supervision afforded an individual on duty vis-a-vis any other corps of the Army. It could be no other way, given the variety, number and complexity of duties, and the ratio of NCOs or Officers to men. Hence it was imperative that a provost be disciplined, trustworthy and well trained. The reality of working with a minimum of supervision was probably a huge factor in influencing Canadian recruits to join the Corps.

Field Company Routine

Table 2 gives an outline of the various Provost units along with some information on the establishment strengths and ranks. Without going into detailed job descriptions, it is appropriate to discuss some of the persons found in the HQ section of a field company. The officer commanding (OC) held captain rank with direct responsibility for all aspects of operations, training and administration. In the words of a statement made later by a famous President of the USA, he might well have had a sign on his desk, (if he had a desk) that said: "The Buck Stops Here". He was assisted by two or three (whether division or corps) lieutenants who were variously assigned the duties of transport, messing and training officer, with the senior being the designated second-in-command (2/IC). Seldom, if ever, will you find even a passing referenceto the toil associated with these mundane but most essential tasks. The term "messing" covered all activity related to the requisition, bulk pick-up, storage, and conversion of each man's ration into some form of edible food. The Messing Officer assisted by the Quartermaster (CQMS) must ensure the company received its full daily ration entitlement. Shortages obviously resulted in less food; and if the daily indent demanded rations in excess of the actual strength on a given day, the result was a decrease at some future date equalling the overdrawn rations. The life of the messing officer was further complicated by something called, "the tuppence-a-penny account". Very briefly, this was an allowance of two and one half pence per man per day to be used to buy items of food to supplement the normal issue rations. All such purchases must be made from the local Navy, Army and Air Force Institute (NAAFI) which stocked such tidbits as HP Sauce, Powdered Eggs and NAAFI Biscuits. Not only was the Messing Officer required to keep a strict accounting of each man's daily entitlement, the amounts spent and balances, but he must also return all boxes and bags and claim a specified credit for them. Last but not least, he must convert the balances in this account from Sterling to Dollars, and vice versa. Incidentally, the ration was scanty, the kitchen equipment was inadequate, the mess hall frequently non-existent and the untrained cook was a "volunteer" member of the Canadian Provost Corps. In fairness it should be said that most of these tedious accounting duties disappeared when a company entered a war theatre, and, overall, the food was adequate.

The transport officer's main concern was keeping the large complement of jeeps and motorcycles in roadworthy condition. The standard of preventive maintenance was only fair, and the repair capability depended on a single corporal mechanic and his tool-kit. There was seldom any suitable hard standings or garage space, special equipment or an adequate supply of spare parts. Most of these problems could be attributed to a completely inadequate allocation of Division repair and recovery resources normally provided by the allocation of RCEME Light Aid Detachments (LADS). Perhaps the biggest single headache for the Transport Officer was the huge effort required to cope with Courts of Inquiry and Accident Reports which were the inevitable aftermath of motorcycle accidents.

The 2IC was normally responsible for personnel, supervision of the orderly room and the various reports and returns such as Part I and Part II orders. He automatically became the A/OC during any prolonged period of absence by the OC. The duties of the Training Officer were handled in various ways such as each officer assuming a share, to rotating this job between all officers. The OC would, in many cases, prepare the overall training programme and allocate time and instructors.

The Corps overseas required about 80 officers when fully developed and up to strength. Nearly all of these were commissioned from the ranks including a total of 48 RCMP members of No 1 Company. The remainder, except for a few posted from Canada, were from the various companies. Candidates for commissioning were selected on the basis of some demonstrated leadership ability, their level of intelligence as revealed by the "M" test, and physical fitness. They were required to pass a written examination which was held periodically at a central location for the candidates from all corps of the Army. The candidates then appeared before an Officer Selection Board (in London) for scrutiny and an interview. On successful completion of these preliminaries he was posted, as an Officer Cadet, to No 1 Officer Candidate Training Unit (OCTU) in Bordon, Hants, for an intense course on "common-to-all-arms" subjects. The course was of seven weeks duration and was really designed to determine the candidate's capacity to function under stress, make logical decisions and solve a few basic military problems. For example, a written test conducted in a steel nissan hut was completed while a machine gun was firing short bursts of blank ammo outside the window. The total intake for one class was about sixty, and it was not unusual for as many as five Canadian Provost Corps candidates to appear on any one of the three or four intakes each year, from 1941 to 1944.

Those who stayed the course were posted in Orders as Lieutenant, Canadian Provost Corps, with an effective date. His pay was credited with the princely sum of 175 Pounds Sterling which was used to purchase the required items of dress and kit from military outfitters in London such as Reid's, Hobson's, Thomas & Stones and Burberry's. Following a short stay at the Provost Depot in Aldershot he was posted to a company for duty.

The field provost company had a Regimental Sergeant-Major (RSM) even though a Warrant Officer Class 1 (WO1) would normally only be allocated to larger, battalion size units of the Army. It is thought to be a carry over from the practice in British RMP companies where this rank was justified for disciplinary duties when dealing with the aberrant behaviour of any senior warrant or noncommissioned officers of the formation. While not required for general disciplinary duties, he was a valuable asset in the company. The RSM kept a sharp eye on almost every aspect of day-to-day activity such as the layout and moves of company headquarters, allocation of quarters, hygiene, camouflage, leave and passes, dress, discipline and duty rosters. He did his turn as Duty Officer and the inspection of quarters, patrols and vehicles. These were strong, self-made leaders who possessed tremendous loyalty to the Corps and "their men". They did not tolerate mediocrity. The following names come to mind; Jimmie Rae – 11 Coy; Bob Wallace – 3 Coy; Hugh McCallum –13 Coy; George Ball – 1 Coy (later DPM First Cdn Army); Oakes – 2 Coy; Dennis Harper – 4 Coy; Rob Staunton – 5 Coy; Bill Knight – 8 Coy and Mac MacNamara – 7 Coy.

The Section Sergeant rated high on any list of really essential positions in a provost company. The Section was the work element and he was its leader. He had to be knowledgeable, alert, energetic, and possess the sometimes conflicting qualities of initiative, compassion and toughness. Some were made sergeants on the basis of their previous military or police experience, and all were, very simply, first-class men. It was normal, in any company, to find sergeants who came from such diverse backgrounds as:

- pre-war service in a NPAM unit;
- service in the RCMP;
- service in a civil police force;
- a supervisor or foreman in civilian life;
- a NCO transfer from another corps.

Perhaps, above all else, he must display a high degree of integrity and self-discipline. The sergeants of the Canadian Provost Corps met all of this criteria, with rare exceptions.

Provost Duties

What we had in Southern England during the first three years of the War was a large and growing body of Canadian soldiers who had suddenly left their jobs, families and homes. They were hastily organized into manageable groups and transplanted, across an ocean, to a strange environment which if not hostile was much different than anything previously experienced. The process of converting a civilian into asoldier is a tricky job under ideal conditions. It requires time, effort, patience and understanding if the sad scenes of pillage, rape and plunder, so prevalent in the seventeenth century, are to be avoided. There were some obvious extremes between his former life as a civilian and that of a soldier in a far away land. He could no longer contemplate the joy of "Mom's" home cooking; the comfort of clean sheets and a soft pillow; the luxury of a hot bath; the comfort and solace received when ill or out-of-sorts or the great feel of

Early Days in the United Kingdom 33

clean clothing to wear. Apart from such creature comforts, he must suddenly adapt to a whole new life style and set of rules. He was subject to a totally different package of regulations and even the language was different, eg: "report to the adjutant at 0900 hours". or "check the petrol in that lorry". If he talked back to the "boss", quit his job, went home or was late for work he could be charged and punished under something called "military law". Add to this the prospect of an uncertain future, boredom, loneliness and a somewhat monotonous routine, and you have the reasons, if not always the justification, for the irresponsible behaviour of some Canadian soldiers. Some mention should be made of the off-duty activities of Canadian troops during those days in England. It would be incorrect to assume they were ill-disciplined generally because within unit lines, on duty or training the discipline was good, in fact often very strict. The problems arose when they were off-duty, on leave or pass away from the unit. Off-duty soldiers flocked to the hamlets, towns and cities where there was no shortage of pubs,[39] dance halls, clubs, canteens, pretty girls and the odd good restaurant. This mix of people and places led to a higher than acceptable incidence of: drunkenness, disorderly conduct, quarrels and fights, property damage, injuries, vandalism, absenteeism and arrest by civil police. In addition to these forms of misbehaviour, mostly offences under the Manual of Military Law (Army Act), the soldier must also adhere to a host of Regulations promulgated throughout the Canadian Army Overseas. Here are a few examples of some rules to be followed:

- carry his steel helmet and respirator at all times;
- carry personal identification (Parts 1 and 2 of the Paybook) at all times;
- be in possession of an authorized pass when away from his unit;
- be in possession of written authority, signed by the CO, when operating a WD vehicle in certain areas at certain times;
- wear only the authorized items of military dress and accoutrements in a prescribed manner.

In retrospect, there was really nothing much a healthy, red-blooded Canadian lad could do if he was to stay out of trouble. It was amazing that the great majority managed to do so.

Each Provost Company was located in the area currently occupied by the units of the formation. This enabled contact and liaison with units which assisted all ranks to gain a good knowledge of their location, organization and activity, even to becoming acquainted with some unit members. This contact proved most valuable then, and later, since it helped provost

TABLE 3
No 10 Provost Company Duty Roster – Week 20–26 April 1942

	DAY / DATE						
DUTY	MON 20	TUES 21	WED 22	THU 23	FRI 24	SAT 25	SUN 26
Town Patrols	A	G	F	E	D	C	B
Mob Patrol & Vehicle Check	B	A	G	F	E	D	C
Training	C	B	A	G	F	E	D
Stand To & Company Fatigues	D	C	B	A	G	F	E
Security Corps HQ	E	D	C	B	A	G	F
Make and Mend and Vehicle Maintenance	F	E	D	C	B	A	G
Day Off	G	F	E	D	C	B	A

1. H Section is on detached duty with 1 Canadian Armoured Brigade.
2. The section on Training will provide TC, as required, for short moves and fd exs.
3. At least 1 corporal and 5 l/corporals of Stand To will be ready for duty, and in their quarters, from 1800 hours onwards.

to understand and respond to what was going on around them. The nature and extent of the provost response, when taken over an extended period, was about evenly divided between disciplinary patrols (Town Patrols), traffic duties, and other police and security duties. As previously stated, one of the problems which confronted the provost company, whether in or out of battle, was to organize itself so as to be in a position to deal with those activities which occurred on a regular basis, as well as those that popped up unexpectedly. The predictable was easy while the unforeseen required some forethought in having a reserve or stand to section ready for duty. Under these circumstances a weekly Duty Roster was developed for the company whereby each Section was allocated a specific duty on each day of the week. Duties were allotted to sections on a rotating basis to ensure an equitable distribution of work and to meet the needs of training, maintenance and some time off. Table 3 is a specimen roster for a corps provost company.

The weekly Duty Roster was a flexible and effective method of ensuring all duties were covered and that each section did its fair share. Most important, it enabled the section sergeant to detail men for specific tasks at least one week in advance. The manpower required and method of carrying out the various duties requires further explanation. While there might be some variation in the nature of provost activity in different formations, the Town Patrol was common to all. One or more "two man" foot patrols were posted in every town or city visited by an appreciable number of off duty troops. To ensure adequate contact and coverage, each patrol was assigned a designated beat which would be patrolled at specified times. Following an inspection by the Orderly Officer, the various patrols were transported by section truck or motorcycle, to the town or towns, usually in time to arrive at the local police station about an hour before sundown. The section sergeant, after a check with the desk sergeant as to any incidents involving Canadian troops, would assign the patrols to their beats where they remained for the next four or five hours until all establishments had closed and the town was quiet.

A patrol on a given night would have occasion to stop and check Canadian soldiers for minor offences such as improper dress, vehicle offences (improper parking or no authorization), or no leave pass or identification. The provost was required to record the full regimental particulars[40] in his notebook which was subject to routine inspection by the section sergeant or a company officer. As is still standard police practice, the pages of the Provost Notebook were pre-numbered to prevent the removal of a page from being unnoticed. Offenders were either informed that the matter would be reported to his unit CO or, for serious offences, were placed under close arrest and held temporarily in the police station until an escort from his unit arrived. In either case a written statement of the incident would be delivered to his unit early the following day. These statements were called "Offence Reports" and were typed on a form, introduced and used by the British Army, called the AFB252. A copy was distributed to the "A" Staff of the formation, the APM and Provost Company file. The unit was required to report the disposition of each case, to the appropriate HQ staff but not, in keeping with modern police procedure, to the concerned Provost Unit. The small villages and crossroads communities were normally covered by a mobile or roving patrol (two men on motorcycles) checking once or twice each night. The size, frequency and duration of town patrols was influenced by a variety of events such as pay day, pub closing time, the arrival of new units or large scale exercises in the area. Whether or not these patrols had a beneficial effect on the maintenance of good order and discipline and prevented a "SCATHING OF THE COUNTRY" is a question best judged by someone other than Provost. Some realities of life in the Canadian Army during those days in England is best illustrated by one or two short excerpts from the *Regimental History of the 48th Highlanders – Dileas* by Kim Beattie, page 97:

The Provost Corporal came before the Colonel for succumbing to the joys of London while on escort duty. He had been despatched to pick up a prisoner, incarcerated for drunkenness. He got his man, but decided the two of them might pub crawl a bit before starting back. That night, the APM at Waterloo Station had to incarcerate the escort and reincarcerate the prisoner. Provost Sergeant Pethwick then had to go to London to be an escort for the escort. The sentence: "reduced to the ranks.

Another incident of a good, old fashioned fight between the "48th" and the "Hastie P's" also bears on these patrols: page 98,

The Hastings resented being called "dumb" Plough Jockeys – to the Brigadier, to boot. There was a pitched battle in a pub near Thursley Common, where a bald headed DCM of the 1914–18 war was luckily the publican. His army experience told him to put the clock ahead and the lights out. This forced the fight out on the road, where the tussle was called off in time to let the combatants vanish into the night as the provost patrol arrived.

The plagiarism of the history of this famous Regiment may, to some small degree, be excused, by a final excerpt:

The convenient term "esprit de corps" explains what they were building. Regimental cohesion, family fellowship and soldierly self respect were taking hold. The stress of the Aldershot winter had marked the malingerers and habitual defaulters, setting them aside for weeding. Some were gone. The great proportion reached out for self respect. Under adverse conditions they were becoming mature soldiers, and the regiment matured and strengthened them.

Another fixed duty required the constant presence of a Provost section at Corps and Division headquarters. These headquarters were invariably located in large, country estates, previously requisitioned by the Government (War Office). It was very much the nerve centre of the formation and was the scene of much coming and going by the commander, his staff and numerous daily visitors. The provost were on duty around the clock on tasks such as: traffic control and checks at the main gate, car parking, checking the identity of all visitors; enforcing blackout regulations and patrolling the grounds during darkness. It was the practice in most Division Provost Companies to detach one section on a semi-permanent basis to meet this need. This was always the case when operating in a war theatre, when the additional task of marshalling, moving[41] and relocating the Headquarters was an important function of the Div/Corps HQ attached section. The situation depicted on Table 3 was the actual case at HQ 1 Canadian Corps when located in England. Provost sections did this duty in turn, on successive days, from 0600 to 0600 hours.

The section detailed for Mobile Patrol and Vehicle Check was responsible for a number of patrols and traffic duties on the roads throughout the area. These were one or two man patrols, depending on the circumstance, and were carried out on motorcycles. The duties were varied and included tasks such as: point duty at busy or dangerous intersections; driver infractions such as speeding and unattended vehicles[42]; traffic duty at supply points or for small convoy movements such as range or training parties. A further task was stopping all Canadian military vehicles and checking the drivers for special authorization on what was known as "gasless Tuesday". This arose directly from the success of the German U Boat sinking of our merchant ships inthe Atlantic crossing, causing among many shortages, a crisis in the flow of gasoline (petrol) to the United Kingdom. To cushion the impact of this general shortage, the Canadian Army issued an order prohibiting all except really essential vehicle trips, on one day each week. A serious view was taken of any contravention which led to the setting up of "check points" where Canadian vehicles were stopped and checked for the required special authorization. The location and timing for these check points was constantly changed to prevent discreet detours by errant drivers. Needless to say the spot selected was always on a lonely, seldom used stretch, at night, and when it was raining.

The training conducted in a field provost company during this period was, for the most part, dictated by formation and unit training exercises involving road movement. On almost any given day there was a variety of such movement ranging from unit range parties of 25–30 vehicles, engineer bridging or mining exercises, moves of tanks to driver training areas, artillery batteries moving to firing ranges and occasionally practice moves of a brigade or division headquarters. The task of the provost section was to ensure, as far as possible, that designated routes and timings were followed, congestion avoided and accidents prevented. The traffic control duties by provost included measures such as : route signing[43], lead escorts, point duty at main intersections and at entry and exit points on or off main routes, one way control at narrow defiles and checking the speed and density[44] of the convoy.

The Section Sergeant, depending on the size and duration of the movement, would conduct a prior recce of the route, brief his men, issue maps or route cards and detail them for individual duties. This type of activity was invaluable training for the section since it provided much needed experience, assisted in developing section drills and, most important, enabled each man of the company to gain valuable knowledge of all units in the formation. This knowledge engendered self confidence and enabled each provost to take individual initiative when on traffic control duty. Terms such as "4th Brigade is moving tonight on Route X," instantly conjured a mental image of the familiar "tac" signs[45] on the vehicles of the Royal Regiment, the Royal Hamilton Light Infantry and the Essex Scottish Regiments, the three battalions in 4 Canadian Infantry Brigade. The familiar "Division Patch" or logo of each Division (Corps or Army) gave him the formation designation. Thus this quick method of identifying unit vehicles was a tremendous boon when directing traffic at intersections, dispersal points or when marshalling units in parking and assembly areas.

The Section on training might well catch other jobs such as VIP escorts, traffic, parking and security duties for conferences, sports days and other special assignments. It was also possible, if not probable, that the absence of any field exercises or special assignments might permit a day on the ranges to sharpen up the shooting eye. In any event training was a continual process in most companies where, as said previously, they learned by doing. The following story[46] lends some perspective to the work of the Canadian Provost Corps during those early years in Southern England. It tells us the trials of a Regiment, when endeavouring to move by road from Aldershot to an area North of Oxford, in May 1940.

The Battalion was travelling by company convoys, and none was immune; they were all on their own and they were all lost. It was not even an exclusive 48th snafu; practically every unit in the Division was also lost, and some of them stayed lost for days. The men gleefully enjoying it but they knew there was some excuse. It was not only the pubs and inns which had become nameless overnight; so had the railway stations and even the churches. All road signs had disappeared; the names of towns had been chiselled from stone facades; the business signs of large commercial firms and even those of the little green grocer, the village seamstress and the apothecary shop had all disappeared. It was as if a genie had waved a wand and wiped clean the face of the English countryside to make everything anonymous.

The anonymity of everything was not the only reason they were lost; also to blame was that most unwarlike device, the complicated highway roundabout. Brigade had assured the Highlanders that guides would be placed to block off all incoming roads, and thus keep the convoys on the right route. But they ran out of guides by the time they reached the big Oxford roundabout, and the convoys promptly went off into the blue in a dozen directions.

This accounts for four of the seven days in what might be called, "a week in the life of a provost". The remaining three days were spent on more mundane, but nonetheless important duties. The Stand-to Section, as the name implies, had to be ready for duty, in quarters, from early evening to midnight. They were a ready reserve or back up men normally called to augment town patrols to cope with incidents such as pub closing brawls or other emergency situations. The section was also called on to deal with incidents such as: road accidents, escorting soldiers under arrest, minor investigations and temporary guard duty. During the day they supplied men for company fatigues which included such glamorous tasks as "policing up" unit lines, "pot walloping" and "potato-peeling" for the company cook and running errands for the Officer Commanding, RSM or company clerk. The section sergeant was invariably detailed as Duty Sergeant of the day.

The men of the Maintenance Section carried out first line or driver maintenance on their vehicle or motorcycle. In the more progressive sections this was done from a check list which included such tasks as: tire check, brake and clutch adjustments, lubrication, topping up oil and petrol and reporting defects to the beleaguered Corporal Mechanic. This was also the day for spending some time washing and pressing clothing, shining shoes, brass and buckles, blanco-ing web equipment and cleaning the service revolver. If he had planned everything carefully and the sergeant agreed, he might be able to get a head start on his day off, normally from 2359 hours to 2359 hours the following day. He might use his day off to visit a friend or relative, scrounge a meal, see a movie or just plain revel in the luxury of this much anticipated free time.

It is emphasized that this duty routine might vary slightly between field provost companies, however it is safe to say each member of every company would have spent the major part of his time on these typical duties. The bottom line was a heavy work load for all ranks, carried out under difficult conditions requiring mental agility and physical toughness. Of course there were a few failures, but the great majority passed the test.

No account of the Canadian Provost Corps would be complete without mention of No 6 Provost Company in London. War-torn London has been the subject of countless descriptions and stories but it is appropriate here to mention two themes. It was a mecca for tens of thousands of Allied servicemen; and it was the central target for the Luftwaffe bombing in 1940 and 41, followed later by heavy attacks from the fearsome V1 and V2 German missiles. It was logical, therefore, that one of the first projects undertaken by the newly appointed Provost Marshal at CMHQ (Colonel A D Cameron) was organizing adequate provost service. No 6 Company was quartered in a former hospital on Henrietta Street just off Covent Gardens market. From its initial start as a small detachment, in 1940, it quickly grew to reach a final strength of 4 officers and 314 men, and was under the direct command of the Provost Marshal at CMHQ. Despite its size, this company was hard pressed to meet the many demands placed on it. It was not unusual, for example, to have up to 50 provost on street and station[47] patrol at one time. Other duties such as escorts and guards for soldiers under arrest required much coordination and manpower. The company also deployed detachments to cities such as Glasgow, Aberdeen and Liverpool to deal with the many thousands of off duty soldiers in Scotland and the Midlands. The Canadian Forestry Corps working in Scotland were on the whole, a well behaved lot. Finally the presence of CMHQ on nearby Trafalgar Square was an assurance of steady employment for another one or two sections. All provost, whether on or off duty, were expected to assist the Air Raid Precaution (ARP) volunteers in their effort, during raids, to extinguish fires started by the dropping of canisters of phosphate by pathfinder planes preceding the main attack. Many provost, not only from the No 6 Coy, but also men off duty from field companies stood fire bomb watch in London during those troubled days.

The provost of this company were subject to strict discipline which demanded a very high standard of smartness in dress and deportment. Close and friendly relations was maintained with the London Metropolitan Police, and in some areas joint Provost/Police patrols were routinely scheduled. Walter Gatehouse, a Canadian serving in the London Metropolitan Police, gives us this interesting account of his initial contact with the Canadian Provost Corps.

I enlisted in the London Metropolitan Police in February 1939 and took training at the Scotland Yard School. On completion of training I was posted to B Division at Victoria, on 5 June 1939. On 7 April 1943, I was granted permission to resign in order to enlist in the Canadian army. I was sent to the Canadian Provost Corps Depot in Aldershot on 8 April, for training and outfitting. I arrived in Aldershot 29 years after my Dad returned to England in 1914, as a Canadian soldier. Incidentally, I was verbally reprimanded by the Chief Constable of B Division for two prior attempts to enlist in the Canadian army without the Commissioner's consent.

I was posted to No 6 Provost Company on 28 May 1943, and subsequently posted to the Glasgow Detachment and promoted corporal. I was promoted sergeant and posted to the Special Investigation Unit[48] at CMHQ, in early 1944. I was posted to the SIU on the continent late in 1944 and returned to Canada in December 1945.

Walter Gatehouse went on to serve the Corps with distinction in places such as Germany, Lebanon, the Gaza strip and at home in Canada. It is impossible to over state the contribution he, and men like him, made to his Corps and country.

No 9 Provost Company was formed in early 1942 to police the Base reinforcement Units located in and around the towns of Guildford, Aldershot, Camp Whitly and Farnborough. It had an establishment strength of 4 officers and 161 other ranks and was comfortably quartered in a well known golf course not far from Guildford. Like No 6 Company, it had a heavy workload of patrols, escorts and security duties. This Company reported to the Assistant Provost Marshal (APM) at Headquarters, Canadian Reinforcement Units located in Farnborough. It was disbanded early in 1946 following the repatriation of the Canadian Army to Canada.

The applicable Canadian law governing military offences, tribunals and subsequent punishment was contained in: The Manual of Military Law, 1929 (as amended), and Kings Regulations and Orders, Canadian Militia, 1939, (KR&O–CAN). These statutes defined, in great detail, all military offences, methods of trial and the scale of permissible punishments. A distinction was made between conduct deemed unacceptable when committed by Service personnel on Active Service, but would be quite acceptable in normal civilian life. These purely military offences included such things as absence without leave (AWOL), leaving a post or picket without authority, insubordination and misuse of military equipment. The offences applicable to both military and civilian life included the more obvious serious crimes of murder, rape, robbery, assault and fraud. A soldier charged with any offence and found guilty could be awarded punishments ranging from a few days confinement to barracks, a fine, extra duties, detention or imprisonment for periods up to months or years. Minor offences were, in general, dealt with at a summary trial by the Commanding Officer who could award a punishment of up to 28 days detention. In the case of a serious offence tried by Court Martial, a sentence of several months or years of detention could be, and often was, awarded.

Finally, it is necessary to explain a further Canadian Provost Corps unit, namely: 1 Canadian Field Detention Barracks. The need for a facility to administer awards of detention was initially met by a Field Punishment Camp in 1 Canadian Division. This ad hoc facility was set up early in 1940 and served as a guardroom and detention facility until No 1 Canadian Detention Barracks was formed, near Grayshott–Headley Downs, in 1940. This was a large facility capable of handling up to 400 soldiers under sentence. It had an established strength of 6 officers (including a Paymaster and Medical Officer) and 171 rank and file. It was commanded by an officer of lieutenant colonel rank, and was controlled by CMHQ in London.

To say that this was not a home of happy campers would be an understatement. The resident inmates were undoubtedly the misfits, malingers and downright criminal element of the Canadian Army overseas. As time passed, so the number of hardened cases increased because the policy was firm during the war years, not to release malcontent soldiers only to have them evade service and start their nefarious activities afresh back home in Canada.

There were several minor and at least two major riots during its four years of existence. The last blow-up came in March 1945, lasted for six days, destroyed everything of value in the buildings and was only quelled by a well armed and organized infantry company led by a well known Brigadier of D Day renown. However, the Charter of Rights and Freedom had not yet been invoked and, in any case, nobody ever said it would be easy.

4

Bumper, Tiger and Spartan

In order to provide background for subsequent Canadian Provost Corps activity it is necessary to describe, in outline, the role and training of the Canadian Army overseas. For the first two and one-half years (to mid 1942) its role was the defence of Southern England. From this time onward the emphasis changed to preparation for offensive action designed, in cooperation with our Allies, to expel the German and Italian Forces from Europe. The ultimate size and structure was decided by the Canadian Government acting on recommendations made by the Chief of the General Staff (Ottawa), Lieutenant General H D G Crerar, and the Commander 1 Canadian Corps (United Kingdom) Lieutenant General A G L McNaughton. On 26 January 1942 Prime Minister Mackenzie-King outlined the Army Programme in the House of Commons, as follows:

During 1942 it is proposed to create overseas a Canadian Army[49] of two Army Corps: one Corps to comprise three Infantry Divisions and two Army Tank Brigades; the other to consist of two Armoured Divisions. In addition, all the additional necessary ancillary units to serve these two Corps will be provided.

The organization of the Canadian Army overseas, as at June 1943, is shown in the following table (Table 4).

The Canadian Army was fortunate to have two able and experienced officers in General A G L (Andy) McNaughton and General H D G (Harry) Crerar, both World War I veterans. Each held senior Command positions which enabled them to manage and direct the Army through World War II; a truly gigantic task. Each was well aware of the importance of *moving* large bodies of troops, weapons and supplies under varying conditions, on a planned and timely basis. Failure in this regard was, and has

TABLE 4

A HQ & FMN	B DATE ORGANIZED	C RANK & NAME OF COMD
First Canadian Army	April 1942 UK	Gen A G L McNaughton
1 Canadian Corps	Dec 1940 UK	Lt Gen H D G Crerar
1 Canadian Inf Div	Oct 1939 CDA	Maj Gen G R Pearkes
5 Canadian Armd Div	Mar 1941 CDA	Maj Gen E W Sansom
1 Canadian Armd Bde	Sept 1940 CDA	Brig F F Worthington
2 Canadian Corps	Jan 1943 UK	Lt Gen E W Sansom
2 Canadian Inf Div	May 1940 CDA	Maj Gen V W Odlum
3 Canadian Inf Div	Oct 1940 CDA	Maj Gen E W Sansom
4 Canadian Armd Div	June 1941 CDA	Maj Gen L F Page
2 Canadian Armd Bde	June 1942 CDA	Brig R A Bradbrooke

(1) Column "A": This was the Order of Battle during the period 1 CANADIAN CORPS was in Italy.
(2) Column "B": Note the late date of forming HQ 2 CANADIAN CORPS. The sequence for arrival overseas was: 1 Division, 2 Division, 3 Division, 1 Armd Brigade, 5 Armd Division, 4 Armd Division and 2 Armd Brigade.
(3) Column "C": These were the Commanders at date of formation. See Appendix "F" to "The Canadian Army, 1939–1945" by C P Stacey, for a list at various times throughout Word War II.
(4) Army Troops: First Canadian Army Headquarters controlled a large reserve of combat and service support units for allocation to corps or divisions, as required by the battlefield situation. For example, HQ First Canadian Army had eight regiments of artillery (about 6,000 men and 168 guns of medium, field, anti-tank and anti-aircraft calibre).
(5) Corps Troops: A more intimate reserve of units for direct support of the divisions was held at the Corps level. The total number of Canadian troops in all of the formations overseas, as at 31 May 1944, was 251,000. This did not include the 6th Parachute Battalion which served under the 1st (British) Airborne Division.
(6) As shown in Table 2, there were three Provost companies plus other C Pro C elements under command HQ First Canadian Army, ie, No 7, 11 and 2 L of C Companies.

always been, a limiting factor in war and was given much attention by such successful Generals as Hannibal, Marlborough, Napoleon and Von Moltke.

What made the MOVEMENT problem new and decidedly difficult for World War II commanders, staff and units was the introduction, for the first time, of a vast array of motor vehicles of every description. Only the "P B I" walked and even they were often moved into battle by trucks and carriers. Add to this the physical problems already mentioned (darkness, road space, no route signs, congestion and inadequate communication equipment) and the results were road "BLOCKS" instead of road "MOVEMENT". It was largely in response to this problem that both McNaughton and Crerar, severally and jointly, ordered several large scale exercises with troops to practice Headquarters Staffs and units in road movement, although each exercise also had one or more contingent purposes. In any event, the Provost Companies were always employed flat-out during these "Schemes". To give the minute details of each exercise would be boring and unnecessary, however, a summary of three or four may provoke nostalgia and serve to illustrate the scale of this effort during the period February 1941 to March 1943.

Exercise FOX, February 1941. An anti-invasion scheme involving move by road to a concentration area northwest of Dover. 1 Canadian Corps, with 1 and 2 Canadian Divisions, was involved. One of the Chief Umpires critiques was, "monumental traffic jams".

Exercise BUMPER, September 1941. 1 Canadian Corps with 1 and 2 Canadian Divisions moved, as part of a large force (ten other British Divisions), to deal with an invasion force north and east of London, in East Anglia. There were huge traffic problems.

Exercise TIGER, May 1942. 1 Canadian Corps with under command 1, 3 and 2 Canadian Divisions and 1 Canadian Armd Brigade participated. This was also an anti–invasion exercise requiring a rapid advance to contact to practice physical endurance and movement. Some Canadian infantry battalions marched for distances up to 250 miles, about the life of a pair of "ammunition" boots. A reduced scale of transport was used and may have helped the attainment of a passing grade for all aspects, including traffic and march discipline. Note: Two Brigades of 2 Canadian Infantry Division were off on special training for what later became the "Dieppe Disaster".

Exercise SPARTAN, March 1943. A large scale test of mobile warfare by tanks moving to an area north and west of London. HQ 2 Canadian Corps, recently formed, was getting its first taste of command and control, as was 5 Canadian Armoured Division, which had not yet participated in a large scale exercise. The purpose of the exercise was to practice movement, tactics and placed special emphasis on the ability of Staffs to "handle" their units. The Exercise Report was not complimentary and cited traffic jams, petrol shortages and breakdown of communications. In fairness, much of this was probably lack of proper equipment, plus the inexperience of the Corps and Division staffs.

In the wonderful world of hindsight it is easy to draw lessons and reach conclusions on measures that could, and should, have been taken to deal with the pervasive problems of road movement. It serves no useful purpose to assess, or even consider blame, however, one has to wonder why it was that the same unsatisfactory routines were followed time after time by the three elements involved, ie, headquarters commanders and staffs, the units and the provost service. Armies are not democratic institutions in that major initiatives come from the top. Headquarter Staffs routinely ordered moves on routes not previously reconnoitred; they almost always failed to recognize that large scale moves at night meant ONE-WAY travel only; and they failed to consider the capability of various types of vehicles to negotiate grades, switchbacks or soft ground. Other staff failures included such things as allocating inadequate dispersal areas for units, poor assessment of route capacities, mixing wheels and tracked vehicles on the same road and making unrealistic time and space calculations in terms of optimum speeds and density of the number of vehicles moved, in relation to available road space.

A most serious deficiency was the failure to produce a standard procedure for road movement. This deficiency was remedied later on, with excellent results. Standard operating procedures (SOPs) for road movements were beginning to emerge late in 1942 and covered such aspects as: standard speeds and density; responsibility for route allocation vis-a-vis Army, Corps and Division; defining maximum number of vehicles permitted to move without HQ authorization (free-runners continued to be a problem); unit drills for marshalling, moving and dispersing off routes (for example, all units were required to have unit guides at start and dispersal points to direct unit vehicles); placing unit identification markers at appropriate places to indicate unit/headquarters location; standard rules for march discipline such as pulling over when stopping, posting sentries and traffic spotters, maintaining vehicle interval, vehicle lighting; allocation by Corps HQ of a main supply route (MSR) and a division centre line for each division; movement priorities; action on enemy air or ground attack and so on and so on.

The SOPs for movement filled in many large gaps in the heretofore hit-and-miss system. It gave units firm guidance for developing training and drills and greatly improved march discipline. Standard Procedures for road movement were an absolute boon to Provost because there was now an established uniform standard and a few sensible rules to follow and enforce.

Before leaving this general subject, it is appropriate to mention some of the problems which hindered Provost in their efforts to contribute to the movement of large convoys by road. The object of traffic control was, simply, to ensure that military vehicles followed the designated route, arrived at the right place, at the right time and in the right sequence. Some of the methods employed by Provost included placing temporary route markers to guide drivers, route patrols to check march disciplines and placing Provost pointsmen at potential trouble spots to prevent congestion at intersections, direct serials and stragglers and keep the traffic moving. The pointsman was an effective method of preventing traffic jams. To be fully effective he must be well briefed and in possession of a marked map and move schedule. He faced many problems during night moves including dust, breathing carbon monoxide fumes as well as the physical danger of being rundown in the darkness. It was unrealistic to expect him to function, without relief, for lengthy periods yet this was often the rule rather than the exception during these hurly-burly days. Provost officers and NCOs soon learned that a "point" to be covered for 24 hours required three men, working in shifts. They also learned that at really busy intersections there must be two men on duty at the same time. This experience resulted in a reassessment of allocating Provost manpower to traffic duties because, in general, we were expecting a section to cover far too much ground. The use of mobile route patrols was instituted to prevent, or minimize, traffic congestion or blocks. The system of road movement then in use is best described as "The Average Speed and Density System". It entailed a fixed order of march at a designated speed (expressed as the distance to be travelled in one hour), and the density, expressed as the number of vehicles per mile of road space. A standard speed and density for convoys might be 15 M1H (miles in 1 hour) and 30 VTM (approximately 60 yards between vehicles). The result was a long, slow moving, snake-like column where if one vehicle stopped all behind it stopped. Stopping and starting created an accordion-like effect, in terms of density and delays. The density factor was a realistic regard for possible interference and damage by the Luftwaffe. Under these conditions the Provost mobile route patrol performed such useful functions as: checking speeds, density and road discipline, providing liaison between traffic posts, dealing with trouble spots and, most important, relieving pointsmen for short breaks.

The posting of route markers and information signs on routes was, and continued to be, one of the more onerous tasks undertaken by Provost throughout the War. It was amazing that Provost accepted what was a major engineering project, namely the manufacture and erecting of hundreds of route signs with little or no material and equipment, and, even more amazing, with short advance notice. The issue section stores for this task consisted of a metal stencil set of letters and numbers, a quantity of discs directional with short (12" wooden stakes), a few heavy metal enamelled plaques, some paint, a roll of white (3") cloth marking tape and about thirty paraffin traffic lanterns. It needs little imagination to conclude that paint, when available, was never the right viscosity (it either clogged or ran), the stencils soon became bent and twisted, the discs were useful but of limited value, and the blank metal sign boards soon lost the outer coat of shiny enamel through chipping and bending. The absolute worst asset was the lantern (Lamps, Traffic Control, MK IV). It featured a circular glass globe which, when turned opposite an aperture, displayed a red, green or white light. The burner contained a small (3 ounce) quantity of kerosene, which would sustain the flame for about three hours. Unless the wick was kept well trimmed and adjusted at regular intervals, the gradual heat build-up thinned out the kerosene which, in turn, quickly increased the flame. If not adjusted, the lantern would "burn-out" after about one hour. You could not light it and leave it. It was also prized by units as a light inside of a 4 gallon nonreturnable petrol can used to mark their HQ location during darkness. It was not unusual to "lose" a dozen or so in an one night move. Material for sign posters was almost impossible to obtain and signs had to be salvaged, cleaned, repaired and reused many times. You became an expert "scrounger" and, indeed, were likely to be congratulated by the APM for displaying this initiative. In theory, it was thought that a section could make up and post a sign in the 'twinkle of an eye'. In practice it took much longer because, after all, paint must dry. The lack of suitable stakes or posts on which to display signs adds further to this tale of woe. Perhaps the biggest single deficiency, particularly in a war theatre, was the lack of suitable traffic control communications. Given that the state of the art radio set then in use in the Canadian Army was the unreliable and cranky No 19 set, there is some excuse for not having a full-time TC net with a link to whatever formation was involved in the movement. Without adequate communication, however, it was simply impossible to keep abreast of changing tactical situations and deploy Provost resources accordingly.

However gloomy the foregoing, let it not be said that the field Provost did nothing by way of remedial action. We have already made reference to Standard Procedures to which there was considerable Provost input. A great deal of the "route signing" dilemma was solved by the introduction of the Division Axis Marker. This was a small, metal (12" x 12") square displaying the Division logo, or patch with an attached Disc-Directional which could be set to point the broad ARROW in the desired direction.

The Axis Marker and Directional Arrow was mounted on a lightweight steel rod. Each section carried up to 150 of these markers which were recovered for further use as the formation moved forward or back, as the case may be. A simple and most effective solution that proved successful through the war. Drills were established to ensure that a section, or sections, could be rapidly deployed in response to situations where little or no warning was received. For example, no duty was finished until vehicles were topped-up, equipment checked, maps issued and folded and everything readied for the next move. A few blank sign boards were carried for use when required and some companies, especially at Corps and Army level, developed some very ingenious methods of fabricating printed route signs. Incidentally, it should be mentioned that the FORMATION PATCH appeared on every sign put out by the appropriate Company. This served as the "signature" of authority for the sign. While Provost never overcame long hours of traffic duty, the Section Sergeants developed systems of relief and rest periods for each man, particularly pointsmen. We never did get a full-blown Provost wireless net, however, much assistance was provided in this area by our great R C Signal units, and also much help was given by temporary use of Recce and Armoured regiment wireless vehicles and personnel. They were experts. As previously stated, an intimate knowledge of all units in the formation was of tremendous *value to each company.*

5

The Dieppe Raid, 19 August 1942

This historic action was the first battle of the new Canadian Army against enemy forces in Northwest Europe. The allied leaders[50] had agreed that a major operation against the German ground forces must be undertaken during 1942. Daring cross-channel raids had already been carried out by British Commandos with some success, and had stimulated the military imagination. The raid was designed to achieve several objectives: to develop equipment and techniques for an ultimate full-scale invasion; to damage and destroy the enemy and enemy installations; to test the Canadians who, in any event, were bored with inaction; to capture a port and, finally, to ease the heavy pressure against Stalin's armies in the east. There is ample evidence that this decision was not taken lightly and that our Senior Commanders[51] agreed.

The Plan called for two brigades of 2 Canadian Infantry Division, the 4th and 6th, with supporting elements of artillery, engineers, signals, service corps, medical and provost. All units of this force had completed extensive assault landing training on the nearby Isle of Wight during the weeks preceding the actual crossing. After nearly three years of relative inactivity, and much repetitious training, it was not surprising that a feeling of boredom and frustration began to emerge throughout the Army overseas. It was most pronounced in the ranks of the infantry regiments but was also prevalent in the units such as provost, where the day-to-day duties more closely paralleled the atmosphere and tempo expected on a battlefield. Corporal Bob Prouse of No 2 Provost Company participated in the Dieppe raid, was wounded and spent the remainder of the war in a German POW camp. His[52] personal view of the prevailing mood was shared by many Canadians serving in the United Kingdom at this time.

Like every other Canadian soldier, I was bored to tears with the long inaction and was itching for battle. When, in the late summer of 1942, we returned to the mainland from the Isle of Wight where the 2nd Canadian Division had undergone intensive commando training and beach landing techniques. I was thoroughly browned off. I had missed the training due to an overload of investigative[53] assignments. I requested a transfer back to the Depot with the idea of joining a parachute corps.

Within the week I was summoned before the OC[54] and advised that I was due to be sent on an officers' training course but that, since I had been bitching about inaction, he would offer me a choice – OTC or going on what he called 'a special manoeuvre'. I chose the latter and within a few days was seated in a truck headed for the Coast with other members of our company, the No 2 Canadian Provost Corps.

The Company was located at a small village near Chichester, Surrey. The OC with one officer, two sergeants, four corporals and thirty-three lance-corporals embarked for the move across the channel on "Jubilee", the codename for this operation. The utmost precautions were taken to maintain secrecy as the success of the mission depended, to a great extent, on achieving surprise. For example, all units were told that the move to the embarkation ports was merely another "Exercise" and were not fully briefed until all had boarded the various craft.

The Force Commander had his headquarters in the destroyers CALPE and FERNIE, the command and alternate command ships. The tanks of the Calgary Regiments were embarked on LCT's (Landing Craft Tank)[55].

The cross-channel convoy which sailed from Portsmouth and other Channel Ports on the evening of 18 August 1942, numbered about 120 vessels, the whole protected by a Royal Navy escort of five destroyers and RAF and RCAF fighter and fighter bomber aircraft. Misfortune followed the operation from the start. One incident which occurred about halfway across, and which undoubtedly ended all hope of taking the enemy by surprise, is described by C P Stacey in his *Canadian Army 1939–1945*, in Chapter V:

All went well until 3:47 a m, but then misfortune struck. At eight o'clock in the evening, we learn later from Field-Marshal von Rundstedt's[56] report, a small German coastal convoy, consisting of five motor vessels escorted by three submarine – chasers, had left Boulogne harbour for Dieppe. This convoy now ran into the extreme leftward group of our Force. The result was that the British escort vessels fought a violent short-range battle with the Germans, and were seriously damaged;

and the craft carrying the Commando were completely scattered. One enemy submarine-chaser was sunk."

The Group Commander of our Group 5 which was involved in this incident was unable to report the matter to the HQ Ship because his wireless was destroyed in the fight with the result that the Force Commander did not receive any account of the event until about 6:00 a.m., by then too late to postpone or change plans.

Corporal Prouse relates[57] his feelings and activity during the crossing:

I tried to shake the feeling as I spread my ground sheet underneath a Churchill tank on Landing Craft No 5. I lay down, pulled my blanket around my ears, settled my head on my steel helmet and immediately fell into a deep sleep.

I was rudely awakened by the staccato sound of gunfire and quickly scrambled from beneath the tank to get a better look at what was going on. It was almost 0400 and the night was blacker than the hubs of hell, but this only heightened the glow of the tracer bullets that filled the air. It was beautiful to watch, something like a July 1st fireworks display, but it was also strangely awesome, especially as we didn't know what was going on and couldn't do much about it anyway. Later we learned that we had run into a German convoy, which eventually broke away from the main action and no doubt warned the German forces ashore what was coming in.

The German forces ashore were formidable. Dieppe was a popular seaside resort town with a wide, pebbly beach. On either side, steep cliffs extended along the waterfront and a concrete seawall ran along the front with a wide esplanade or promenade just in front of it, above the water at high tide. The river Arques emptied into the Channel, on the east side, and there was a fairly good, though small, port facility. The high ground on each side, the seawall and open beach area provided unhindered fields of fire for all types of weapons. The beaches and seaward areas were covered by guns of all calibers, including coastal, medium, field and antitank batteries. Many of these were turreted and protected by concrete bunkers overlooking the sea front. Machine gun posts were, in most cases, also trained on the beach approaches and were secured in concrete pillboxes. A German infantry division comprised the main defensive force. It was well supported by additional heavy artillery, mortars and a battalion of tanks. The German Airforce (Luftwaffe), although outnumbered overall, was very active during the initial landings and later.

The landings were slated for the period just prior to first light so as to

The Dieppe Raid   53

take advantage of darkness for the final approach. Timings were thrown off somewhat by a ten minute delay in the arrival of the tanks, through no fault of theirs. One thing was certain, the leading and all subsequent assault troops and their craft were subjected to murderous fire before they reached the shorelines, and for as long as they moved across the beaches. Corporal Bob Prouse explains the approach and ensuing battle:

The dawn broke and we sighted the coastline of France. The outlines of buildings were becoming dimly visible, particularly a large structure that was our destination and that, we learned later, was the casino.

Suddenly – all hell broke loose. The air was filled with the hum of bullets sounding like a swarm of angry bees. Mortar shells were exploding all around us and strike bombers dive-bombed to beat hell. As we drew closer to the shore the Navy gunner who had been handling the Bofors gun suddenly disappeared in a puff of smoke. As the ramp of our landing craft was lowered at about 0540, the men in the front row started to fall. Others, myself included, tried to hug the side of the craft.

Finally I got tired of being a sitting duck and ran to the front, stepping over all the bodies. I was up to my thighs in water and still don't know how I got ashore without being hit. I threw my body on the coarse gravel beach and squirmed my way towards the concrete seawall. I had to get through a mess of barbed wire already strewn with bodies and finally pulled myself up to the wall where a soldier lay dead, draped over the barbed wire that ran along the top. I made may way to a burning scout car which afforded some protection. I flopped down behind it and found three or four men from our company. There was a blinding explosion as a mortar shell hit the scout car. All I could feel was a numbing sensation in my legs as shrapnel entered my flesh.

These scenes of terrible destruction and death, narrated by   Cpl Bob Prouse, are described more fully in his book *Ticket to Hell*, published in 1982 by Van Nostrand Beinhold Publishers, Toronto. His acccount of this disastrous battle includes at least three seperate instances were Allied forces struck back at the enemy, in some cases with telling affect.

I could see that some of the tanks had made it ashore and were churning up the gravel. They would turn and fire, then head up the beach a few yards and repeat the procedure. One tried to breach the wall but the tracks spun on the concrete as it tried to climb at a dangerous angle. It finally gave up and backed onto the beach, repeating its fire-and-spin technique.

A little later he had this to say about the Naval supporting fire:

Looking out over the water I could see our Navy bombarding the town and could hear the whistle of shells going over our heads. This was great but it did not cause any lull in the heavy fire that rained down on the beach.

Finally, near the end of the ordeal, he tells us about a further blow struck at the enemy:

I gradually became aware of a familiar drone and looked skywards. For the first time since landing I could see a squadron of Spitfires heading our way. They peeled off and took after the Stukas and, in nothing flat, two German dive bombers were hit and started to fall with black smoke pouring from them. One dived into the sea and the other came down in a slow circle.

This one-sided battle ended about noon on 19 August. Bob Prouse, although badly wounded, survived and spent the rest of the war in various German prison camps. Of the 4,963[58] all ranks of the Canadian Army embarked on the evening of 18 August, 2,211 returned to England; 589 of these were wounded but survived while in 28 cases the wounds were fatal. A total of 1,944 Canadians were taken prisoners-of-war, at least 488 of them wounded. There were 907 Canadians killed at Dieppe.

Included in these numbers were the 41 members of the Canadian Provost Corps who embarked for the Dieppe Raid on 18 August 1942. Of that number 22 returned to England; one was killed; 18 were taken prisoner of which 7 were wounded. Their names, by category, were subsequently published in Part 2 Orders of No 2 Provost Company:

Killed in action
Lieutenant Peter S Oliver

Prisoner of war
L Cpl R Baddley
L Cpl C E Buck
L Cpl R A Crawford
Sgt A Edgar
Cpl F E Goldie
L Cpl H W Glynn
L Cpl A C Jessop
L Cpl W Moloon
L Cpl J D Noble
L Cpl R H Pearson

Disembarked wounded
Cpl L W Oakes
Sgt D E Sands
L Cpl I E Thompson
L Cpl W D Ramsay
L Cpl J Thevenat
L Cpl F J Wheaton

Disembarked unwounded
Captain E H Stevenson
L Cpl D H Beattie
L Cpl F A Causton
L Cpl W R Escott
L Cpl V Harding

L Cpl A C Russell
L Cpl R E Cresthwaite
L Cpl W H Dignam
L Cpl J A Furnell
L Cpl W J Greer
L Cpl H W Manchester
Cpl A R Prouse
L Cpl J Rogers

L Cpl K A MacMillan
L Cpl J C O'Connor
L Cpl R C Tressider
L Cpl J C Webb
L Cpl R P Ford
L Cpl S W Gouldie
L Cpl C R House
L Cpl W J C Martin
L Cpl E T Woods
L Cpl J H Stako

Back at No 2 Provost Company, even though those who returned from the debacle on the Dieppe beaches told the sad story, it was sometime before the fate of *the nineteen* was known. News eventually came that Lt Pete Oliver had been killed and the remaining 18 were prisoners of war in a German POW camp. The Company, now in billets in Bognor Regis, organized a fund raising project to provide comforts and parcels for their comrades suffering the loneliness and privations of POW camps. Parcels arriving from Canada were saved and auctioned with Captain Stevenson as auctioneer. Items such as cigars went for £1.10 each and were thrown back for reauction. Such was the brotherhood and courage of these fine men who had suffered much for the cause, and asked nothing in return.

6

Sicily, Italy and Goldflake

No 1 Provost Company left England, for the second time, during early July 1943. The Division landed, as part of a larger Allied force, on the Southern tip of Sicily on the westward side of Cape Passero, on 10 July. This well-documented operation needs no further explanation here beyond mention of those aspects which impacted on Provost. The landings across the beaches met light opposition from the Italian forces but much tougher fighting came later in the rugged terrain inland. A further feature affecting No 1 Company was the organization and control required to deal with the mass of vehicles, guns and supplies coming ashore. Everything must be moved over the beaches, offloaded then reloaded for the maintenance and resupply of the Division. This process continued throughout the campaign and created steady employment for No 1 Company. The surrender of considerable numbers of enemy created the need for establishing a PW Cage and attendant escort and guard duty.

The advance inland was steady, despite some tough battles on easily defended hilltop towns such as Ispica on 11 July, Grammachele on the 15th[59], Caltagirone on the 16th, Leonforte on the 22nd, Nessoria on the 28th and Regalbuto on the 17th August, 1943.

Control of traffic on the narrow, winding and often unpaved Sicilian roads presented the usual problems and the Company was busy marking the Division centre line both UP and DOWN, controlling at the numerous defiles and, in general, keeping the single route open. Pointsmen worked long hours when the dust and hot weather were the biggest enemy. In self defence, the pointsmen wore handkerchiefs over their faces and, dress regulations notwithstanding, soft neckcloths to prevent chafing. Another novel aspect of these operations was the introduction of mule trains to pack ammunition and supplies cross country. A great idea in so far as Provost were concerned because there was no dust, no traffic jams and no point duty involved.

This campaign was successful but not without cost in lives. Canadian casualties included: 562 killed, 1,664 wounded[60] and 74 taken prisoner. The Germans and Italians commenced the evacuation of Sicily on 11 August and, under cover of intense gunfire from the mainland, were able to ferry their defeated armies across the narrow Messina Strait to the Italian side. The campaign concluded when US and British troops met at Messina on 17 August.

Space does not permit a detailed account of every action of the Italian campaign from September 1943 to February 1945, when all Canadians in Italy departed for Northwest Europe. In any event this is fully covered in The Official History, *The Canadians in Italy 1943–1945*, by Col G W L Nicholson. We will, however, discuss a few highlights involving Canadian Provost Corps units and the part they played. The assault of 1 Canadian Infantry Division, across the Messina Strait on 3 September, was designed to secure a lodgement area South of Naples, clear the "Toe" of Italy and advance northward on the Adriatic coast. Italy surrendered to the Allied powers on 9 September and was out of the War. Henceforth, the sole opposition was a formidable German Army which contested every yard of ground in this mountainous and, therefore, easy to defend country.

For the next month No 1 Provost Company was spread over a large chunk of Southern Italy. Sections were allotted to the widely dispersed Brigades of the Division. This dispersal greatly allayed traffic problems but it created the need for thorough route reconnaissance and traffic posts at vital intersections. The advance was steady and resulted in the successive clearing of places such as: Gambarie, Locri, Catanazaro, Crotone, Villapiano, Nova and then inland through Sant'Arcangelo, Potenza to Melfi which was cleared on 26 September. The Division then moved, via Highways 93 and 16 through Foggia and halted short of Campobasso which was taken, following a concerted attack, on 14 October.

This movement puts into perspective the work of No 1 Company. In a period of six weeks they had moved the Division over 370 miles, as the crow flies, twice that when including the turns, switchbacks and detours. This represented countless hours of point duty, placing and recovering hundreds of route markers, dealing with accidents, casualties, prisoners, dust and grime, sometimes confusion and always danger from shellfire, teller mines and the like. They also earned the confidence and respect of commanders, staff and units. Brigadier Chris Vokes, then commanding the Division in an acting capacity due to the temporary absence of General

Simonds, reveal[61] a keen appreciation of the importance of unrestricted movment and the importance of effective traffic control by provost.

We had continually to wait until our trucks could cover the miles to bring up food and ammunition and other wherewithal we needed to continue advancing. The roads were often in poor shape. They were holed from mines that had been exploded. They were sometimes washed out from sudden rain. They were diverted along new paths when bridges were blown. Near Foggia, the Germans had blown all the road bridges so diversions were constantly built – bulldozed through the river beds. Most diversions were single-lane. This meant that traffic had to alternate: that vehicles had to take turns moving north and south. The alternation was accomplished by having barriers at both ends of the diversion and radio-equipped Provost corpsmen acting as traffic police.

My orders were that traffic control would be absolutely tight, that my Provost corpsmen, of however humble rank, would demand absolute obedience from commanders of convoys of vehicles *whatever* their rank and, most important, that nobody and nothing would stop for any cause in a one-lane diversion. This day a unit of the 8th Royal Air Force was on its way through the diversion headed for the airfield near Foggia, which we had captured. The RAF unit halted in the diversion for a tea break.

The Provost at the Foggia end pressed his radio switch and called his cohort at the other end.

"Nothing's coming through!"
"Has to be."
"No. Nothing."
"I sent some limey fliers along, don't you see 'em?"
"Nope."
"Well, hell! They're in there."
"OKay, I'll go find out what's wrong."

He found out. Every last man was halted for a tea break. Men, vehicles and equipment clogged the diversion, motionless. He sought out the senior officer, who proved to be a wing commander equivalent to a lieutenant colonel. My provost lance-corporal was eleven ranks below. The provost explained that stopping in a diversion was against orders in this sector – nobody could halt. The wingco said it could not be helped as they were having a brew-up and they would proceed when it was over. The Provost undid his holster flap, drew his pistol and pointed and the officer's belly. "Sir", he began politely enough, "kindly put down your — tea mug". My corpsman knew the lubricating word too, and was skilled in its use. "Get into your — truck, with your whole — lot and get a — move on, or I will see to it here and — now that you will be carried out of this — diversion, feet — first." The wingco got pretty wrathy, but he moved, and smartly. Shortly thereafter I got the report from my provost, as well as a nasty postcard from him complaining in great detail about his ill-treatment. I tore it up. My corpsman was absolutely right".

The point to be made here is that the whole-hearted support of the commander, whether in peace or war, is absolutely essential. The job of a military policeman was difficult under any circumstance, without the Commander's support it was impossible. With minor exceptions, we are happy to say, it was always forthcoming, if not always with the enthusiasm displayed by General Chris Vokes.

We leave 1 Company and the Division at Campobasso for the time being. Headquarters 1 Canadian Corps and Corps Troops, 5 Canadian Armoured Division and 1 Canadian Armoured Brigade arrived in Italy, via the port of Naples, during November 1943. Included in this large infusion were No 3 Provost Company, No 5 Provost Company, 1 Canadian L of C Company[62] and 2 Canadian Detention Barracks[63]. 1 Canadian Corps was temporarily located in Catania and Taomina in Sicily, with No 3 Company in these pleasant towns. 5 Canadian Armd Division was located in Caserta, near Naples. Due to delays in receiving their tanks, vehicles and equipment they remained there for the next three months. The Canadian Holding and Reinforcement Unit, for reasons not clear to this writer, was located across the Mediterranean at Phillipeville, in Tunis. This Unit was later relocated in the main Canadian Base area, near Avellino.

The 11 Infantry Brigade of 5 Armd Division was equipped and saw action in the Arielli sector during January 1944. 5 Canadian Armoured Division moved, in late February, to the Altamese area. 1 Canadian Corps was then located in the Santa'Arcangelo, about 50 miles south of Potenza on Route 92. This gave both 5 and 3 Companies some practice in the problems of traffic control over road conditions described previously by Chris Vokes. Meanwhile, 1 Provost Company was, once again, engaged with traffic problems created in the drive to capture Campobasso and clear the area up to the Biferno River. A description of the roads is given in "The Canadians In Italy", page 235.

The axis allotted to the Canadian Division was singularly devoid of alternative routes. The main road from Foggia to Vinchiaturo (Highway 17) ran westward in the most serpentine fashion into the heart of the Sannio Mountains Climbing out of the plain, twelve miles west of Lucera, the highway twisted and turned up the rugged escarpment, following a sinuous course which doubled and sometimes more than trebled the airline distance between the hilltop towns along its route. This mountainous terrain, in which all vehicle movement was confined to the road, naturally favoured the defender; and he was further aided by the barrier of the Upper Fortore River and its tributaries which flowed across the Canadians path.

Campobasso fell on 14 October after very heavy fighting, and the Biferno River was secured on 4 November 1943. The Division then crossed the Moro River near the east coast and, during the last 15 days of 1943, fought the tough battles which ended with the capture of Ortona on 26 December. Some innovations by 1 Provost Company included the use of No 22 radio sets for T C at defiles and road recce from spotter aircraft. The Service Corps (RCASC) employed up to 370 mules to pack ammunition and supplies over the mountains. Although exact figures are not available, the strength of 1 Company had declined steadily since crossing into Italy on 3–5 September. During the next five months the Division was in reserve prior to the Liri Valley campaign, which started 11 May 1944. During this respite most of the men of 1 Company were able to spend a few days of R and R in Campobasso, which had been developed as a recreational and administrative area for Canadians. Of great importance during this lull, the Company received three full *sections* of Canadian Provost Corps reinforcements[64] with Lt Q E Lawson in charge of this welcome group.

By 1 May 1944 the Canadian Corps, with both Canadian Divisions, was located over the Moro River. It was preparing to fight its first major battle, as a Corps of two divisions. This was a major attack up the valley of the Liri River. Once again a large concentration of Allied Troops was faced with the task of fighting forward for a distance of about 40 miles, through two heavily defended German positions, the Gustav and Hitler Lines, with the enemy in control of the heights on either side of the Valley[65]. These difficulties were greatly exacerbated by the absence, once again, of anything resembling an adequate road network. There was a single road up the valley and it was simply impossible to provide road space for not one, but two Army Corps, the 1 Canadian and 13 British. On at least one occasion there was a total of five divisions, plus corps troops, using, or attempting to use, this single route. Page 446 of "The Canadians In Italy" contains a graphic description of this situation.

During the pursuit from the Hitler Line traffic congestion had caused many delays for, as we have seen, the narrow Liri-Sacco, with its one good highway, provided limited road space for a parallel advance by two corps.

These operations ended following the breaching of the Hitler Line on 22 May, the capture of Pontecorvo on 24th and the pursuit by 5 Canadian Armed Division across the Melfa River on 5 June 1944. The casualty list was extensive and the Provost had their share. Lt Johnnie Myers, L Cpl Ken Dalbenas, Pte Len Eisenman, L Cpl Gerry Gauthier, L Cpl Bill Graham, L Cpl Tony Krasniuk, Cpl John Nelson and Cpl Don Stackhose were killed on duty. The men of No 1, 3 and 5 Provost Companies worked around the clock throughout this period. There is not the slightest doubt that but for their efforts the traffic congestion on the Liri Valley would have been much worse. Major Anthony J Scotti, MC, CD[66] tells of improved methods instituted to preclude traffic blocks.

Lt Col L H Nicholson[67], APM 1 Canadian Corps, was instrumental in obtaining additional resources. No 35 Traffic Control Company was formed from personnel and equipment of Nos 1 and 5 Light Anti-Aircraft Regiments; these two units being largely unemployed due to total Allied air superiority. HQ 1 Canadian Corps formed a Traffic and Movement Centre which, effectively, coordinated all road moves in the Corps area. No 5 Provost Company obtained, on permanent loan, the resources required to operate four Traffic Control Posts, around the clock. This consisted of 4 officers and 20 other ranks, all trained as radio operators and 4 x 22 radio sets and the necessary vehicles. Never again were we criticized for not having control over our traffic movement. In fact, Field Marshal Alexander stated later, during a visit to Canadian Formations, that he was not once delayed on the roads in the Canadian area.

Tony Scotti also shares a little humour.

Lieutenant Eric Morkelberg, Canadian Provost Corps, arrived at the Reinforcement Holding unit in Tunis. He had missed the recreational bus and had to walk back to Base. However, being tired he decided to have a rest beside the road and he dozed off. When he awoke he was amazed to find himself "bootless". Eric was a man of ample proportions, 6'5" tall and size 14 shoes. Someone stole his boots off his feet whilst he slept. He arrived in Italy, as a reinforcement, wearing tennis shoes as there was not one pair of size 14's in the theatre.

The next major action by the Canadian Corps was the assault on the Gothic line from 30 August to 3 September 1944. The fact that D-Day landings had taken place on the coast of Normandy on 5 June, and that Rome had fallen on 4 June 1944, did not deter the German armies will to fight in Italy. The Gothic Line was heavily defended and extended across the waist of Italy, running east-west just north of the Foglia River. The Corps, with 1 and 5 Divisions, advanced to the Foglia River on 26 – 29 August. The attack, with heavy artillery support, broke through on 1 September and our troops reached Cattolica, on the Adriatic coast, three days later. Once again the enemy line had been smashed. There were few, if any, traffic problems as all concerned staff, commanders and provost had learned how to cope.

Despite heavy rains in September, which created river torrents and washouts, the Canadian Corps advanced from the Marechia to Riccione. It took Rimini with 5 Armoured Divisions advancing as far as Mauro by 20 October. Sounds easy, but Provost still talk of mired tanks and guns, enemy shellfire and cold, wet nights. The days of the Canadians in Italy were drawing to a close. The last major operation was clearing the flat plain area between the Montone and Sennio Rivers, past Ravenna, on the 2–6 January 1945. The 5 Armd Division units reached Sant'Alberto on the Valli di Comacchio (Adriatic) on 5 January 1944.

Goldflake was the codename given to the transfer of all Canadians in Italy to northwest Europe, in February and March 1945. This move by road, rail and sea must rank as one of the largest, longest and fastest of any in military history. The term "all Canadians" included not only the Corps, two Divisions and one tank Brigade of the Field Force, but countless tons of equipment and several thousand troops of the base and maintenance areas required loading and transport; units such as General Hospitals, Leave Centres, Stores Depots, Detention Barracks and Workshops had to pack and go. The plan, which must be kept from the ears of the German High Command, called for move by road from the present locales to the seaports of Naples and Leghorn. Then by sea transports to Marseilles, followed by road and rail to assembly areas near Renaix, Belgium. The first convoys of 1 Corps and 1 Division left the Ravenna area on 15 February, sailed from Naples 22 February, disembarked Marseilles 24 February, stayed for two days and arrived in Belgium on 4 March 1945. The tanks of 5 Canadian Armd Division and 1 Canadian Armd Brigade were embarked at Leghorn, offloaded and reloaded onto transporters and trains at Marseilles and moved by road or rail to Belgium. On arrival in Belgium the whole of 1 Canadian Corps, the two Divisions and the Armd Brigade was placed under the operational control of HQ First Canadian Army. Thus, for the first time in history, Canada had a complete army of two Corps in the field.

Needless to say, the Canadian Provost Corps played a significant role in this remarkable military move. Routes from battle-field positions to

Naples/Leghorn must be signed and manned. Staging areas enroute to and at seaports required tight control and adherence to move tables. A point of interest arose when, suddenly via moccasin telegraph, absentees and deserters began flocking into the Base areas to get a free ride back to "wherever". The route from Marseilles to Renaix, via Lyons and east of Paris, was signed with a special "G F" marker by 35 Traffic Control Company, along with five, spaced out, staging areas along the way. The Corps was, once again, fully operational on 15 March 1945 and would soon participate in the final liberation of Holland.

7

Northwest Europe, June 1944–October 1945

Normandy and Caen

Apart from a passing reference to the Canadian formations which took part in the so-called Second Front, this phase of the Canadian Provost Corps history will dwell exclusively on dates, places and events where provost were involved. The detail of the many battles fought during this campaign by the Canadian Army is in any event well documented. This omission is not in any way a denigration of the fighting qualities shown by Canadian soldiers from the beginning to the end of this history making campaign. By 6 June the last Exercises were completed and Nos 2, 8 and 13 Provost Companies were living in sealed, tented camps in and around Dover, with their parent formations. See Table 2. No 4 Company, with No 3 Canadian Infantry Division, was located near Portsmouth and No 11 Company, with First Canadian Army, was near Mickleham, Sussex. At first light on 6 June six battalions of 3 Canadian Infantry Division landed on a five mile stretch of beach in Normandy, including the coastal towns of Vaux, La Valette, Courselles, Bernieres and St Aubin.

The six sections of 4 Company were embarked in separate landing craft in keeping with the practice of not having all eggs in one basket. Sergeant W.E.R. (Ray) Chambers[68] of "D" Section described the crossing.

> There were five members of No 4 Provost Company aboard our craft, myself and four Lance Corporals. There was also 18 Platoon, D Company of the Highland Light Infantry of Canada (HLI of C), as well as small groups from other units. All told, there were about 105 passengers. The idea, of course, was that if we were unable to land, there would be people in other landing craft who could carry on with the job that needed to be done when we did land.

The English Channel was very rough and everyone seemed to be seasick. The stench in the ship was horrendous. With the folding bunks so close together, and the buckets overflowing with vomit, it quickly became unbearable. At that point I asked the Officer in Charge, from the HLI of C, if my men and I could go topside to get some fresh air. He said yes, with the condition that we, in turn, do just one thing for his men. It was planned that the HLI of C was to go ashore with folding bicycles, which were being stored in the bow of the ship behind canvas screens. In the interest of order and time, he asked if we would pass these folding bicycles over the screens during the landing. I said we could certainly do that. So, after touchdown, my men and I stood behind the canvas screens and handed the bicycles over the screens to the HLI of C men as they went down the ramps one either side of the bow. As soon as that was done we went through the town of Berniers sur Mer and reached our rendezvous spot in Beny sur Mer before nightfall. All our section and all our vehicles were ashore and ready to go.

No 4 Company dealt with a few POW, which meant holding them inside a house or courtyard until they could be backloaded. Routes off the beaches were marked and critical points manned. Sergeant Giles accompanied the Commander of the 8th Infantry Brigade, Brigadier K G Blackader, on an anti-sniper patrol using a 6–pounder A tk gun towed behind Giles' jeep. Apparently every church steeple received a round or two, just in case.

Another incident worthy of recall occurred when Lieutenant Howard German and RSM Dennis Harper of 4 Company were jumped whilst in a jeep near Beny sur Mer, and taken prisoner. Lieutenant German, a fast talker and aided by some incoming Canadian fire, convinced his captors, some 17 Jerries, that their position was hopeless with the result they, in turn, surrendered to him. Perhaps this is an example of the "morale factor" in war.

The next Canadian Provost Corps unit across was No 13 Company on 29 June, followed by 2 company on 7 July, 8 company on 17 July and 11 company, with HQ First Canadian Army, on 20 July, all with their parent formations. Mention should be made of the routes, embarkation and methods of getting the follow-up formations from the Dover area to the Normandy beaches. These units travelled by road from Dover, via Canterbury, through London to the Embarkation Area at the Tilbury docks on the Thames River just east of London. There were some problems. The putty-like material used to waterproof vehicles resulted in the loss of some heavily loaded jeeps and trailers due to overheating. Replacements were not immediately available. Another source of trouble came from the damage caused by the V-1 German Rockets (Buzz Bombs), many of which landed in and near the dock area. Lance Corporal Vince, of No 8 Company, was killed and two other were injured from this source. Although transport ships were scheduled to match incoming units, there were some "glitches". For example, units were scheduled to remain in their assembly areas for at least 24 hours in order to complete the final phase of waterproofing, draw French francs, turn in their Pounds Sterling, and other such details. No sooner had No 13 Company settled for a night's rest when the order came over the loudspeaker for Serial "X"[69] to proceed immediately to Pier "Y" for loading. This caused a scramble in the blackout, however the vehicles: 3 ton and 15 hundredweight trucks, 28 jeeps and trailers and 96 Triumph motorcycles were loaded by huge cranes onto the deck and into the holds of the transport. A sleepy Field Cashier was awakened in his bombproof bunker and produced, without hesitation, a large cotton bag full of French francs, being equivalent at the prevailing rate of exchange to the total British pounds owing to or turned in by each member of the Company. The Orderly Room Corporal (Cpl Keelan), the RSM and OC later held a pay parade in the middle of the English Channel. On arrival, at a point about one mile offshore near the beach area, the smaller LSTs came alongside and the vehicles were smartly offloaded by the ship's booms. The 96 motorcycles were placed on a huge "Rhino" barge. The tide was ebbing by the time it reached the beach at about 1945 hours. This created a huge problem in getting the machines off, owing to the barge's inability to moor with its ramp out of the water. After several bike had drowned the day was saved by Lance Corporal Wright who rode the bikes, at high speed, for the full length of the barge, then literally jumped the water and landed them on the sandy beach. The last elements of the Company reached the assembly area near the village of Thaon, by 2230 hours on 29 July. The noise of artillery and the long streamers of light caused by tracer bullets did not make for sleeping.

Despite the rapid build-up of Divisions and Corps Troops, there were very few traffic problems in the initial bridgehead. The country was flat and open with a good road network. The City of Caen and the line of the Odon and Orne Rivers was the immediate objective. About this time the Provost pointsmen came up with a novel and effective technique for preventing German artillery fire, which was zeroed in on almost every crossroad in our forward areas, from wreaking damage on our traffic passing through the intersection. It was an observant corporal in 4 Company who noticed that a salvo of 6 to 8 rounds would come in at precise intervals. He, therefore, could halt all traffic and take cover himself when the next "stonk" was due. This technique was used with much success at the crossroads near Buron, which was under enemy observation for his OPs in Colombelles.

Operation Goodwood, on 18 July, was a massive attack over the Orne, east of Caen, designed to dislodge the Germans to the south of this city. Three British armoured divisions (7th, 11th and Guards) moved laterally from west to east across the maintenance routes of 2 Canadian Corps. No 13 Company was flat out for two days dealing with halting all of the maintenance traffic, which had to be diverted to enable these divisions to get into position for the assault. This attack, by massed armoured formations, was stopped by the overpowering fire power of well positioned German Tiger tanks with their deadly 88 mm guns. Needless to say, there were heavy tank losses and many casualties. It was clear by now that the formidable German Panzer (Armoured) Divisions were now on our front. Once again, as in Sicily, dust and dysentery seriously hampered provost, particularly pointsmen as they were frequently forced by the "call" to leave their points for short periods, at the most inopportune times. This meant that the Section Sergeant was often forced to post two men on a point where normally one would suffice, thus quickly reducing his manpower resources. As usual, there were many rumours that the Germans had poisoned the wells[70] and streams. Some even went so far as to say this was done to force the Canadian troops to drink Calvados, the local fermented apple cider, which was unspeakably strong and foul tasting. Whether true or not, a certain amount of this potent elixir was consumed, in any event.

The ancient Norman city of Caen was located about twelve miles inland from the Canadian beach area, on the Orne River. Like so many French cities, all roads converged at this point like the spokes of a wheel. It will be remembered by provost as the mother of all traffic bottlenecks. The Allies must get through this obstacle in order to gain access to the open country beyond. Commencing on 8 July, and continuing for almost three weeks, a total of four infantry and two armoured divisions[71] supported by hundreds of corps artillery guns and heavy bombers from the RAF Bomber Command, were engaged in the battle for Caen. The adjoining suburbs of Colombelles and Vaucelles, south of the River Orne, must also be cleared. Caen was captured following a heavy attack by over 450 bombers on the evening of 7 July, which reduced much of the city to rubble and completely closed all streets and roads. It took our engineers with bulldozers two days to clear a route which would enable a bridge to be built over the Orne. A Bailey bridge was erected across the Orne by a company of 2 Canadian Corps Engineers and was ready for traffic on the morning of 19 July. A further attack resulted in the capture of the high ground west of the Orne, including the towns of Vaucelles and Colombelles.

This action resulted in the first sizeable number of captured enemy prisoners of war, some 460 on 19–20 July. No 13 Company quickly constructed the *first* of many PW Cages. The compound was located in an open area about the size of a football field, with the boundary marked by white tape suspended on stakes. A complete provost section, with one provost officer, was assigned full-time to this function. The procedure which quickly evolved soon became standard. On arrival, usually escorted by infantrymen, the PW were segregated by officers and men, counted, formed up in one or more ranks, searched and marched to the appropriate area in the compound where officers and men were again segregated[72]. It was also important to appoint a senior German commander for both groups, who was made responsible for organizing all internal administrative matters such as requesting medical care for wounded or sick, distributing food (biscuit and bully), water and spades for digging slits and constructing latrines. Provost with stens were stationed at alternate corners and an escort was on hand to parade those selected for interrogation to the Intelligence Interrogation Officers' tent. An interpreter, if required, was found from the PW group. Often he would be the person nominated as the POW Senior. It was a principle the PW were moved out of the forward areas quickly. The system developed utilized empty 2nd line RSASC trucks returning to rear area supply depots. The Provost Officer or NCO 1C PW would make requests, as required, to the CRASC at Rear Division for an appropriate number of trucks based on 30 POW per truck. A provost jeep escort would accompany these trucks to the Base Area Cage in the Army or L of C area. It is strange that the provost engaged in this task had little or no prior instruction; there was no standard procedure and it is highly unlikely that anyone in a field provost company below officer rank had ever seen the 1936 Geneva Convention Relative to the Treatment of Prisoners of War. It was largely a matter of using good 'horse sense' and setting the job done.

The RCE Bailey bridge over the Orne was ready for traffic on 19 July, by which time a sizeable bridgehead over the Orne had been secured. This bridge was christened "CHURCHILL" and was later flanked by its mate "WINSTON" in order to permit two-way traffic across this defile. A special traffic control system was organized to control the huge volume of tanks, trucks, guns, ambulances and people involved in the breakout operations south of Caen. This involved five sections of 13 Provost Company as well as the Division Companies. Waiting, or "laying-up", areas were located well back of Caen itself so that units and headquarters could be available as required. Another smaller waiting area was established closer to the bridge sites where vehicles could be held for short periods, ie, supply convoys, ambulances and free runners. Wireless silence was necessary so the next best alternative for passing move orders was provost on motorcycles and unit DRs. All of the routes leading to the bridges were narrow, bulldozed lanes through huge piles of rubble and, therefore, were one-way only. This defile control problem was gradually eased with the clearing of additional routes and, as mentioned, the construction of "WINSTON" bridge. A further bridge, farther upstream on the Orne, was built for 2 Canadian Infantry Division, on the western outskirts of Caen and this also relieved the congestion at "WINSTON" and "CHURCHILL". In about two weeks it was possible to sign good UP and DOWN routes from the outskirts of the city to and from the bridges.

In preparation for the attack on Verrières Ridge, south of Caen, a huge ammunition dumping programme was organized. Over 400 truckloads were moved from the beach area, through Caen and into a large factory area south of Colombelles. This was done over a period of three consecutive nights. The DUMP area was somewhat farther forward than desirable, but there was no other option. A section of 13 Company was employed on traffic duties in the Dump area to assist in getting loaded trucks to their offloading areas, and back to the DOWN route for another load, in the dark. The dumping programme was nearly complete after three nights, and then it happened. Some US Airforce Bombers were returning in the early morning from an aborted night raid when they spotted this huge dump area which they mistook for an enemy supply base. They released the bomb loads with great accuracy and effect, blowing up and exploding the major portion of the ammo so laboriously gathered for the next major offensive. The 13 Provost Company section was in the area getting ready for some breakfast and clean-up when the bombs came down. The Sergeant quickly recognized the situation and the men moved with commendable speed into previously recc'ied slits. Fortunately there were no provost casualties however the section lost one jeep and two motorcycles in the exploding inferno, which lasted over three hours.

During the lengthy period of training and work in England, the Provost Companies endeavoured to develop a drill or system for every anticipated situation. While most situations were covered, there was always something new cropping up. One of these was the requirement in a Field Provost Company for an organized system of requisitioning, distributing and recovering map sheets. As far as provost were concerned, everything happened on the roads. With a few exceptions all of the areas in France, Belgium and Holland, over which the Canadian Army, moved were well mapped by good, accurate 1:50,000 G S Ordnance Survey maps. These were generally available on demand to the Division/Corps Map Store. It is probably correct to say that most companies did not ascribe the importance deserved to this subject and, hence, at some time were caught short and ordered or distributed the wrong sheets. Furthermore, it was absolutely essential that every Canadian Provost Corps officer and man be thoroughly trained and practiced in using the G S Survey map. He must, if catastrophes were to be avoided, be able to plot accurate grid references, follow a route by day or night, measure gradients and distances and, above all, double check all map references. The following example of issuing an incorrect reference, and the consequence thereof, is given by Sergeant Ray Chambers of 4 Provost Company.

In the latter part of July 1944 I was handed a map reference sent down by the APM from Divisional Headquarters, which ordered us to set-up traffic control at a new one-way bridge which had just been built. We were, at that time, situated near Colombelles, just outside of Caen. I located the map reference on the map and it looked to be pretty far out to our left, near a town called Troarn. Accompanied by two Lance Corporals I started out for the bridge. We had to go four or five miles down a good road towards Troarn and, as we drove, we noticed to our right that a British brigade seemed to be forming up for an attack. They were under very heavy shell and mortar fire. Just as we entered the outskirts of Troarn a British Captain stepped out from behind a brick wall and stopped us. He asked us where we were going and I showed him our map reference and the map. He said that an error had been made and that the bridge we were headed for was still well inside enemy territory. He advised us to return for verification of the map reference.

On our way back, with the attack continuing all around us, we were stopped by a British Infantry Medical Corpsman and asked if we could take a couple of their "walking wounded". We escorted the wounded men to their Advanced Dressing Station and then returned to Division Headquarters. Upon our return we checked with the APM and found that his original map reference was out by ten grids, and that the bridge where traffic control was needed was almost within sight of Division Headquarters.

The fierce battles to clear the Caen are were no sooner over when yet another problem reared its 'ugly head'. Large numbers of inhabitants were rendered homeless by the destruction of their city. Panic-stricken they began to move out of the devastated area, at first in a trickle which soon became a torrent. The refugees used the only roads and streets available, namely our main operational routes, especially the good Caen-Falaise highway as well as our only good lateral route running east-west across the southern edge of Vaucelles. They carried what personal possessions they could salvage and travelled by every conceivable means including bicycles, on foot, in mechanically unfit cars and horse or ox drawn carts. The result was a serious obstacle for our military vehicles, and there thousands, using these roads both night and day.

The initial provost response was to stop them from getting on the routes, which was like trying to stop water from leaking out of a sieve. Posting signs, in French, directing them away from the area was tried without success. The best results came from heavy route patrols combined with pointsmen at strategic points. the fact that they gradually built up into a large group, moving in column, helped provost patrols to cope as they could be spotted quickly and dealt with. The provost patrols had some success by explaining why they must not use the road and then leading them off on some track or side road. We were conscious of the plight of these poor people. They had lost everything, including family, friends and relatives and were only doing the sensible thing, which was to flee and seek safety somewhere.

At least one provost patrolman knew what to do. As a farm lad from Western Canada he knew about such things as "king pins", "lug bolts" and "axle pins" on farm wagons. When he had trailed a group off the route and halted them near a farmyard, he simply removed the axle pins from each cart and threw them, as far as he could, into a nearby wheat field. This rendered the cart immobile since any movement would result in the wheel falling off. He was probably justified in taking this action. In any event, he explained he had given the driver a sporting chance as he could probably recover the pin by a diligent search. One sometimes had to be cruel to be kind and the priorities in this case seemed quite clear.

Quesnay Woods, Falaise and The Gap

The next major objective of 2 Canadian Corps was the capture of Verrieres Ridge, a high feature running across the Canadian front, about three miles south of Caen. It was secured after some heavy battling by Infantry and Armoured Divisions on 21 July. Both 2 and 3 Canadian Infantry Division suffered casualties in places such as St Andre Sur Orne, Marton-de-Fontenay, Hubert-Folie and Bourguebus. Another 600 – 700 German PW were processed through the Division and Corps cages by the Provost Companies. The Caen bottleneck was now solved by adequate two-way routes into and through the city. The main Corps axis was the Route Nationale, a good highway which ran southeast of Caen through Falaise, Argentan and eventually to Paris. This did wonders to alleviate the constant press for road space in the Corps area and it translated into a marked decrease in traffic problems for provost.

Headquarters First Canadian Army became operational on 23 July and was given command of 2 Canadian Corps (2 and 3 Canadian Infantry Divisions, 4 Canadian Armoured Division and 2 Canadian Armoured Brigade) as well as 1 British Corps (3 Infantry and 11 Armoured Divisions). This brought our buddies in No 11 Provost Company into the fray. The Company had been busy for the past week assisting in the never ending traffic problems occasioned by the constant shuffling of armoured and infantry divisions fore, aft and laterally. The build-up over the beaches continued full blast throughout July and into August with men, vehicles, guns, ammo, supplies and petrol coming ashore.

The next objective was Falaise, about ten miles south of the current front. The German Panzers were fighting from well prepared defensive positions on either side and on the Highway. A two phase attack, by four divisions under 2 Canadian Corps, was carried out on 8 and 10 August. It was not successful despite massive artillery and heavy bomber support, over 460 guns and about 500 light and heavy bombers of RAF Bomber Command. The attack was made at night, aided by low beam searchlights. The dust and darkness were probably factors in not achieving success. Nevertheless, the bombers hit their targets in good order as did the deadly 88 mm German guns which knocked out 47 tanks of a Canadian armoured regiment.

One of the really tough defended areas was the Quesnay Woods, about halfway between Caen and Falaise astride the highway. Two Canadian Corps planned and carried out another major attack on 14 August, code-named Operation Tractable. Once again the plan called for bomber support on the pre-selected targets, just prior to H Hour[73]. This time the attack was made in daylight and the bomber run was on time. Red smoke shells were dropped as markers by the Pathfinders, and then it happened. The attacking troops were buried in a hurricane of exploding bombs long before they crossed their start lines. The first few bomber flights had delivered their loads on target but, for some reason, the succeeding bombers released their explosives prior to the target area. This progressive "back-up" action, whereby bombs fell short, resulted in many Canadian casualties. We now know that a Canadian officer from a reconnaissance regiment had been captured by the Germans a few days before. The problem was, he not only carried a marked map but also a copy of the complete operational plan. Another possible cause of this debacle was that the German defenders lobbed their own coloured smoke shells back on us, thus accounting for the early release of bombs by the pilots of Bomber Command.

The tremendous force of exploding bombs hurled large equipment, such as 5.5 inch artillery guns and large lorries, high in the air. There were craters everywhere, some the size of a two-storey house. The World War I trauma called shell-shock was soon apparent following this bombardment. Men with no visible wounds were found in a dazed, numb state. Some walked aimlessly about, others remained in a slit-trench or hole where they had taken refuge and all stared ahead, in a trance-like state. Three sections of No 13 Company were engaged in keeping the main Caen-Falaise road open and getting ambulances forward and back again with the wounded. Sergeant George Blythe, NCO IC "B" Section, No 13 Provost Company was able to assist one unfortunate infantryman.

I met a soldier around the Falaise Gap wandering in a daze. He turned himself over to me to be arrested. He said, "I'd sooner be shot in one piece than to go back there again". I tried to explain to him that if I placed him under arrest, he would be charged with desertion. He simply repeated the same words, "I'd sooner be shot in one piece than to go back and face that again". As you know, most provost sergeants, senior NCOs and officers were allowed one bottle of alcohol per month. It happened that I received my monthly ration that same day. I suggested to him that we have a couple of drinks, that he should have something to eat and a night's rest and we'd have a little chat in the morning. I told him that if he decided to go back in the morning, I would take him back to the unit myself and I would speak to his major. After a good night's sleep he had second thoughts about it and was quite happy to go back to his unit. I explained to his major that he had just got lost and was trying to find his way back to the unit. I never did meet the chap again, but I was happy to be in a position to be able to help him. I felt great satisfaction in seeing the lad get back to his unit. The policing end of it was important, but it was just as important to be able to help others, and there were many instances where I could be of help.

The offensive by the Canadian and Allied forces continued towards Falaise and the River Dives. All Canadian formations were involved in an all out push to capture Falaise, and of great urgency, to link up with the rapidly advancing armoured divisions of General George Patton's Third US Army somewhere southwest of Falaise. Our forces, from left to right, were: 3

Canadian Infantry Division, 2 Canadian Armd Brigade, 4 Canadian Armed Division, 1 Polish Armd Division (under 2 Canadian Corps) and 2 Canadian Infantry Division. On our right we had 53 and 59 British Infantry and 11 British Armed Division also moving around Falaise to the west and south. A brigade of 2 Canadian Infantry Division, following a heavy artillery programme by our field and medium guns, captured Falaise on 17 August. A 2 Provost Company pointsman, on duty in Falaise at a crossroads where fires were still burning on each side, was photographed by a Canadian PR officer. This photo appeared in several papers as well as in the official history. The Provost Companies were hard pressed to keep track of "who was going where", as divisions were leapfrogging, crossing others' main axis, regrouping and, literally, making "U" turns. Once again it falls to the redoubtable Sergeant Ray Chambers to explain how his provost section met this challenge.

One of our basic jobs was traffic control and the marking of UP and DOWN routes on our Axis of Advance. But when the action was fluid, time was very short and we had to improvise.

During the breakthrough south of Caen we were given the Start Point, the Route and the Dispersal Point, then told the Recce troops in front of us to 'get on with it' because the first vehicles were due at the Start Point in a matter of minutes. We were putting up the Start Point signs with the first convoy about one hundred yards away and so, with the jeep leading and me reading the map, we started out. As we came to an intersecting road or path I would point. The L/Cpl immediately behind the jeep would park his bike and take over control of that intersections. He knew the direction the vehicles were coming from and where they were going, as well as all our unit vehicle signs. Later on, if that same road was going to be used by our Axis of Advance, it would be properly signed and manned, as time permitted.

This same method was used at times when we hit the Polder country of Northern Holland, where the land was flat and you could see for miles ahead.

Elements of 4 Canadian Armd and 1 Polish Division met a unit of the Third US Army driving up from the south, at the village of Chambois, on 19 August. Chambois was the most southerly of three villages located on the Dives River. Trun and St Lambert sur Dives were equally spaced about three miles apart and this area became known as the Trun-Chambois Valley. It was carnage such as few had ever seen. The German Panzers, knowing they were being encircled, fought furiously to break out eastward and escape. Many did, but they were subjected to constant attack by our fighter aircraft which, by now, were flying out of a landing strip southeast of Caen.

They absolutely destroyed the luckless German columns fleeing to the east on any available road or track. There can be no better explanation of the finale of the battles in Normandy than that given by our Official Historian[74], Colonel Charles P Stacey.

During the five days, ending at 6:00 pm on 23 August, 28 officers and 13,475 other ranks passed through First Canadian Army's prisoner-of-war cage. Many more, of course, were picked up by the other converging Allied armies. As well, the German armoured formations were mere shadows of themselves after the battle; and we have ample evidence to show how terrible was the slaughter of the unfortunate German infantry. Across the whole region where the Gap[75] had been, the green uniformed corpses lay thick; at one place, just northeast of St-Lambert-sur-Dives, an observer on 22 August saw "hundreds of dead, so close together that they were practically touching". From this appalling charnel-house there rose, to offend the heavens, a stench that was strong on the nostril, even of people in light aircraft above. Every road and byway was blocked with ruined or abandoned German vehicles. In the Gap area British investigators found 187 tanks and self-propelled guns, 157 lightly armoured vehicles, 1,778 lorries, 669 cars and 252 guns. A grand total of 3,043 guns and vehicles[76]. The heaviest concentration was south and southwest of St Lambert. Much of the German transport had been horse drawn; but no exact count was made of carts and wagons, for the investigators found that "the stench of dead horses was so overpowering that where there was any number of horse drawn vehicles, that area had to be passed with all speed.

At least one section of No 13 Provost Company can attest to this vivid description of the "charnel house". In the rush to move quickly to the Seine River, the next objective, a mild dispute arose between 1 British and 2 Canadian Corps staff as to who would have priority for the one good road leading out of the immediate Gap area. "E" Section was detailed to move into the area quickly and secure this route for 2 Canadian Corps, their masters. They left St-Pierre-sur-Dives, farther north, at about 0730 hours on 11 August. On reaching St Lambert the "stench" was so overpowering that the sergeant wisely pulled back, as had every human being in the area, soldiers and civilians alike. He reported back to company headquarters where the RSM complained loudly of "a strange smell". The odour was so pervasive that it still clung to the vehicles and clothing of the "E" Section provost. As RSM's are want to do, he ordered everyone to take a bath. In this hard fought campaign, there were many obstacles placed in the path of provost including buzz bombs, soft sand beaches, our own bombers, dust, dirt and dysentery. Why not dead horses?

The Seine, Channel Ports and Antwerp

The next phase of the campaign was largely devoted to chasing the defeated Seventh German Army across northern France, Belgium and to Holland. This is not to say that it was a cakewalk because the enemy seized every opportunity to delay and stop the pursuit. He laid land mines, the deadly Teller mine. Every bridge, road or rail, large or small, was blown and he would slow or stop our advance by small, well placed rearguards that were often strong enough to cause a major deployment of our leading brigades. The cities located on the Channel, all seaports, he defended with large garrison forces to prevent our gaining the use of a port as a forward supply base. The supply lines of the Canadian Army, at one time, stretched all the way from the Normandy beach to Antwerp. An armoured division required 15,000 gallons of petrol to move 10 miles, which translated to 25 x 3 ton RCASC trucks each carrying 150 x 4 gallon jerricans[77] (ie: 600 gallons). Rations and ammunition were equally as important and expensive in terms of the truck-miles-time equations. Much of the strategy on both sides, would revolve around the Allied armies' efforts to shorten their supply lines by securing a shipping port such as Le Havre, Boulogne and Antwerp.

The pursuit, or chase, was often, as noted previously, rudely interrupted, however, what a welcome relief from the Normandy plains. The countryside was rolling, green and dotted with farms, orchards, streams and, above all, friendly, smiling and hospitable habitants. It was quite inspiring to see the odd hastily constructed sign saying: "vive le canadien". Provost section cooks (cum-truck drivers), always skillful foragers, found a plentiful supply of eggs (les ouefs), fresh bread (du pain) and cheese (le fromage), much of it presented as a gift from a smiling farmer or shopkeeper.

With this overview of the Canadian Army's activity during late August and September, it is timely to recall a few previously unrecorded incidents and events where the men of the Canadian Provost Corps were players. The first stop after the Gap was near the town of Ste-Foy-de-Montgomerie. No 13 Company Headquarters, plus two sections, bivouacked overnight in a pear orchard about 2 miles north of Ste Foy. Following a trip to Corps Headquarters nearby, and a good hot meal, the orderly room corporal ushered in a local habitant who was anxious to give some information. After a short walk along the road towards St Foy he pointed to a large touring car which was laying upside down on the side of the road. It had the swastika logo and the other markings which indicated that the former owner was a German officer. Our friend then stated, quite gleefully, that this was the car in which Field Marshal Erwin Rommel[78] was seriously injured when strafed by an Allied fighter, in mid-July. This new friend never did divulge his motive for imparting this information, but he was proud. The Corps axis from Chambois ran east through Orbec, Bernay, Brionne and up to the Seine near Elbeuf, below Rouen. On about 27 August, the Commander 2 Canadian Corps, as he sometimes did, went forward for a fast look as his divisions closed up to the Seine. He was accompanied by an engineer, signals and provost officer. This trio preceded him in jeeps ahead of his Staghound scout car. As they barrelled along the open road about 4 miles short of the River the Provost Officer suddenly spotted about twelve tanks, line astern, coming toward them. The question of whether they were friend or foe was resolved when the large, white logo of the Allies, the five pointed star, became visible. Nevertheless the trio pulled up and stopped, as did the staghound driver. By the time the Corps Commander had climbed down from the turret, the lead tank upon seeing us, pulled smartly off the road and quickly performed a classic "circle wagons" manoeuvre with each tank facing outwards. A very young United States Armoured Corps lieutenant got out of the lead tank, approached Lt Gen G G Simonds, saluted and, in a pronounced southern drawl, said: "Good afternoon General, we have just liberated Elbeuf for you all". The General quickly got to his staghound and roared towards the Seine with the trio frantically trying to catch up in their jeeps. As Robbie Burns said: "The best laid plans of mice and men gang aft agley".

On this day the OC 13 Provost Company was leading his small Headquarters group (QM truck, RSM, Orderly Room, MT truck and two provost on MC's just in case). As they approached the town of Bernay, west of the Seine some 25 miles, a large crowd in the centre of town forced a halt. After a short while it became apparent what the fuss was about. A group of French Resistance Fighters, wearing berets and armbands, were in charge of a solitary German soldier, obviously a prisoner and not too happy. The leader approached and requested permission to ride with us to the next village where his prisoner would be interned. He was carrying, of all weapons, a Sten Machine Gun (gas-pipe special) and was very regimental and all business in his voice and posture. The offer was declined, however this was not to be the last episode involving German prisoners and the local Resistance people. This FF1 Leader had every right to be proud.

While this phase might have had the appearance of a peacetime tourist caravan, nevertheless there was a serious side for provost. The tremendous litter of German transport and tanks could be found on every road eastward of the Gap for about forty miles. The pursuing Canadians, travelling in daylight, simply wormed around burnt out tanks and lorries and kept going. It would be sometime before road clearing operations were completed. In the meantime, those using these roads at night suffered frightful accidents caused by crashing into these unseen derelicts. At least six provost were badly injured and two, one each from No 8 and 13 Provost Companies, were killed. Shades of the concrete road blocks in England, which also took a toll.

One outcome of this experience had important overtones for provost. The very real problems of road clearance had not, as yet, been seriously addressed by Canadian staffs, however, it was decided at Headquarters 2 Canadian Corps to take remedial action. A system evolved whereby the Royal Canadian Electrical and Mechanical Engineers (RCEME) workshops, who carried huge "wreckers"[79] for this purpose, would detach one or more of these to the Corps provost company and to Division Companies where warranted. From this time forward 13 Provost Company had at least one of these Recovery Vehicles and crew, which was attached to one of the sections. It proved a most valuable addition to the efforts of provost in clearing "dead" vehicles off the routes.

The vanguards of 2, 3 and 4 Canadian Divisions and 2 Canadian Armed Brigades reached the Seine on 26 August. The Germans fought a fierce rearguard action to buy time to get their own troops across the river. The fighting was especially heavy opposite 2 Canadian Infantry Division, on the left across from Rouen. For once the Germans could not be accused of blowing the bridges since the Seine River bridges, throughout its entire length, had been long since demolished by the Allied bomber interdiction programme which started before D-Day. Our infantry crossed in storm boats and assault crafts. A Canadian Engineer Company of 2 Canadian Corps constructed a large, tank-carrying raft which successfully moved a regiment of 4 Armoured Division across on 26–27 August. In what has to stand as a remarkable feat, the Engineers constructed a pontoon bridge[80] across the Seine at a point just north of Elbeuf. It was started on the late afternoon of 27 August and was ready for traffic, including tanks, at 10:00 hours 28 August. The river here is over 400 yards wide with a strong current. Stringing anchor cables, mooring the large "pontoon" boats and laying the deck, all done in the dark, was another remarkable achievement by our efficient and stalwart Canadian engineers. They were noted for their achievements. The Division provost companies were kept busy on traffic duties which, in the main, consisted of assisting in getting units to the crossing sites. The first provost across were sections from 4 and 8 Companies and it was their task to assist in assembling units in their proper concentration areas, prior to moving forward.

It fell to 13 Company to organize a defile control system, along the lines of the Caen experience. A notable difference was that there was very little "return" traffic, a decided advantage. A series of "Marshalling Areas" were established and signed. First an area for the large number of RCASC bridge carrying equipment was located close to the bridge site. A series of MAs, marked "A", "B" and "C" were located farther back and were designed to hold the Division, Corps and Army units waiting their turn to cross. It is regrettable that statistics were not kept, however, the movement across this bridge continued night and day for one week. One of the important tasks of the provost pointsmen at the bridge entrance was to ensure that heavier types of vehicles were kept spaced out in order to prevent overloading at one point. A famous photograph shows the Office Caravan of General Crerar crossing over. This was a huge vehicle, in both weight and bulk. The provost on duty halted it, sensibly, and requested clearance from the Engineer Duty Officer before sending it across. The picture shows the caravan canted upwards at a 30° angle, due to its weight, which pushed the pontoon's floats down to water level. A lusty cheer could be heard when its driver finally passed the off ramps, and we, once again, had the Army Commander safe on dry land.

The helter-skelter race across northern France continued with the Canadian Army moving east and north, up the Channel coastal area. Dieppe, not far from Rouen, was reached by 2 Canadian Infantry Division on 1 September. The Germans had departed. Elements of 4 Canadian Armoured Division reached the Somme River, south of Abbeville, on 3 September and 3 Canadian Infantry Division stopped short of Boulogne, farther west of Dieppe. This city was heavily defended, as was Abbeville on the Somme. The tanks of 11 British Armd Division[81] reached the outskirts of Antwerp on 4 September, where they met some stiff resistance. The people of Dieppe gave the men of 2 Canadian Infantry Division a very warm welcome, there were cheering crowds everywhere. General Crerar authorized the GOC of 2 Division to mark this occasion by calling a two day halt and organizing a suitable victory parade. The members of 2 Provost Company had an opportunity to survey the scene where their colleagues, two years previously, had suffered so much disaster. Captain H C (Chris) Forbes, OC 2 Provost Company, described the return to Dieppe[82].

Corporal Russell, who had been to Dieppe in 1942, rolled up to the outskirts again, this time from the landward side, with three armoured cars of the 8 Recce Regiment. Russell had marked the route for the Division to follow. One car moved forward to clear out three stay-behind German machine gun posts in the city, and Russell followed it, putting up his signs. That meant only one vehicle preceded 2

Company on the victorious return to Dieppe of the 2nd Canadian Division. A search of the Canadian military cemetery in Dieppe revealed Pete Oliver's grave to be No 479. Patrols and route signing was carried out in frantic preparation for a victory march.

On Sunday, 3 September, the Division held a memorial service at the cemetery and a victory march through Dieppe. The Dieppe veterans of 2 Company were photographed at Pete's grave and the picture was later published in the Canada Weekly and the Toronto Star Weekly. This necessitated a lot of work for 2 Company, who badly needed a breather after the long dash from Falaise.

Chris Forbes' last sentence expresses, directly perhaps, a somewhat unfair situation which arose every time a Division was ordered to a rest or refit posture. During such periods everyone EXCEPT PROVOST were refreshed by rest and recreation, good baths and clean clothes. This, inevitably, resulted in soldiers getting into trouble and, hence, increased rather than decreased the tasks of provost on patrols and checking out reports of troop misconduct. This is amply illustrated previously.

The reason why some cities and towns were stoutly defended by the Germans becomes clear when the events of that time are explained by later historical research. C P Stacey records[83] that Hitler had designated certain French ports a "fortress" to be especially defended to the last. On 4 September Hitler issued this directive.

Because of the breakthrough of enemy tank forces toward Antwerp, it has become very important for further progress of the war to hold the fortresses of BOULOGNE, DUNKIRK, the CALAIS defence area, WALCHEREN Island with FLUSHING harbour, the bridgehead at ANTWERP and the ALBERT CANAL position as far as MAASTRICHT.

Those soldiers of the Canadian Army who were involved in the fierce battlelines at the preceding named places, will testify to the fact that these orders were carried out 'to the letter'.

One small bit of satisfaction on the part of Canadians who had suffered attacks in England from the low flying "buzz" bombs, launched from sites across the Channel, was to pass by several of these totally destroyed sites located between Dieppe and Calais. It was also awesome to look at hundreds of deep bomb craters which pockmarked the area of each site. One could imagine how many bombs it took before a direct hit was registered. But it was comforting to know that the long suffering people of London and suburbs were at least reprieved from this menace[84].

Abbeville was taken by 4 Canadian Armoured Division following a sharp battle. It was here that a misread report from the Recce regiment, through 4 Division to 2 Corps, resulted in near catastrophe for two sections of 13 Provost Company. The report stated Abbeville and Pont Remy were free of enemy. In fact, there was still a strong German rearguard in Abbeville. At the request of Corps headquarters two sections of provost were dispatched from the Corps headquarters position near Neufchatel, to commence a preliminary recce in anticipation of a night assault and bridging operation over the Somme at Abbeville. The Provost officer and his two sections were rudely greeted by heavy German fire on arrival at their destination. The 4th Division then moved on and quickly captured Bruges and Ecloo, in Belgium. One of the stories here attests that a German field hospital was overrun in captured Bruges. To the astonishment of the South Alberta Recce Regiment of 4 Armed Division, they found the hospital treating both German wounded and, surprise, two or three Canadians who were wounded, presumably taken prisoner and carried back to the hospital.

After leaving Dieppe on 4 September, the next task given 2 Canadian Infantry Division was to capture Dunkirk, one of the fortresses. It was a tough nut and, after some unsuccessful assaults, it was decided to bypass this city and contain it (seal it off) with a small mobile force. The Division then moved to the Antwerp sector.

About this stage of operations yet another serious problem reared its head. Long lines of supply, previously mentioned, were taxing the RCASC resources to the limit. The demand for the three basics: rations, ammunition and petrol was far outstripping the supply. A senior "Q" officer at Headquarters First Army put it about right when he said, "a ten ton truck is now worth more than a tank". To further add to the problem of a strong pursuit, the demand for engineer bridge equipment was very heavy owing to the myriads of bridges, in this part of the world, over rivers, streams and canals; all blown by our enemy. Finally, No 84 Group Tactical Airforce assigned, to support First Canadian Army, also required huge amounts of summer-felt track and other material used for the repair and construction of forward airstrips. Nonetheless, our RCASC columns were magnificent. Almost every driver spent from 12–15 hours per day in the cab, snatching a few winks whenever they could. This, on top of lifting tons of ammunition, rations and jerricans, full and empty. Rations were drawn 4 or 5 times per week from a preselected "Supply Point"[85]. The provost companies never went hungry and often our lance corporals on the road would request a couple of jerricans of gas (petrol) from a halted column. Never a problem, except they insisted on a one-for-one exchange of jerricans. Their motto was most appropriate: "CAN – CAN DO – NO CAN – NO CAN DO".

The first Hitler "fortress" to be captured was the city of Boulogne, on the Channel about halfway between Dieppe and Calais. The attack by 3 Canadian Infantry Division began on 17 September and continued, against strong enemy resistance, for five days when it was finally taken. Once again the defences, mainly on the high ground ringing the city, were 'softened up' by a force of over 700 aircraft from RAF Bomber Command, which dropped over 3,000 tons of bombs just prior to the attack. Another feature was the use of long-range, 15 inch, coastal artillery located east of Dover across the Channel, to shell targets in Boulogne. They did this with good effect. Over 9,500 POW were taken and processed through 13 Provost Company's cage on 22 and 23 September, the largest number since the Gap. The cage was located in an open field south of the city and required the support of an additional provost section due to the crush of work involved in the sorting, counting, searching, securing and backloading this large, but docile, group. It required over 300 x 3 ton RCASC trucks to transport them to the rear army cage, over a two day period. It was here that the provost received some criticism for co-opting a group of eager FFI (freedom fighters) to ride the POW laden trucks as guard escorts. However, the storm from Headquarters 2 Canadian Corps soon blew over, and it did save countless man days of provost work for a company already stretched very thin. This was also one of the few times that the services of our own Medical Corps were used to look after the approximately 250 wounded German soldiers at a POW cage. Our own casualties, killed, wounded and missing, was about 650 total. So much for a trade-off in war.

The next fortress was Calais, and this task also fell to the good, old reliable 3 Division. It too was defended by a determined German force of about 7,500 troops in well prepared defensive positions. Once again these were hammered by RAF bombers prior to the attack. The battle lasted from 25 September to 1 October, when the German commander surrendered. An important aspect of this victory was that it finally silenced about ten large calibre German coastal batteries, which had regularly shelled Dover across the 15 mile narrow Channel. It also resulted in another 6,000, very subdued, POW at the Corps cage. One older German Wehrmacht[86] member, when being searched, asked the Canadian Provost Corps officer, speaking to him in English, if he could have a cap as his had been lost. The officer, Lieutenant Blackie Paige, showed compassion and granted this request. He then asked this POW if he thought Hitler would soon surrender. His reply, which undoubtedly expressed the sentiment of a large segment of the German Army, was "Hitler does not know enough to surrender".

Before leaving the Seine and Channel ports area there are one or two tales, involving provost, which should be told. The first involves a private of a United States Army Infantry battalion who was lost and/or isolated from his unit near Elbeuf, on the west side of the Seine. Accompanying this thrust, a "patented Patton ploy", was a battalion of motorized Infantry from the 29 United States Infantry Division. This occurred on or about 24 August. The United States Combat Team turned about, as directed when contact was made with the Canadians, and returned to the United States Third Army area much farther south. Private Eddy Slovik had arrived, in a United States army truck with a group of reinforcements for a battalion in the 29 United States Division in the Elbeuf area. Unfortunately, this small convoy of reinforcements was caught in a heavy German artillery barrage just as they were debussing. In the confusion that followed Private Slovik and a mate took cover in some stone buildings. They never did find the rest of their group who had, as mentioned, pulled out quickly. Those two frightened novices spent the night under cover. The following morning they started to look about and soon spotted a small group of Canadians. Coming from Detroit they recognized these men as friends and overcame their apprehensions long enough to ask for water. They had found the small section headquarters of Sergeant Kingswell and "H" Section of 13 Provost Company. Lance Corporal Gordon, who was preparing to go out on duty, made the two wayfarers welcome and turned them over to Lance Corporal Code, the section cook, who gave them coffee and a breakfast of bread, eggs, fried Spam and jam. This pair remained with "H" Section and made themselves useful by assisting with all sorts of chores and 'flunky' jobs such as cleaning traffic lanterns, making route signs, washing and pressing clothes and peeling potatoes for Lance Corporal Code. After about ten days, Sergeant Kingswell, who had been left to look after the Seine pontoon bridge traffic, brought them to company headquarters near Abbeville and reported their presence. By now they were solidly settled and were enthusiastic and useful members of the section. Private Slovik even made "potato pancakes" for the men. By all accounts, they were 'mouth watering'. However, it became clear to the company commander that they must be returned to their unit, which was much farther south across the boundaries of Second British Army and First United States Army. They both agreed to proceed on their own and were given a small German amphibious jeep, extra petrol, a box of 'C' rations and a map with the route marked on a road running straight south past Arras. They were to follow this road south until they came across a United States Army formation, where they would ask for assistance in locating their unit. They were even given a letter of identification explaining their situation, which was stamped and signed by the OC. So, the problem was solved. Not quite. Three days later they once again turned up at "H" Section, which they found by driving up the signed Corps axis route until they came to the familiar "H Section 13 Provost Company" sign beside the route. They were fast learners. Their return was reported by Sergeant Kingswell who stated he had doubts about their enthusiasm to return to their outfit. The OC then went official by having a priority message sent, through the long channel, back to Headquarters SHAEF and down the United States chain to 29 United States Division. This resulted in two US Army MPs arriving by jeep at company headquarters, then near Bruges, about two weeks later. They took custody of the pair, gave us a receipt, informed us that these two men were listed as deserters, and departed. The sequel to this story resulted in incredible notoriety for this whole affair. Private Eddy Slovik was tried on a charge of desertion, court-martialled and was subsequently executed[87] by firing squad during February 1945. He was the only United States Army soldier executed for desertion in World War II.

The port facilities of Antwerp were vital for the Allies. The Germans knew full well that we could not move much farther towards German soil unless this port could be used to shorten our long and tenuous supply routes. The city is located on the Scheldt River, about fifteen miles in from a point where the estuary narrows from the North Sea. The seaward channel is flanked on the north by the Island of Bevland and WALCHERN, and on the south by the so-called Breskens Peninsula, which was a flat, water covered polder about twenty miles in length. It was these two approach areas that the Germans defended with everything they could muster. It took 3 Canadian Infantry Division on the Breskens, and 2 Division at Bevland and Walchern, almost all of October and into November to finally dislodge the enemy from these bastions. As always, the Germans fought on ground which favoured the defence. When this bitter and bloody fighting was over, on 8 November, the port was opened to our shipping. Colonel C P Stacey relates the cost.

Thus, with the approaches[88] to Antwerp free of the enemy, and the country up to the Maas similarly cleared, the Battle of the Scheldt was over. It had been a hard and bloody business.

From 1 October through 8 November the First Canadian Army, on all its fronts, had taken 41,043 prisoners. Its own casualties, for the same period, were computed as 703 officers and 12,170 other ranks killed, wounded and missing. Of these, almost precisely half–355 officers and 6,012 other ranks–were Canadians.

Before leaving the Scheldt, we really must include another incident, as related by Sergeant W E R Chambers, NCO IC "D" Section, No 4 Provost Company.

At about the time of the Breskens Peninsula attack I was attached to the Company Headquarters for a couple of weeks, while my section, deemed to be the most experienced, was placed under a newly promoted sergeant.

During the time I was instructed to lay a traffic route in the vicinity of the town of Ecloo in northern Belgium, which was to be used by convoys the following day. A corporal and I started out to sign the route, which was a sturdy two-way metalled road good for heavy traffic. We experienced some trouble getting our metal sign holders into the verges, as they were very hard. We were signing the UP and DOWN routes at the same time and came to a set of inter-urban tracks that ran parallel to the road for some time. As it was easier to get the metal sign holder in between the tracks, rather than on the verges, we put our DOWN signs on the track up to the point that it wandered off left of our route.

We completed signing the route and came back down the route, checking all signs as we did. We found the DOWN signs on the tracks to be pointing 'every which way'. Of course we immediately thought our signs were being sabotaged, and decided to go after the saboteur. We hid the jeep and settled down into the ditch, waiting for our culprit. Eventually a small inter-urban car came down the tracks. The old motorman at the helm would stop, diligently pull up our signs, go the length of the trolley and then put our signs back. Of course, during the transfer the round arrows would fall off and he would patiently put them on again in a different hole. We had to re-lay that particular section of the DOWN route.

The people of the countries through which we passed looked upon war from a fatalistic point of view. A farmer near St Omer, south of Calais, provided us with water from his well and said it was good as the Boche had used some that very morning. When asked for his opinion on the constant coming and going of armies, he replied, "First the British, then the Boche, then the Boche and now the Canadians-it makes no difference". His great grandfather would very likely have expressed the same view.

The Canadian Army was now extended from Normandy to Antwerp and beyond along the line of the Maas River, through places such as Breda, Tilbury, Schertogenbosch and Nijmegen. The ill-fated Arnhem battle was fought from 16 to 26 September, when three Allied parachute divisions (82 and 101 United States and 1 British)[89] landed in the Graves, Nijmegen and Arnhem areas to secure a bridgehead from which to launch an assault on the Ruhr Valley, Germany.

The defeat of the Allied paratroop forces was largely due to the inability of a British armoured column to travel the distance, which would enable them to "link-up" and support the lightly armed paratroopers who were fighting against German panzer units. This epic, if ill-conceived, operation has been dramatized in the book and movie A Bridge Too Far. Although this effort failed, it did secure objectives, such as the bridge at Nijmegen, which was of considerable value to later operations.

The build-up of First Canadian Army included additional Canadian Provost Corps units to cope with the ever expanding lines-of-communication, variously called the "rear", "base" or "maintenance" area of First Canadian Army. With the opening of the port of Antwerp our lengthy supply routes were shortened. Nevertheless there was virtually no place in the long, narrow pathway made by the Canadian Army's movement along the Channel coastline where one could stop without seeing some military installation. The list was neverending and included a vast array of ordnance depots; petrol, ration and ammunition dumps; vehicle and tank workshops and replacement units; hospitals; reinforcement depots and a host of administrative and logistic headquarters for command, planning and control. Needless to say, these areas were busy around the clock with much traffic, both human and mechanical. This scene resulted in the planned move of two additional provost companies from England to the continent during the months of September and October.

No 7 Provost Company was organized on a field war established in England in late 1941. It augmented No 9 Provost Company in providing military police support for the CRU Base Area. It was located at Crookham Crossroads, near Aldershot, in a former golf course. This unit was sited near Ghent on its arrival in Belgium, and placed detached sections in the neighbouring towns of Ghent, Bruges and Antwerp where the men performed town patrol, traffic and security duties in much the same manner as in England. There was, however, one important difference. The supply of gin, cognac and wine available to troops on leave or rest caused some wild brawls, which occasionally resulted in indiscriminate shooting incidents. One such incident took place in Ghent late one evening, just as the Commander-in-Chief, Field Marshal Montgomery, was travelling through in his staff car. Having witnessed this personally it was not surprising that a "rocket" came down, through channels, which eventually reached all

Canadian formations. More on this later, however, such activity meant steady employment for No 7 Company from this time forward.

No 2 L of C Provost Company was formed in England early in 1944 and was designed for duty in the First Canadian Army L of C area. Its war establishment differed somewhat from a field company in that it had only one officer, the captain officer commanding, and a reduced scale of vehicles. For example, there was only one jeep in company headquarters and one light truck plus six motorcycles per section. Regimental Sergeant Major (RSM) Arthur S Bird[90] contributes this account of 2 L of C Company activities on the continent.

Prior to the move to France, one section under Sergeant Jock MacPhail was attached to Headquarters, 2nd Canadian Echelon[91] to provide a protective guard for a number of Canadian Army Women's Corps personnel on the strength of that unit. I am not sure, but I think the section remained there until it settled in Brussels.

As the company Sergeant Major, I was ordered to take the walking party of the unit to France, to be followed a week or so later by the OC and the rest of the unit. On arrival in France I had some difficulty finding a unit that would provide rations and quarters. We finally wound up with a British MP company for a week or so until the rest of the unit arrived. All sections were then detached from company headquarters, performing mostly traffic control duties. One section had the unenjoyable task of guarding the dead bodies of Canadian soldiers killed by General Kurt Meyers' men[92].

One section, under Sergeant Ted Broughton, was posted to Paris for duty and remained there until the unit was disbanded. We reached Brussels a few weeks later and located the unit a few yards off the main street, three blocks from the centre of the city.

Although we had a number of French speaking personnel on staff, we found it necessary to engage two civilian interpreters. We also added, to our investigative staff, Sergeant Rene Van de Waller from the Belgian Gendarmerie. We dressed him in Canadian battle dress and beret, but he wore the Gendarmerie cap and shoulder badges. I must add that he was a great asset to the unit. The unit establishment changed from one to three officers, and the WO2 rank was changed to WO1.

Brussels was a major leave centre and, needless to say, we were kept very busy. Our guard room was usually full and was cleared out once or twice per week by vehicles from Ghent. Sergeants Sleeman and Newman were in charge of two sections in Ghent and, as this city was the reinforcement area for the Canadian Army, much action took place there. Some of the written reports received from Ghent read like the wild west gun fighter days. In fact, one of our officers, Lieutenant MacDonald, was shot the knee during one of these shoot-outs.

I left the unit the end of November 1945 and arrived in Edmonton 1 January 1946, having left that city with the Loyal Edmonton Regiment on 15 December 1939.

Regimental Sergeant Major Bird goes on to relate another story which typifies the tenor of these times.

I was the Sergeant Major of No 2 L of C Provost Company in Brussels in 1945. One night, around midnight, a Canadian major, well under the influence of alcohol, was driving a jeep in small circles on the main street. He seemed unaware that the steering wheel was chained to an eyebolt on the outside of the jeep as an anti-theft device. He was taken to our Guard Room and the Duty NCO came next door to awaken me and report the case. I grunted sleepily and gave the usual order, "Lock him up. I'll see him in the morning."

At 5:30 am the next morning the Sergeant again aroused me and said, "What are you going to do about that Major you locked up last night?" "What Major?" I exclaimed, and was up and dressed in seconds. As we all know, it was a definite "no-no" for a Sergeant Major to incarcerate a commissioned officer!

I got the Major out of the Guard Room and brought him to the office, where we had coffee. He wanted to know if there would be any charges and just what might happen. I assured him that the case was closed and there would be no written report. The Major heaved a big sigh of relief–and so did I.

Reference was made to an incident in Ghent which elicited a sharp response from the Commander-in-Chief (F M Montgomery) to senior Canadian commanders. As usual, this created a flurry as to who was involved, what action was being taken and please report back. The DAPM Army Troops with No 7 Provost Company spent much time compiling and reporting statistics on crime and punishment in this area, stepping-up patrols generally, even placing some local bistros out-of-bounds. The Commander, 2 Canadian Corps, for his part, called in his senior A and Q Staff Officer, Brigadier Daryl Laing, a former Halifax lawyer, and ordered him to "tighten up" discipline in the Corps. The Brigadier, in turn, decided to institute a system which would crack down on anyone driving a Canadian military vehicle in the general area of Antwerp. Provost would concentrate on fractions such as speeding, double-banking, illegal halting, smoking whilst driving, being in an area which his work order did not cover, and so forth. Further, instead of the Provost Offence Report going to the unit, a system of "Roadside Courts" would dispense justice on the spot. To this end some four or five office lorries, complete with typewriters and clerks, would be located in strategic spots. A well briefed officer[93] of captain or major rank in each "Court" would receive the charge directly from the provost patrolman who would also escort the defendant to this place of justice. The defendant, sometimes objecting, would be found guilty and the presiding court officer would then forward the necessary documentation to the appropriate unit. The somewhat puzzled commanding officer was then obliged to award punishment and advise the Corps APM and DAQ accordingly. It may sound improbable, but it happened, and this procedure was actually initiated. Needless to say, it was short lived as the Judge Advocate General's office at Headquarters First Canadian Army found, as almost every provost lance-corporal well knew, that this whole business was highly illegal and contained many contraventions of the rules of evidence and powers of officers other than Commanding Officers to conduct summary trials. While it may have been an extreme case of over reaction by some senior commanders, suffice to say, this theme was repeated many times during this long war, always, it seemed, punishing everyone except the odd undisciplined soldier. Drunken soldiers who indiscriminately fired their weapons should have been charged with a serious offence and dealt with, not by a Commanding Officer's summary trial but by Field-General Court Martial. It was not just another "ho-hum" offence.

About this time in the NWE campaign another, not entirely unexpected, problem began to emerge. So far there had been little call for a detention facility on the Continent due to the high standard of discipline in Canadian units, and the continued use of Headley Downs MDB, back in Grayshott, for the odd case resulting in an award of detention or imprisonment. This satisfactory state of affairs began to change with the sort of situations described previously. Accordingly the DPM, First Canadian Army, obtained authority to organize a detention barracks in the Theatre. No 2 Canadian Detention Barracks, with a Canadian Provost Corps staff of three officers and thirty-four sergeants and corporals, was established and operating by 1 October 1944. It was located in the town of Voght, near Tilburg, in what had been a former German internment camp. This was a large installation built for this particular purpose by the German Todt organization. With very little modification, it was well suited for its revised role. Major Charles Rochon was the commandant and it had an authorized maximum capacity of seventy detainees. The daily programme included early reveille and roll call, PT, breakfast, morning inspection in barracks, close order drill, shower parade, make-and-mend, lunch parade, sick call, more PT, lectures, drill parade, inspection and roll call, supper parade, free time and lights out. A principle of any detention programme was that the life of a detainee should be busy, with emphasis on keeping fit, clean and be at least as uncomfortable as his fellow soldier living in a foxhole. Good conduct and behaviour when undergoing detention was rewarded by earning marks for remission of the original award, that is, time off for good behaviour. This facility remained in this location until July 1945 when it was disbanded with whatever residue of detainees being moved to Headley Downs in the United Kingdom.

One of the reasons the Nazi regime of Germany was able to withstand the might of the armed forces of the world for so long was due to their policy of using slave labour battalions for doing almost all of the sedentary tasks associated with their military effort. This included building the defensive positions along her borders and at all strategic locations, construction and repair of docks, roads and railways, as well as working in heavy industrial mills and foundries. Estimates vary as to the total numbers of these forced labourers but a generally agreed figure is over one million. They included citizens pressed to German military service along with Czechoslovakians, Russians, Dutch, French, Belgiums and people from almost every country in Europe and Western Asia. These so-called "TODT" organization workers were controlled and supervised by the German OKW (High Command) and were, very simply, slaves. Not surprisingly many of these used the ebb and flow of battle to escape the talons of their ruthless masters. The provost became involved frequently when these poor wretches would arrive at the PW Cage, sometimes dressed in German military garb, as prisoners of war. What to do? At first we took little notice but, eventually, there were many convincing cases where it was obvious the individual was not correctly classified as a POW. However, at our level we had no alternative but to backload them with the ordinary German PW and report each case, which usually came to our notice by way of an earnest and direct complaint of the individual. In a few cases certain individuals would be held for further questioning and review by intelligence and officials of the liberated country. Some were out-and-out spies while others may have been influential and patriotic officials. All of these Displaced Persons (DP's) asked nothing more than to be returned to their home and native land. Some were held for short periods in Charlie Rochon's rest camp, at Voght. Two sturdy fair-haired Russian boys, about 15 years of age, somehow escaped from the German army unit, where they had been employed as a cook and shoemaker. They were picked up on the route by a patrol from No 11 Provost Company and brought to company headquarters near Antwerp. Alex and Ivan remained with their provost friends for the next several months. Alex continued to help the company cook and Ivan repaired the shoes most expertly. It was a sad day when they had to be turned over to the Civil Affairs authority for, it was hoped, repatriation. RSM James "Jimmie" Rae, of No 11 Provost Company, and Captain Eric Porter[94], the Officer Commanding, can vouch for these two young lads.

An arrangement was made between the commanders of First United States Army and First Canadian Army during November whereby the newly formed 104 United States Timberwolf Division would, temporarily, take over a sector facing the Maas River in Holland. This deal contained benefits for both sides because the three Canadian divisions, while not severely taxed at the moment, were, nonetheless, tired and beaten up following the tough Scheldt Estuary campaign, and 3 Canadian Infantry Division, in particular, needed a rest. The 104 United States Division, for its part, had not yet been "blocked", and a short stint in a relatively quiet sector was just what was needed. The hand over was made with No 11 Provost Company assistance on the routes in and out. In order to bring the 104 Division staff abreast of our way of doing things, a liaison team from 2 Canadian Corps was stationed with their opposite members for a few days to brief them on the way we went about our business. The provost representative on the LO team naturally briefed the Division MP Company and G2 staff officer on our system of road movement; including route signing. The United States Division MP Company, as a matter of policy, does not manufacture or erect route signs, however, they paid strict attention and made notes. Our provost officer could scarcely believe his eyes the next morning when, on being asked, he visited the MP Company headquarters and there, neatly stacked and complete with supporting stakes, were piles of Timberwolf logo axis markers, Division headquarters markers and a large pile of blank signboards. The company commander informed us these had been made up last night by the workshop of the Combat Engineer Battalion. I guess envy gets you nowhere, but it does raise the question of why, with virtually no resources, our field provost companies were saddled with such a major engineering task as manufacturing route signs.

8

The Reichwald, Hochwald, Groningen and Victory

The Canadian Army in Northwest Europe was not involved in any major operation from the clearing of the Scheldt Estuary on 8 November to the opening battle for the Rhineland on 8 February. This relatively quiet interval was most welcome as it afforded the battle-weary divisions some time to recuperate and refit. It also allowed a build-up of supplies and equipment in depots as far forward as Antwerp. The huge tonnages required could now be delivered by ships through this large port. The obvious benefit for provost was a much diminished requirement for traffic control, due to shorter maintenance routes. The German Army opposite the Canadians, east of the Scheldt and north of the Maas River and up to Nijmegen were, we hoped, also happy to sit still. However, it was not to be. A force of two German Panzer armies launched a major attack on 16 December against the First United States Army sector farther south in the Ardennes Forest region of Belgium. This attack was something of a desperation move which was designed to encircle the First Canadian and Second British Armies and recapture Antwerp. It created a stir. It might have succeeded except for a very stalwart defence by the United States forces. This whole German assault ended in total defeat on 26 December. It necessitated the move of our 4 Canadian Armoured Division to the area of Boxtel, in a blocking position, with the resultant traffic control effort by No 8 Provost Company. All Canadian formations were placed on stand-to-alert, which upset some planned Christmas Day activities to say nothing of gaining any rest and relaxation.

General Crerar, and his staff at Headquarters First Canadian Army, was given the task of planning and, subsequently, carrying out a large scale offensive designed to clear the enemy from the Nijmegen salient up to the Rhine River near the town of Wesel. This entailed an advance of some 45

The Reichwald, Hochwald, Groningen and Victory 93

miles, on a ten mile front, over incredibly difficult terrain. The general axis ran southeast from Nijmegen through Cleve, Udem, Xanten and Rees to Wesel. The ground on the left flank was a narrow strip of marshy, flooded land about three miles wide and extending along the west bank of the Rhine. The area was bisected by two heavily wooded forests, the Reichwald and Hochwald, both on lateral ridges running across the axis of advance.

The Germans had developed a series of defensive lines across the front at intervals of 10 to 15 miles, always placed in front of a natural obstacle with open fields of fire. Small villages and farmhouses were heavily fortified by barbed wire, minefields and gun emplacements and, at one point, included the northern end of the highly publicized Siegfried Line. A further deterrent was the weather, which was cold, wet and foggy. The will of the German army to resist was certainly not diminished by the fact they would be fighting the Canadian Army, for the first time, on German soil. As usual the road network was not adequate for the vast array of military traffic. The few existing roads were designed for the carts and wagons of this farming region and quickly became rutted and holed quagmires when subjected to heavy vehicles and tanks. This "vast array"[95], or the order of battle, was comprised of 2 Canadian Corps (Lt Gen Simonds) and 30 British Corps (Lt Gen Horrocks) with a total of six infantry and two armoured divisions plus the large contingents of artillery, engineers and other support troops, including 2 Canadian Armoured Brigade. Air support in the form of saturation bombing, tactical fighter strikes and reconnaissance, was made available throughout the campaign.

The provost of 11 and 13 Provost Companies were kept busy on traffic control duties for a large scale "dumping" programme prior to the start of "VERITABLE", the code-name for this operation. Huge quantities of ammunition, petrol and equipment spares were stockpiled in the rear area from Schertogenbosch to Nijmegen in preparation for this offensive. It is doubtful whether any Canadian Military operation, Vimy a possible exception, was ever so carefully planned as "Veritable". H Hour was set for 1030 hours (10:30 a.m.) on 8 February 1945. It was preceded by a massive bombardment by our field, medium and heavy artillery as well as saturation bombing of the towns of Cleve and Goch by RAF Bomber Command aircraft. It was calculated that 1,034 artillery guns and 769 bombers were active in this preliminary deluge of fire support for our infantry. The initial attack was made by troops of 3 Canadian Division on the left (flooded area) with 2 Canadian Division following up to lead the assault farther ahead. The British divisions had the task of moving through the initial enemy positions and clearing the enemy from entrenched positions in the

Reichwald. The initial progress was quite good but the going soon got tough. Some of the towns, such as Goch, required bulldozers to clear a route through the rubble caused by the pre-attack bombardments. Once again the German troops fought fiercely and counter attacked whenever our troops forced their way onto an objective.

 A feature of this entire operation, which seriously hampered the ability of Canadian infantry, was the inability of Canadian tanks to move over the water-laden low areas. In general, the plan called for a series of deliberate attacks by successive infantry tank groups, which were designed to maintain constant pressure against the enemy. Time after time these actions by our troops were delayed or aborted because the tanks became mired and immobile in the ooze. Units of 2 Canadian Infantry Division came into action about 12 February in the area between Cleve and Goch, the former town being cleared by the 15 Infantry Division on 10 February. Meanwhile, 3 Canadian Infantry Division, which had reached Emmerich on 14 February, attacked astride the route between Cleve and Calcar with 2 Division on its right. After fierce fighting and heavy casualties, particularly by 2 Canadian Division, the line of the main lateral road between Calcar and Goch was finally secured on 20 February.

 The next main objective was the Hochwald, which was a wooded ridge extending across the Canadian's front. Operation "Blockbuster" was then launched by Simonds. This attack was designed to clear the heavily fortified town of Udem, secure the Calcar-Udem ridge, clear the Hochwald Forest and drive through to Xanten. The regrouping required for this operation placed 2 Canadian Division left with the task of assaulting the defended German line in front of the northern Hochwald sector. The 3rd Canadian Division was moved to the right and given the task of clearing Udem and securing the right flank. The 4th Canadian Armoured Division was brought forward for its first action in Veritable. From an initial concentration area on the slope of the Calcar-Udem ridge, about 4 miles short of the Hochwald, it was to clear the western end of the ridge and than attack the southern sector of the Hochwald and seize positions astride the railway where it passed through the Gap. This so-called Gap, which played a dominant part in the ensuing battle, was a natural opening or cleft which ran through the southern end of the Hochwald feature, adjacent to the railway.

 Life for these Canadian soldiers, whether in or out of battle, was most unpleasant. The concentration area for units of 4 Armoured Division was clogged with guns, vehicles, shell craters and roofless farm buildings. A 4th Division unit diarist talked about the area becoming more and more congested as streams of vehicles continued to struggle along the mired roads and the guns, now numbered in the thousands, deployed and redeployed for the battle ahead. The inability of tanks to move in the low-lying areas (all of the area in front of the Hochwald) was soon apparent. This deprived the Algonquin Regiment (4 Armoured Division) of essential tank support for their task of seizing ground in the Gap area. Simonds hit upon a novel plan. The tanks supporting the Algonquins would move along the railway embankment. The plan was to convert this railway embankment as an axis for tanks and later use as a maintenance route. The engineers would tear up the track so the roadbed could be used for traffic.

In retrospect, the din and fog of a battle during darkness, which prevailed at times in the Normandy campaign, was a mere Sunday stroll compared to the utter desolation and confusion which characterized this battle. Even though most attacking units had to cope with rain, darkness, loss of direction across the muddy fields and the explosion of shells, our own and the enemy's, it was the lot of the Algonquins to suffer all of these misfortunes. The SL (start line) for their attack was southwest of the town of Kirsel, with H Hour at 3:30 a.m. on 26 February. The necessity of moving forward, across a low muddy valley, at night was dictated by the enemy's excellent defensive position on high ground from which he could direct deadly fire during daylight. A vivid description of the problems faced in even "forming-up" for this attack is described by Major George Cassidy of the Algonquins in *Warpath: The Story of The Algonquin Regiment, 1939–1945*. "The night set in dark and rainy with an icy breeze. The road axis was, by now, a perfect welter of vehicles nose to tail inching their way by fits and starts toward the shell–illuminated southeast. They were baffled again and again by the mud and general confusion."

Lieutenant George Wilkinson, No 8 Provost Company of 4 Canadian Armoured Division, spent a very long night trying hard, with the help of a provost section, to assist in the difficult task of getting these huge war machines (tanks) forward.

4 Armoured Division had passed through the Reichwald Forest and was moving south of Cleve on the Bedburg/Loisendorf road. It was decided that 4 Armoured Brigade should advance cross-country, over farmers' fields, at night using white tapes to guide the tanks over three separate routes. The move started around 2200 hours in cold, wet weather. The ground had become so soft from frequent rains that only two or three tanks could follow each other without bellying. As each tank stuck the following tank would bypass it, then stick. By early morning only a handful of the Brigades' tanks had made it to the start point, while the rest floundered about in a sea of mud, spinning their tracks and belching smoke.

Further details of the part played by No 8 Provost Company, during the battle for the Hochwald Forest, are contained in a written account by Lieutenant Wilkinson. His vivid description is attached as Appendix "B".

The enemy's fierce defence of their positions in front of the Hochwald came with the knowledge that this was the last obstacle in the path of the Canadian Army, to the Rhine River. Canadian units, claiming "HOCHWALD" in the Battle Honours of their Regimental Colours, will long remember that hard won honour, units such as the Algonquins of Northern Ontario; the Lincoln and Wellands of the Niagara Region; the Argyle and Sutherland Highlanders of Hamilton; the Lake Superior Regiment from the Lakehead; the 29 Armoured Recce Regiment from Southern Alberta and all of 4 Canadian Armoured Division. Equal contribution was made by units of 2 Canadian Division on the left sector, units such as the Essex Scottish of Windsor; the Royal Regiment of Canada of Toronto; the Royal Hamilton Light Infantry from Hamilton; the Calgary Highlanders of Calgary; the Black Watch from Montreal; the Cameron Highlanders of Winnipeg and the Regiment De Maisonneuve of Quebec. There were, of course, many others from supporting arms and services who braved the dangers and hardships in this test of wills. The enemy gave way after five days and nights of continuous fighting. It remained for 2 Canadian Infantry and 4 Canadian Armoured Divisions to advance and clear places along the Rhine, such as Xanten, Veen and Winnenthal, while 3 Canadian Infantry Division units cleared the southern portion of the Hochwald (termed the Tuschen Wald) and, finally, Sonsbeck where they were pinched out by the advance of 30 Corps, on the Canadian's right.

The Hochwald was not without a few tense moments for the battle-tested provost of 4 Company in 3 Canadian Infantry Division. Having cleared the town of Udem the Division moved its forward brigades into position for its assault through the south end of the Hochwald. As a result of a blunder by someone, we may never know who, there occurred one of the most improbable traffic snarls of history. A lengthy column of 3 Division met an equally long column of 4 Division head on in a situation where neither could pass or turn around. The story has already been narrated by Lieutenant Wilkinson (Appendix "B"). The 3 Division version is given by Sergeant Chambers.

In the early spring of 1945, between the town of Udem and the Rhine River, Lieutenant John Dowsett[96] and I were laying a route for 3rd Canadian Division, who would be bringing up supplies for the build-up needed for crossing of the Rhine. Just to the south of Udem we noted a road that went down an escarpment of about

The Reichwald, Hochwald, Groningen and Victory 97

30 feet and then entered a swampy area. To the left of the point, where the road made a dip into the swampy area, we also noted an abandoned railway embankment. Further reconnaissance of the road showed that it took a dogleg turn to the left and married up with the abandoned railway line, at a town near the Rhine, in the direction we wanted to go. Since the road going through the swampy area was only good for one-way traffic, we decided to use it as a one-way route UP. The embankment would serve as a one-way DOWN route, so there would be no need to have traffic crossing. We signed and lighted our routes that way.

After things were in place, and the traffic was flowing smoothly, we bedded down for the night in an abandoned barn in the swampy area where we could keep an eye on traffic. At first light we came out of the barn and looked at the embankment. Vehicles and trailers of all kinds, as far as we could see in either direction, were at a standstill. Two convoys were nose-to-nose on a 30 foot embankment with nowhere to go. I was later told that a staff officer had decided that the UP traffic should use the embankment, rather than the road, as it was much shorter, and had changed the signs accordingly. It took many men, and nearly a full day, to sort out that mess.

The Rhineland campaign was concluded on 11 March when Canadian, British and 9 United States Army Troops, coming up from the south, met in front of the German town of Wesel. It had been a terrible struggle and victory had its sad aftermath. It had been costly, as revealed by Canada's military historian Colonel C P Stacey. The total casualties of the British and Canadian armies for the period 8 February to 10 March were 1,049 officers and 14,585 other ranks. Canadian losses numbered 379 officers and 4,925 other ranks of which 243 officers and 3,395 other ranks were incurred during this same period. A casualty, it should be explained, was any soldier listed under one of the four categories: Killed, Died of Wounds, Missing or Wounded. The Canadian infantry battalions suffered paralysing casualties, none more so than the Algonquins. Their sobering list from 26 February to 10 March was:

Killed in Action	69
Died of Wounds	8
Wounded	166
Missing	49
Total Casualties	292

The loss inflicted on the enemy was much heavier. During the whole period, from the beginning of "Veritable" until the German withdrawal east of the Rhine, First Canadian Army captured 22,239 prisoners,[97] and the estimated enemy losses in killed and long-term wounded at 22,000.

The British and Canadian formations of 21 Army Group (Montgomery) now lined the west bank of the Rhine from Nijmegen to Dusseldorf. The stage was set for the final campaign of World War II in Europe, which begin on 23 March 1945.

The 6th British Airborne Division[98] was again employed in the Rhine crossings. It dropped on strategic road and rail junctions and other positions on the east side of the Rhine, across from the Wesel sector. The Canadian Paratroop Battalion[99] landed on the right flank of the DZ (Drop Zone) with the task of defending the main crossings against German counter-attack from the south. The unit diarist reported[100] that, "prisoners were quite a problem because they numbered almost the strength of the battalion", and "Germans were killed by the hundreds". The usual heavy artillery supporting fire was provided by our guns. The main attack was made by three infantry divisions, from left to right: The 51st British Highland, 43rd British Wyvern and 3 Canadian Infantry Division. A variety of craft was used to cross the fast-flowing Rhine, which was about 500 yards wide at this point. Provost, as well as the Royal Military Police of the British formation, were flat out on traffic control duties involving moving troops and vehicles forward from rear marshalling areas, loading in the proper craft, crossing and then to forward assembly areas across the river. Much of this was done at night and navigation was greatly assisted by a new light called "Tabby", which was invisible unless seen through special glasses. It was Caen all over again, with technology and organization. These complicated operations went off without a hitch and all divisions were soon driving inland behind a fleeing enemy. Sergeant Chambers provides this insight on the crossing of 9 Canadian Infantry Brigade.

When the Allied troops were getting ready to cross the Rhine River, at a town called Rees, my section was attached to the 9th Canadian Highland Brigade[101] which, in turn, was attached to the 51st Highland Division of the British Army for the purpose of assisting them in the crossing.

We sat on the west bank of the Rhine and watched as the glider borne and paratroops went in and, later, after darkness arrived, we headed for our crossing area. We waited behind the west dyke until we were herded, with our jeeps, into a Buffalo, which is a lightly armoured vehicle which can propel itself through water. The noise from the shelling was terrific and it was impossible to hear anything else. Finally we felt the vehicle climb up the bank and come to a halt. The back door was let down and we drove out into a hop field on the east bank.

The Reichwald, Hochwald, Groningen and Victory 99

Later, after the bridgehead had been enlarged and secured, two floating bridges were built for the UP and DOWN routes. We went to work doing traffic control on the bridges and approaches for a few days until our brigade went back to 3rd Canadian Division and we went on, through Emmerich and north into Holland.

The leading brigade of 2 Canadian Infantry Division crossed the Rhine in the Rees sector and started an advance northeast, which ultimately ended with the capture of Groningen (Holland) and Falkenburg, near Bremen (Germany) on 14 April and 30 April, respectively. The Rhine crossings at Rees were very successful. No 2 Provost Company and two sections moved across the Rhine in the evening. They moved too far along the road towards Emmerich, with the result that they were shelled during the night and had to move back into the Division area in the early morning. 31 March 1945 found 2 Provost Company handling traffic on the Arnholtulft highway.

On 2 April 1945 the division was pretty well stretched out with forward elements following the fleeing enemy very rapidly and the rest of the Division clearing up "left behind" enemy pockets of resistance. One of these pockets was in Doetinchem, an old Dutch fortress city. A company of young German paratroopers, armed to the teeth, held the sturdily built town hall in the centre of the town. No 2 Provost Company signed a route through the suburb of the town and maintained traffic control points within a few blocks of the heavy street fighting.

On the morning of 7 April 1945 Sergeant Fife was I/C (in charge) of the leading section of 2 Provost Company. Captain Lee[102] had intended to go up to the Shipbeck Canal in the early morning to determine whether the engineers had completed the bridge they were building. However, when Lee received word to go on leave, RSM George Oakes went up in his place. Oakes picked up Sergeant Fife and they drove up to the canal in their jeep. Oakes and Fife noted that the engineers had been delayed by enemy action and had not even started to build the bridge. They decided to back up and turn around. In doing so the left front wheel of the jeep fell off the hard surface of the road and ran over a Teller mine. The jeep was blown completely upside down and landed on the opposite side of the road. Sergeant Fife was killed. RSM Oakes was badly wounded and pinned under the jeep. Some engineers saw the explosion, proceeded to the scene and rescued Oakes, who lived to tell the tale. He truly lived on borrowed time, having been previously wounded at Dieppe. Oakes and Fife were very popular in the company and their loss was deeply felt by all.

(On) 13, 14 and 15 April the Division approached Groningen. There was heavy street fighting. The town blazed furiously from uncontrolled fires in the marketplace. Many Germans gave up the fight and poured into the POW cage. Recce elements, speeding through outlying areas, were constantly radioing for Provost assistance in handling POWs, but none could be sent as everyone was just too busy. The town was finally captured. Sergeant's Gouldie and Brawn, with their sections, moved in on 16 April to try and maintain some semblance of discipline. The town was in a "freedom" mood and really threw their doors and hearts open to the Canadians. No 2 Company had never been this busy.

The (first) elements of 2 Division moved into Haselunne, Germany, on 19 April 1945 and the balance arrived during the next two days. On 25 April the welcome news came through that the Americans and Russians had linked up. No 2 Provost Company had a lot of work to do in connection with slave workers the Germans left behind, and also displaced persons. Local German civilians were complaining of the slave workers stealing, looting, murdering and roaming the country at will. All complaints were handed over to the Military Government, unless Canadian troops were involved. The Military Government established displaced persons camps, to which all slave workers were directed. They were very difficult to control as they did not want to remain in camp but preferred to travel homeward in gangs, wreaking vengeance on the Germans enroute.

On 7 May six men from the company went into the German occupied area and escorted the German Commanders into Oldenburg, where they signed the unconditional terms of surrender. Lieutenant George Hodgkiss, from 13 Provost Company, arrived on 9 May and took control of the Information and Complaint Office. Provost Headquarters moved into the hospital building.

In the meantime, Headquarters 2 Canadian Corps, along with 4 Canadian Armoured Division, had moved up and over the Rhine in early April.

Headquarters[103] First Canadian Army was located near Hengelo, Holland on 14 April and remained there until 6 June 1945. By a quick glance at a map of Holland it is easy to understand why a main supply route was required through Emmerich, on the Rhine. Now we return to our friend, Sergeant Ray Chambers, for his final comment on the drive of 3 Canadian Infantry Division from the Rhine north to the northerly tip of Holland, which ended near the city of Aurich.

A day or so after 3 May 1945 my section was called back into company headquarters. We were rested there for a day or two and were then instructed to proceed to a town called Aurich, which is about midway between Wilhelmshaven and Emden in Northern Germany. At Aurich we were to take over suitable quarters for the Provost company headquarters. I can't remember if an officer was with us. All I can remember is that we had to travel a very circuitous route as there were very few bridges left intact and the road verges were stilled mined, as were many of the roads. There were still a good number of small German units around, all heading towards Aurich, and all still armed. Eventually, after using the same roads as the German troops were using, we came to Aurich. We took over a good sized hotel in the centre of the town for company headquarters, and I took over a small hotel next to the Police Station for my section.

It was quite interesting to watch the German troops, in small groups and fully armed, marching through Aurich towards a naval barracks located on the northern outskirts of the town, where they would then leave their weapons.

During that time there were a few small groups of Polish ex-prisoners of war in the area who were trying to break into the stores, and any of the other buildings, in hope of finding food. Fortunately several of the men in my section came from the prairie provinces and could speak Russian and/or Polish, so we didn't have too much trouble. The company headquarters arrived shortly after that.

Meanwhile 4 Canadian Armoured Division was playing its part in this advance northward. The Division crossed the Rhine on 2 April and began a rapid drive along the general axis of Doitenichem, Lachem, across the Twente Canal near Delden, Almelo, Meppen, Sagel to the Kusten Canal at Edewechterdam, near Oldenburg. They had reached Bad Zwischenahn on 14 April, about the same time that 2 and 3 Canadian Infantry Divisions, further west, had reached their final objectives. The enemy made a determined stand on the Kusten Canal. However units (Algonquin, Lincoln and Welland Regiments) of 4 Canadian Armoured Division launched a successful attack and breakthrough on 16 April. This was the last major battle for these three Canadian divisions. It had been a long, hard struggle since Normandy, almost one year ago. As Sergeant Chambers stated "We managed to get a couple of day's rest". Sadly, it was during this operation, near the town of Sagel, that Sergeant George Buttimer, of No 8 Provost, was killed on 10 April. He came so close to seeing it finished. Later, on 6 May, Lieutenant George Tomalin, of No 8 Provost Company, reported to No 2 Provost Company in Oldenburg. He had been taken prisoner on 11 April and held in a German camp near Wilhelmshaven. Sadly, Lance Corporal D H Birch, who was with him at the time, was killed by a burst of machine gun fire from an enemy rear guard. He was driving the jeep when they ran into this outpost.

We left 1 Canadian Corps with 1 Canadian Infantry, 5 Canadian Armoured Division and 1 Canadian Armoured Brigade in Belgium, following their long journey from Italy. Head-quarters 1 Canadian Corps became operational on 15 March 1945 and was placed under command of General Crerar's First Canadian Army. It is worthy of note that, for the first time in history, Canada now had an army of purely Canadian content in a theatre of war, that is to say: First Canadian Army (General H D G Crerar); 1 Canadian Corps (Lieutenant General C Foulkes); 2 Canadian Corps (Lieutenant General G G Simonds); 1 Canadian Infantry Division (Major General H W Foster); 2 Canadian Infantry Division (Major General A B Matthews); 3 Canadian Infantry Division (Major General D C Spry); 4 Canadian Armoured Division (Major General C Vokes); 5 Canadian Armoured Division (Major General B M Hoffmeister); 1 Canadian Armoured Brigade (Brigadier R A Wyman); 2 Canadian Armoured Brigade (Brigadier J S Booth).

1 Canadian Corps was given the task of clearing out the German forces still in Holland. They held good positions behind their "Grebbe" line, which extended northwest from Nijmegen to Amersfoort, southeast of Amsterdam. This operation involved an attack by 5 Canadian Armoured Division on 2 April, which was designed to capture Arnhem, then advance north through Deelen, Otterloo, Voorthuizen, Putten to the town of Harderwijk. The start line for the 1 Division attack was the road between Zutphen and Deventer. This assault was designed to capture Apeldoorn and advance westward through Barneveld to Amersfoort. Both operations were successful despite some stiff fighting, along with the usual problem of finding ground that was not marshy or flooded for the tanks of 5 Armoured Division. By 25 April this large area of Holland was fully occupied by our friends from Italy. An incident occurred on the night 16–17 April that was a first for Canadians in World War II. The Germans launched a sharp counter attack towards Ottorloo, which was occupied by the headquarters of 5 Canadian Armoured Division. Everyone, including staff officers, clerks, signallers, cooks and the APM and Provost Section, was obliged to become "instant" infantrymen on order to hold their ground until a company of the Westminster Regiment[104] came to their aid. It was during this encounter that Captain Thomas E Clark, the officer commanding No 5 Provost Company, and a veteran of Italy, was killed.

As early as November 1944 there were indications that the people of Holland, especially in the large cities still occupied by the German Army, were starving. Four years of occupation and war had almost completely dried up normal food sources. The Germans, as we have seen, systematically flooded large areas of reclaimed agricultural land, deliberately commandeered food supplies for themselves, and made off with large numbers of livestock for their own use. The Allied commands were certainly aware of this problem and, after much negotiation, it was decided to provide "relief" supplies of food to some of the most critical areas. Headquarters First Canadian Army succeeded in contacting the German Reich-commissar, one Seyss Inquhart, and a truce line was arranged in the area over the Waal River near Tiel. The Canadian Army, under the direction of General Crerar, delivered over 10,000 tons of food supplies to distribution centres inside the German lines on 25 – 28 April 1945. Further relief food was also delivered to the cities of Apeldoorn and Hilversum during this period. There were also large scale "food drops" by parachute into the cities of Amsterdam and The Hague by the Allied airforces. The nature and extent of this melancholy story was made clear by this report[105] of a Red Cross official, at the end of March 1945.

The physical situation of the Western provinces has reduced the inhabitants almost to a primitive state. They are obliged, in the struggle for existence, to engage in the black market, in usury and even in theft; men eat flower bulbs. The bombed houses are pillaged and looted of all combustible material. The trees in the gardens are cut and carried away by night. Horses killed in bombardments are immediately cut up by passers-by. The bread wagons in the cities can only circulate at 4:00 o'clock in the morning because, if they go about in broad daylight, crowds threaten to attack and plunder them.

These scenes were extremely hard for all Canadians to endure. Units shared their rations, but this was only a 'drop-in-the-bucket' in terms of allaying the terrible hunger of these brave people. No 11 Provost Company, in one instance, moved the company headquarters to a more remote area, rather than observe the pitiful stares of hungry children who would gather near the cookhouse at meal time.

The provost of every company were heavily engaged in a multitude of duties, such as those experienced by No 2 Provost Company in the Groningen area. The German Army SURRENDERED, unconditionally, on 8 May 1945. Lieutenant J A Dowsett of No 4 Company provided an escort and guard at the signing ceremonies at Aurich. Our 1st Canadian Parachute Battalion, after a long 280 mile dash, had reached Wismar, on the Baltic Sea, and had shaken hands with the advancing Russian army on 4 May. The Deputy Provost Marshal of First Canadian Army personally headed the guard and escort[106] for the infamous Seyss Inquhart, who was later tried for war crimes.

The men of the Canadian Provost Corps who participated in this long and bloody campaign could now relax, if not physically at least in terms of tension. All ranks, without exception, had been living on the edge for many months. Men like Fife and Buttimer never complained and never flagged or failed. They deserved a soft bed, in a hotel such as that found by Sergeant Ray Chambers, in Aurich. They could now afford the luxury of thinking about home, in Canada, and their loved ones.

9

Repatriation

Everybody wanted to go home. The Canadian government and Defence Department had been planning the ways and means of doing this, for the past year. There were many factors bearing on this problem including the fact that the war against Japan was still raging; the extent of a requirement for a Canadian Occupation Force in Europe; the size and shape of a yet to be determined regular or peace time army; the priorities for returning all overseas service personnel and, most important, the availability of ships. The priority question was settled by a policy of "first in – first out". Each soldier was given a "point" score based on length of service overseas, the Pacific force option and marital status. The soldier was required to choose one of the following options: immediate release, continuing service in the Pacific[107], continuing service in a Canadian Occupation Force or continuing service in an Interim Force.

These policies, coupled with the World War I experience, created a demand for additional provost units in England. There had been one or two incidents in 1918–19 when Canadian soldiers, awaiting return to Canada while living in miserable camps in Wales, had engaged in a mild mess hall disorder. The result was extreme overreaction by camp officials, which ended in several Canadians injured and three dead from the gunfire of British soldiers and military police. It was therefore decided that the rehabilitation depots would be properly run and provide decent amenities. It was also planned to form two additional provost companies in England to ensure that any disciplinary problems would be dealt with by the Canadian Provost Corp as opposed to British authorities. The great majority of provost in the field companies, as well as those in No 6 and 9 Companies, were all "high pointers" and were, therefore, eligible for immediate repatriation.

The plan for organizing the additional provost companies and provost reinforcements was developed at CMHQ by the Deputy Provost Marshal (Colonel A D Cameron) and the headquarters staff. Rather than expand the small existing provost depot, already operating in Aldershot, it was decided to form a full scale Canadian Provost Corps Training Depot which would be capable of handling an intake of up to 180 recruits at one time. It was to be staffed by selected Canadian Provost Corps officers and NCO's. The provost recruits were to be selected from low point infantry and armoured corps reinforcements in England and transferred to the Canadian Provost Corps. Two Canadian Provost Corps officers, an NCO clerk, CQMS (Quartermaster) and a RSM were posted to the Provost Depot and began to work. By the end of March this team, assisted by the newly appointed commanding officer, had developed an approved war establishment,[108] secured and occupied accommodation in the Wellington Barracks Lines in Aldershot and, vide CMHQ, had issued posting orders for most of the staff and instructors. They had also developed a six week training programme. The first recruits began arriving by mid April and by 1 May there were 160 new members of the Corps undergoing training in this quickly assembled facility.

The quality of recruits was first class. When requested, the staff of the Headquarters Canadian Reinforcement Units (See Table 2) would arrange a schedule of visits to various reinforcement depots by Canadian Provost Corps officers in order to interview prospective recruits. The criterion for selection was that the soldier must have volunteered for this duty; he must have a clean conduct sheet and meet the medical and physical standards for the Canadian Provost Corps. The two provost captains originally posted to the depot worked at this task, in relays, and often interviewed up to 60 applicants in one day. Needless to say, the Corps was the recipient of a great many excellent military policemen. Several went on to serve in the Regular army in later years, with higher rank and responsibility. This provost training depot remained active until it was disbanded in January 1946. It trained a full complement of corporals and lance corporals for two newly formed provost companies, No 14 and 17 Companies, as well as over 130 reinforcements for No 6 Company in London. The latter company was one of the last to be disbanded and these reinforcements replaced "high point" men being repatriated.

Aldershot had been a 'garrison' town since the days of Wellington's army. It was designed and operated for soldiers. This large base depot featured rows of two-storey barracks with adjacent paved parade squares. It also had numerous civilian businesses which ran largely to military outfitters, cinemas, fish and chip stalls and the ubiquitous pubs. By midsummer of 1945 it was bursting at the seams with Canadian soldiers in varying stages of repatriation process. There was a large scale riot on the night of 4–5 July. It started near the railway station, around 8:00 pm, when a relatively small group of Canadian soldiers started a brawl in an amusement hall, which spread rapidly along the main business section. The local provost patrols could not cope as the original rioters were joined by others and the situation was soon out of control. Windows were smashed, shops were ransacked and pubs were taken over. There was much shouting and shoving and fighting along the congested downtown streets.

The Canadian Provost Corps Training Depot was soon involved. The Duty Officer received an urgent phone call from HQ CRU at 9:15 pm, requesting all available provost assistance in dealing with this disturbance. Fortunately the Commanding Officer and several officers were in at the time. After a quick trip to the riot area a plan was developed. Every available provost, staff and trainee alike, was placed on ready alert. A platoon of RCASC 3 ton trucks was requested, and soon arrived from the local supply and transport centre. The plan called for successive trucks, each carrying a squad of six provost under an officer or NCO, to move to the outskirts of the main riot area. The idea was for the provost, operating in pairs, to move in and seize a rioter designated by the squad leader and move him (back first) to the truck. After being loaded the rioter would be guarded by a two man team still in the truck. Each truck load was then taken to the Maida Barracks square, which was some distance away, where they were deposited inside a previously constructed and guarded compound pending a further check. The plan worked and was further refined by selecting only those rioters who appeared to be ringleaders. The casual onlookers that are always found at these scenes began to disperse. After about three hours the crowd dispersed; the provost patrols from 14 and 17 Companies were again in control, and the compound at Maida contained an assortment of humanity numbering close to two hundred people. Tables were set up and the task of compiling a list of this "bag" began. Illuminated by vehicle headlights it was truly a comic opera scene because not everybody brought here forcibly was a Canadian soldier. There was the odd British and United States Army soldier, two or three sailors, a few civilians, including shopkeepers who were trying to protect their wares. One gentleman complained that he had just got off the train from London when: "This great Canadian seized me and shoved me into a lorry filled with soldiers".

As riots go, this one could have been worse. There were few injuries, there was no shooting or burning and, while it was night, the area was fairly well lit by the odd illuminated building, such as the cinema. All but a handful of those detained and removed from the scene were released to their units the following day. The following comment, made by C P Stacey at page 433 of his official history, *Six Years of War*, is worthy of republication.

Notwithstanding the speed with which the repatriation mill had begun to grind, one unpleasant incident took place among the troops awaiting return. There was rioting in Aldershot on 4 and 5 July, and much damage was done to property (by 31 March 1946 Canada had paid $41,541 to meet damage claims). This would have been deplorable under any circumstances; it was particularly indefensible in that it took place so soon after the end of hostilities and at a time when the movement back to Canada was developing rapidly. General Montague expressed the opinion that the ringleaders in the disturbances were certain Pacific Force volunteers "whom I cannot describe otherwise than as racketeers". (There was a suspicion that some men were volunteering for the Pacific Force merely as a means of getting back to Canada at an early date.) In fact, of the six soldiers convicted by court martial as a result of the riots, three were Pacific volunteers. Most of the six had long records of misconduct. The citizens of Aldershot magnanimously forgave the many misdeeds of the few and on 26 September conferred "the freedom of the borough" on the Canadian army overseas.

Our historian does not mention it but, for the next few days, those Canadians who lived and worked in Aldershot were not too anxious to display the "CANADA" badge on their shoulders. But, as he has stated, the good citizens of Aldershot were most generous in their understanding.

From January to August 1945 there had been a trickle of 'high point score' provost returned to Canada. Many had been away since late 1939 and early 1940, a five year period. The field provost companies were disbanded during the period August through October. All personnel were processed for repat in accordance with their chosen option. An APM and a six section provost company was formed for service with the Canadian Army Occupation Force (CAOF), which was roughly the size of an infantry division. The CAOF was located in northwestern Holland, not far from Bad Zwischenahan. It was based on 3 Canadian Infantry Division and given the title: 3 Canadian Infantry Division (CAOF). It remained operational, dealing with and regulating relations with and between Germans, looking after large numbers of displaced persons and ensuring the security and good order of the area. The CAOF was withdrawn beginning April 1946 and was disbanded on 20 June when the last of its troops were returned to Canada.

Before leaving the Continent one last incident involving a provost company is recorded. The terms of the general surrender on 8 May included the disposition of those German troops of the 88th German Corps still located in Western Holland. They were ordered to return to a demobilization area near Hamburg, using two specific routes through Holland. No 3 Provost Company of 1 Canadian Corps was given the task of keeping them on the routes and, of more importance, checking each German vehicle and unit for 'booty' and valuables taken from the impoverished Dutch people. Checkpoints were established and large quantities of material ranging from jewels, art and even household fixtures were recovered. The provost, at checkpoints, also recovered a large number of draft horses, which were identified by the markings and brands supplied by the Dutch authorities. RSM Bob Wallace of 3 Company, himself an old Alberta ranch hand, recalled, with much glee, several cases where the 'recovered' horse was taken out of the team pulling a heavily laden wagon and its place was taken, between the shafts, by several members of the Wehrmacht. It was this sort of incident that engendered the enormous outpouring of goodwill and friendship by the people of Holland towards the Canadians. This feeling was mutual and is still manifested nearly fifty years later.

One of the last duties given to provost during the repatriation phase was the provision of an escort for a large group of Canadian soldiers under sentence. It was necessary to make special arrangements for this group, some 317 strong, due to the fact that they were, largely, the worst criminal element of the Canadian Army, most having been sentenced by Court Martial to lengthy terms of IMPRISONMENT, the most severe award in the scale of authorized punishment. The task was to bring them by train to Glasgow from the Headley Downs Detention Barracks in England, under a strong provost escort. The Deputy Provost Marshal at CMHQ managed, after much negotiation, to secure their passage back to Canada on a Royal Navy Escort Carrier, which was on loan from the United States Navy and had been operating in the Indian Ocean.

This carrier was the HMS "KHEDIVE" and was being returned to Norfolk, via Halifax, by a Royal Navy sailing crew. They were not too happy to be suddenly given a rather dubious group of passengers for this voyage across the Atlantic, in the dead of winter. It was scheduled to sail out of Glasgow on 3 January 1946, and sail it did. The escort was organized by the DPM. It consisted of five officers and 18 senior NCO's, all Canadian Provost Corps due for repatriation. Corporal Elwood V Christensen[109] of the Glasgow Detachment, No 6 Provost Company, recalls his involvement in this project.

In December 1945 I was stationed in Glasgow, Scotland, at No 2 Detachment of No 6 Company, Canadian Provost Corps. We had received orders that on 31 December 1945 we were to have our full complement of personnel at a specific dock at the Glasgow harbour for a security function.

Two large lorries loaded with bulk provisions from England would arrive at the docks early in the afternoon of 31 December. A civilian dockyard workgang was to load these provisions on board a ship berthed at the dock. This ship, a "Liberty" type vessel constructed as a small airplane carrier, had been stripped of its armaments and planes in preparation for its return to the United States. On this voyage the ship was to serve as a troop carrier for a number of Canadian Army personnel being returned in custody to Canada, having been previously convicted of various serious offences.

On arrival of the lorries the workgang, with the aid of a tall shipyard crane, commenced loading the provisions into the ship. Our function was to check the shipping bills against the provisions numerical count and to make sure that all food went directly from the lorries to the ship. Those sides of beef, bacon, etc. were certainly mouthwatering to see.

Late in the afternoon the work gang foreman called a halt to their work stating they were finished for the day and would be leaving at once. When questioned by the detachment sergeant the foreman stated it was New Year's Eve, and that was the end of the matter. When the crane operator descended from his control cabin a discussion ensued between the sergeant and the crane man; this ended by the worker climbing up to his cabin again, where he stayed until the loading was completed.

There was still a large part of the second lorry's load to be transferred, so who was going to do the work? The provisions could not be left on the dock; they had to be secured aboard ship in preparation for the Canadian troops arriving on 2 January 1946. We were informed that no help was available from the minimal crew that the ship was carrying.

There we were, turned out as usual, with our polished boots, brass, sparkling white webbing and pressed uniforms, as befitted a "Provost". Approximately three hours later we did not look or feel quite so "spiffy", but we certainly did get a taste of postwar, peacetime manual labour. By the time we had secured dozens of cartons, sacks of vegetables, slabs of meat in the bowels of the ship we all found and felt muscles we didn't know we had.

By approximately 19:00 hours we were able to return to our detachment quarters and, those not assigned duty, went on to celebrate New Year's Eve as only one can in Scotland, though I suspect a little subdued after their earlier workout. I know I slept most of the next day–off duty, of course.

The rations and supplies referred to by Corporal Christensen were required due to the fact that the KHEDIVE had been stripped in preparation for being layed-up at Norfolk, Virginia. Hence, it did not have its full complement of supplies or staff so these Canadian Army personnel had to provide their own rations and cooks for the 317 passengers, using the ship's galleys and facilities. The OC Troops also had an RCAMC Medical Officer and orderly, along with necessary medical supplies. Sleeping quarters for the SUS[110] were arranged in the hangar deck, now devoid of aircraft, and they were messed in an adjoining area. The Canadian Provost Corps officers and men were billeted in the regular ship's company quarters and took their meals in the appropriate galley or wardroom. The SUS arrived by LMS train about 16:15 hours, 2 January, and were brought aboard in single file. This operation went smoothly and by 17:00 hours were all secure and comfy in their assigned spaces. The first meal parade was also uneventful, perhaps because the food was excellent in both quantity and quality, which continued to be the case throughout the voyage.

The sea was fairly calm for the first day, however, the North Atlantic was rolling from then on, as was the Khedive. The OC Troops contact was with the First Mate, who turned out to be of Canadian origin. He was most helpful in every way. The captain, a salty old naval officer, remained on the bridge, or in his quarters, and relayed the odd command through Commander Mackenzie, to the OC Troops. His chief concern, understandably, was that the "NO SMOKING" rule be strictly enforced. He did, however, agree to two smoking parades per day, on the top flight deck, following the organized exercise (PT) period for the SUS. The provost staff could smoke in the mess room, but not in their quarters. A "sick call" was made twice daily by the Duty Officer, but the incidence of SUS reporting sick was extremely low. There were, mercifully, very few cases of seasickness despite a normal rough North Atlantic sea in mid winter.

Somewhere about the halfway point of crossing, the soldier element on board witnessed an unusual event. The ship came to a dead stop, turned into the wind and, for the next two hours, jettisoned the contents of its large "Avgas" fuel tanks into the ocean. This was necessary in view of the fact that the tanks must be empty when putting in at Norfolk. It brought back memories of "gasless" Tuesdays during the days in England when the German wolf-packs were sinking our ships, oddly in these very sea lanes.

It was about two days out of Halifax that the OC Troops received some startling news. Simply put, the latest head count that morning revealed one missing SUS. The count was repeated twice again, each with the same results, 316 not 317 heads. What to do? With the captain's consent a thorough search of the ship was carried out. The NOMINAL ROLL, held by the OC Troops, was checked again and again. Members of the SUS in the missing persons alpha grouping were interviewed, but nothing was learned. Visions of an Official Court of Inquiry, and a long delay in Halifax, were passing through the minds of the OC Troops. The problem was solved, at least for the moment, by simply striking a line, in ink, through the missing man's name on each of the six copies of the nominal roll, and initialling and dating the entry. At least in this way the deficiency would not be passed on to the Canadian Provost Corps escort taking over at Halifax.

A final incident occurred during the docking at Halifax. It seems this was the first time ever a carrier had pulled in at this particular pier. There was a roof on a shed which protruded past the outer edge of the pier's sea wall. The high superstructure of the Khedive did a remarkable job of shearing this roof off, amid much crashing and falling of lumber, onto the pier itself. We felt sorry for the captain who, like the OC Troops, was the victim of sheer bad luck. The handover of the 316 SUS to a waiting escort, under Major Stock of 33 Provost Company, went quickly. Both groups boarded trains for points west. Major Stock, and escort, for Montreal and Toronto where the SUS were again incarcerated. The Glasgow escort, a really happy lot of campers, were home. P.S.: The question of the missing SUS was never, as far as can be determined, raised again.

The vast majority of Canadian servicemen were brought home by three or four prewar passenger liners, such as the Queen Elizabeth, Queen Mary, Isle de France and the Neiuw Amsterdam. These speedy liners plied back and forth across the Atlantic carrying up to 10,000 delighted passengers on each trip of about five days duration each way. Some idea of the speed of the repatriation can be determined by the following statistics. On VE Day there were 281,357 Canadians in the United Kingdom and on the Continent, excluding the Canadian Army Occupation Force in Holland. By March 1946 only 17,745 remained to be returned, and only 630 all ranks, mainly in London, remained in January 1947. Canadian Military Headquarters was closed during 1947 and would, henceforth, be known as the Canadian Army Liaison Establishment (CALE) in London.

10

The War in Canada

There exists a certain tendency among the battlefield veterans of World War II to disparage the efforts of the Services here in Canada. In fact the soldiers, sailors and airmen of the fledgling Royal Canadian Air Force were, in the fullest sense, essential troops. The civilian population also bore the brunt of rationing[111] and many other restrictions caused directly by the need to fuel the total war effort. The National Resources Mobilization Act[112] of June 1940 required the compulsory registration of *all* persons aged 16 and over. Most males in the younger age group were liable for military service, but only within Canada. This was followed, in October 1941, by the National Selective Service Act[113] which gave the Director of Selective Services, under the Wartime Prices and Trade Board, authority to place Canadian citizens in jobs deemed essential to the war effort.

The following vivid description of the overall economic scene in Canada is given by Desmond Morton in his book, *A Military History of Canada*:

Eleven million Canadians, eight million of them over eighteen, could not meet all the military and civilian needs. From June of 1940 the crisis grew. With it the demands of total war came home to Canadians as they never had in the earlier conflict. Exhortations by government committees and councils gave way, in October 1941, to National Selective Service (NSS). Resolutions in 1942 brought most Canadian men, and then women, under NSS control. By September, when young women were ordered to register, no able-bodied man aged seventeen to forty-five could drive a taxi, sell real estate, or help produce beer, toys, sporting goods, or a further list of non-essentials. From 1 September 1942 no one could be fired or quit a job without giving Selective Service a week's notice.

It is also well to remember that the size and role of the Canadian Army

TABLE 5
Major Training Centres in Canada – November 1942

Type of Centre	NUMBER (Each Type)	Location and Allocation
Basic training	41	BC-2, Alta-4, Sask-3, Man-2, PEI-1, NB-2, NS-2, Que-10, Ont-15
Corps training	29	RCA-7, RCAC-2, RCE-2, RCIC-10, RCCS-1, RCASC-2, RCAMC-1, RCOC-1, C PROC-1, CWAC-2
Trade / specialist schools	10	Small Arms (2), Dvr Maint (2), RADAR, Motor Mech, Parachute, Junior Ldrs, Chemical Warfare, Motorcycle
Vocational schools	11	Toronto, London, Kingston, Montreal, Quebec, Halifax, Saint John, Winnipeg, Saskatoon, Edmonton, Vancouver
Officer training	4	Kingston, Brockville, Gordon Head, Three Rivers
Miscellaneous	4	Administration, Combined Ops, Battle Drill, S-8 Trade School (Hamilton)
Total	99	

in Canada, from 1939 to 1946, was comparable to the overseas contingents. The threat of an attack on the Canadian home land was a distinct possibility from September 1939 onward. It was not diminished by subsequent events such as Stalin's pact with Nazi Germany early in 1940, Pearl Harbour and the Japanese occupation of the Aleutians, as well the odd German U Boat sighting in the St. Lawrence River. Our Canadian Military planners, quite sensibly, developed sizeable Home Defence Forces to cope with these external threats. There was also a requirement to develop, from scratch, a large number of supply depots, command headquarters, maintenance facilities, recruiting and placement centres and, above all, a huge TRAINING capability.

The composition of the Home Defence Force is shown, in detail, in Appendix "E" to *Six Years of War* (C P Stacey). However, it is appropriate to outline the size and scope of the Pacific and Atlantic Commands charged with this task. Atlantic Command HQ in Halifax was responsible for the eastern maritime area including Newfoundland. In addition to the 7th Canadian Division at Debert, Nova Scotia, it maintained a total of ten infantry battalions and thirteen artillery regiments (coastal, field and anti-aircraft) deployed in locations such as Newfoundland, Goose Bay, Sydney, Halifax, Shelburne, Saint John and Gaspe. The 7th Division deployed three infantry brigades, each of three battalions, in Debert NS and Sussex NB. Pacific Command in Vancouver controlled two divisions, the 6th and 8th, with their HQs at Esquimalt and Prince George, both in British Columbia. All told, this command controlled a total of twenty-one infantry battalions in five brigades with a further ten regiments of artillery. Elements of this force were deployed at Vancouver, Vernon, Esquimalt, Port Alberni, Nanaimo, Prince George, Terrace, and Prince Rupert.

The sequence of training for the tens of thousands of reinforcements required for the overseas and home formations and units started with recruit, or basic, training followed by special-to-corps/ arm training at the appropriate centres. In addition there were centres for officer training, vocational and trades training, CWAC, educational and other special facilities. The training effort can be judged by a glance at Table 5.

The development of the Corps in Canada paralleled the growth of the Army. The presence of army units in such previously isolated communities as Rouyn, Terrace, Capreol and Grande Prairie almost always necessitated some attendant provost service. The result, as shown in Table 6, was a gradual growth in the overall strength of the Corps as well as changes to the type and role of the various units.

The Provost Marshal reported to, and dealt directly with, the Adjutant General on provost policy. He was authorized to consult with district officers commanding on matters related to the duties, employment, training and accommodation of provost, and the operation of detention barracks. He was also designated Officer Administering the Corps and was responsible for a wide range of administrative matters such as: enlistments, promotions up to WOII, records and documentation, and the promulgation of Standing Orders for dress, discipline and equipment of Corps personnel.

The reports[114] of Colonel Puize clearly show that provost personnel, at all levels, maintained active cooperation and exchanged information with Naval Shore Patrols; Air Force Police; RCMP; Provincial, Municipal and Railway Police, and with the headquarters of foreign forces authorized to operate in Canada. In the interest of uniformity he issued written orders which detailed the duties and responsibilities of the DAPM's, Provost Company Commanders and Commandants of Military Detention Barracks.

The Provost Marshal's staff, as of October 1941, consisted of a lieutenant colonel APM, two captains, an adjutant and quartermaster, respectively. Another officer of lieutenant rank, a warrant officer Class I and additional

TABLE 6
Development of The Canadian Provost Corps in Canada from 1940 through 1943

Type of Unit	Number of Units	Authorized Strength as at					
		JULY 1940		OCT 1941		AUG 1943	
Corps HQ & PMs office	1	4	13	15[a]	10	16[a]	20
Internment camps	15	75[b]	450	–	–	–	–
Military Detention barracks	11, 22 & 22	–	208	–	363	18	340
Provost companies	12, 15 & 18	24	1054	42	1427	34	2045
Reinforcements	–	–	–	3	88	35	450
A-32[c] Canadian provost corps training centre	1	–	–	–	–	18	135
		103	1725	60	1888	121	2990
		(1828)		(1948)		(3111)	

a. Includes 11 DAPM's in the Districts
b. The administration of Internment Camps by Canadian Provost Corps ended 30 June 1941
c. A-32 Training Centre became operational in Camp Borden on 1 November 1942

clerical staff were added in October 1942. The Provost Marshal's office in Ottawa was originally located at 95 Rideau Street. On 3 August 1941 it moved to the Motor Building at 238 Sparks Street and, again on 16 July 1942, to the Department of Mines building at the corner of Sussex Drive and George Street. The final move was to 312 Laurier Avenue East, during August 1945.

The eleven DAPM's were carried on the HWE of the Provost Marshal and were posted for duty with the Military District Headquarters. Five held the rank of lieutenant colonel (Halifax, Saint John, Montreal, Toronto and Vancouver), while the remaining six were majors. The DAPM was advisor to the District Officer Commanding on all provost matters. He administered the provost units in the district and was responsible for their supervision and efficiency, in accordance with the policy established by the Provost Marshal and approved by the Adjutant General. DAPM's had considerable latitude in channels of communication, as revealed in the following quote from the statement of "Duties of a Deputy Assistant Provost Marshal" recorded in Colonel Puize's resumed history of August 1943.

He will deal directly with the District Officer Commanding and may correspond directly with the Provost Marshal and Officer Administering the Canadian Provost Corps, with the Heads of Services and Departments and Officers Commanding units throughout his District, on all subjects connected with his duties.

These channels corresponded closely with those of his counterpart in the overseas army. The key words are "subjects connected with his duties". It goes without saying that in situations where servicemen or women are involved in frays, disorders, accidents or are under arrest, the matter must be dealt with promptly.

Just as the section was the workhorse of the field provost company, so the detachment carried the load for the Home War Establishment Company. Early in 1941, after the organization of the original twelve provost companies, detachments[115] were gradually posted from companies to key cities and towns in the military districts. In May 1941 a total of fifty-one such detachments, averaging ten other ranks each, were posted throughout Canada. As the strength of provost companies increased, and as additional companies were authorized, detachments grew in number. In December 1941 there were sixty-five detachments with a total strength of 1,469 all ranks. By the end of August 1943 there were eighty-three detachments, totalling 2,079 all ranks, operating in the various commands, districts, camps and areas.

The role of these detachments was the maintenance of good order and discipline among the troops in their area. They patrolled the areas frequented by off-duty troops and, generally, performed provost duties,[116] as listed below:

(a) patrolling trains, streets, steamships, railway stations, docks, bus terminals and other areas;
(b) directing military traffic and controlling movement in operational areas;
(c) investigations in relation to absentees and deserters and in respect of mishandling or theft of army stores, supplies and equipment;
(d) locating and apprehending absentees and deserters;
(e) investigating offenses against military law and order;
(f) escorting prisoners of war and refugees from camps to camps, from

camps to ports of embarkation and from ports of disembarkation to camps;
(g) assisting and cooperating with civil police in the prevention of civil offenses by soldiers;
(h) cooperating with the police bodies of the other armed services;
(i) by their presence, act as deterrent to would-be offenders against military law and order;
(j) assist and aid naval ratings, soldiers and airmen whenever possible and necessary;
(k) guard and train soldiers under sentence, including naval ratings and airmen in military detention barracks.

Reports and records prepared during the early years of the war clearly show that the Corps in Canada had its fair share of growing pains. It is also evident that the Provost Marshal dealt with these in a timely and forthright manner. He spared no effort to ensure that the Canadian Provost Corps was organized, trained, equipped and deployed in a manner consistent with its responsibilities. He maintained close contact with the Adjutant General and staff at army headquarters, and was in constant touch with the district DAPMs. He initiated several directives and orders which were promulgated throughout the army by the Adjutant General branch. For example, the procedure for dealing with absentees and deserters, contained in a Canadian Army Routine Order (CARO) of August 1943, was based on recommendations made by the Provost Marshal.

Initially, the absence of a corps training centre, where recruits could be trained to a uniform standard, created a problem. The large number of recruits allocated to HWE provost companies, nearly 2,000 by the end of 1942, strained the meagre training resources available to DAPMs and company commanders. There are no reliable statistics, but only a small percentage of new recruits were former policemen or had any military training. The whole question of minimum standards for Canadian Provost Corps recruits received considerable attention during the first two years, from June 1940. While recruits for field provost companies had to be category "A", and fit for battle conditions, those for HWE companies could be of a lower physical standard. In September 1941, following representations by the Provost Marshal, the medical category for HWE provost was raised from "B" and "C" to "A", and the necessary implementing orders were issued by the Adjutant General. This was an enormous help to the Canadian Provost Corps units which, hence-forth, received recruits who were physically capable of performing their demanding duties. A minimum height requirement of five feet, eight inches was also established, and the minimum M Score for provost was raised from 115 to 125, effective 10 March 1943.

A training manual, dealing with provost duties in Canada, was prepared by the Provost Marshal's staff, commencing March 1941. It was approved by the Directorate of Military Training and issued to all Canadian Provost Corps units, in October 1941. This "Manual Of Provost Training, 1941" was also used at A-32 from November 1942 onward. The manual, together with the issue of numbered Corps Circulars and Corps Standing Orders, proved invaluable in achieving a uniform standard for the performance of provost duties. From November 1942 all provost personnel (HWE and OS reinforcements) were given special-to-corps training at A-32 Canadian Provost Corps Training Centre at Camp Borden.

As noted above, A-32 Canadian Provost Corps Training Centre was authorized under War Establishment Cdn/V/229/1 of 10 October 1942 and it commenced operating on 1 November 1942. It was designed to produce, each month, 80 OR reinforcements and 50 OR for HWE units. It also conducted "Special-To-Arm" training for Canadian Provost Corps Reinforcement Officers. Recruits allocated to the Canadian Provost Corps were received from Basic Training Centres and at a later date provost from HWE companies, for refresher courses. The duration of the course for Overseas Reinforcements was three months, and for HWE ORs it was four weeks. During the period November 1942 through August 1943 it trained 485 OR reinforcements, 438 ORs for HWE units and 31 reinforcement officers. It seems there was some lack of communication between CMHQ in London and Army Headquarters in Ottawa with regard to Canadian Provost Corps Officer reinforcement quotas. It is not known whether this was due to lower than anticipated wastage rates, or fewer officers required overall. In any event, reinforcement officers of lieutenant rank were being produced on both sides of the Atlantic in excess of the number required. As Canadian Provost Corps reinforcement officers completed training at A-32 they were attached to HWE companies for duty until posted overseas. This led to complaints from these officers who considered it unfair that the overseas requirement for reinforcement officers was being met by the commissioning procedure in the United Kingdom. They were available, trained and eager to proceed overseas instead of languishing in a HWE company. The outcome of this was an arrangement whereby 50% of the overseas officer reinforcements required would come from each source. The situation of having a surplus in Canada began to right itself following the incidence of Canadian Provost Corps officer casualties in 1944–1945, along with the programme of returning high-point Canadian Provost Corps officers to Canada on rotation leave, commencing March 1945.

The necessity for military detention barracks has often been queried by various members of the military establishment. There are several logical reasons, however, the basic one is simply because a term of "Detention" is authorized, by law, as one of the punishments that can be awarded service personnel for contravening the rules and regulations for good order and military discipline. From the outset of World War II it was apparent that there was an immediate and continuing need for detention facilities in Canada. At the Army Headquarters level the question was whether to have several smaller barracks, located close to large troop concentrations, or a half dozen large scale barracks. The decision went to smaller barracks, but more of them. Existing buildings could be easily converted to this use, it saved much time and travel expense and, most important, experience had shown that large concentrations of prisoners, whether civil or military, were more liable to disorders and were difficult to control.

The progressive build-up of detention barracks is shown at Table 6. The maximum of twenty-two MDBs, with a total Canadian Provost Corps staff of 18 officers and 340 OR was reached in August 1943. The cell (room) capacity ranged from a low of 20 at Sydney NS, to a high of 141 at Camp Borden, for a total cell capacity of 1308. Each military district and large camp (Borden, Petawawa, Valcartier, Debert, Sussex and Dundurn) had one or more detention barracks. The commandant of the larger MDB's was an officer of captain or lieutenant rank, while the five smaller ones were administered by a warrant officer Class 1. Staff was provided on a scale which enabled three eight hour shifts each day, with a higher than usual ratio of staff-sergeants, sergeants and corporals. An additional officer of lieutenant rank was added to the DAPM's staff to coordinate all activities related to detention, in the district. He was designated "Officer-in-Charge of Administration, MDBs", and was also appointed Accounting Officer for the barracks controlled by a warrant Officer. He reported to the DAPM. The procedures followed for the day-to-day routine was contained in the manual "Regulations and Instructions For Detention Barracks and Branch Detention Barracks, 1939", and were closely followed at all times.

The commandant of a military detention barracks had no power to punish a detainee but he could, in accordance with Regulations, suspend privileges, order a restricted diet or withhold marks earned for time off awarded for good behaviour. The local headquarters in the area was responsible for detailing a visiting officer whose duty it was to inspect the barracks and inmates at least once weekly, ask for complaints and, generally, monitor the current programme. It was a general principle that the daily routine of a detainee should be at least as rigorous as that pertaining in his unit on its worst day. Rules, no matter how trivial, were strictly but impartially enforced. Much emphasis was placed on cleanliness, physical fitness and good behaviour. Detainees serving lengthy sentences were encouraged to take correspondence courses, available from the Education Services, and to generally upgrade their scholastic standing. A medical officer and padre visited the barracks daily, or on request. Finally, detainees were trained in basic recruit subjects (drill, small arms, military law, etc) and senior NCOs on the staff were sent on special courses to qualify as instructors.

Not surprisingly, the administration of the overall detention programme was confronted, from time-to-time, with outside interference and other problems. One such incident bears mention. In November 1941, and again in April 1942, the Provost Marshal made strong recommendations to the Adjutant General that the practice, by camp and district staffs of detailing soldiers in detention for fatigue duties outside the compound of the barracks, should be discontinued. These extraneous duties, it was pointed out, were contrary to Regulations, interfered with the training programme in effect at the MDB and prejudiced the safe custody of detainees. As a result of these representations CARO 2025 of 3 June 1942 was issued. It prohibited the practice of using detainees "for extra-mural fatigues outside the confines of the Detention Barracks".

There is no question that this detention programme made a significant contribution to the overall discipline and effective use of manpower during World War II. The following statistics, covering the period 31 August 1941 to 31 August 1943 (24 months), are of interest.

Admitted to MDBs	33,514
Average length of sentence	26 days
Percentage of offenses:	
Absence without leave	72%
Conducts to the prejudice good order & discipline	10%
Drunkenness, theft, assaults, desertion	12%
Other	6%

Colonel P.A. Puize commented on this programme in his final report. Typically it is an understatement.

Conditions in Military Detention Barracks have substantially improved. Diet for soldiers in detention is now identical to that applying to all troops. Soldiers under sentence are now given full basic training, with the object of making them better soldiers and better fitted for duty in the ranks of their units.

One of the early and short lived tasks of the Canadian Provost Corps was the administration of internment camps. The war cabinet in Ottawa implemented a programme of interning (confining) persons in Canada suspected of, at best, disloyalty and, at worst, being potential saboteurs. The RCMP and local police were given the job of identifying and incarcerating suspects. We have no interest in discussing the merits of this action, however, one of the first tasks given the Provost Marshal was the administration of several internment camps that had been hastily formed across Canada. A force of 75 officers and 450 men of the corps was employed on this administrative duty from August 1940 to 30 June 1941. The Provost Marshal had disagreed with this role for the Canadian Provost Corps from the outset. Happily, he succeeded in convincing his mentors in the Defence Department of this view with the result that provost were relieved of this duty which was assumed by the newly formed Veterans Guard of Canada. These camps were designated as Camp "A", "B", "C", etcetera, and were located as follows.

Camp A – Farnham, Que K – Kananaskis, Alta
B – Fredricton, NB M – New Toronto, Ont
C – Gravenhurst, Ont N – Newington, Que
D – (not known) P – Petawawa, Ont
E – Espanola, Ont Q – Monteith, Ont
F – Fort Henry, Ont R – Red Rock, Ont
H – (not known) S – St Helen's Island, Mtl, Que
I – Isle ax Noix, Que W – Neys, Ont

(Eight in Ontario, four in Quebec, one each in New Brunswick and Alberta)

On 26 June 1941 the government announced its intention of forming a Canadian Army Women's Army Corps (CWAC). The first recruits were enrolled the following September. They were employed in Canada, initially, but a total of 1,944, all ranks, served over-seas from November 1942 onwards. By war's end the corps reached a strength of 652 officers and 13,282 other ranks.

These female soldiers received basic training at two CWAC Basic Training Centres located at Ste Anne de Bellevue, Quebec and Kitchener, Ontario. By January, 1942 plans had been made to train and employ CWAC personnel in various trades to replace Category A men, who could then be posted to active field duty. The first such course was conducted, starting 12 November 1942, at the Edmonton Wing of 13 District Depot, where 15 selected CWAC completed a clerks course. CWAC were trained to replace RCASC drivers, RCAMC orderlies, as well as in technical areas such as wireless operators and many other trades and specialties.

It should come as no surprise that members of the CWAC occasionally contravened the mass of rules and regulations considered necessary for good order and military discipline. In addition to being subject to the edicts of Kings Rules and Orders and Military Law, these young women sometimes found it difficult to accept the complete uniformity of dress demanded by their superiors. Dress regulations specified the precise details of all items of dress. The skirt hem must be 16 to 17 inches from the ground; gloves, when not worn, must be carried in the left hand (leaving the right hand free for saluting); and, most serious of all, the cap must be tilted at a 15 degree angle over the right eye. In addition to these somewhat minor infractions there were a significant number of more serious breaches such as, being AWOL, pilfering and involvement in various degrees of disorderly conduct. The Provost Marshal's request to employ CWAC as military police was approved in July 1942. The initial training course was held for 72 CWAC volunteers at Fort Osborne Barracks, Winnipeg, under the direction of DAPM of MD 10, Major W S Jones. The basic prerequisite for acceptance as a CWAC Provost required good physical stamina; between 25 and 35 years of age; and good conduct and character. This one month course commenced on 13 August 1942 and included intensive sessions on security, safety, military law, ranks and badges, grievance and the army organization structure and customs. As evidence that training was serious and demanded a high standard by all ranks of the Provost, only 62 of the 72 of these enthusiastic volunteers were graduated as qualified military police, and ready for patrol, escort and security duties.

Volunteers for CWAC provost duties with the Canadian Provost Corps was continued until the end of the war. Exact numbers are not available but it has been estimated that by the end of 1944 there were 450 to 500 CWAC employed in provost companies across Canada. They were trained by the local provost company initally but, starting in August 1944, a special CWAC Provost Course was organized at A-32 Canadian Provost Corps Training Centre in Camp Borden. A total of six courses, each four weeks duration, were conducted during the period August 1944 to April 1945, for a total of 108 CWAC graduates.

One of the early "originals" was W1201 Corporal Vivian M Howard of

Galt, Ontario. She enlisted in London 11 May 1942 and completed basic training at Ste Anne De Bellevue by the end of June. She applied for provost during a short stay at the Thames Valley Military Camp near London. Posted to 30 Provost Company in London, Ontario in September 1942, she was employed, initially, in the office of the DAPM on administrative and clerical duties. She attended the first provost training course held at Wolsley Barracks in July 1943 and, henceforth, until her release from the Canadian Army on 1 February was employed full-time on provost duties. Vivian married Harold Bancroft, a RCAF veteran, and now resides with her husband in Strathroy, Ontario. She is proud of her service with the Canadian Provost Corps and recalls many unusal incidents, in the course of duty, during her years as a provost.

During the Summer of 1943 I was detailed for escort duty involving travel to the USA. Word had been received at HQ MD 1 (London) that a CWAC absentee had been apprehended by the local US authorities and was being held by US MPs at Fort Sheridan, Illinois. My order directed me to proceed by train, via Detroit and Chicago, and return this absentee to Kitchener. Apart from a mistake in the train schedule from Chicago to Sheridan the trip down was uneventful and I arrived in Fort Sheridan (Military Camp) in the evening. I was met by the US MPs, given a huge meal, and quartered for the night. The MPs took the absentee and I to the train the following morning. Despite a couple of train changes, the return trip was eneventful and I was met at the border (Windsor) by our own provost patrol. We arrived in Kitchener later that day and my duty was finished when this absentee was handed over to her unit. The thing I remember most vividly about this particular duty was the outstanding courtesy and cooperation shown to me by the various USA authorities, including railway agents, civil and military police and immigration officials.

Members of the CWAC Provost were authorized to wear the Canadian Provost Corps lanyard and MP armband. They were given extensive powers of arrest and authority over all CWAC personnel. Canadian Army Routine Order (CARO) 4368, which sets out the details of their employment, powers and duties, is republished.

4368 – C.W.A.C. PROVOST

R.O. 2443 is hereby cancelled and the following substituted:
1. For the information of all concerned, selected personnel of the CWAC are being posted for duty with the Canadian Provost Corps as Provost personnel.

2. C.W.A.C. Other Rank personnel will be posted to the C.Pro.C. Company with which they are to be employed and will be shown as attached back to the appropriate C.W.A.C. Administrative Unit for such purposes local conditions may warrant. The extent of such attachment will be at the discretion of the district Officers Commanding concerned. C.W.A.C. Provost will not, however, be accommodated in the same quarters as other C.W.A.C. personnel. If no separate accommodation is available, they will be placed on subsistence.

3.(a) The duties of C.W.A.C. Provost will, insofar as the extigencies of the Service permit, be restricted to C.W.A.C. personnel and they will generally exercise all the powers, rights, privileges and duties of soldiers detailed to perform the function of Military Police. Insofar as the Provost Marshal may direct, C.W.A.C. Provost as Service Police may exercise the rights and duties outlined in R.O. 3252. C.W.A.C. Provost will NOT, however, perform any of the duties outlined in R.O. 3773 in as much as the rights and privileges conferred therein are confined exclusively to members of the C.Pro.C.

(b) C.W.A.C. Provost will, while on duty, be identified by the Arm Band worn by personnel of the C.Pro.C.

(H.Q. 54-27-111-111)

The CWAC Provost were an enormous asset to the Canadian Army in general and the Canadian Provost Corps in particular. They regularly patrolled the streets, railway stations and terminals to enforce regulations and settle disputes. The author of "ATHENE", the Story of the Canadian Women's Army Corps", at page 171, makes the point that these "Provost", in addition to their normal disciplinary duties, rendered an invaluable service to new CWAC recruits and trainees by informing them of the correct dress, manner of salute and the fine points of military discipline and customs. They served with dedication and contributed much to the cause of good order in the Canadian Army.

In the spring of 1941 the corps assumed responsibility for the movement in Canada of prisoners of war. It is somewhat surprising to find that POW, in sizeable numbers, were lodged in POW camps in Canada as early as 1941 and 1942. They were moved by rail from Halifax. There was close liaison between the provost and railway officials at all levels. The railways organized special trains and adjusted timings at the request of the Provost Marshal. Arrangements were made for meals and ablution facilities, however, no special provision was made for sleeping or dining as a POW lived in his allotted seat throughout the trip. Windows were "blocked" shut, emergency switches were disconnected and, once aboard, the POW did not detrain until the destination was reached.

The average train was made up of seven cars, each carrying about forty POW. It was not unusual for as many as ten trains to leave Halifax during one 24 hour period. The average provost escort was three officers and fifty men per train. Escorts were detailed from nearly every provost company although, as might be expected, the majority came from Nova Scotia, Quebec and New Brunswick provost units. The procedure followed by provost escorts was detailed in Standing Orders for POW Movements, issued by the Provost Marshal. These instructions covered such things as take-over; records and documentation; seating of POW in trains; number and duties of provost; shift changes; detraining and liaison with train crews. The Canadian Provost Corps officer in charge of the escort was required to complete a report and forward it, through provost channels, to the Provost Marshal. Escorts were required to deadhead back to Halifax, immediately after each completed movement, during periods of heavy POW traffic. A recurring complaint of escort personnel, especially during hot summer weather, was the lack of fresh air in the ancient, closed passenger cars. This problem was partially solved by the issue to provost of light-weight summer drill uniforms. It was also arranged, with railway officials, to have the window blocks on one car removed during return trips. We do not have complete statistics, however in a twenty-eight month period, from May 1941 to August 1943, the following figures are given:

Total POW train movements	99
Total POW	26,142
Average duration of each movement	8 days
Average strength of each C Pro C escort	3 & 50

The exact number and location of each POW camp is not known. However, most were in remote areas of Quebec, Ontario, the Prairies and British Columbia.

The life of a Canadian soldier in Canada was reasonably predictable. He would rise at reveille, wash, don his uniform, eat, work, train and indulge in much barrack room banter. He cleaned everything including the barrack room, parade ground, his kit and equipment, vehicles, the flagpole and walkways. If lucky, he might get to enjoy the sheer delight of a leave or weekend pass. It was also an absolute certainty that he would make several trips on Canadian National or Canadian Pacific Railways, whether on duty, leave or on draft to a new location in Canada or overseas. Regardless of the reason for his travel, it created an extraordinary feeling of euphoria to be moving on the train. Perhaps for this reason, and sometimes because of previous over indulgence, there was much damage done to the passenger cars of the CNR and CPR trains, all of it caused by the boisterous behaviour of troops. The railway officials complained loud and long to anyone in the Defence Department who would listen. This problem, ultimately, came to rest in the Adjutant General office and quickly, from there, to the Provost Marshal.

The first Provost Train Patrols were initiated over the 1940–1941 Christmas and New Year's period. The procedures for these patrols was arranged between the Directors of Investigation and Chief Passenger Agents of both railways and the Provost Marshal. The details included: the routes, trains, times of patrols, issue and control of railway passes, liaison between provost and railway officials and train conductors, arrangements to communicate with provost station patrols by CN and CP Telegraph, reserved seats (always in the first car) for patrol personnel and the changeover, at divisional points, for relief patrols. It worked. The railways were highly complimentary and there was a marked decrease in incidents involving troops on trains.

A permanent schedule of train and station patrols was inaugurated during 1941. The procedure was simple and most effective. A train patrol, depending on the circumstances, would consist of at least two, and as many as seven, provost. The patrol entrained at the point of origin and stayed on duty for a period of 24 to 36 hours, when it would be relieved by a patrol from another company, usually at a main station such as Montreal, Toronto, Port Arthur, Winnipeg, and so forth. An initial tour of the train was made soon after leaving the point of origin, and again after each stop at main stations. If it became necessary to place a soldier under arrest the next station patrol would be advised, via the conductor, and the offender would be handed over when the station was reached. Too much booze was the major cause of trouble, and also the reason for placing soldiers in custody. It was found that large drafts, under control of unit officers and NCOs, were not nearly as troublesome as small, independent groups and individuals.

As time went one these patrol procedures were developed and further refined. The following measures, to deal with this general problem, were implemented:

- An army order required all soldiers, other than formed drafts, to show their pass and railway ticket to the gateman, and a notice of this effect was posted at entrances to station platforms;
- An information booth, manned by a Canadian Provost Corps NCO, was

installed in most of the large, mainline terminals. These booths provided much valuable information to the travelling soldiers, such as bus schedules, hostel and canteen locations, desirable lodgings and general information. They were well patronized by all servicemen.

- In September 1941, at the request of the Provost Marshal, a circular letter (HQ 6614–12) was promulgated to all military districts. It emphasized the duty of all officers to counsel troops under their command against the consumption of liquor on or prior to boarding trains.
- A meeting of senior Canadian Provost Corps officers and rail-way officials was held at the Provost Marshal's office in January 1943. The schedule of train patrols was reviewed and revised to meet current conditions.

Some idea of the way the 2,076 all ranks of the HWE provost companies spent their time can be gleaned from the following statistics compiled in August 1943 by Colonel P A Puize. The man-hours devoted to train and station patrols clearly indicate the relative importance of this duty.

Statistics – HWE provost companies
May 1941 to August 1943 (28 months)

Daily Duty	Total (28 Months)	Average
Daily street patrols		
– Cities and towns patrolled	–	72
– Provost on this duty	–	566
Train patrols		
– Trains patrolled	952	34
– Provost on this duty	–	115
Station patrols		
– Stations, bus terminals & docks (daily)	–	65
– Provost on duty (daily)	–	180
Prisoners of war		
– Number of POW	26,142	264
– Provost on duty	–	53
Military detention barracks		
– Admissions	33,514	–
– Provost employed	–	358

Daily Duty	Total (28 Months)	Average
Investigations		
– Related to provost duties	88,158	–
– Others (RCN, RCAF, Civil)	11,438	–
Arrests		
– Absent without leave	37,959	–
– Drunkenness	11,945	–
– Others	18,202	–
(Incl.: Civil cases, fighting, assaults, theft, etc.)		

The corps in Canada continued to function to meet the many demands placed on it throughout the war. Regrettably Colonel Puize was forced to retire due to ill health in September 1943. He turned over his duties to his deputy, Colonel G T Goad, who was appointed Provost Marshal on Colonel Puize's retirement. Colonel George Thomas Goad served for two years until October 1945 when Colonel Leonard Hanson Nicholson was appointed Provost Marshal of the Army. Provost HWE units were phased out in concert with the overall rundown of the Canadian army following the defeat of the Axis Forces (Germany and Japan) in May and August of 1945. They had served the cause of Canada, their service and the corps with distinction. It is regretted that space does not permit mention of the many individuals who made outstanding contributions. Frequent mention of Colonel Puize does, perhaps, partially atone for this omission. He symbolized all that was worthwhile in the Canadian Provost Corps.

11

The Interim Force

All of the field provost companies and most of the HWE units were disbanded by the end of 1945, as were most of the detention barracks in Canada. The few remaining Canadian Provost Corps units were gradually reduced to nil strength as the Canadian Army literally evaporated. Colonel L H Nicholson replaced Colonel T Goad as Provost Marshal during October 1945. He had the unenviable task of dealing with the residue of the Corps at war's end and planning for a somewhat uncertain future. Colonel "Nick", in his usual down-to-earth fashion, dealt with both aspects with much wisdom and forethought.

Brooke Claxton became the Minister of National Defence in MacKenzie King's government, and Lieutenant General Charles Foulkes, former Commander of 1 Canadian Corps, was appointed Chief of the General Staff (CGS) for the Army, both by early 1946. In order to ensure there would be sufficient soldiers for a yet to be determined continuing Regular (permanent) Canadian Army it was decided to give all soldiers an opportunity to voluntarily defer their release until 30 September 1946. Those who did so were designated as "Interim Force" and would be eligible to serve in a yet to be defined Regular Army. For a variety of reasons there were many who did so. Those who had been Permanent Force prior to 10 September 1939 were also retained, since this group already had service to count towards a service pension. The overall strength of the army as at 30 September 1946 was 31,042, made up of 17,682 general service, 12,306 interim force and 1,042 NRMA personnel. On 30 September 1947 the total strength of the Canadian Army was 14,683 all ranks. The manpower ceiling for the continuing, or regular, army was set at 25,000 all ranks which included 117 all ranks of the Canadian Provost Corps. This was a dramatic decrease in numbers and it meant there would one member of the Corps for every 200 peacetime soldiers as opposed to one for each 100 wartime army ranks.

The question was, how would this small remnant be selected, organized and deployed. The selection process presented some problems but proved the easier of the three to manage. It was decided that A-32 Training Centre in Camp Borden would be used a holding unit during the reorganization period. By April 1946 it had been reduced until only the commanding officer and a handful of NCOs remained. Members of the Corps accepted for the Interim Force were posted, supernumerary, to A-32 in Borden, where a newly appointed Interim Force major was given the task of selecting provost personnel, by ranks and numbers, for the first peacetime units of the Canadian Provost Corps, up to and including the rank of lieutenant. There were problems since the numbers and ranks of these Interim Force provost bore no resemblance to the vastly reduced regular army requirement. For example, there were over 450 applicants for 117 vacancies. In the warrant officer situation there were seventeen warrant officers Class 1 for just six vacancies in the proposed Plan "H" establishments.[117]

The commanding officer of A-32 was also given the task of disbanding several HWE provost companies whose residue of personnel were posted to A-32 for disposal. This meant countless Courts of Inquiry and Committees of Adjustment to finalize canteen accounts, nonpublic funds, stores and other assets. Life for those aspiring to serve in the regular forces was further complicated by the sudden departure, without immediate replacement, of supporting services such as personnel selection officers, padres and pay-masters. The newly appointed commanding officer of the A-32 Unit was his own paymaster for a period of two months. The duties of pay sergeant, it must be recorded, were most ably performed by Acting Sergeant Laurie Paulhus because, after several pay parades for this large and diverse group, the value of signed Acquittance Rolls and Cash On Hand came out exactly even.

It was necessary to organize an assessment programme to evaluate the skills and knowledge of the many applicants for the limited number of vacancies. This accounted for what must have seemed senseless, regimental parades, drill and mutual instructional periods, all designed to assist the evaluation process. Applicants were informed of the decisions made as to the rank and appointment they would be offered as soon as possible, but usually within a six week period. Should an individual not be offered a position in his current rank, he had the option of accepting regular service in the Corps, but at a lower level rank. Many very capable warrant officers and NCOs accepted service in a lesser rank. Others decided against further service and requested discharge, which was, invariably, granted. Several privates requested "farm leave" since this had been previously granted whilst serving in another unit. At least one such applicant appealed to his Member of Parliament after his request had been denied. At least one capable lieutenant, a former Permanent Force soldier, accepted a position as a warrant officer. He went on to become a lieutenant colonel in the Canadian Provost Corps. This brings up what became known as the "pension prisoner" syndrome, so-called because the former Permanent Force soldier had already acquired considerable service towards pension and was most reluctant to give up his opportunity to continue as a career soldier. It seemed unfair that many good men were forced to accept lower rank rather than be discharged.

A new command structure for the Canadian Army was announced in June 1946. There would be five commands, each controlling one or more areas, each to be commanded by an officer with the rank of Major General or Brigadier. He was responsible to the next superior for all military matters pertaining to the Canadian Army, within the geographical boundaries of the command or area. The following chart shows this command structure which absorbed the previous military districts.

COMMAND/AREA	GEOGRAPHICAL REGION	HEAD-QUARTERS
EASTERN	Maritime Provinces	Halifax
New Brunswick	New Brunswick	Fredericton
Newfoundland*	Newfoundland	St John's
QUEBEC	Quebec Province	Montreal
Eastern Quebec	Eastern Quebec	Quebec City
CENTRAL	Ontario	Oakville
Western Ontario	Southwest Ontario	London
Eastern Ontario	East Ontario	Kingston
Central Ontario	Central & Northern Ontario	Oakville
PRAIRIE	Manitoba & Saskatchewan	Winnipeg
Saskatchewan	Province of Saskatchewan	Regina
WESTERN	Alberta & British Columbia	Edmonton
British Columbia	Province of British Columbia	Vancouver

*Newfoundland from 1949

Prairie command included the northwestern region of Thunder Bay, in Ontario

Western command included Yukon and the Northwest Arctic Territories

The real problem now confronting the Provost Marshal and his staff was the manner in which the one hundred and seventeen all ranks allocated to the Canadian Provost Corps should be organized. How could they provide some form of meaningful provost service to the newly formed Regular Army of some 25,000 all ranks? On the one hand it was clear that duties related to prisoners of war, large scale training, military traffic control and, hopefully, discipline would either disappear or become low priority. It was equally clear that detention facilities would be required, not only to deal with the residue of detainees from the war but with the distinct problem of absentees and deserters in Canada. More on this later, however, experience told us that the apprehension, escort, confinement and trial of absentees was, and would likely continue to be, expensive in the use of provost manpower. Records are not completely reliable, however, there were over 24,500 absentees and deserters, mostly in Ontario and Quebec, at war's end. A further provost problem was already surfacing, namely, the large scale, almost wholesale, theft of Department of National Defence stores and equipment from camps, depots and the locations of former units. The haste with which units were disbanded made this plunder almost inevitable. The War Assets Disposal Board had been set-up to dispose of the millions of items , ranging from wartime buildings, vehicles, plumbing and electrical fixtures, and a myriad of other items made scarce by wartime shortages. An incident in a large camp illustrates this point. War Assets were selling the temporary "H" huts built for barracks, mess halls and stores. Most buyers simply loaded the building on long, lowbed trailers and towed them away. One such "buyer" was stopped by a Canadian Provost Corps officer as he approached the main gate leaving the camp. He could not, when asked, produce the yellow Release Certificate issued by the local War Assets representative. Further inquiries quickly revealed that the "H" hut on his trailer was simply stolen. This thief had banked on not being challenged if he drove into camp, loaded and drove off with one half of a "H" hut. His assessment of the low risk was well founded. There were no provost around and the soldier guard at the gate, if there was a guard, was probably due for discharge in a few days and had little interest in the protection of DND property. Lance Corporal A B (Robbie) Robertson tells about the general situation which prevailed along the Pacific coast of Western Canada.

The war in the Pacific ended with total abruptness. There was no 'winding down' or 'phasing out'. One day we were in a war footing, expecting orders for our 6th Division to form up and move "somewhere", and the next day Japan had surrendered and the war was over. Army camps and installations all along the Pacific coast were emptied with astounding speed as troops, many of them conscriptees, were sent home for discharge. Weapons, vehicles, rations, electronic gear were left with minimal security, at best, and totally abandoned, at worst.

I was a lance corporal in the Victoria section of 41 Provost Company, wearing General Hoffmeister's 6th Division multicoloured patch. Instead of embarking for the Pacific theatre I spent months "riding from garrison to garrison" on a Harley-Davidson trying to stem the massive scale thefts and pilferage taking place. Wartime rationing and shortages on civvie street created the demand, and an almost complete lack of security created the opportunity. So our daily patrols and checks amounted to little more than showing the colours, but we did the best we could.

It would be irresponsible to state that this sort of thing was a deliberate policy on the part of the Government of Canada. However, people like C D Howe, who had worked with such vigour to accelerate Canada's industrial output for war, was now working nonstop to convert to the needs of peacetime life. So what did it matter if bren-gun carriers were sold to unsuspecting farmers as tractors; or that truckloads of electric fan motors from army kitchens were acquired by construction entrepreneurs; or that porcelain washroom fixtures, only available to the military, could now be obtained legally, or illegally, by potential tourist camp owners? One suspects that the intricacies and delicacies of a strictly military nature were far removed from the thoughts of the prime minister and most of his cabinet. The CGS received less than half of the soldiers he requested. The Canadian Provost Corps was not the only element to suffer from dramatically reduced manpower. The combat component of the regular army was fixed at three infantry battalions, two armoured regiments, a field artillery regiment, a locating battery, two light antiaircraft batteries and a few supporting services. Most corps allocated a good proportion of available manpower to the establishment of a training school and instructional cadres for the reserves.

The final organization for the Canadian Provost Corps of the CA(R) was completed by July 1946. It utilized the 117 positions as follows:

Provost Marshal's Office	2 (1 RSM & 1 Sgt)
The Canadian Provost Corps School	5 (Capt, WO 2, 3 Sgts)
Five Detention Barracks	85 (Lt, RSM & Approx 15 OR)
APMs Commands	5 (OR Clerks)
Special Investigators	3 (WO 2 & 2 Sgts)
No 6 Provost Company	17 (1 Capt, WO 2, 15 OR)

The Provost Marshal[118] was established in the rank of lieutenant-colonel. There were four Assistant Provost Marshals with the rank of major, one each in the Provost Marshal's Office and at the headquarters of Western, Central and Quebec Commands. The Assistant Provost Marshals for Eastern and Prairie Commands held the rank of captain. In what must be seen as a really shrewd move, the Provost Marshal and the six assistants were carried on strength of the Branch of the Adjutant General at Army Headquarters, Ottawa, thus saving seven establishment positions for the corps. In any event, to quote Sergeant Ray Chambers on D-Day, "We were ashore with all our men and vehicles, and ready to go".

Converting to peacetime status was a new and interesting experience for the great majority of Canadian soldiers. The date set for the changeover, from Active Service to Regular Service, was 1 October 1946. Beyond some rumours, most officers had not been notified whether or not they would start a career in the Regular Army. One heard much about careers and interesting and glamorous appointments in far-off places. More to the point, the scale of pay and allowances was completely changed; a slight increase in the former and a huge increase in the latter. There was to be a married allowance, kit allowance, subsistence allowance, separated family allowance, isolated post allowance and risk allowance. On the debit side, monthly deductions were made for income tax, pension contributions and, later on, for unemployment insurance. Incremental increases were also made for each year in rank. Additional pay for trades/specialty qualification was authorized. The trade of Service Policeman was authorized, for all ranks below warrant officer, for the Canadian Provost Corps, with gradations from Group 1 to Group 3. All told this made for a fairly decent bimonthly pay package, even for a lance corporal. Perhaps the most positive aspect was that all service counted toward a pension. Soldiers were enrolled for specific periods, usually for an initial three years, with an option of release on completing the term. Also of importance, those enrolled in the CA(R) were permitted to purchase, for a nominal fee, their period of war service, which could be as much as six years, a real incentive. Other benefits for the soldier included full, free medical and dental care, paid leave for four weeks each year, compassionate leave when justified and the privilege of living with his wife and children, if married. It sounded like a good deal and, for the most part, it was a good deal. The members of the corps enrolled in the CA(R) were, in keeping with the prevailing custom of the day, obliged to take the Oath of Allegiance to the King. The actual wording was: "I... , swear by Almighty God, that I will be forever faithful and bear true allegiance to His Majesty King George VI, his heirs and successors according to law, so help me God". This oath could be attested by an officer of field rank (Major) or above. If, for any reason, the person attested objected to the Christian oath, he would make a solemn affirmation, ie, "I ... do (solemnly swear) etc, etc". It seemed like a solemn decision and, indeed, for the new members of the first peacetime Canadian Provost Corps, it proved to be just that.

12

Absentees and Deserters

Throughout recorded history there have always been soldiers who left their units or place of duty, be it barracks, camp or battlefield, without permission. The Canadian Army has had more than its share of absentees and deserters. On the face of it, any soldier who goes AWOL is disloyal and shirks his duty. This is not always the case. Many otherwise conscientious and well motivated soldiers have taken this extreme step because some personal, family or financial problem could not, or was not, readily resolved. History tells us that the problem of soldiers going AWOL was prevalent in most armies of the world, and is not just confined to Canada. Both sides in the United States Civil War of 1861–1865 had large scale absentee and desertion rates. Certainly it was cause for concern in the British Army from Marlborough to Wellington, and on to Haig. There has always been a trickle of Canadian soldiers who, for whatever reasons, have gone AWOL from their units. Another facet of the problem in the Canadian Army is the fact that very few soldiers go absent when stationed outside of this country. For example, out of the 370,000 Canadian soldiers who came to Britain during World War II only 239 were charged with desertion.[119] When the Canadians left Italy there were only 153 left behind. At war's end in Europe, although exact statistics are not available, there were less than 500 Canadian absentees and deserters in all of Europe. By contrast, the number absenting themselves from army units in Canada during World War I, and again in World War II, was extremely high. There is no doubt this was a direct result of the Military Service Act of December 1917 and the National Resources Mobilization Act of June 1940, followed by the Conscription Referendum of April 1942. In both instances large numbers were either "draft dodgers" or went AWOL in Canada following enlistment. Statistics are somewhat meaningless when not related to a normal base, however, from June 1917 to November 1918 there were 29,278 draft evaders and absentees APPREHENDED in Canada. As late as February 1946 there were 24,500 absentees and deserters still at large in Canada. During the period July 1942 to August 1943 there were 29,985 absentees in Canada, of which 29,462 were apprehended or surrendered.

The military police of both wars were given the job of apprehending absentees and returning them to units. During World War II arrests and charges laid for absence without leave accounted for over fifty percent (50%) of all offences committed by servicemen. Drunkenness was number two. The Provost Marshal has always been involved in the handling of absentees. Early in World War II he was made responsible for maintaining a record of all absentees. The system was simple but effective. The apprehension of absentees and deserters was made the sole responsibility of the Canadian Provost Corps in July 1942. The revised procedure was promulgated in Canadian Army Routine Order (CARO) 3464 of August 1943. Units were required to report each instance of a soldier being AWOL, at the expiration of 48 hours. This was done by completing Military Form B-483, showing the soldier's regimental particulars, unit, address of next of kin, his physical description and date of absence. Copies of the MFB 483 (Notice of Absence Without Leave) were distributed to the Provost Marshal at Army Headquarters, the Deputy Assistant Provost Marshals of military districts and the records officer of the command or district. Another form, MFB 483A, Cancellation of Absentee Notice, was issued by the unit when, or if, the absentee returned. The Provost Marshal's office issued a weekly summary of all MFB 483s to all DAPMs. This kept all provost across Canada informed and up-to-date on new and cancelled notices. The DAPMs of districts in which the next of kin was resident were obliged to initiate an investigation as soon as possible. This system worked and was continued, largely unchanged, in the Canadian Army (Regular) following the war. It was successful in keeping the number of outstanding absentees at low level, thus greatly improving the effective working strength of the army. The quick reaction by provost was, undoubtedly, a contributing factor in the considerable number of absentees who returned, after a few days, of their own volition. Others, perhaps due to shortage of funds, would surrender themselves to civil police or provost units, thereby assuring paid transportation back to their unit. Canada is a wide, wide land.

Lance Corporal (later Major) A B Robertson of 41 Provost Company gives this account of his experiences during this era.

When the war in Europe was climaxing there were still thousands of absentees, deserters and draft evaders on the books. Casualties in Europe had brought an urgent demand for replacements and the apprehension programme was stepped up in response. The draft evader problem was left to the RCMP and Provincial Police, but the provost had a major role in rounding up the deserters.

There were problems, not the least of which was the practice of travelling in military vehicles and wearing uniforms complete with white gaiters and webbing. Talk about conspicuous. I recall driving down a lane leading to an isolated house near Quesnel, BC, where a deserter was reported to be staying. As we neared the house our man left by the back door, donned snowshoes and took off into the woods. We didn't catch him.

Native Indians had a strong proprietary attitude on the reserves even then. Twice we attempted to arrest one native soldier who was wanted for desertion, and some other criminal offence. Both times we were turned away by a rather formidable gathering of the tribe. Our MP brassards and military warrants didn't impress them at all and we, eventually, had to obtain the assistance of the RCMP.

The absentee problem surfaced again when recruiting opened up for the Korean War. When 2PPCLI left for Fort Lewis, enroute to Korea, almost a battalion strength were left behind 'on the loose'. We made absentee sweeps in rural Alberta and rounded up panel truck loads. In most cases they would be summarily tried, given a short sentence and released from the army in a matter of days. Strangely a large number of absentees were veterans of World War II who, apparently, found that a second helping of military life was one too many.

Lieutenant Colonel Howard Baker provided this "insight".

There were always lots of AWOLs and "deserters" to be picked up in any large city, and Montreal in 1940 was no exception. A special AWOL squad was organized to cope with the problem, consisting of a sergeant and six husky military policemen. They soon learned all the ruses used by absentees to avoid arrest and return to their units. One of these ruses was to 'shack-up' with their girl friend, and not in the homes of either his parents or wife.

Receiving a tip that one soldier they were looking for was living with his girl friend, the squad paid a visit to her apartment about 2:00 am one morning. The sergeant of the squad was over six feet tall, weighed over 200 pounds and was rather good looking. After ringing the door bell, repeatedly, the door was eventually opened by an attractive young woman wrapped in a bathrobe, which she was holding in place with both arms.

She vehemently denied that the missing soldier was in her apartment so, finally, the sergeant asked, "Do you mind if I have a look?", wanting to search the apartment. Instead, and much to the pleased surprise of the sergeant, she smiled, replied

"OK", pulled the sides of her bathrobe wide open and stood naked before him! After a moment he assured her he just wanted to have a look around the apartment, did so and found the AWOL hiding under her bed.

While the basic approach to absenteeism remained fairly constant, there were some policy changes made in the method of dealing with the problem. Following the war a policy of releasing absentees "in absentia" was adopted. This had the effect of reducing to zero the outstanding World War II absentees, ie, the 24,500 in Canada. Another important result was that these absentees were no longer a charge against the overall manpower ceiling prescribed by law. In August 1946 Privy Council Order No 3264 declared that all members serving on Active Service and who were AWOL as at 1 October 1946 were deemed never to have served. In December 1953 a policy was adopted whereby all personnel of the Active Force (Korean War enrollments) who were AWOL for more than twelve months were released in absentia. This took care of a large number of absentees and deserters from the Korean Force, many of whom were in the United States. The reference for this action is File HQ 255–1, TD 69 (Adm B) of 22 December 1953. Again in March 1961 the release of absentees, in absentia, was authorized for all service personnel (army, navy and air force) when the period of continuous absence exceeded six months. This action was taken by the Personnel Members Committee (MC Meeting 11/1/60, Item 4) as a means of reducing the number of outstanding absentees so as to keep these "non-effectives" as low as possible within the tight manpower ceiling.

The AWOL problems of the Canadian army did not, unfortunately, disappear at the end of war and start of peace. Neither the new recruit nor the old sweat adjusted quickly to the new-look army. The much discussed Canadian economy, under the guiding hand of C D Howe, developed quickly to the point where jobs were plentiful and wages were high in relation to the pay of a private soldier. More significant perhaps, there was no longer the mystique or glamour of adventures in far-off lands to motivate the aspiring warrior, only dull parade square bashing and endless routines. In any event, the incidence of absenteeism continued to be high, not only from infantry units but other corps, both arms and services. During the period 1947 to 1950 the number of absentees from the Light Anti-aircraft batteries stationed at Picton reached thirty-five percent (35%) of the unit's strength.

Canada's response to the outpouring, on 25 June 1950, of a formidable force of Communist soldiers across the 38th Parallel into South Korea, included a hastily formed, self-contained brigade group. All told, this force would require an additional 10,000 soldiers. As usual they would be "volunteers". When the required numbers were not forthcoming the minister directed that standards be lowered, and all who applied would be accepted. Further, to accelerate the process, the normal administrative steps such as a medical examination, documentation and personnel selection would be dispensed with at the recruiting depots. The result was chaos. Many went AWOL the day after attestation, some went home when army life palled, some enlisted while under the influence and, promptly, left when sobered. Many waited until they were midway through training, both in Canada and later in Fort Lewis, Washington, before taking off. This latter group, by far the largest, continued to be a problem until the "Release in Absentia" Order of December 1953 was promulgated. An account by Sergeant Walter Gatehouse, Canadian Provost Corps, then employed in Central Command working out of Oakville, Ontario, illustrates the no-nonsense approach taken by the United States officials and Canadian Provost Corps when dealing with these AWOLs.

Our liaison with the civil police in places such as Toronto, Hamilton and London in Ontario, and Niagara Falls, Buffalo and Erie on the USA side of the border, was excellent. There was one instance where the police in Niagara Falls had notified the Command APM they were holding a Canadian soldier, later determined to be an absentee. When I arrived, by DND vehicle, at the United States Customs an official refused access of a military vehicle. So we parked and phoned the appropriate police station. They readily escorted not one but two absentees to the border, took a receipt and handed them over. I called the APM at Oakville to report the apprehension and was advised to stop in Hamilton and pick up another absentee being held[120] by the Hamilton Police on a charge of drunkenness. I stopped at Hamilton and picked- up this one, then, with the three on board, drove back to Toronto. The cells at No 1 Police Station in downtown Toronto were full, in fact packed, so my only alternative was to drive on to Camp Borden and lodge them at 12 Military Detention Barracks, the closest guard facility. I arrived at 12 MDB about midnight. After a long argument with Sergeant Benny Hewitt as to his acceptance of a soldier who had not been convicted, and for whom I had no committal order, I left for home in Toronto.

Another case in which officials from three countries became involved, occurred in 1948. The APM Central Command was notified, through somewhat roundabout channels, that the military police in London, England were holding a Canadian soldier believed to be a deserter, one

Gunner R G Lake of the Royal Canadian Artillery. Sure enough, Gunner Lake was listed as absent from World War II days in Belgium. He had, it seemed, surrendered himself to the Belgian Police in Antwerp and they, in turn, had returned him to England via a regular air flight from the British Army of the Rhine, to London. In any case, there followed an exchange of cables between Army Headquarters, Ottawa and the War Office in London which resulted in Gunner Lake being placed aboard a TCA aircraft and flown to Halifax, thence by rail to Toronto under a provost escort. The whole cost borne by the Department of National Defence. A few days after his incarceration in 12 MDB Camp Borden, the Commandant, Lieutenant T J Quirk, reported that there was something not quite right about Gunner Lake in that he spoke with a most distinct cockney accent. Since he was born near Kingston, Ontario, and had never lived in London, this seemed strange. After much further questioning he (Lake) confessed that he was not the "real" Gunner Lake, but was a British Army absentee who had agreed to assume Lake's identity, and surrender to the authorities in Belgium. He finally gave a regimental number and name which was verified, by more cables, to be that of a deserter from the British Army of the Rhine. There followed a further exchange of cables between Ottawa and London of the "we don't want him, you can have him" theme. The matter was finally dropped, and he remained in Canada. The final outcome meant complete success for Gunner Lake and his accomplice. One got to stay on in Belgium and the other realized his goal of departing the British Army and resuming life in Canada.

These are but a few of the sometimes humorous, but often tragic, stories seldom mentioned in polite military circles. The philosophy of the absentee apprehension programme in Canada was, and still is, based on the quick return of an absentee to his unit. It has been found that the longer he remains away the less likelihood there is of him becoming an efficient soldier. It must also be stated that a significant number of absentees surrender themselves or return to their units for a variety of reasons such as persuasion by relatives, fear of punishment, inability to find civil employment or simply over-staying their leave. Absentees live as best they can. Some travel from relative to relative, others take up part-time jobs and a percentage turn to crime and end up in civil court and jail.

There has always been a great deal of conjecture about the causes of absenteeism in the Army. In order to determine, with some degree of accuracy, the reasons that soldiers go AWOL, the Provost Marshals' office conducted a study in 1960 to determine the main causes. The method adopted was to complete a brief questionnaire for each absentee who surrendered to, or was apprehended by, provost. This questionnaire was completed for

409 absentees during the period 1 November 1959 to 1 June 1960, with the results tabulated below.

SERIAL	REASONS GIVEN	NUMBER OF ABSENTEES
1.	Pressure or worry caused by family problems	81
2.	General dislike of army life and discipline	80
3.	Dissatisfaction with location and life in unit	51
4.	Overstaying leave with no intention of absence	45
5.	AWOL as a possible means of gaining release	41
6.	No particular reason	26
7.	AWOL to seek civilian employment	19
8.	Never intended to become a soldier	17
9.	Homesick	16
10.	Dislike of officers, warrant officers & NCOs	13
11.	Low pay	11
12.	Financial problems	9

The vast majority, over seventy percent (70%), of absentees were recruits in their first six to eight months of service. Most were infantrymen from large training depots as opposed to the infantry regiment in its home station. This was also the case in World War II when hundreds of disgruntled recruits went AWOL from one of the forty-one basic training centres in Canada. This fact led to a conclusion which was forwarded to the Adjutant General and General Staff Branches at Army Headquarters.

The first month of a recruit's service must be devoted to a period of initial orientation for which a separate syllabus of training is arranged. During this stage the tempo is relatively slow and some mistakes are acceptable. The fundamentals must be explained and practised. He should be introduced to his corps and should commence elementary military training on routines, the meaning of military terms, care and cleanliness of himself and equipment as well as military customs and discipline. At the end of this stage his morale should be high and he should have confidence in himself and be ready to commence more intense recruit training. The aim of this orientation training is to introduce the recruit to the Army and his corps, and to condition him mentally and physically for intense recruit training.

There is strong evidence to suggest that the greatest single problem in the adjustment of a young lad, from a civilian to a soldier, is the sudden and extreme change from one way of life to another.

13

Beginning the Resurrection

Despite the austere appearance of Canada's postwar military establishment, there was general agreement by its leaders that life in it should be upgraded. The Chief of the General Staff and his planners at Army Headquarters lost no time in developing plans and programmes that would make service life more attractive and, at the same time, improve equipment, tactical doctrine and training. It was to be a truly professional army in every respect. The Minister, Brooke Claxton, was a former Montreal lawyer who had served in the 1914–18 CEF as a sergeant in the artillery. He was an enthusiastic supporter of these goals and, indeed, the originator of this general concept. Among other ideas for change, he opened the National Defence College in Kingston in 1948 as a place where senior officers, senior civil servants, foreign military officers and corporate executives could discuss the political, economic, social and strategic aspects of war. A first for Canada. The Royal Military College at Kingston was reopened to produce officers for the three Services (Navy, Army and Air Force). Each Corps of the Army (RCAC, RCA, RCIC, RCASC, etc) would have its own training school which would be responsible for *all* aspects of training related to its basic functions, including training and qualification of recruits, tradesmen, junior and senior leaders and officers. Perhaps the most dramatic change came with the decision made in February 1947 to adopt American[121] weapons, vehicles and equipment. There were several reasons for this decision, but the most compelling one was that it would be readily available in a crisis.

The food, pay, accommodation and training of the soldier received prompt attention. New standard design quarters that were spacious, bright and well ventilated were approved and constructed over the next six years, as were standard mess halls with modern kitchen equipment. Lecture training buildings and administrative facilities would replace the tattered old tar paper huts of the war years. Married quarters were constructed in most of the permanent camps, together with schools and chapels, recreational facilities and shopping centres. Now the married soldier had breakfast at home with his family before leaving for duty. A scale of graded trades pay was introduced, which provided for progressive increases upon qualification up to Group 4 level. The ration scale was revised by highly qualified dietitians which, together with new messing facilities and well qualified cooks, provided excellent food both in quantity and quality. Believe it or not but soldiers in barracks were provided with white sheets and pillow cases, laundered at public expense. A new, well-cut, lightweight uniform was authorized for all ranks for dress wear and when walking out. All ranks received a monthly clothing allowance, credited to their pay account, from which to purchase all clothing items, at a nominal cost. Finally, there was an annual leave entitlement of four weeks with provision for further compassionate leave when justified by circumstances. Of course not all of these changes took place overnight, however, by the end of 1948 many had been introduced. The first of the new standard design buildings were completed by the fall of 1950 and others quickly followed.

A decision was made to fill unit positions where the function or service required a tradesman to perform duties that were normally basic to another Corps. This meant that all unit regimental police vacancies must, henceforth, be filled by Canadian Provost Corps Service Policemen.[122] Similarly, all cook positions would be RCASC, vehicle mechanics RCEME, storemen RCOC and so forth. This made good sense, however, the recruiting and training of these vacancies placed quite a strain on the limited resources of the Canadian Provost Corps School. It took another four years before all of these positions, approximately 12 sergeants and 52 lance corporals, were filled with qualified Service Policemen. The Command APMs, in keeping with the general impetus given the postwar Reserves of the Army, were busy forming the first ever Reserve Provost Companies in the various Commands across Canada. Each Company was entitled to a qualified Canadian Provost Corps instructor in the rank of sergeant, and a Canadian Provost Corps corporal, vehicle mechanic and driver. This established a requirement for another ten Canadian Provost Corps vacancies.[123] Another three Canadian Provost Corps instructors were, by agreement, employed at the RCMP Depot in Regina. This temporary need arose because the Force was under strength at War's end and required time to rebuild their instructional cadre to prewar levels. This was an interesting assignment which was most capably filled by Canadian Provost Corps instructors. Warrant Officer (later Major) Lorne Henderson, the small arms instructor, had this to say about this duty.

In early January 1946, I was one of a group of candidates from various components of the Interim Force which was assembled at Camp Borden to undergo assessment as instructors in physical training, foot drill and small arms at Depot Division, RCMP, Regina, Saskatchewan. The numbers were, eventually, reduced to three on the reorganization of the Interim Force to the Regular Army. The remaining three were WO1 Ernest McNamara, Staff Sergeant Philip Gagnon and myself. Each was reduced one rank to conform to the new establishment rank structure and transferred to the Canadian Provost Corps.

During their tenure, of about five years, this cadre instructed a variety of classes including the RCMP College classes, part 1 training (new recruits), part 2 training (advanced recruits) and refresher courses. The members of the cadre were well respected and completely integrated within the Depot training establishment. I was appointed team captain of the Depot and "F" Division Rifle and Revolver Club, which captured more than their fair share of prizes at the Saskatchewan Rifle Association competitions held annually at Camp Dundurn, Saskatchewan.

Further increases to the overall Canadian Provost Corps establishment were made from time-to-time, including an increase of another 17 all ranks to the Canadian Provost Corps School. This was welcome, but it still meant that the School staff was hard pressed to cope with the ever increasing training load. Another substantial addition was the formation of the NDHQ Security Guard in 1948. It would be quite correct to say that this requirement arose as a direct result of the early manifestations of the Cold War. The Berlin blockade started early in 1948 and, with it, a growing realization that Stalin, far from demobbing the Soviet Armed Forces, was doing exactly the reverse. Despite the shattering revelations of the recent Gouzenko case, the Canadian Government was slow to respond. In any event, the Americans, from the President on down, began to wonder why they had been so hasty in disbanding their Armed Forces. As we have mentioned, the relations between the Canadian and United States Services were close. Following a visit by a team of USA technicians and service officers to Army Headquarters in Ottawa, early in 1948, it became apparent that the general security of the DND complex in Cartier Square, Ottawa, was almost non-existent. Apart from a few Commissionaires, nobody was even remotely concerned about security of property, personnel or documents. The Chiefs of Staff Committee quickly moved to remedy

Beginning The Resurrection 147

this situation. The result was that a Security Guard of 51 all ranks of the Canadian Provost Corps, with another 50 Corps of Commissionaires, was formed at the Canadian Provost Corps School. It moved to Ottawa during December 1948. Warrant Officer Class 2, Arthur S Bird[124] provided the following graphic account of some of the growing pains involved in organizing and operating this new unit of the Canadian Provost Corps.

In an atmosphere of growing mistrust of our former allies, the USSR, the Americans expressed dismay with the standard of security at Canada's National Defence Headquarters in Ottawa and demanded that action be taken to remedy the situation. Thus, the NDHQ Security Guard was formed in Camp Borden during the latter part of 1948. As there were not enough serving members within the Provost Corps to detach for these duties, at that time, some of the NCO's and nearly all of the men were recent transfers from various units within the Canadian Army. The unit consisted of a captain, officer commanding, one WO2, one sergeant clerk and three sections each of one sergeant, one corporal and fourteen privates.

One of the sergeants,[125] prior to joining the Security Guard, had been employed in the Minister's office at NDHQ, and his detailed knowledge of the buildings was invaluable. On occasion he was known to supply stationery not normally available to lesser beings.

This Security Guard moved to Ottawa in December 1948 and the first priority was to get the men settled in private accommodations, as rations and quarters were not provided. It was then revealed that the Guard would provide physical security during the "silent hours". This included patrols and punching time clocks throughout A, B and C buildings. Periodic checks were to be made on the 'militia building', and one man would be on duty at the Historical Section on Gloucester Street. All these functions were carried out.

Apart from a number of disciplinary and personnel problems, the unit attracted a lot of attention at Headquarters. Most of this was due to the OC of the Guard, who insisted on a high standard of discipline and general deportment. He became quite upset by the low standard of dress of the other ranks of these three services and, in particular, the failure of other ranks to salute commissioned officers. He tried to redress this laxity and, where applicable, charges were laid and forwarded to the appropriate authorities.

The problem of providing rations and quarters continued for some time, and was finally solved by the provision of single quarters and rations in the building at 312 Laurier Avenue, East,[126] which was also the location of the Provost Marshal. This was not a popular duty due to perpetual night shift work, as well as the dull routine of patrolling the stuffy halls of these old buildings and parking cars during the morning rush. However, this basic unit is still functioning some forty-five years later.

There was little change in the detention policy or programmes as a result of the start of a Regular continuing army. The five barracks were not overcrowded, however, they continued to do a brisk business mainly because of a decision, in 1947, to make this a tri-service function. The Air Force had two or three detention centres which operated on an irregular basis. The Navy administered detention aboard ships or at shore based stations. At a meeting of the Chiefs of Staff Committee it was agreed that the Army would assume responsibility for detention facilities for all of Canada's armed forces. A sensible decision since these facilities were already in place. It was also noted that the law and attendant regulations required no change to put this policy into practice. There was little initial impact in terms of increased admissions, however, it, undoubtedly, increased the overall size of the detention programme, over the long haul. There were, of course, a few administrative details to iron out such as admission and release procedures, training programmes for detainees and the kit and equipment carried by detainees when admitted to detention. We previously touched on the legal aspects of soldiers sentenced to a term of detention. The procedure was covered, in great detail, in the *Manual of Military Law*, which was reprinted for use in the Canadian Army in 1941. It listed the offences related to military service, as well as those punishable by ordinary law; the procedure for bringing an offender to trial was detailed; it listed the circumstances when a summary trial by a Commanding Officer was in order, as well as the occasions when the trial must be by a properly constituted Court Martial; the maximum and minimum punishments were prescribed for each type of offence; and it also set out the rules of evidence and the elements to be proved whenever a soldier appeared before a military tribunal. The authority of the Commandant of a Detention Barracks to admit a soldier under sentence of detention was Form G (Form of Commitment to Detention Barrack on Award of Detention by Commanding Officer), duly signed by the CO. A similar form, with slightly varied wording, was also used when the soldier was: sentenced by Court Martial (Form K) to a sentence of military imprisonment; transferred from one Detention Barrack to another (Form D); being admitted for temporary custody in a civil prison or jail (Form Q). Several other forms were used to reverse the procedure and order the release of a detainee from detention. If this appears to be somewhat convoluted, it is only because it really was a bit twisted. However, the whole intent of these rules was to ensure a uniform and fair method of dealing with the soldier who had been charged and convicted for an offence under military law. The detailed procedure for invoking all military law was contained in a large volume of attendant regulations entitled *Kings Regulations and Order for The Canadian Army, 1939, as Amended*. The Regulations for the committal of soldiers under sentence were contained in Sections 585 through 589 of that reference.

We have already described, in the chapter on Repatriation, the return to Canada in January 1946 of a large number of military criminals who had been sentenced overseas to serve varying periods of imprisonment. No 12 Military Detention Barracks at Camp Borden was the only detention facility which was also a designated Military Prison. Consequently, most of this group were admitted to 12MDB with the prospect of either being released, following a review, or transferred to a Civil jail. Lieutenant (later Major) Thomas J Quirk, a veteran RCMP and Canadian Provost Corps officer, was the Commandant at this time. He tells this interesting story:

As you know, the inmates of the prison were not "S.U.S." but civilians discharged from the army but subject to military discipline and regulations. When I took over there was a prisoner with a lengthy record including, I think, a couple of escapes from prior incarcerations. This man was considered a high security risk and was surly and uncooperative. On looking at his history, and speaking with the lad, I gathered he was a very intelligent man. During a lengthy period on the loose in Europe he ran a smuggling operation with his own fleet of stolen vehicles, during which time he posed as a sergeant-major in the Canadian Provost Corps. He told me that he always made a point of being very well turned out–short haircut, clean shave, well pressed uniform, plus a variety of phoney documents as required. A tall, well built man, I am sure he presented a soldierly figure, unlike most absentees and deserters who tended to get very scruffy in appearance. He was, ultimately, betrayed by a spurned girl friend, it seems. At the time there was no establishment for a batman so I asked him if he would like to act as batman for me. This he did, in a most meticulous fashion. My sam browne belt, boots and the chin strap on my cap were boned and shined to a high degree and he kept my living quarters in immaculate condition. There was no authority for a "Trustee" at the prison but, as this chap had quite a bit of freedom in looking after his duties, this was, in effect, what he was. When I took three weeks leave to visit the west coast, I told my "batman" I was instructing the staff to permit him to go about as usual during the daytime. I further told him I was well aware that he could, if he wished as an accomplished escape artist, take-off with my civilian clothing and even my car during my absence. I further informed him that, should he do this, no blame would be placed on the staff but, as the one totally responsible, I might well be court martialled. All I asked was his word that he would not attempt to escape during the time I was away. This he gave me. On my return I found that my entire living establishment (attached to the office) had been completely redecorated in expert fashion. On enquiring, from my pseudo batman (I will call him "Smith"–not his real name), I asked "Smith" about this and was told he had gone over to the paint shop, got the necessary equipment and undertaken the job himself. I may say that "Smith" had given me quite a bit about his childhood and later life, indicating that he had been brought up in a Maritime orphanage where, I gather, the atmosphere was anything but pleasant. In view of his excellent service to me I said that if he wished he could peruse any of my several hundred books when he had time. When the balance of his sentence was finally remitted I asked him the day he left whey he had never attempted to escape, to which he replied, "Well Sir, you are the first one who ever gave me a decent break.

The first Provost Marshal's Conference held in the Regular Army was assembled at Camp Borden from the 16th through 19th March 1949. The lengthy agenda covered a large number of items related to the organization, training, duties and general efficiency of the Corps. The detailed minutes of this conference are reprinted as Appendix "A" to this volume. Although not specifically designed for this purpose, this conference laid the foundation for the continuing existence of the Corps in the Regular Army. These minutes revealed the general state of the Corps, some current problems, together with some proposed courses of action. It is noteworthy that progress had been made in several areas during the past two and one-half years since 1 October 1946. Perhaps the most significant gain for the Corps was a growing realization throughout the command element of the Army that a well organized provost service was essential to its well-being.

The problem of the initial inadequate manpower allocation (117 all ranks) was partially solved by a considerable increase, including an additional seventeen positions at the School. This permitted greater capacity to train provost to a specific standard in the new trade of Service Police. The overall situation, in regards to the latter, was revealed by the following figures:

Present established positions	288
Restricted employment ceiling	230
Qualified Group 1 Service Police	99
Qualified Group 2 Service Police	23
In-Training (recruits and plan H)	77

Most of the Agenda items indicated the decisions made and further action required, and need no further elaboration. However, a few general conclusions may be in order. It is clear that all officers of the Corps were working hard to resolve the concurrent problems of (a) keeping abreast of the day-to-day provost tasks, and (b) laying the groundwork and formulating plans and policies for a really viable Corps of the Regular Army. The routine duties of the NCOs and men of the Corps, always the bottom line, were analyzed and proposals made to ensure a consistently high performance. The inadequate manpower was of great concern to all officers. Well supported submissions were required in order to adjust and increase resources in line with work loads. The training and qualifications of *all ranks* was a matter for concern. Mention is made of GSPS 40 regarding the qualifications of officers. This General Staff Policy Statement simply stated that every officer in the rank of lieutenant to major must now formally qualify, by Army-wide examinations, for the next higher rank. Those aspiring to go on to higher rank and senior appointments must graduate from the one year course at the Canadian Army Staff College, in Kingston. The prerequisites for attendance at the Staff College were the same for all officers. The upper age limit was 34 years, must pass an entrance examination and be recommended by the appropriate senior commander and the Corps Director, in this case the Provost Marshal. Failure to qualify for the next higher rank resulted in compulsory retirement when reaching the age limit set for each rank. The age limits were as follows: for lieutenants – 45; captains – 47; majors – 49; lieutenant colonels – 51; colonels – 53 and for general ranking – age 55. The reasoning behind this policy was to ensure that the officer establishment, especially in the upper brackets, was not clogged with aging men who were not physically capable of field duty and, more important, were resistant to change. This policy was accepted throughout the Canadian Army by all officers. It was applied with consistency and fairness.

The cornerstone for the development of efficiency in the Army was the Rank or Trade Standard. Each Corps was required to produce, in accordance with an Army-wide standard format, a Standard which denoted the SKILLS and KNOWLEDGE required for each rank below warrant officer, and for each trade/specialty in the Corps including the various progressive levels of each trade. The standard was used to evaluate the soldier's standing; it was invaluable for the development of training courses and career paths for everyone. It enabled Corps Schools to set the aim and scope of training curriculums and assess the final qualification reached. Now each private must qualify for corporal rank by attending and passing a Junior NCO course. Similarly, the corporal must qualify for sergeant rank at a

Senior NCO qualifying course. These courses were far from being a sinecure. The candidate was required to demonstrate his ability to lead a provost section or detachment, instruct on a few basic subjects, organize and supervise work projects and duties common to the Corps, and prepare duty rosters, provost reports and basic returns. He was also required to have a fair knowledge of the overall organization of the Army and a good knowledge of military law and its application. In other words, the NCO must be qualified to perform the day-to-day tasks he would encounter in the Corps. Regrettably, there was no "Grandfather" clause for the NCO who had been promoted prior to this more formal procedure. While most of the existing NCOs in the Corps had learned their trade very well in the "school of hard knocks", there were some, through no fault of their own, who had been promoted before their time. It probably took about six or seven years before the NCOs and, indeed, the officers were fitted into the appropriate niche. This was an Army-wide dilemma and not something that was solely the concern of the Corps.

The training and qualification of provost in the new trade of Service Policeman received much attention during the March 1949 Conference. It was necessary to be realistic when establishing Standards, or Specifications as they were termed. Perhaps the most difficult problem in the Corps, throughout World War II, was the difficulty engendered by the low literacy standard of many recruits entering the Corps. While we did have an adequate IQ level, there was no pre-enlistment screening as to oral or written communication skills. Not surprisingly, it was not uncommon to find a few in any Canadian Provost Corps unit who had little formal schooling. They simply could not compose a simple report and only gave verbal evidence with much difficulty. This continued to be a problem during the first few postwar years. In the absence of firm pre-enlistment educational standards, these low literacy recruits, allocated to the Corps from recruiting depots, were reallocated to other Corps following an assessment period at the Canadian Provost Corps School. This was often not easy since the recruit invariably, manifested a strong desire for service as a policeman and, failing that, life as a civilian. Furthermore, it was always a fact that the youngsters of Canada did not flock to the colours during periods of rising economic growth. The postwar era was certainly such a period. There was another very good reason for ensuring that the Service Policeman was well qualified. This hinged on the fact that the new National Defence Act would soon become law and replace the old, and much revised, British Manual of Military Law adopted for use in Canada by the Militia Act of 1929. The new and revised Code of Service Discipline replaced the previous Sections

4 to 44 and, among other twentieth century refinements, prescribed the powers of arrest and general authority of Service Policemen. For example, it stipulated that: "A member of the Canadian Provost Corps, mustered in the trade and on duty as a Service Policeman, could, for cause, arrest, interrogate and detain all persons subject to the Code of Service Discipline". It was, therefore, of the utmost importance that every service policeman be well qualified in every aspect of this demanding duty.

The matter of Special Investigators to deal with the more serious and complex cases was discussed at length. It is, perhaps, noteworthy that, despite the restricted establishment, there was unanimous agreement that at least two well qualified investigators were required in each command. The importance of continued close liaison with the RCMP and the Provincial and Municipal Police was emphasized.

The matter of the Corps dress, insignia, accoutrements and symbols received a great deal of attention. Given the Corps' newness, its far-flung deployment and the recent dramatic changes in the Army, it was not surprising that there was lack of uniformity in some areas. In addition, items such as buttons, belt buckles, whistle lanyards and a Corps tie had not yet been designed or approved for wear. A brass button[127] (4 sizes) was subsequently approved by the reigning Monarch vide the College of Heraldry, London, England, since the design included the Royal Crown. A very handsome molded brass belt buckle followed, also displaying the crowned lion and maple leaf with the inscription "Canadian Provost Corps". The tie featured alternate navy blue, gold (narrow) and scarlet diagonal stripes with a white silk lining. It was approved for wear in 1950. A light red, braided cotton lanyard, to be worn on the left shoulder, was authorized for all ranks about the same time. Brass shoulder titles [C Pro C] were designed and approved for issue to all ranks for wear with serge or tropical worsted uniforms.

The original Corps cap badge and collar-dogs were continued without change except that for a short period in the mid-fifties, a dark bronzed replica was produced and worn when on duty. It was not popular and was discontinued about 1960. The whitened web belt and shoulder strap was continued for all ranks when on duty. However, one or two APMs voiced complaints that other units had, on occasion, usurped this Provost custom, which was designed to distinguish the service policemen at all times. In any event, this was never a serious problem.

Following the approval of a distinctive Mess Kit for officers and blue Patrol dress for officers and NCOs, it became necessary for all officers to purchase an approved Corps sword, sash, scabbard and other accoutrements for wear during ceremonial occasions. The infantry pattern sword, with nickel and leather scabbards, was approved for Canadian Provost Corps. This was a fairly costly item, however, thanks to our presence in Europe and Asia it was possible to make significant savings by purchasing these items outside Canada in well established military outfitters located in places such as Hong Kong and Germany.

The March 1949 conference was also notable for the introduction of two other important features of Corps tradition, namely, a Corps March and a Corps Motto. First the March – the initial thought was to have an original composition rather than borrow one of the time honoured marches of military history. This approach was not successful despite the cooperation of the Director of Bands at Army Headquarters and CSM Fred Nelson, Canadian Provost Corps, both graduates of Nellers Hall in London. Success came in 1952 when Major Bob Luker, in Winnipeg, heard a stirring piece over the air. He was so impressed that he finally obtained a recording from the station. This music, after follow-up investigation, proved to be a very old German wassail song written by one Ernst Laukien. Further investigation elicited the information that it had been arranged in its current form by Boosey & Hawkes, London. In any event, *Through Night to Light* (Durch Nacht zum Licht) became the official music of the Canadian Provost Corps. It was a lilting, stirring march without lyrics, but certainly original and very popular with all ranks. Finally, the question of the Corps Motto was quickly decided with the suggestion by Lieutenant Colonel Jim Stewart that it should be *Discipline by Example*. It would be impossible to imagine a more appropriate phrase to describe a basic guide to govern the thoughts and actions of every Corps member. Further, it was agreed that no attempt would be made to translate this meaningful phrase into latin. It required no translation.

There was a resolve to establish and maintain high standards and improve efficiency. Slow but steady progress had been made during the first three years of the Corps peacetime existence. It had been a period of learning to cope with austere military budgets. However, the tight purse strings would soon be loosened and the Canadian Provost Corps would come a little closer to acquiring resources to match its mission.

14

Provost in the Militia

As stated in the March 1949 Conference Summary, there was now, for the first time in history, a reasonably healthy complement of Militia Provost companies across Canada. By the end of 1948 there was at least one company in each of the five Army Commands. The militia had always been the nucleus of Canada's army since the War of 1812, and continuing through the Northwest Rebellion of 1885, the Great War of 1914–1918 and again from 1939 to 1945. This is neither the time nor place to discuss, at length, the issues surrounding the size, role and cost of a Canadian Militia in today's world. A case can be made for a larger, better trained and equipped and, hence, more costly militia with a smaller cadre of Regulars to provide a command and administrative element. Similarly, it can be and is debated that, because of the nuclear threat we must have adequate "forces-in-being" since the time element will not longer permit a lengthy mobilization period. Professor T C Willett, of Queen's University and author of *A Heritage at Risk, 1987*, commented on the social and community aspects of the militia during an address made to the January 1989 meeting of the Conference of Defence Associations.

Until the Korean War, when the Regular Force began to outnumber it, the Militia was Canada's Army. It symbolized the nation's identity and brought the various social classes and ethnic groups together in a national organization. At one time membership was not easy to achieve in the city regiments, and was a hallmark of one's worth as a man and as a citizen. Hence, it was sought after by the up-and-coming youngsters who needed to establish their credibility in the community. Through the militia the roots of the Army were deep and pervasive. The link with the community was close, and most politicians knew something about the army, even if they didn't help it much in peacetime. Perhaps this was because the Canadian Public hasn't taken the threat of war seriously since the Fenian raids in the late 1860's. It still doesn't, and therein lies a real problem as armed forces become more expensive and remote from the citizenry.

It was quickly decided after World War II that there would be, once again, a substantial reserve component. Pay was authorized for 150,000 reservists, roughly organized to form the nucleus of two Corps, each of three divisions. Each Command Headquarters was responsible for all units within its geographical boundaries. Units were located, often crowded, in prewar armouries which seldom were the right size or in the right location. Most units were allotted at least one Regular officer or NCO, and they met one evening each week to carry out individual training and perform administrative tasks such as recruiting, completing reports and returns and a hostof miscellaneous duties, some of a military nature, some not. The reservist was enlisted for an indefinite period and if he grew weary of life in this environment simply failed to appear again on subsequent parade nights. This occurred occasionally in Canadian Provost Corp Militia units, but never with the frequency that the reservists departed the larger Corps. All ranks were paid at the going rate for his equivalent in the Regular Army, on the basis of one-half day's pay for each militia drill, duty or training parade attended with his unit. They were issued with basic kit and clothing such as battledress, boots, shirts, head dress, great coat, web equipment, kit bag, blanket and the badges, patches and buckles common to his Corps and unit. The larger units had their own officers' and sergeants' messes, complete with a license to sell beer and spirits. Most units operated a canteen for the men, with the profits used to provide various amenities not otherwise provided at public expense. The militia "drop-outs" almost always failed to turn in the items of kit and equipment, and even firearms, issued to them. This resulted in provost patrols from the local detachment making an effort to recover the items and return them to the militia unit. Lance Corporal Robbie Robertson describes his efforts to recover .303 Calibre Lee-Enfield rifles from former members of the Canadian Rangers in the remote areas of British Columbia.

One duty which seemed never-ending was the recovery, from non-effective militia personnel, of weapons and personal kit. In most cases the investigation would start with a letter of request and a list of outstanding gear from a Militia unit company. Usually these cases involved nothing more than enquiries to locate the non-effective member and a visit to his or her residence to pick up the kit.

In the mid-fifties a little variation cropped up when NDHQ took a look at the Canadian Ranger programme and found that many Ranger personnel, and their weapons, had not been heard from for a considerable period – years in some cases. Due to the nature of the programme very few Canadian Rangers could be located by directory checks, especially in the Yukon and Northwest Territories. Our investigators did track many of them down and did recover numerous .303 Lee-Enfield Rifles. Very few of the recovered rifles would ever be reissued, however, as unusual modifications to make them more suitable for hunting, was the norm. 'Cabin Fire' was the reason given when an amazing number of Ranger personnel were unable to produce their weapons.

In 1960 I despatched an investigator to the Queen Charlotte Islands to account for some non-effective Rangers. After a lengthy period on TD, at 'higher rate' and expensive transportation costs, the net gain was seven Rangers accounted for and seven rifles recovered including one charred relic from a 'cabin fire.'

Improper possession or use of military (DND) equipment was listed as an offence in the Criminal Code of Canada, but offending Reservists were rarely prosecuted. It was not easy to prove since the items in question had been issued to the reservist in the first place. Secondly, judges and magistrates were reluctant to deal with these cases. On one occasion when a charge had been laid for a serious and blatant case involving firearms, the presiding judge dismissed the charge and remarked that this was persecution not prosecution. It is a strange commentary, but it is a fact that a large segment of the Canadian public do not consider the misappropriation of Government property to be in anyway improper.

What came to be known as "Summer Training" or "Summer Camp" was conducted under Command arrangements for all militia units. These large scale concentrations were held at a convenient central camp and the training was usually during the month of July. One of the largest of these concentrations during the years 1947 through 1950 was at Camp Petawawa, in Central Command, from early July to mid-August each summer. The requisite staff and instructors were made available from the staff of Command Headquarters, the pooling of all A & T Staff, and the full-time employment of selected militia officers, warrant officers and NCOs. In addition to the large number of militia units in the Command, all artillery and some armoured regiments from Eastern and Quebec Commands also came to the Petawawa concentration. Units arrived in regular weekly intakes for five days of intense training designed, for the most part, to practice units in their normal war roles under conditions made as realistic as possible. The infantryman fired his weapons and prepared positions, tank crews moved the tanks and fired a few rounds, as did the gunners of the field and medium regiments. Engineers bridged the Petawawa River, signallers laid cable and operated radio networks, RCEME recovered heavy vehicles from bogs, and the provost signed routes and performed traffic control duties for the moves of Divisional Headquarters and other practical exercises. This training culminated in an impressive Firepower Demonstration each Friday evening. It was staged in a long narrow strip of land about two miles in length, flanked on one side by the Ottawa River and on the other by a low escarpment. Live ammunition was fired from each type of infantry, artillery and armoured weapon. It lasted about one and one-half hour and invariably attracted a large crowd of spectators, including the Minister, Brooke Claxton, on two or three occasions.

A summary of all Militia Summer[128] Training concentrations held across Canada during July 1956 is shown in the accompanying chart.

The following account of the summer concentration for the Canadian Provost Corps units of Central Command was provided by Lieutenant Colonel John J Platt[129], the APM.

Summer-camp training for Central Command Militia Provost Units was held at Blackdown, Camp Borden, from 21 to 28 July 1956. Units attending were No 2 Provost Company (Militia), Toronto, Commanded by Major E K Maxted, No 6 Provost Company (Militia), London, with a detachment from Guelph under command Major E J Lautenschlager. A Group of individuals from 12 Militia Group, Ottawa, also attended. Training and conduct of the Camp was combined under the command of myself. Emphasis this year was placed on training and qualifying Junior and Senior NCOs. Good results were obtained in both courses. The new soldier was given a course of training in basic provost subjects such as map using, road reconnaissance, traffic control (point duty) and route signing. Officers and NCOs already qualified were attached to local Regular Force Provost units, or given appointments within the Camp organization to practise them in administrative tasks.

The Conference Summary of March 1949 reveals the interesting fact that the combined strength of the eight newly formed Reserve Provost Companies now exceeded that of the Regular Corps units, ie, 342 versus 280 all ranks. Once the APM had obtained authority to organize a company it was really remarkable how quickly it went ahead. The initiative was with the APM who, after ascertaining that the unit was included in the Command Reserve order of battle, requested formal authority to proceed. This was almost always forthcoming, provided there was a suitable officer available as Officer Commanding, that adequate local accommodation existed and the proposed unit was sanctioned by Army Headquarters. The Provost Marshal controlled the allocation of the number designation for

Command	Locations	Units attending
Eastern	Camp Utopia	7 Infantry Battalions (NS, NB, NFLD, PEI)
		2 Armoured Regiments
		RCASC Column
		RECEME
		No 5 Provost Company
		Dental Corps
	Aldershot	COTC Cadets
		CWAC
		Army Cadets
		Junior NCO & Recruits – all Units
	York Redoubt	Harbour Defence Artillery Batteries
Quebec	Valcartier	15 Infantry Battalions
		Signal Regiment
		RCASC Column
		RCEME Units
		No 3 Provost Company
		No 4 Provost Company
Central (Province of Ontario)	Camp Petawawa	9 Armoured Regiments (Ontario)
		6 Armoured Regiments (Quebec)
		13 Artillery Regiments (Ontario)
		3 Artillery Regiments (Eastern)
		6 Artillery Regiments (Quebec)
		RCE (Engineers)
	Camp Niagara	15 Infantry Battalions (Ontario)
		CWAC
		Chaplains
	Camp Petre	6 Light A A Regiments (Ontario)
		5 Medium A A Regiments (Eastern)
		3 Light A A Regiments (Quebec)
	Camp Borden	3 Signal Regiments
		4 RCASC Columns
		720 RCAMC Personnel (Canada)
		2 RCEME Workshops
		No 2 Provost Company
		No 6 Provost Company
		and Guelph Detachment
		5 C Int C Companies (each command)
Prairie (Manitoba and Saskatchewan)	Camp Shilo	5 Armoured Regiments
		5 Artillery Regiments
		8 Infantry Battalions

Command	Locations	Units attending
	Dundurn	RCASC Units REME Units 13 Provost Company CWAC 2 Machine Gun Bns
Western (Alberta and British Columbia)	Camp Wainwright	4 Armoured Regiments 4 Artillery Regiments 8 Engineer Squadrons 3 Signal Squadrons 6 Infantry Battalions 7 RCASC Companies 5 RCEME Technical 2 Dental Units
	Vernon	No 8 Provost Company CWAC Officer and NCO Courses

each company, thus avoiding duplication. The Reserve Provost Company establishments were identical to the wartime field companies except that the all companies were entitled to four officers, with the OC a major and the 21C a Captain. There were a number of former Canadian Provost Corps officers living in almost every large town or city in Canada so it was not difficult to find officers, at least initially. The same was true for senior NCOs. The junior ranks of private, lance corporal and corporal, although not quite as enthusiastic, nevertheless, came forward in moderate numbers. A special effort was made to ensure each A & T staff position was filled with a well qualified Regular Force provost sergeant. One of the main attractions for the private was checking-out on a motorcycle. Unfortunately, obtaining jeeps and motorcycles was sometimes a problem since these vehicles were not always available. Nonetheless, these companies were real assets to the Corps at this stage of its development. They provided much needed services during concentration and exercises and maintained a good standard of training and performance. The following narrative reflects the life and times of the Guelph Detachment of 6 Provost Company (Reserve) during the period 1956 to 1960. The author, Captain James V Findlay[130] had this to say.

This detachment was an authorized strength of three Sections from 6 Company, stationed in London, Ontario. It had no commissioned officer and was going to be abandoned if one could not be secured. At that time I was serving with the 11th Field Regiment RCA and the CO asked me if I would transfer to the Provost to save the detachment. A move that was good for me, I'm not sure what it did for the Corps.

This interest of the CO of the 11th Field in maintaining the presence of the Provost in the Garrison, along with the Medical Company of the RCAMC, is ample proof of the spirit of cooperation within the Garrison. It developed within the Detachment a strong feeling of purpose and desire. At summer camps we were always attached to the 11th for rations and quarters.

It is interesting to note that with the changes in the Militia and the Detachment and the Medical Company ceased to exist, that the 11th arranged for a Provost badge and a Medical badge to be mounted behind the bar in the Officers Mess to hang with pride beside their illustrious RCA badge, and which still hangs with pride today.

There was a small town atmosphere in Guelph which we all enjoyed. Of course it did help us greatly that Ted Lamb was the Chief of Police and also our RSM. This enabled us to work very closely with his force, other local police forces in the area and the OPP.

This Detachment's one claim to fame is that Colonel Bill McCullough started his military career here, left to join the Active Force and was Director of Security on his recent retirement.

It was my pleasure to command the Detachment for four years until I moved from Guelph in 1960.

One of the little publicized contributions made by the Canadian Provost Corps Reserve is mentioned, in passing, by Jim Findlay. Apart from the original World War II Canadian Provost Corps veterans, the various companies were later blessed with an infusion of excellent leaders. Several officers held important full-time positions in various Police Forces and in the world of business and commerce. For example, Lance Corporal R T (Bob) Grogan, of 13 Provost Company (R) in Winnipeg, a former midshipman in the Royal Canadian Navy, went on to become the Director of Security for the Canadian Armed Forces. As already mentioned, Lance Corporal William J (Bill) McCullough of 6 Provost Company (R) later succeeded R T Grogan in the same senior Canadian Forces appointment. Incidentally, Bill McCullough was awarded the Meritorious Service Cross for courage and leadership during a tour of duty in Beirut, Lebanon from 1982 to 1984. This prestigious award was not introduced in the Canadian Armed Forces until June 1984, hence Bill McCullough and Sergeant L D Abbott were the first recipients of this award, a unique distinction for the Corps. Major

John A Fullerton was one of the early Commanding Officers of No 2 Company (R) during the late 60s. He had prior service in the Corps and served full-time for many years as a Commissioned Officer in the Ontario Provincial Police. Like so many others in the Corps he served his community as a volunteer, having assumed the onerous responsibilities of Area Commissioner for the St John Ambulance Brigade for Central Ontario. Jack was also Aide-de-Camp for the Lieutenant Governor of Ontario. He retired from the Canadian Forces Militia with the rank of Lieutenant Colonel, in 1982, as commander of the local Service Battalion.

The strength of character, determination and versatility of most Canadian Provost Corps Reservists of that era is exemplified by the life of Alexander Gordon Cameron. He was the last Officer Commanding No 2 Company (R) during the transition period of militia organization, commencing in 1966. Sandy was born in New York City on 19 December 1933, of Scottish parents. The family returned to Glasgow prior to World War II where young Sandy grew up and received his early education. He evinced a fondness for military type life, at an early age, and became an active member in the Life Boys and the Boys Brigade. At age fourteen his father's business took the family to Liverpool where he enrolled in the Liverpool City Police Cadet Corps. Following three years as a police cadet he enlisted, at age eighteen, in the Royal Air Force Police where he served for the next three years. After another year as a constable in the Liverpool police he returned to the United States in 1955. He came to Canada in 1957 and joined the Trans Canada Pipeline Corporation; construction of the pipeline had just been completed. He remained with Trans Canada Pipelines for the next thirty-four years, retiring as a senior manager in Toronto in 1990. He joined No 2 Provost Company in 1960 and was later commissioned in the rank of lieutenant. He describes his service in the Canadian Provost Corps Reserve and his eventual transition into the unified Security Branch Reserve of the Canadian Armed Forces.

In August 1963 I was commissioned as a lieutenant in the Canadian Provost Corps and posted to No 2 Provost Company as Transport and Training Officer. The OC was Major John Fogg and the second-in-command was Captain Peter Marshall. The unit was located in the College Street Armoury in downtown Toronto. I joined the newly formed 1st Toronto Service Battalion[131] in 1966, during the reorganization of the Militia, as adjutant. Shortly after this a Security Platoon was formed and I became its 2 I/C in the rank of captain. All members of the Platoon were required to qualify in the new standards and trades of the Security Branch, which I did on numerous weekends, at the School of Intelligence and Security in

Camp Borden, during 1968 and 1969. Lieutenant Colonel R I (Bob) Luker, MC, CD was the School Commandant at this time. I spent four years at Headquarters, Central Militia Area as the Area Security Officer, and was succeeded in this appointment by Major Fred Jones, a former Canadian Provost Corps Regular officer. In October 1970 I was appointed Officer Commanding the Administration Company in 1 Service Battalion, and in 1981 as Deputy Commander of this unit. In October 1985 I was appointed Commanding Officer of 1 Service Battalion, was promoted lieutenant colonel and served in this appointment until my retirement in April 1988.

Before leaving the subject of Provost Militia it is necessary to record another aspect, namely the periodic training of volunteer RCMP constables at the Canadian Provost Corps School. Colonel Leonard H Nicholson returned to the RCMP in May 1946 and was appointed Commissioner of the Force in 1951. His six years in the Corps gave him an appreciation of the recurring cycles of war and the inevitable involvement of the RCMP. In any case, he decided it would be wise to maintain, within the Force, a cadre of men trained in some of the military skills not overly emphasized in their normal police training. With the full agreement of everyone in the Defence Department it was arranged that up to sixty constables would undertake a course at the School designed to upgrade their skills and knowledge of current small arms; basic army organization; map using; chemical, biological and nuclear (NCBW) warfare; movement and traffic control; and, of course, PT and close order drill. The duration of the course was three weeks during which the RCMP candidates were lodged in single quarters at the School and followed the daily prevailing routine. An RCMP officer would accompany the group to take care of any RCMP administrative details such as pay, mail, records and so forth. The first course, all volunteers, was conducted at the Canadian Provost Corps School in Camp Borden, August/September 1952. The forty-eight constables were well motivated and the course was a success. Superintendent Gerry Mudge, a former RCMP from No 1 company, was the resident liaison officer and made a considerable contribution through his vast knowledge of the Corps. The Commissioner came down for the final parade and was most pleased with the results. A further two courses were organized, one in the Fall of 1954 and a final one in September 1957. This training was of some direct benefit to the Force and it held enormous potential for the Corps and the Army. All told, about 150 RCMP constables completed this programme.

Canadians, and Canada's governments, have always adopted a laissez-faire attitude towards the Militia during periods of relative peace and stability. Professor Willet correctly makes the point that escalating costs for the Regular Force has resulted in a progressively smaller budget for the Reserves. This is well illustrated by the gradual reduction of the Reserve component of Canada's Army from 155,000 in 1947 to 27,000 today. The argument most frequently put forward for this drastic reduction is that there is no point in authorizing a large number of militia units, all of which are vastly understrength. This misses the point. The point is that the reason they are understrength is because service in the Militia is singularly unattractive for the average Canadian youngster. If it is politically unacceptable to have compulsory military service, then other incentives must be introduced to ensure proper manning levels for the Reserves. The Conference of Defence Associations has made repeated representations, over the years, that this be done. Some of the incentive measures, none of them costly or disruptive of current policies, include:

- An income tax break for reservists, allowing a tax deduction equal to the amount of their service pay;
- Financial assistance for the continuation of their training and education, either academically or technically, following a specified term of service;
- A universal law requiring all employers to permit the attendance of reservists at annual training concentrations;
- Providing units with adequate training equipment and facilities;
- The introduction of a Service Contract that is legal and binding. Reservists should have the option of serving for varying periods of time, stated in years, in order to fit militia service into their life agendas. Contracts must explain the commitments, benefits and responsibilities of service and the penalties for failure to attend training parades or duties.

Those who were members of Canadian Provost Corps Militia units deserve a special niche in our history. They were an important part of the Corps who did their job cheerfully and well, often under difficult circumstances. They were worthy successors of the wartime field companies whose titles they inherited.

15

Korea

The North Atlantic Treaty Organization (NATO) was the result of worldwide aggressive action by Stalin's communist regime. The USSR had not downsized their armed forces following the war, and they continued to occupy countries such as East Germany, Poland, Roumania and the Baltic Republics in Europe, along with Manchuria, Mongolia and North Korea in Asia. They were vigorously developing and supporting a number of surrogate Communist states around the world. They possessed the devastating nuclear bomb, from 1949 onward. Stalin had openly revived the Comintern in order to spread subversion and revolution, especially in the emerging states. China, under Mao Tse Tung, would soon be a Communist state in full control of its teeming millions. It was against this background that delegates from ten European nations, along with the United States and Canada, met in Paris during April 1949. The outcome was the collective defence alliance called NATO. It was based on the principle that any attack on one would be construed as an attack on all. Each nation was bound to contribute to a standing, permanent military force which would function under a single unified command.

With the NATO force offering much determined resistance in western Europe it was not too surprising that armed Communist aggression should erupt in far off Korea. The June 1950 invasion of South Korea by a strong Soviet trained and equipped North Korean army is now common knowledge. What is not so well known are the events leading up to the division of Korea into the Communist North and USA controlled South, immediately following the Japanese defeat in August 1945. Following the defeat of Germany in May, Stalin ordered several Soviet Combat Divisions into Manchuria. This move was not entirely unwelcome by the US Chiefs of Staff who were still faced with a formidable Japanese war machine. The USSR became very active in this theatre immediately after the two bombs were dropped on Japan in early August. Joseph C Goulden, in his book *Korea, The Untold Story of the War*[132], gives this account of subsequent reactions.

... two days later the Soviets finally entered the Pacific war, far too late to be of any practical military value, but a 'de jure' fulfillment of their Yalta pledge. On August 10 the Japanese sued for peace and several divisions of Russian troops began a rapid drive through Manchuria, bound for Korea.

With peace, the issue of the surrender of the large Japanese forces in KOREA became an urgent matter. The nearest United States troops were in Okinawa, some 600 miles away. It was clearly in the United States interest to establish a presence in the long Korean peninsula as far north as possible. The problem was whether they could get their own forces, in reasonable numbers, into Korea in sufficient time to forestall the rapidly approaching Soviets. Goulden continues his narrative.

The military view was that if our proposal for a demarcation line for receiving the surrender greatly over-reached our military capabilities there would be little likelihood of Soviet acceptance – and speed was the essence of the problem.

After talking, Rusk and Bonesteel recommended the 38th parallel, even though it was further north than could be realistically reached by United States forces in the event of Soviet disagreement. They chose this line because "we felt it important to include the capital of Korea (Seoul) in the area of responsibility of American troops".

To Rusk's surprise, the Russians accepted the 38th parallel without hesitation. Formal orders went out from MacArthur on September 2, the day the Japanese signed the surrender on the USS Missouri in Tokyo: Japanese soldiers north of the 38th parallel would surrender to the Russians; those to the south, to the Americans.

The foregoing account of how Korea, long enslaved by Japan, came to be divided at the precise time in its history when there was realistic hope of attaining its freedom, is one of the more distressing outcomes of World War II. It is still divided at near the 38th parallel after forty-seven years.

Prime Minister Louis St Laurent spoke to the nation on 7 August 1950. He emphasized the importance of Canadians assuming responsibility for the defence of Canada and also cooperating with our Allies to halt the spread of Communist aggression around the world. He made the point that Canada could no longer depend on the Royal Navy for the protection of our sovereignty. He stated that a defence budget exceeding three billion would be approved for the expansion of Canada's Armed Forces (Navy, Army and Air Force), including the immediate raising of an Army Brigade for service in Korea. The fiscal austerity experienced by Canada's military leaders was further, and dramatically, relieved when Brooke Claxton announced, on 5 February 1951, that starting at once the Royal Canadian Navy would get up to 100 ships, the Army a full infantry division and the Royal Canadian Air Force up to 40 squadrons. The total cost would be five billion over three years. It was now clear to all Canadians that Canada would once again be involved in global military ventures. It was the beginning of a whole new era for everyone serving in Canada's armed forces.

In Ottawa it was quickly decided to raise a brigade group, as part of an United Nations force, for action in Korea. This force would be predominately American, albeit there were eleven nations contributing to it at various times. The Canadian brigade was named: 25 Canadian Infantry Brigade (Special Force). It was to consist of three infantry battalions, an armoured squadron, an artillery regiment, an engineer squadron, RCASC transport company, a RCEME workshop, a Canadian Provost Corps detachment of two sections and a headquarters. The total strength was to be about 8,000 all ranks, the majority to be raised by a recruiting drive which commenced in early August 1950. In order to give recruiting some impetus it was decided to call back into service several notable World War II officers. Brigadier John Rockingham and Lieutenant Colonel James Riley Stone were foremost in this category, although a fair number of soldiers in many higher ranks came to this new brigade from the Militia or were war veterans not yet settled.

Once again Canada's military assets were at a very low ebb. The supply of such essentials as weapons, vehicles, ammunition and even boots and combat dress was scarce or nonexistent. Following the initial announcement there was a flurry of recruits reporting to the small, understaffed Personnel Depots which were incapable of handling the crush. The Depot located at Chorley Park in Toronto, which was geared to process about six people each day, was suddenly confronted with ten times that number. The result was a progressively larger backlog of Special Force applicants. At one stage there were over two hundred people lying about, in various states of sobriety, on the well-kept lawns at Chorley Park. It required a special squad of provost from the school in Borden to restore order. This scene was repeated across the country. When brought to the attention of the Minister he reacted by ordering all recruits to be attested for service without benefit of even the most elementary administrative screening. They were not given a medical examination or any of the basic checks designed to determine their usefulness as soldiers. They were given a transport warrant and told to report to Camp "X". On arrival at the camp, often without advance notice, hastily formed reception areas, manned by Regulars, had to compile nominal rolls by asking men their names. There were no beds, stores, mess halls or cooks. They had no regimental number and many had not been assigned to a corps or unit. Some stated they had enlisted on a dare, or when drunk, and demanded to be returned to their home town. One agitated World War II veteran stated he had left without informing his family, during his lunch break at work, and had not even shut off his truck motor. It took weeks to sort out this tangle and would take years before the unsatisfactory aftermath of these hasty recruiting measures was finally put to rest. It must be emphasized, not all of those engaged for service in Korea were misfits or delinquents. The majority, especially the veterans, served with distinction.

The provost element[133] for the Brigade was designed to be self-contained (able to work on its own) and have the capability of providing something like the services considered necessary during the past war. The fact that it would be serving alone, in a difficult environment on the other side of the globe, was also taken into account. The officer commanding held the rank of major and would also serve as the brigade APM[134]. The transport was also somewhat changed. Each section had five M38-A1 cars (5-Cwt) jeeps each with a ¼ ton trailer. There were no motorcycles. A jeep was provided for each officer, a 2½ ton 4 x 4 truck for the headquarters and another ¾ ton 4 x 4 for the orderly room/office. After much debate it was decided to issue each service policeman with a standard 9 mm pistol with a further three Sten guns per section. The World War II battle dress was augmented by a denim combat jacket and trousers with peaked, baseball type caps of the same material. The new design, higher top, boots were an improvement over the World War II "ammunition boots" and puttees. Each was issued with an excellent, standard design parka and sleeping bag. Two-man pup tents were also available but were never very popular.

This Canadian Provost Corps unit was formed at the school in Camp Borden. The officers and senior NCOs were all experienced Regulars or veterans. The junior NCOs and men were quickly recruited and at Camp Borden by the end of September 1950, where they were outfitted and underwent some serious training under the keen eye of Major Bob Luker, the recently appointed and most capable officer commanding the new unit. Enrolment in the Special Force was voluntary, the term of service being 18 months or "such further period as may be required". By 26 August, notwithstanding the difficulties described above, the number of enlistments had reached 8,000. The entire Brigade Group[135] moved to Fort Lewis,

Washington during November 1950, where they would be equipped and carry-out more unit and formation training. Each unit received its entitlement of vehicles, guns, small arms and other items from United States sources. In almost every case this United States equipment was superior to our own equivalent. The 2½ ton 4 x 4 truck, in particular, with its powerful motor and traction provided by dual tandem rear wheels, was a 'God send' in the rough terrain of Korea. The Provost Corps Detachment was soon, as usual, busily engaged in traffic and disciplinary duties in the pleasant countryside of the State of Washington, in such places as Yakima, Walla Walla and even as far as Seattle, Oregon. The training facilities for the brigade were quite adequate. The artillery regiment (105 mm gun/howitzers), armoured squadron (76 mm gun–Sherman tank) and antitank platoons of the infantry battalions (75 mm recoilless rifles) carried-out firing practice at Yakima, about 80 miles from Fort Lewis. The Service Support units, including 25 Provost Detachment, performed the same duties as would be required of them in action.

It is appropriate, at this stage, to return to Canada and relate to a disciplinary problem which, inevitably, involved the Corps. The formation of the Brigade and subsequent movement of sizable bodies of troops necessitated much troop travel back and forth across Canada. As in World War II, the Adjutant General was receiving complaints from the Canadian National and Canadian Pacific Railways about rowdiness by troops and damage to railway property. It is difficult to determine whether the problem was serious or whether the Railway officials were playing it by the rules established during World War II. One suspects the latter because they actually suggested that "Train Patrols" be reactivated to deal with the problem. In any event, the decision was taken later in 1951 to initiate train patrols on main lines, the main variation being that this time the patrols would be made up of Army, Air Force and Navy military police. Lieutenant R T (Bob) Grogan[136] (later Colonel Grogan) gives the following account of this activity:

In late 1951 members of the Canadian Provost Corps, together with their counterparts from the Royal Canadian Navy and the Royal Canadian Air Force, commenced performing Tri-Service Train Patrols on mainline transcontinental passenger trains of the Canadian Pacific Railway and the Canadian National Railway. The program was instituted following a coordinating conference convened by the Provost Marshal (Army) at Ottawa, who would be overall functional authority for the program.

Each railway, through its Police Director, issued the required number and types of passes to PM (Army). These were then issued, on a strict accountable basis, to

Command Provost Marshals for subsequent distribution to Command and Area Provost organizations, from whence the scheduled patrols would operate.

As an example of patrol operations, Prairie Command Provost Company organized and scheduled patrols which operated eastward from Winnipeg to either the Lakehead (CPR) or Sioux Lookout (CNR) and westward to either Regina (CPR) or Saskatoon (CNR). Commands coordinated their patrols with one another to ensure appropriate patrol coverage, particularly for larger troop movements or to deal with troublesome military travellers. With regard to the latter, serious offenders were usually removed from the trains and deposited into the custody of civil or military police along the route through requests for assistance transmitted via the train conductor.

Tri-Service Train Patrols were supplemented by Station Patrols at major railway terminal points where scheduled stops of approximately twenty minutes to forty-five minutes occurred. The dress and deportment of all ranks who detrained were monitored and corrected, if necessary, and observable purchases of liquor and beer were confiscated before the offending military passengers reboarded the train. Appropriate reports were submitted to the offender's superiors. Often Draft Conducting Officers would opt to take their troops on a short route march during a stopover. The station patrols facilitated those marches on public roadways by arranging traffic control coverage with the local police, sometimes on very short notice.

Perhaps an obvious comment on these patrols is that, for the first time ever, the railway officials conceded that not only soldiers, but on occasions sailors and airmen, crossed the line of good behavior. If nothing else, it shows that colours other than khaki are sometimes compromised. Perhaps the Halifax riot of May 1945 was also an influence in this venture. In any event, the Provost Marshals, over the years, had received much cooperation from the Railway Directors of Police and Criminal Investigation, John Belanger of the CPR and Ed Spearing for the CNR. They were always helpful when asked for assistance. For example, their cooperation did much to resolve some movement and security problems in conncection with the huge army display during the centennial year of 1967.

Earlier reference is made to the hasty recruiting procedures and lack of proper initial screening procedures. The Special Force had an effective strength of approximately 8,000 men prior to its departuure from Fort Lewis. Another 500 were either absent without leave or had deserted. Another 1,500 had been discharged as unlikely to become effective soldiers, some for medical reasons others for continued misconduct, while a significant number were borderline criminals. Those AWOL would continue to cause problems for the Corps, as well as the police of both Canada

Military policemen at Camp Borden, May 1916. Standing, L to R: Cpl Carl Harvey, Pte Mercer Hamilton, Pte Fred Pierson, Pte Eddie Walsh. Seated L to R: Pte Mel Martin, Pte Forbes, Unidentified. (Pte Forbes was from Midland, Ontario; the other identified were from Tottenham, Ontario).

'E' Section, 3 Provost Company, Salisbury Plains, August 1941

Officers, WO1 and NCO's, 11 Provost Company, Juniper Hall, Surrey, June 1944. Seated L to r: Lt M Fitzgibbon, Lt B W E Lee, Maj J R Stewart, Lt Col George Ball (DPM). Capt Pat Byers, Capt Eric Porter (OC), Lt C Newman. 2nd row: RSM Jim Rae, Sgts Hanna, Sims, McKnight, Canning, McArthur, May, Ssgt Sherrit. 3rd row: Sgts Moore, Rinker, Petterson

Refugees at Caen, July 1944

Maj-Gen Keefler, 3 Cdn Inf Div awaits von Straube's surrender, May 1945

CWAC Provost, A-32 C Pro C Training Centre, Camp Borden, September 1944. Cpl V Howard is shown third from right, second row.

CGS' conference (26 officers), June 1947. L to R: Capt Lou Bourgeois, Maj Bill Lee, Maj Joe Lawson, Col Mike Dunn, Maj Don Pilley, Col Mike Brennan, Lt Col Buster Phillips, Lt Col Paul Triquet, Lt Col Donnie Buell, Col Bob Moncel, Maj Don Cheatley, Lt Col Bruce MacDonald, Lt Gen Charles Foulkes (CGS), Lt Col Ken Coats (obscured), Lt Col George Stevenson, Maj Tony Scotti, Maj Radley Walters, Maj Harold Hagey, Maj Gen Chris Vokes (GOC), Capt Tom Quirk, N/K, Brig George Kitching, N/K, Maj John Beswick, Maj Gord Kirk, Capt Jack Fraser, Capt Ross Elmer.

Twelve C Pro C subalterns at RMC, Kingston, August 1952. Standing: Lts Jim Lumsden, Walt Dabros, Jack Dunn, Jack Turner, N/K, Dave Stone, Gord Perry, Bill Fay, Capt Lorne Henderson, N/K. Seated: Capt Norm Easthaugh, Lt Col Tommy De Fay, the author, and Capt Bob Grogan.

Officers of No 2 Provost Company (Militia), Toronto, November 1959. L to R: Maj Ted Maxted, Maj Jack Oliver, Brig Forbes West (guest of honour), Maj John Tweddle, Maj John Fogg.

The Provost Marshal conference, December 1956. Seated, L to R: Lt Col A R Ritchie, Lt Col A J Scotti, Col A J Stone, Lt Col JJ Platt, Maj T J Quirk. Standing, L to R: Maj B W E Lee, Maj R I Luker, Maj J M Walsh, Maj C A Breakey, Maj J R G Surprenant, Capt E A Wilson, Maj E M Hills.

Presentation, Cambridge Challenger Bowl, C Pro c (S), April 1956

Prime Minister Louis St Laurent and the military police bodyguard in Korea, March 1954

Cpl Mitchell, RMP, Cpl Butler, C Pro C, and Cpl Wright, RAAPC

Col S Jarrell, USMPC (with the author, centre of photo) visits C Pro C (S), May 1958

Guard of honour for CGS at C Pro C (S), April 1958

Nicosia Provost Zone Unit – a veritable United Nations of military police from Canada, United Kingdom, Denmark, Sweden, Finland, and Eire – in Cyprus, August 1964. Cpl Bob Thomas is sixth from left in the back row.

UN Secretary General Dag Hammarskjold visits UNEF military police in Gaza, 1957. He is greeted by Capt R F Woodburn.

Senior officers of the C Pro C, Camp Borden, October 1964 L to R: Lt Col R I Luker, Lt Col B W E Lee, Col L H Nicholson, Col AR Ritchie, Col A J Scotti

Col P A Puize and Col L H Nicholson at the dedication of the memorial cairn, Camp Borden, June 1965

and the United States for years to come. The "Release in Absentia" order of December 1953 never really solved the problem of the Canadian soldiers who went absent from Fort Lewis. The majority were unaware of this policy and, as frequently happened when arrested by various United States police for some offence, would be returned to the nearest Canadian military authority for disposal.

In Korea the United States forces had survived the initial onslaught of the ten North Korean divisions. Aided by a British brigade, an Australian battalion and greatly strengthened by the arrival of some of their own fighting formations such as the 1st Marine, 1st Cavalry, 3rd, 7th and 25th Divisions they totally defeated the North Koreans and drove them north to the Yalu River near the Chinese border. The country was completely devastated by war. Seoul was a heap of rubble, every village was burnt, millions of people were homeless and suffering from cold, hunger and disease. The Communist North Koreans committed acts of brutality and were completely merciless. The South Koreans panicked and used any means available to flee the advancing Communist invaders. People who could find no means of transport put their belongings on their backs and trudged south. Most of the members of South Korea's National Assembly in Seoul had departed ahead of the advancing North Korean tanks. Those who chose to stay were rounded up and shot by the North Korean invaders. The small and ill-trained South Korean army was powerless to stop the invaders and had no option except withdrawal, although there were many acts of bravery by small groups and individuals. Some of the tactics used by the North Koreans are described by Joseph C Goulden[137]:

Enemy soldiers stripped off their clothing, camouflaged their bodies with mud and tried to slip through United States lines. A group of eight or ten soldiers would attack and then raise their hands in surrender. When American fire stopped, and men moved out to accept their surrender, a company-sized North Korean force would launch an attack from a concealed position. Groups of fifty or more North Koreans would launch suicidal banzai charges. While United States soldiers concentrated fire on this group other forces would slip around the flanks and attack. Many North Korean soldiers carried civilian clothing, the white pyjama-type garb traditional in the South. They slipped out of their military uniforms when they wished to avoid detection.

A Canadian Advance Party[138] of 350 all ranks sailed from Seattle during late October. The intention was that the main body should go to OKINAWA for further training, and thence to Korea. By the time the advance party reached Japan certain changes of plan had developed. In view of the prospect of early victory, and an apparent lessening in the need for further ground forces, the immediate Canadian commitment was cut to one battalion. The Advance Party then sailed to Pusan where it arrived on 7 November. The Canadian battalion selected for immediate service in the Far East was the 2nd PPCLI, commanded by Lieutenant Colonel James R (Big Jim) Stone, DSO, MC. They sailed from Seattle on 5 November aboard the American troopship "USS Pte Joe Martinez". They arrived in Pusan on 18 December 1950. By this time the massed Chinese Peoples Army, which had entered the War, had advanced to a line 40 miles south of Seoul. So much for the theory that more troops were not needed in Korea. The 2nd PPCLI underwent a period of realistic training and orientation near Taegu, moved into the line under the command of a United States Division in February and took part in two or three actions against the Peoples Army. On 22–24 April 1951 they fought their now historic battle at Kapyong. They successfully defended key positions near the junction of the Pukhan and Kapyong Rivers northeast of Seoul and prevented a general advance by the Chinese.

The Brigade Group, commanded by Brigadier John M (Rocky) Rockingham, CBE, DSO, ED, sailed from Seattle from 19–21 April on three American troopships: Marine Adder, General Patrick and President Jackson. The Brigade arrived in Pusan on 4 May. By the 28 May the Brigade, rejoined by the Patricias, and was in action immediately south of the 38th parallel, near the junction of the Imjin and Hantan Rivers. No 25 Canadian Provost Detachment experienced the luxury of driving north as free runners as United States military police provided traffic control on the one main route used by the Brigade. A welcome respite, which permitted time for some useful orientation in this unfortunate land. It is not our purpose to deal with the actual fighting war during the next two years beyond those events which impacted directly on provost, nor is there any need to do so since it has been thoroughly covered in many excellent histories.

It is impossible to understand the full meaning of a Canadian soldier's life in Korea without having some knowledge of the country, its climate and people. The map shows Korea as a long, narrow peninsula attached to southern Manchuria. The climate ranges from extremes of cold, snowy winters to hot, humid summers, a more temperate spring and a dry, hot autumn. There is a monsoon season of about six weeks duration from mid May through June during which it rains as it rains no place else on earth. The country, by our standards, was primitive. With minor exceptions, it is entirely mountainous with numerous river valleys and re-entrants which flood during the monsoons. The only roads were constructed by United States Army Engineers using bulldozers and graders. These were simply ridges of piled earth with a high, narrow crown and a deep monsoon ditch on each side. There was no electricity or water outside of the half dozen larger cities. The rural areas were dotted with villages, with buildings constructed of wooden frames covered with baked mud walls and thatched roofs. They were surprisingly comfortable. The climate was one of extremes and it was cold, with frost and snow in January and February. A pleasant spring season was followed by a summer of extreme 110 degree F. heat and torrential rain. The fall season was quite pleasant. The diet staples were rice and fish, always in good supply. The country was divided into administrative districts called "myons", each controlled by a myon chief. The South Korean government of President Syngman Rhee, during the few years since 1945, had established basic control of the country with an elected assembly, a national police force and local governments. The people were hardy, energetic and resourceful and were fiercely patriotic which many years of Japanese domination had not quelled. Almost every village had one or more schools. The local schoolhouse was always one of the first reconstruction projects during the rebuilding phases following the ebb and flow of battle. It was heartwarming to see hundreds of children moving across the paddies to and from their classes.

Compared to the recent European experience this was not a war of movement. This did not result in any lessening of traffic control duties for provost, but simply changed the emphasis. The network of routes, described above, were permanently marked using a system similar to that used on highways in America. For example, to go from Ouijongbu to HQ 25 Canadian Infantry Brigade take Route 33 to 3X, left on 3X to 11C, north on 11C to 2Y (across Pintail Bridge), left on 2Y to HQ 25 CIB. The emphasis was now on marking the location of headquarters installations and numerous short detours caused by washouts and erosion. Another task for 25 Provost Detachment was manning a number of checkpoints on the routes. Some of these were temporary, such as those set-up to stop traffic on narrow, one-way sections of a route in order to permit a priority column to clear. A general "no light line" was established well back from the front. It was critical that all headlights be turned off when moving forward of this line during the hours of darkness. These points were covered by provost to ensure compliance. Roads were frequently blocked by vehicles, both tracked and wheeled, sliding off the narrow crown of the road and coming to rest in the monsoon ditch. This required active provost route patrols and quick action to prevent further tie-up of movement, particularly during darkness. It was impossible for any vehicle to move off a route, even for a short distance, without a previous reconnaissance. To do so invited rolling down a mountain-side or sinking in a flooded rice paddy. Consequently, everything happened on the roads. There were a few Chinese POW taken by the Canadian battalions and these were quickly evacuated to the 1st United States Corps Prisoner of War cage, further to the rear.

By and large, the men of 25 Provost Detachment adjusted well during those first months. There were a few cases of severe diarrhea and two men were evacuated due to minor injuries incurred in a vehicle accident when their jeep was forced off the road by a fast moving 2½ ton truck[139]. Both returned to the unit after a short stay at the Canadian Field Ambulance. The perennial problem of dust once more reared its ugly head. The dust of Sicily and Normandy was nothing compared to the dense clouds of fine particles stirred up by moving tires. Its affect was magnified by the stifling heat during the day, and it made driving at night synonymous with Russian roulette. The supply system was plugged into the United States Army pipeline except for mail, clothing, rations and reinforcements. The system worked quite well. All Canadian troops were paid in military script vouchers called Military Purchase Certificates (MPCs), which were valued at the equivalent United States dollar. There was not much a soldier could purchase in any event, unless there happened to be a nearby American Post Exchange (PX). The current issue of MPC was withdrawn and replaced from time-to-time by the United States authorities. This measure was designed to prevent black marketing or illegal profiteering by manipulators. The withdrawal was always done without any warning or advance notice so that a hoarded quantity of MPC script would be worthless and could no longer be redeemed for United States dollars.

The next development of major importance to provost was the integration of all British, Canadian, Australian and New Zealand troops in Korea to form I Commonwealth Division (1 Comwel Div). This concept originated in the War Office in London and was agreed by the governments of Canada and both ANZAC countries. It was implemented in July 1951 in Korea. Two of the necessary three infantry brigades were already in being, the 29th British Brigade and the Canadian 25th Brigade. The third brigade was a composite of British, Australian and New Zealand units and was named the 28th Brigade. The commander was an Australian brigadier with a mostly Australian staff. It had two British infantry battalions, one Australian battalion, a New Zealand artillery regiment and a NZ Service Corps company and Signal squadron. The Division was commanded by a British officer, Major General A J H Cassels, with a mixed staff of British, Canadian and ANZAC officers. The divisional "Service" units included both national and Commonwealth units and sub-units. For operations the Comwel Div was placed under control of Headquarters 1st United States Corps, a relation which was to continue throughout its 3½ years of existence. The divisional front, at this point in time, extended about 6 miles westward from the junction of the Imjin and Hantan Rivers, generally north of the lower Imjin. This line was slightly north of the 38th parallel and remained much the same for the next two years. Hence, it was not a war of movement in this sector, albeit there was much hard fighting in the days ahead.

A divisional provost company, consisting of a headquarters section and eight sections, was formed from five British RMP (military police sections), the two Canadian sections of 25 Provost Detachment and one Australian section of the Royal Australian Army Provost Corps. These sections were similar in terms of numbers, ranks and vehicles with a strength of 15 all ranks (Sergeant, 2 Cpls, 12 L/Cpls) and five jeeps per section. It was decided that the APM of the Division would be British, while the Officer Commanding 1 Commonwealth Provost Company would be the current Canadian APM of 25 Canadian Brigade. The second-in-command and one lieutenant to be British, with another two lieutenants, one Canadian and one Australian, completing the company headquarters officer slate. The RSM and CQMS were to be British, and the remaining company headquarters section was a composite of British and Canadian tradesmen. The WO2 (Company Sergeant Major) of 25 Provost Detachment was moved to the Korea Detachment of a British Special Investigation Unit (SIU) reporting out of the Commonwealth Base Headquarters in Kure, Japan. The decision as to the make-up of 1 Commonwealth Provost Company was left to Major Luker and Major Rawlings, the senior Canadian and British provost officers on the spot. The company was fully operational by September with sections deployed, more or less on a permanent basis, as follows:

    One Section (Br) at Div HQ
    One Section (Br) at Rear Div HQ
    One Section (Br) at HQ 29 Br Bde
    One Section (Cdn) at HQ 25 Can Bde
    One Section (Aust) at HQ 28 Aust Bde
    Two Sections (Br) at Coy HQ
    One Section (Cdn) at Coy HQ

The administration of the Company was done on a composite basis wherever practical. For example, there were common messing arrangements for each of the three national groups, officers, NCOs and men, as well as common QM stores and MT lines. The orderly room was, in fact, three offices in one since the records, reports, returns, pay, medical and personnel accounting procedures were different and required a competent clerical staff from each national group. It should be mentioned, however, that the Australian Provost officer did most of the day-to-day administration for the Australian Section in addition to his other duties. The second-in-command was the principal administrative officer and looked after the camp layout, medical, casualties, rations and messing, quarters and sanitation, water supply, hygiene and all wholly British administrative matters. The RMP lieutenant was appointed Transport Officer, while the Canadian and Australian lieutenants supervised the day-to-day activities of the various sections. The background, training and motivation of these men presented an interesting study in contrasts. The British army was now composed of national servicemen (drafted) except for the odd veteran officer, warrant and non-commissioned officer. The men met the standards for the Royal Military Police and, in fact, often possessed a much higher educational standard than either his Canadian or Australian counterpart. They had all received military police training at the RMP Depot in England and, with one exception, were able to perform provost duties with little supervision. The exception was the ability to operate and maintain a vehicle, where they were somewhat lacking. They were otherwise reliable and carried out their duties cheerfully. The members of the Canadian Provost Corps were undoubtedly better trained on the whole. If there was one specific weakness it was a tendency to complain about the weather, the food, the war and their lot generally. But when the chips were down they got it done. The Aussie MPs were, without question, diamonds in the rough. Some had seen duty in the Reserves or police, and a few were experienced veterans. Given a minimum of instruction and guidance they were first rate military policemen and were most reliable. The Canadian Provost Corps member was, by far, the better paid and equipped, however, it was sometimes difficult to overlook the fact that his opposite number in the RMP got just as tired, cold, wet and dispirited on point duty at the other end of the bridge. While there were some differences in the preferences for food, entertainment and life style between the nationals, they pulled together quite well and certainly, insofar as doing the basic job was concerned, there was no problem. The only problem was the inordinate amount of time spent on daily administration. There was also a variation in time spent on training a new man before he could be posted for duty. This was a neverending chore.

If there was one problem above all others in 1 Commonweath Division Provost Company, it was the loss of efficiency and morale caused by the rotation system. The policy for each of the nations was roughly the same; when a soldier had completed one year in Korea he was returned to his homeland and a replacement was sent out to take his place. In large units, such as infantry battalions and artillery regiments, a complete unit was replaced by an equivalent unit. Thus, the 2nd PPCLI, being the first over, was replaced by the 1st PPCLI in November 1951. The officers and men of 1 Commonwealth Provost Company were rotated on a one-for-one basis, after completing one year. This meant that there were always some counting the days until "home go", some enroute and some arriving in this austere and sombre land. This was not good for morale since the newly arrived member, in addition to feeling low about his ordained one year stay in this strange environment, was forced to listen to the rejoicing of the ones about to leave. Secondly, it meant that there was a direct loss of manpower occasioned by the time lag between departures and arrivals, plus the fact that it took at least one month of orientation before the new arrival was functioning at full efficiency. However, given the circumstances, there was really not much to be done about the problem. It should also be mentioned the overall affect this had on the Corps in Canada. The trained replacements for overseas rotation came from the only source available, the static provost units in Canada. Even when they were up to strength, and later with increased numbers, these units bore the brunt of the time lost due to lengthy leave entitlements of the returning men. Indeed, in due course, this deficiency was recognized as an army-wide problem and the overall manpower allocated to the Corps was increased to provide for this factor. It would have been more efficient to form complete provost sections in Canada and use them to replace sections returned on the rotation.

No account of the Canadian Army's participation in the Korean War would be complete without mention of the contribution made by Korean personnel serving with Canadian units. The 2nd PPCLI, in keeping with the practice of nearly all United Nations forces, had employed Korean labourers to carry ammunition and supplies over the rugged hills. These "bearers" were exceptionally strong and displayed great endurance in carrying loads, often equal to their own weight, over long distances.

During the course of the campaign the Korean Service Corps (KSC) was formed in the ROK Army. The 120th KSC Regiment was attached to 1 Commonwealth Division to provide non-combatant duties such as domestic services, cleaners, drivers, mechanics, cooks and, most important, interpreters. 1 Commonwealth Provost Company were allotted 17 KSC who were attached for all purposes (rations, duty, clothing and shelter) except pay. They were supervised by the appropriate company staff and employed as follows: 2 cooks, 5 cleaners, 2 runners, 4 driver/mechanics, 2 waiters, one houseboy (OCs orderly) and one interpreter. They were quartered in their own squad tents, prepared their own meals and observed the same camp rules followed by all members of the unit. They were all proficient at their jobs and were diligent, cheerful workers. Pak, the interpreter, spoke, read and wrote good English. He was raised in the region and was a walking encyclopedia of local knowledge. If, as frequently occurred, the Company Investigator was stuck on a case of theft or lost weapons it was invariably Pak who suggested a fruitful lead. In one case where a large canvas bag full of soldiers' mail went missing it was Pak, after a short visit to a local village, who recovered it and the culprit. He was absolutely indispensable in the many day-to-day dealings that the provost had with local people and the ROK Army. Another KSC personality was Chung, the OCs orderly or houseboy. He was a young orphan boy when befriended by Major Bob Luker on the arrival of 25 Provost Detachment north of Seoul in May 1952. He remained with the unit for the next three years serving each of the four Canadian majors who commanded. He awakened his charge in the morning, brought shaving water, a hot cup of tea, cleaned the brass and shoes, pressed uniforms and kept the quarters (office lorry) spotless. He was very proud of his olive-green denim uniform, his cap and kit which was issued to him and he wore the Corps badge with great pride. Normally Chung was very quiet and seldom spoke but he came to the "major OC" one day in an excited state. He had received word from somewhere that his grandmother might be living in a village about 40 miles distant. He was despatched in a jeep with Pak and a Corporal to check and find this close relative if possible. It was possible and Chung found his grandmother. This was, perhaps, one of the few happy events in Chung's life since the Communists destroyed his village and killed his parents nearly five years previous to this reunion. Everyone in the Company was happy for him, and the key word was "everyone" of these men from a half-dozen separate countries. It may be that this incident explains, in some small way, the reason why soldiers from so many countries of the free world came to this sad land of their own free will.

This integrated provost company was involved in some unusual events during the next three years. The next major event in Korea was the establishment, by the Corps, of a Field Detention Barracks. The conditions under which front line soldiers must live, especially during the winter months of December to March, were almost intolerable. It took a great deal of stamina and courage to live in a foxhole all day, patrol during the night in enemy territory or stand-to on piquet duty. There were two major problems. The weather, which was cold and wet without let-up, and, secondly, about 100,000 members of the Chinese Peoples Volunteer Army on the opposite side of the hill. The CPVA invariably attacked at night, either in force, or with a great clamour and blowing of bugles, as a feint. In spite of the effort made to alleviate the situation by such means as hot meals, frequent reliefs and dry clothing, the morale sank and, inevitably, a few engaged in malingering. The less hardy reported sick, feigned injury and even committed a minor offence in order to evade the unpleasantness. In any case, spending a few days in the guard tent was vastly preferable to the foxhole. Reports soon reached Army Headquarters where the Adjutant General, as recommended by the Brigade Commander, directed the Provost Marshal to establish a detention barracks in Korea. It was quickly decided the capacity would be 50 detainees with a Canadian Provost Corps staff of 2 officers, a RSM and three guard shifts of 1 S Sgt and 4 NCOs each, plus the necessary cooks, clerks and storeman. This unit, commanded by a captain, was organized from the staff of existing barracks and arrived in Korea by early May 1952. It was designated No 25 Field Detention Barracks and was located on the northeastern outskirts of Seoul. The compound was constructed by United States Army Engineers and was enclosed by a perimeter wire fence. The detainees were quartered in the regular 8-man squad tents with a frame building for ablutions, cookhouse, unit office and orderly room. The daily programme kept the inmates fully occupied from reveille at 0530 hours to lights-out at 2100 hours, with emphasis on physical training. It was the intent that life in detention should be at least as onerous as that of a front line soldier. It was arranged that soldiers sentenced to detention by British or Australian units could also be admitted to 25 FDB, and this occurred from time to time. This Detention Barracks continued to operate until July 1955, but on a reduced scale for the last seven months. It did a first class job.

Japan was the stepping stone for the vast majority of United States and Commonwealth troops in Korea. The Americans had well established garrisons since 1945, so it was natural to continue these as the main supply, communications and reinforcement bases for the Korean forces. The British, Canadians and Australians also formed a Japanese Base, the British Commonwealth Force Korea Base Units (BCFK) with its headquarters in Kure, on the southeastern coast of Honshu near the ruins of Hiroshima. The introduction of a seven day (R & R)[140] leave period in Japan for all troops in Korea meant that there would be a large number of Commonwealth and United States soldiers in Japan at any given time. HQ BCFK arranged leave and recreation centres in places like Mia Jima, Kobe, Kyoto, Tokyo and Kure. This led to the formation of a second integrated Commonwealth Provost Company composed of RMP (Br), C Pro C (Cdn) and RAAPC (Aust) personnel. The Canadian Provost Corps element consisted of about 23 all ranks, including a major, captain, lieutenant and 20 other ranks. There were detachments in Tokyo and Kure. Needless to say, these provost were fully employed rescuing Korean warriors from small and musty Japanese cells. The Royal Australian Air Force flew a regular DC3 shuttle service from Kure to Kimpo Airport in Seoul. This flight was a sobering experience for the odd Commonwealth soldier placed on board because he had missed his scheduled transport back to the Imjin hills. The DC3 was not heated, the cabin was not pressurized, it had bench seats along each cabin wall and it made a "character building" landing at Kimpo.

The war dragged on for another two years, with countless bloody battles for some obscure hilltop. If you were on top of the hill, you controlled the immediate region. The most severe fighting took place in a relatively small area termed the "Iron Triangle". In the final analysis it was the superior, massed artillery fire and excellent close air support of the United States forces that defeated the Chinese armies. They fought fiercely and massed infantry for an attack. Small groups would infiltrate at night and set ambushes on roads. They had well trained mortar crews, some artillery, which gradually improved in quantity and quality, and a few T-34 Russian tanks. The infantrymen carried large quantities of ammo for their good automatic rifles, as well as grenades. They did not depend on roads to move, and each soldier carried a ration of rice to last for 4 or 5 days. It was stated, and easily believed, that they followed Mao Tse Tung's relentless tactics, which were:

        Enemy advances – we retreat
        Enemy halts – we harass
        Enemy tires – we attack
        Enemy retreats – we pursue.

Their main weakness was the inability to move their artillery into good fire positions, and in the air their pilots were no match for United States and United Nations flyers. The match-up of ground forces at the end of 1952 was:

Chinese Armies	900,000
North Korean Army	270,000
	1,170,000
United States Army	330,000
Republic of Korea (ROKA) Army	370,000
*Other United Nations Troops	45,000
	745,000

*Britain, Canada, Australia & – 1 Comwel Div and New Zealand
*Turkey – 1 Indep Inf Bde
*Miscellaneous (India, Greece, Norway, France)

Negotiations for a cease-fire and an armistice began in 1951 at the United Nations. This led to meetings between United States, North Korean and Chinese delegates at Panmujon, near the 38th parallel in August 1951. The major stumbling block was the prisoner of war repatriation problem. To begin with, neither North Korea nor China were signatories of the Geneva Agreement on Prisoner of War treatment. Thousands of prisoners captured by United Nations' forces were South Korean servicemen and civilians conscripted into the Communist armies. These conscripts made it clear they did not want to be repatriated to North Korea. North Korean agents were infiltrated into our Prisoner of War camps with orders to silence these unwilling converts. In order to counter the infiltration tactics, all NKPA and CPVA prisoners were moved to Koze-Do Island, off the South Korean coast. Hardcore Communist leaders and agents continued their terror tactics against these South Korean prisoners of war, committing atrocities and murdering several of them. A United States Marine Regiment was sent in to restore order, which it did after killing 85 Communist ringleaders. The prisoners of war were then separated into two groups, under an United Nations Observer Team. The reluctant Communists in one, and the "repatriables" in the other. The "repats" (Communist) group was, eventually, released near Panmujon under United Nations Observers. The "non-repats", about 22,000, were finally released in April 1954, following nearly three years of stubborn resistance to this action by the North. It was probably the first time in history that prisoners of war were used as a tactic in war. Without question, it delayed a cease-fire by nearly two years, during which thousands were killed on both sides. The final count of those killed, as at the time of the Armistice Agreement on 19 July 1953, is given below:

United States Forces	33,630
Republic of Korea Army	325,000
United Kingdom	935
Other United Nations Forces	720
Canadian	312
North Korean Army	370,000
Chinese Army	830,000

The Truce Agreement established a new demarcation line between the North and South, which was the forward position held by the United Nations Forces, slightly north of the former line of the 38th parallel. The "demilitarized" zone, or DMZ, extended clear across the Korean peninsula and was, in effect, a no-man's-land strip about one mile in width. It was marked with large, permanent signs in both the English and Korean languages, placed at 3–400 yard intervals. There was to be NO MOVEMENT of any description into the DMZ by either side. Fifty years later these markers, or their replacements, are still in place.

Neither side moved so much as one gun, tank or carbine from their positions occupied on 19 July. It was a long period, one year to be exact, of uneasy truce. During this period the United Nations Forces, including 1 Comwel Div, reconnoitred and developed strong lay-back defensive positions known as the Kansas Line. The rotation continued and the third round of infantry battalions arrived in Korea during May 1954. As usual, the overall result of the cessation of the "shooting" war was a sharp increase in work for provost. One of the tasks, which was to take up the entire company, was the periodic practice deployment of all divisional units to new prepared positions on the Kansas Line. This exercise was started by the transmission of the code word "SCRAM" to all divisions in 1st United States Corps. This triggered the packing- up and movement by every unit and headquarters to their new positions. It greatly resembled a huge can of wiggly worms. The timings for each unit were critical and the traffic control was difficult, particularly as this usually took place at night. For the first time, really, Canadian troops were, once again, finding ways to get into trouble. Some went AWOL and lived as best they could in the villages. The incidence of road accidents soared as, following a visit to the "Rec Centre" or another unit, drivers threw caution to the wind when "jeeping" back to their unit lines. Always lurking in the background was the knowledge that a huge mass of Chinese soldiers were across the valley and who, from time to time, would start blowing their bugles around midnight. There was no way of knowing whether this was meant to keep us awake or to deter us from aggressive action. The former was suspected. Smart new signs were posted throughout the Division area to mark units, boundaries, the DMZ, checkpoints and other installations. A large new Recreation Centre was built by joining several quonset huts near the centre of the area. It was complete with a movie theatre, dry and wet bars, snack bar, library, quiet room and games room. This place really "rocked" on pay nights and kept Sergeant Twist and his Australian Section busy restoring and maintaining order. All troops were welcome but it became so popular with the neighbouring United States Divisions that it was necessary to arrange, through the United States Provost Marshal of 1st United States Corps, to have a United States MP patrol called in each night. Lieutenant Colonel L C (Larrupin' Lew) Williams was, in fact, our immediate superior and nobody could ask for any better. After one year of the uneasy truce, and one more rotation, PEACE broke out on 17 July 1954 when the final agreement on cessation of hostilities was signed.

The period of uneasy truce brought a crescendo of tasks and problems never before experienced by provost. In some cases there was considerable doubt as to whether the problem was a legitimate concern of I Commonwealth Provost Company. Take the case of the corpses which appeared in shallow waters of the Imjin following the spring thaw. The river broadened for a stretch below Teal Bridge so that the rocky bottom was exposed, along with whatever flotsam or jetsam that had been carried by the spring and monsoon flooding. Amongst this debris would appear, usually in March and again in July, the bodies of dead soldiers. Since it could not be assumed they were not of United States or Commonwealth origin, it was essential that an effort be made at identification. Notwithstanding the protests of the OC Commonwealth Provost Corps and the Division APM, the task of doing this most disagreeable job fell to provost. The initial retrieval was done by rowing a flat bottomed boat to the spot, securing the cadaver in a wire mesh basket and towing it ashore for examination. Identification was simple if the decomposing was not in an advanced state, or if there were clothing remnants available. In some cases the identity discs were still attached or the shoes were obvious. The drill was to notify the appropriate military authority when nationality could be established. In the event it was Chinese or North Korean the cadaver was burnt on the spot using quantities of petrol. In one case, perhaps the only Canadian one, there was no question the body was that of a Canadian soldier. The problem was how to get a positive and personal identification. It was decided to place the body in the refrigeration unit at HQ 1st United States Corps. This was done. When freezing was complete our SIU man, WO2 Ray Chambers, was called in to recover a fingerprint by using the cadaver spoon method. The print was sent to the Canadian Armed Forces Identification Unit (CAFIB) in Ottawa, where the fingerprint files for all Canadian Armed Forces personnel were held. The report came back and, sure enough, it was a Canadian soldier who was missing from a well known infantry battalion for the past five months. The fact of this success did wonders to reduce the sheer nausea of this unwelcome task. A family in Canada now knew what had happened to their son.

Most of the contact between the soldiers of the Commonwealth Division and the military police was not due to a general lack of discipline but rather by problems of an administrative nature peculiar to this theatre. It has been stated that everybody rode about in vehicles and everything happened on the roads. Casualties, both human and mechanical, reached unacceptable levels due to vehicle accidents. The causes were manifold and included: reckless driving; vehicles in poor mechanical condition; washouts during the monsoons and the narrow dirt roads and monsoon ditches. In any event, it was decided, against the advice of the Canadian APM, to impose a maximum speed limit of 25 MPH within the boundaries of 1 Commonwealth Division. The enforcement problems were caused by the rather lighthearted way most COs viewed speeding tickets issued by provost. Some units, mainly British, awarded a severe reprimand. Others required the attendance of provost to give evidence with the resulting drain on manpower. Others simply dismissed charges, while a very few would ground drivers and award fines. When the APM recommended a follow-up for the disposition of all speeding violations issued by provost, there was much "taking it under advisement" but no action apart from issuing yet another Division Order drawing attention to the fact that "speeding" was a serious offence. This fact was well known to everybody including the CRE (Senior Engineer) who saw that large trucks pushed the earth from the road crown into the ditches. The CREME (Senior Repairman) knew his Workshops could not keep up with the wrecks towed in. The ADMS (Medical) saw the bleeding bodies being repaired and evacuated. All of the above blamed the provost for not enforcing the speed limit, despite issuing over 300 offence reports in one month. And so the beat went on and we did the best we could.

A second, more serious, problem was casualties caused by venereal disease. It was not confined to any national group, or groups, and it reached astronomical proportions. An infantry battalion, which shall be nameless, had 30% of its personnel infected at the same time late in 1953. Whatever the initial source it was certainly compounded by prostitutes, both local and emigres from Seoul, who plied their trade in the rear area villages. No amount of orders, such as placing villages out-of-bounds, counselling sessions or military police action would halt or make cohabitation unpopular. A plan was finally devised to deal with this problem in 1 Commonwealth Division area. The "sexies" would be apprehended by military police (notwithstanding no law was broken) and brought to a central treatment centre for medical inspection. If infected the individual would be evacuated to the Civil Affairs hospital near Ouijongbu, operated by the 1st United States Corps. If not infected the person was simply released. The prime movers of this plan were the Divisional ADMS (Chief Medical Officer), the 1st United States Corps Civil Affairs unit and the Canadian APM. It had the tacit, if not the written, support of several senior officers. A tented camp (the treatment centre) was set-up in the village of Sin-San-Ni. It was staffed by three Korean medical students who were briefed and supervised by the ADMS and provided with the necessary medical supplies. A Vice Squad was formed by 1 Commonwealth Provost Company consisting of a Sergeant (NCO 1C) and three Lance Corporals. This squad made the rounds of the villages where they questioned (vide an interpreter) the known or potential sexies and brought anyone who offered no objection to the Treatment Centre. The Centre, supervised by a United States Civil Affairs Officer, was well equipped and kept immaculately clean. It had its own showers, kitchen and bath facilities. The plan worked, and this process went on with a minimum of fuss or bother. More amazing, when the word spread, many of these unfortunate girls came in on their own. The VD rate among the troops started to decline as did the infection rate of sexies passing through the Treatment Centre. For example, the Vice Squad Report for February 1954 listed 340 admissions of which 312 were infected. The Report for September 1954, when the Centre was closed, showed 128 infected out of 224 admitted. In any event, this positive, if somewhat irregular, action achieved its basic aim

Early March 1954 brought the news of Prime Minister Louis St Laurent's planned visit to 25 Canadian Infantry Brigade in Korea. This was to be the first time ever that our Prime Minister would visit his troops in a war theatre. The Brigade Commander, Brigadier Jean Victor Allard, formed a team to organize and supervise the arrangements for his three day stay. The OC 1 Commonwealth Provost Company, CO 2nd Black Watch and the

DAQMG were given this responsibility, along with the Commander himself. The Prime Minister, and his party, arrived by RCAF aircraft at KIMPO Airport, near Seoul, about 1000 hours on 7 March. He was met by Brigadier Allard and left immediately by staff car for Headquarters 25 Canadian Infantry Brigade, then located about 45 miles north, just over the Imjin River. An escort of two jeeps and six men commanded by the OC 1 Commonwealth Division Provost Company was provided. Another escort by 622 United States Military Police Company (courtesy of Lieutenant Colonel Lew Williams) assisted until the main Route 33 Checkpoint at Ouijongbu was passed. His visit was a source of real joy for all Canadians. He visited, again with the same escort, all units in the Brigade and insisted on having lunch with the men in their mess tents. He was interested, and most perceptive, in everything he saw. The highlights of his visit included a jeep ride up a steep slope to the Naechon Observation Post (OP) where he could observe through binoculars, a large camp of Chinese Peoples Army across the valley. The Brigadier arranged a full course mess dinner complete with the Band of the North Staffordshire Regiment. He spoke after dinner and told how much he had learned, that this was his first ever visit to a military unit, and that he now felt he understood something about the way a military force functioned. He departed from the A10 Division Landing Strip, across the road from HQ 1 Commonwealth Division Provost Company, in a helicopter supplied by the 1st United States Marine Division. Very important persons, or VIPs as they are termed in military parlance, come and go at regular intervals. For most Canadians who were in Korea during Prime Minister St Laurent's visit this was very special. In particular, the three[141] members of 1 Commonwealth Division Provost Company who stayed with the Prime Minister throughout his visit as his personal bodyguard will always remember receiving his thanks and warm handshake as he departed.

The problem of North Korean agents slipping across the lines into the south has been mentioned in connection with the prisoner of war repatriation. This activity caused much alarm amongst the South Korean authorities, and was certainly bothersome from a purely military viewpoint. Since the North Korean looked the same, spoke the same language and dressed the same as a citizen of the South, it was not very difficult to infiltrate. This infiltration was happening across the peninsula, hence it was an Army-wide problem for United Nations and Republic of Korean Army forces. The decision was made at 8 United States Army[142] Headquarters to counter this threat. The plan was to establish a line across the country termed the "Stay Back Line", with each Division made responsible for posting patrols

No. 番號	1 COMWEL DIV PROVOST COY. 英聯邦第1師團憲兵隊 No.　COY. U.N. SECURITY GUARD. 第　中隊 英聯邦 第1師團 所屬 ATT 1 COMWEL DIV. 유엔 保安 警備隊	
RANK　　　　NAME　　　　　　IS A MEMBER OF THE U.N. SECURITY GUARD ATTACHED 1 COMWEL DIV. HE IS AUTHORISED TO HALT, DETAIN OR APPREHEND UNESCORTED MEMBERS OF THE R. O. K, A, K. S. C. AND INDIGENOUS CIVILIANS WITHIN THE DIV. AREA. ANY QUESTIONS AS TO HIS AUTHORITY SHOULD BE REFERRED TO THE UNDERSIGNED. HE IS AUTHORISED TO WEAR ITEMS OF MILITARY CLOTHING.		
階　級　　　　　　姓　名 上記者는 英聯邦第一師團憲兵隊所屬 유엔保安警備隊員임을 證明함 上記者는 英聯邦地域內에있어서 護衛되여있지않는 韓國軍 徵用者 一般軍屬에對하여 停止 拘留 逮捕할權限을갖음 上記者의身分에對하여 質疑가有할時는 憲兵隊로問議하시앞 上記者는軍服着用을許可함		
HEIGHT 身　長 _____ WEIGHT 体　重 _____ BUILD 体　格 _____ MARKS 特　徵 _____	MAJOR 少　領 OFFICER COMMANDING 憲 兵 隊 隊 長 1 COMWEL DIV, PRO: COY; 英聯邦第一師團憲兵隊 AUTHORISED WEAPON 武器携帶許可 NO. 番　号 CALIBRE 口　經 MARK AND TYPE 記　號　　類　型	

Identification and warrant issued by the OC I Comwel Div Pro Coy to each member of the UNSG patrolling the Stay Back Line, 1954 to physically monitor any unauthorized crossing. The SBL was continuous and Divisions would ensure there were no gaps at Division boundaries. The manpower for this task would be provided by a special South Korean Army unit termed the United Nations Security Guard (UNSG) who would hire, at United Nations expense, ROKA veterans, former members of the National Police, or persons judged interested and trustworthy.

This programme was implemented in 1 Commonwealth Division during September 1953. About 260 UNSG personnel were deployed in the Division, about 180 along the SBL and another 70 at installations such as reserve ammunition dumps. They were organized as a quasi-military force into three companies, each with three or more platoons. A leader, or company commander, was appointed for each company and platoon.

Each platoon put out three two-man patrols. These interlocking patrols worked in shifts around the clock, thus making it difficult for line crossers to escape detection. This operation was initially organized by the GSO II (Int) at Division Headquarters, and the day-to-day supervision was given to the OC of the Division Field Security Section, commanded by a British captain and consisting of about six other ranks. For a number of reasons, one being the rugged nature of the terrain in 1 Commonwealth Division area, the system never did get underway. Much of the problem was caused by sheer difficulty in reaching the SBL. The line was over the high KAMAKSAN mountain in the centre of the Division area. This made it difficult to check or visit UNSG now deployed. The task of administering this UNSG force was transferred to the OC 1 Commonwealth Provost Company in late January 1954.

This was not an easy or temporary duty. The problem was further clouded because the OC of the FS Section was ill and had been evacuated. It took almost two weeks for the OC, assisted by two Company officers and two sergeants, to complete a reconnaissance, walk the ground, visit the UNSG leaders and, generally, get a handle on things. There were a few UNSG along the line living, as best they could, in locally constructed bunkers. When discussing the situation with Captain Choi, a former Myon Chief and intelligent man, it was obvious that the first task was to provide for their daily food, clothing and equipment. We were somewhat astounded, during a subsequent discussion with the GSOI[143] of the Division, that this was also the responsibility of the OC Provost Company. The detailed Administrative Instruction was eventually produced. Among other details it made the Division Supervisor responsible for the rations, clothing, pay and training of all UNSG allotted to the Division. It specified what the rations would be, pay scales, where and how to get boots and used United

States Army combat clothing. There was even a scale of vehicles, about one ¾ ton truck and one jeep per company. Little of this had been procured or issued. The second in command, Captain Gerry Scott-Wylie, and staff at company headquarters took on the administration problem. The OC and two sergeants, accompanied by the UNSG Company and Platoon officers, reviewed and revised the patrol beats so that each was about 4 to 500 yards one-way. A marked map, showing the patrol bounds, was posted at each Platoon HQ "hoochie". A number of field telephones and batteries were obtained along with rolls of cable. With some instruction from an efficient Signal Corps sergeant, the UNSG, under Choi and Kim, laid a line across the SBL and soon had a most effective telephone communication system. This enabled company leaders to call the OC Provost Company and vice versa. Clothing was requisitioned from a 1 United States Corps Supply Depot, a parade was organized and items issued by our CQMS. The Company Leaders (Choi and Kim) really did most of this and, of course, they had plenty of help. The 21C issued rations of rice, dried fish, kimchi and tea twice weekly to the Company Leader who, in turn, reissued to each Platoon. Pay was handled by the 21C. It was a remarkable sight to see him set out with burlap sacks full of highly inflated Won, to pay the UNSG. Again he made up an Acquittance Roll with each member's name and amount. This was turned over to the Leaders who paid each man in the Company and returned the signed Ack R to the 2/1C. The Leaders were left to organize the patrols, which they did most efficiently. Each Platoon was visited, accompanied by Choi or Kim, at least once each week. There was no point in trying to catch them off guard because of the telephone line and their own moccasin telegraph, however, there was never one instance where the patrols were not on their allotted routes.

Regrettably the UNSG Group allotted for guarding the Division installations was not so successful. In spite of our best efforts we constantly received complaints of missing petrol and even unit stores. It turned out that the UNSG Leader, sent by the UNSG Battalion in Seoul, was simply a scoundrel. The last straw was his habit of withholding a portion of each UNSG's pay for himself. We returned this entire crew to UNGG HQ in Ouijongbu, but not before this Leader attempted to sell the company jeep on the Seoul black market. While we were happy to be rid of this rogue, and his accomplices, it was with genuine regret that we informed Choi and Kim, on the SBL, that the UNSG would be disbanded on 1 November 1954. During the eight months of operating they had detained over 60 line crossers. While the majority were locals returning to their farm or village, a total of six North Korean agents were caught by this group of loyal men. It was probably worth this extraordinary effort, but we will never be certain.

The winding-down process started in September, after what seemed an age of wishing and waiting. Canadian units started to leave by early October. The plan called for a battalion-size group to remain in Korea for a further period, and all other Canadians to be home by Christmas. All stores, weapons and vehicles of United States Army pattern were returned to designated United States Depots. Our Ordnance Corps did a great job in compiling lists of items and arranging schedules. More to the point, the ever generous Americans allowed a credit equal to the full, new value of each item, be it a 2½ ton truck or tent.

The Canadian Provost Corps members of 1 Commonwealth Provost Company were either listed for return to Canada or to remain as a member of a continuing provost unit. This unit would have two sections, one C Pro C and one RMP, to look after a small Commonwealth Brigade slated to remain for a further period.

The continuing provost unit was called: The Commonwealth Division Independent Provost Company, for reasons narrated by Lieutenant J J Hooper, Canadian Provost Corps. Jim remained with this unit for another six months and gives us this illuminating account of its activities during this period:

In the fall of 1954, 1st Commonwealth Division was reduced to a modified Brigade Group, although the formation nomenclature "Division" was retained. Lateral divisional boundaries were redefined inward but forward and rear boundaries remained essentially the same. The new divisional sector was reduced in area to about 60 square miles (4 miles x 15 miles). The Provost element was reduced to an independent unit consisting of a small headquarters and two police sections. The Canadian Provost Corps provided the unit second-in-command and one of the police sections. The unit was located close to Division Headquarters at the north end of Gloucester Valley.

Provost duties did not diminish proportionately with the overall reduction of troops. Traffic control and vehicle road patrols continued to make up the bulk of provost activity. The dust raised from dry dirt roads was blinding and stifling and sometimes dangerous. Disciplinary patrols in local villages were carried out to safeguard soldiers (and their clothing and equipment) from the attractions available therein. The village of Sinsan-ni comes to mind in this regard. A provost "presence" was invaluable and essential to maintain effective liaison and sources of information. Criminal investigations were often expected because of the "local knowledge" of the investigation.

Although the war was over, the possibility of it starting up again was ever present. Formation Headquarters and Signals elements exercised constantly and these exercises always included provost for route signing, traffic control and security support. A night crossing of the Imjin River, in which provost provided support by taping boat entry areas and personnel on both the near and far shores of the river, is one example of our operational support role.

Korea, postwar, was a lovely, boring experience and anything that might cause a laugh or induce a smile was most welcome. Road signs in Gloucester Valley lent themselves to this type of diversion, and two examples come to mind:
1. One bit of black humour read "Drive Carefully You Might Hit Your Replacement."
2. Another was a series of three signs warning of dangerous driving conditions ahead. The first warned of "Soft Shoulders." Below the printing was a picture of a body's bare shoulders.

The second sign warned of "DANGEROUS CURVES." Under this was a picture of another well developed body displaying her charms.

The third sign stated, simply, "Watch Out For Children."

Provost efforts were not always seen as being beneficial to the troops–especially by the troops. Notwithstanding, some activities had to be carried out, among these being the removal from the divisional area of certain young ladies who were providing favours to the troops. On one occasion, as these bodies were being loaded onto the back of a 2½ ton truck for the journey back to I Corps at Ouijongbu, one of them, with baby in arms, called out "Me no sexy, me mama-san". To emphasize her point she bared a breast and proved to those present that she was a nursing mother. Such a demonstration had to be appreciated and she was not sent back to Ouijongbu.

I served as 2 1/c with the 1st Commonwealth Division Independent Provost Company from the fall of 1954 to July 1955 in the rank of Lieutenant. I retired from the Canadian Army (R) in April 1970 as a Planning and Projects officer with the Chief of Personnel Branch in the rank of Major.

Jim Hooper has the distinction of being the last Canadian Provost Corps officer to serve in Korea. He disbanded the unit and returned to Canada in July 1955. All told, from 1950 to 1955, a total of 16 officers and 248 other ranks of the Corps served in Korea. Of them it can be truly said, "they paid their dues". It was no place for the young or neurotic.

16

NATO

Canada's commitment under the NATO Alliance of April 1949 was honoured in 1951 when each of the three Services (Navy, Army and Air Force) contributed a sizeable force for deployment in Europe. In February 1951 Brooke Claxton announced rearmament in no uncertain terms. The Navy would rebuild its fleet, the Army to be expanded to a modern infantry division with all necessary support infrastructure, while the Air Force would have up to 40 squadrons with 12 of these slated for the NATO force in Europe. The defence budget would be increased up to $5 billion to defray the costs, over a three year period. The formations slated for Europe would function as part of a multi-national force designed to defend central European countries against any aggressions, covert or overt, by the sabre-rattling USSR. There would be a Supreme Headquarters Atlantic Pact Europe (SHAPE) commanded by, in the first instance, General Dwight D Eisenhower, who came out of retirement from the president's chair of Columbia University.

The Canadian Army, having just completed raising and training the 25th Infantry Brigade Group for Korea, must now repeat this process and form another brigade group for Germany. Thus 27 Canadian Infantry Brigade was formed in the Summer and Fall of 1951 and was in the Hannover region of northwest Germany by the end of November. There was considerable discussion and some differences of opinion as to whether these Canadian forces would (a) be trained and ready in Canada to move overseas to Germany, or (b) be attached to a British or an American force for operations. Guy Simonds, who was now chief of the General Staff[144] (CGS), took the position that the Brigade Group must reside, work and train in Germany under overall command of the British Army. Foulkes, now Chairman of the Joint Chiefs, favoured leaving the troops in Canada ready for immediate move and to operate under the overall command of the Americans. The result was a compromise whereby the Canadian Brigade functioned under the British Army of the Rhine, while the 12 RCAF squadrons of F-86 Sabre Fighters were closely linked to the United States Air Force. Both elements would be stationed in Europe. In order to avoid some of the trials and tribulations experienced during the recruiting for 25 Brigade, it was decided to revert to the World War II manning system for 27 Brigade. The idea was to recruit from Reserve units to the fullest extent possible. The call went out for volunteers to serve for a minimum eighteen months, including one year abroad, in their present or higher rank.For example, each of four Reserve infantry battalions was asked to provide one company to form an infantry battalion for 27 Brigade. Thus, 1st Highland Battalion was raised from the Seaforths (Vancouver), Canadian Scottish (Victoria), North Nova Scotia Highlanders (Amherst NS) and the 48th Highlanders (Toronto). The authorization of the "kilt" for ceremonial wear may have been an inducement but, in any event, each of these companies was soon recruited to full strength. Other units were made up of a mixture of recruits from civilian life and a smattering of reservists, with some commanders, staff officers and technicians from the thinly stretched Regular Army. The Brigade was equipped from the War Reserve stocks of vehicles, weapons and guns held in two or three large Depots in Central Canada.

The Canadian Provost Corps unit was identical to 25 Canadian Provost Detachment, which was developed six months previously for KOREA. The commanding officer of No 1 Provost Company (Reserve), located in London, Ontario, was appointed to command No 27 Brigade Provost Detachment. Recruits were posted to the unit, which was formed at the Canadian Provost Corps School in Camp Borden. While exact figures are not available, it is known that about 50% came from various Reserve Provost Companies with the remainder a mix of men off civvy street and the odd transfer from other Corps. The vehicles and equipment were issued prior to leaving Borden which greatly assisted in the conduct of training for the unit's primary role of field operations. In the light of future events, it would have been more realistic had the major emphasis been placed on purely police and disciplinary patrol duties, which were to keep this provost unit very busy during the next year. In any case, 27 Brigade Provost Detachment was settled in Hannover, Germany by the 23 November 1951. This was the start of a lengthy period of over 40 years continuous service with the Canadian Army NATO force in Germany.

The Brigade occupied barracks in what had been a large German base during World War II. Hannover had been an air force target during the war and was still in the throes of rebuilding. It was a bustling city, by any standard, with unlimited opportunities for well paid Canadian soldiers to spend their money. The "Gasthofs" (German pubs) were numerous and, apparently, stocked with an unlimited supply of strong German brews. There is an equation here someplace. Simply expressed it was: bright lights, numerous gasthofs and large numbers of friendly females, TIMES, a large number of newly arrived Canadian soldiers, EQUALS, a very large disciplinary problem. This problem was destined to keep provost fully employed 24 hours each day. Short of confining all troops to their quarters, and even this drastic measure was applied, there was simply no way to curb the high incidence of drunkenness, brawling and general rowdiness. The somewhat bewildered local German police (polizei) were happy to report each case to the Canadian APM, Major George Hodgkiss. Fortunately, or perhaps unfortunately, the offence of drunkenness was not viewed with the same degree of disfavour as it would receive in Canada. It was not a particular sin to sing, talk to strangers or embrace a member of the opposite sex on a night out. Nevertheless, they drew the line at fighting, breaking windows or other violent acts. The provost patrols were busy returning those under arrest to their units. The hastily formed guardroom was seldom empty. The job of provost was not made easier by the fact that the Commander was aware of the importance of Canadians displaying a high standard of discipline, good manners and deportment in this International milieu. However, as the units settled in, and busy schedules of work and training were established, so the incidence of disciplinary cases declined. The Hannover experience made it clear to senior Army planners that the whole question of maintaining a considerable force in Germany would have to be reviewed.

There were several disadvantages to the current situation, apart from a temporary discipline problem. If, as originally planned, all troops would be returned and replaced by equivalents from Canada every year, then it was obvious that a much larger pool of trained replacements was required than now existed in Canada, ie, one division of three brigades. One year rotation meant that there must be a minimum ratio of 3 to 1 (home and overseas) if the soldier was to spend one year away for every three years at home. Bearing in mind that Korea was still going strong, it was apparent that the overall manpower of the Army must be increased. Furthermore, the Hannover region was not suited for the field training necessary to fit a mobile brigade group for its anticipated role. Following a hard sell by the CGS in Ottawa it was agreed that the Army would be increased by another three infantry battalions, one armoured and one artillery regiment, bringing the total arms units to 12 infantry battalions, three armoured regiments and four artillery regiments. Further increases were also authorized for Corps such as Canadian Provost Corps, where rotation was done on an individual as opposed to a unit basis. Finally, the decision was made to extend the normal tour in Germany from one to three years for all ranks. Married men would be authorized to take their families with them, at public expense. Following extensive negotiation with the German government in Bonn, arrangements were made for the construction of a new Canadian Camp in Westphalia Province. The area selected was near the town of SOEST, with subsidiary camps at Werl, Hemer and Iserlohn. It would be built by Germany on a cost sharing arrangement and was to include a full range of buildings for single quarters (barracks), stores, training and administrative buildings, housing for married personnel, schools for dependent children, chapels, recreation centres and a "Maple Leaf" shopping centre. Built to Canadian specification this new base was to be ready for occupancy by mid 1954.

The first rotation of 27 Brigade unit took place in November 1952, and all elements of the new brigade were in Germany by Christmas, including the replacements for the Provost Detachment and the new APM, Major B W E (Bill) Lee, the former CO of the Canadian Provost Corps School. The time of the Provost Detachment was about evenly divided between so-called camp policing and traffic control duties for the many moves and tactical exercises of Brigade units. Much progress was made in establishing contact and good working relations with local German authorities and some general thorny problems of jurisdiction, especially with respect to travel on German streets and roads by Canadian military vehicles. The enforced mobility of Canadian Forces had given the officers and men of the Corps a comprehensive understanding of National diversity and the compromises necessary to work in harmony with people of different cultures, backgrounds and languages. Perhaps the most important lesson learned by members of the Corps was that, other than for law and order situations, military police must never use or condone force in the resolution of disputes or issues. Major Bill Lee was a staunch proponent of this philosophy and did much, during his tenure, to advance it.

It is one thing for the Armed Forces of a country to serve in the territory of another in times of war; it is a much different situation during conditions of peace when sovereign rights must be protected. None of the European nations, especially those occupied by the enemy, were overly concerned about questions of protocol of the jurisdiction of allied troops in their land during the war of 1939–45. However, the North Atlantic Treaty of 1949 provided for each member nation to station troops in western European countries for "collective" defence against the threat of attack by the USSR. As explained elsewhere, Canada's military contribution, commencing in 1951, provided a military force of Navy, Army and Air Force being more or less permanently stationed in several west European countries. Furthermore, the dependents of Canadian troops were also located with them in the various camps and bases. In order to define the status of such forces while in the territory of another party to the NATO Agreement, each member nation signed a further "Agreement Between The Parties To The North Atlantic Treaty Regarding The Status Of Forces Agreement". This Agreement was written in clear terms and defined the rules to be followed for living, travel, law enforcement and jurisdiction of both the SENDING and RECEIVING states. Some of the highlights were:

- members of a "sender" state must respect and obey the laws of a "receiver" state, and refrain from political activity;
- military members could move from one state to another on production, when demanded, of an authorized identity card; civilian dependents required a passport;
- "receiving" states could either accept a valid driving permit or licence issued by a "sender" state, or issue its own without a fee or test. As previously noted, the Canadian Provost Corps Platoon in Germany issued Driver Permits to Canadian Army drivers and their dependents;
- military members must wear uniforms when crossing a frontier as a unit or formation; service vehicles are required to have a distinctive national marking;
- military members may carry arms when authorized by orders;
- the military authorities of the "sender" state have the right to exercise all criminal and disciplinary jurisdiction, conferred on them by their own military law, within the "receiving" state;
- the "receiving" state has jurisdiction over the military or civilian members of a "sender" state with respect to offences committed within the territory and punishable by the law of the "receiving" state.

The Agreement goes on to provide for consultation, cooperation and the implementation of its terms in connection with such matters as arrest, custody, speedy trials and interpreters. It also outlines the procedure for settling claims for damages made by one state against another, the use of local civilian labour, the purchase of goods and services, the use of local facilities and customs regulations. Of much importance to provost, the

Agreement specifically authorized military police of each party to maintain law, order and security in the camps or bases occupied by their own force. Outside the premises military police may be employed to maintain order and discipline subject to mutually satisfactory arrangements being made with the authorities of the "receiving" state. This amounted to a formal requirement to carry out liaison between provost and German local police on an ongoing basis. These close working relationships were invaluable in maintaining trust, goodwill and cooperation in often difficult circumstances. It is not putting it too strongly to state that a major portion of the success of NATO was due to the Status of Forces Agreement, a most practical and sensible document. Much credit is also due to the military police who had a great deal of responsibility for its day-to-day application. This Agreement contains twenty (XX) articles in fourteen pages and was signed on 19 June 1951, in London, by representatives of Belgium, Luxembourg, Netherlands, Norway, Portugal, Great Britain and the United States of America. It has been promulgated throughout Canada's Armed Forces as Appendix XIV of Queens Regulations and Orders.

The first rotation was completed during November 1952. The new units were only in Hannover for a short period due to the fact that the new brigade camp at Soest was ready for occupancy except for the dependents housing. The whole of the Brigade, now 1 Canadian Infantry Brigade, moved from Hannover and was settled in Soest, Hemer, Iserlohn and Werl by mid December 1953. Major J A (John) Dowsett took over as the APM from his previous post at the Canadian Army Liaison Establishment (CALE) in London, just across the English Channel. Needless to say the provost were busy with traffic duties during the move, which was completed smoothly in three days. The families of married men started to arrive early in the new year. Although married quarters would not be ready for another six months, dependents were moved subject to the proviso that they had secured satisfactory accommodation in the Soest area. A significant number took up residence on this basis and moved into married quarters as they became available. Some families found their local rental arrangements most satisfactory and life "on the local economy" pleasant so that there would always be a sizeable number opting for this lifestyle. Many enduring friendships between Canadian and German families grew out of this situation. It should be mentioned that a rental deduction was made from the soldier's pay when the family were occupying married quarters on a DND establishment.

We have dwelled on the matter of families living on Canadian military bases because this was to have a profound affect on the duties and responsibilities of provost, both at home and abroad, for years to come. It was a "good news–bad news" situation. The benefits of the policy were manifested in improved morale, discipline, less time loss and more money saved by the soldier, not to mention his absolute peace of mind. The "downers", from the policing point of view were: stray dogs, kitchen fires, vandalism, family squabbles, truancy and public safety problems. In other words, a large Canadian military base was beset with exactly the same amount of human intransigence as that found in any village or town of comparable size in Canada. The lion's share of dealing with these problems fell to the resident Canadian Provost Corps unit.

The third rotation took place late in 1955. By now the Canadian NATO Brigade in Germany was well established and thriving. It will be noted that the "tour of duty" had been extended to three years due to the policy of all married ranks being accompanied by their family. There were also many additional benefits from this policy, one of the most important being that it gave the commander, staff and units sufficient time to become oriented and develop the routines, training and technical skills so necessary for the success of a disparate force such as the NATO army. In the long run it was probably cheaper to do it this way and, most certainly, less dislocation in the lives of a great many Canadians.

A few changes were made in the size and shape of the Canadian Provost Corps element of the Brigade. A Field Detention Barracks was formed and was operational by July 1953. This was a functionally designed building located in Fort Henry (Soest). A feature of its design was a round, central rotunda with cell wings running out like the spokes of a wheel. This made for good access and control, however, it required a slight increase guard staff over the linear corridor type building. As in Canada, it also received RCAF detainees from No 1 Air Division, located a little further south. As a result of the "family in residence" policy, and resultant workload this imposed, the provost detachment strength was increased by an increment of one officer and 26 other ranks. This meant that there would always be a police detachment present on the base during the many field exercises, which required the provost sections to carry-out their regular operational role. The title of the unit was now changed from "Detachment" to "Platoon" as more descriptive of its size and role.

The fourth rotation was completed in November 1958 when 4 Canadian Infantry Brigade Group took over from the 2nd at Soest, Hemer, Werl and Iserlohn, which was the Armoured regiment's camp. Major J M (Jim) Walsh took over as APM of the Brigade Group, which was commanded by Brigadier Cameron B Ware, a veteran infantry commander from the Sicily and Italy campaigns of World War II. Jim Walsh had commanded No 8 Provost Company of 4 Canadian Armoured Division during the Riechwald, Hochwald and western Holland fighting in Northwest Europe. One of his officers, Captain W J (Walter) Dabros, who went on to reach Brigadier General rank, wrote a most comprehensive article for the Canadian Army Journal issue of 1961. He describes the activities of the Brigade Provost with great clarity and insight. This excellent article, which reflects the hitherto unheralded contribution made by the men of the Corps who served in this NATO Brigade, is reprinted as Appendix "C" to this history.

The regular three year "rotations" continued and, indeed, became a focal point for service in the Canadian Army. The main feature of the tour in Germany was training, and it was this aspect that greatly improved the overall professionalism of the Army. A number of factors contributed to the high standards which were achieved. The absence of long, cold Canadian winters meant more training time; the training facilities were first class; new equipment[145], weapons and vehicles could be tested and absorbed successfully; it provided the opportunity to work with our allies as part of a large, integrated command. Finally, and most important, it enabled the new tactics of dispersal and rapid concentration which arose from the always present threat of the nuclear explosion on the battlefield, to be practised and refined. As a result, this relatively small Brigade Group became a most efficient fighting force.

Much thought and discussion, by the Canadian military, arose out of the prospect of nuclear explosions on the battlefield and the probable effect on tactics, organization and equipment. In general it resulted in smaller but highly mobile formations such as brigade groups. There must be no large concentrations of troops for lengthy periods of time; concentration had to be achieved in terms of time and space, which meant units and formations travelling much greater distances into battle. The problems of command and control became increasingly difficult, requiring greater initiative by junior leaders. The provost of the NATO Brigade were involved in many exercises designed to practice these concepts. It was now commonplace to think in terms of a 100 mile road and cross-country move of a formation. This doctrine, and the manner in which it affected the employment of provost, is clearly illustrated in this account given by Captain André D (Andy) Gauthier[146] during his tenure as commander of No 4 Provost Platoon in 1964.

Shortly after I assumed command of 4 MP Pl in 1964 in Soest (Germany) we were involved in a major exercise with a tactical move of the Brigade's 1,400 vehicles over several routes and a long distance. As everyone connected with controlling road movement knows, route signing is a critical (albeit unglamorous) factor in success. In those days MP route signs were made of plywood and sets of these signs were carried by one jeep-team designated the "Signing Party" in each of the platoon's three sections. The Signing Party's quarter-ton trailer was crammed with these heavy, bulky signs plus the wooden stakes and tools needed to mount them. All other jeep-teams in the platoon carried a variety of personal and platoon stores and equipment with no room for signs other than a few "emergency" ones such as the Disc Directional.

Once I had given my orders for the Brigade's move, the Sections headed off to man and sign their assigned routes. As I was driving down the main axis I learned by radio that a change in the tactical picture necessitated a drastic change in this route. As luck would have it I arrived at the key road junction where this change needed to occur. Together with my MPs on point duty at the turn we removed the Disc signs leading up to the previously planned turn (and the confirmation signs after that turn) and substituted "straight ahead" signs for the new direction. This exhausted the few emergency signs both our jeeps carried! Meanwhile, the old route was still being signed dutifully by the Signing Party that had no radio by which I could recall them (each five-jeep section had only one radio–in the Section Commander's jeep)! While our immediate actions would redirect the coming traffic on the new route, we had no more signs with which to mark that route along its entire length. For lack of such signs I had to commandeer a number of troops, which I dropped off along the new route, as Pointsmen. The move was a success but I was left with a burning desire to correct the huge problem of inflexibility caused by our route signing materials and their concentration in only three of our 17 platoon vehicles!

After that exercise I researched what other NATO MPs were using as signing material and found that USMPs had just started experimenting with a few (very costly) aluminium signs and some cardboard "Scotchlite" reflective material covered signs. Some quick experimentation at home led me to try sheets of oiled Stencil paper, available in our Brigade. We found that this paper could withstand rain for several hours and could resist "curling" in the wind if made more rigid by mounting it with a slight ridge or kink to it. Moreover, we discovered that paper signs could be mounted (and later removed) much faster than plywood signs using a stapler or masking tape instead of plywood's nails and hammered stakes. The greatest benefit which immediately accrued to paper signs, however, was the dramatic reduction in bulk and weight of a given quantity of these versus plywood signs (see photo comparison). With their introduction a small box in each of our 17 platoon vehicles, henceforth, carried the paper equivalent of the entire stock of plywood signs previously available within 4 MP PL! Never again were we caught in the inflexible bind of having only three jeeps capable of signing routes. While this achievement may not quite rank with Atomic Fusion, it considerably eased our "Policeman's Lot"!

The fact that Andy Gauthier "commandeered" some troops to act as route guides speaks for itself. One can see eyebrows being raised, however, he got it done, surely the bottom line. That he also did something about equipment deficiencies and provost deployment drills tells us something about his dedication to getting it right. These were indicators of the professionalism that was becoming apparent in all ranks of the Corps. This three-year tour in Germany was a heaven-sent opportunity for all ranks, from Major to Lance Corporal, to grow and mature in their chosen career path.

17

Towards Professionalism

If there was complete unanimity on any one aspect of Canada's peacetime Army it would be the concept of professionalism. Commencing with the expansion of the early 1950s there was a growing desire by all ranks, from the CGS down to the private, to achieve and display skill and efficiency in their chosen profession. Our soldiers were serving in multi-national forces in Korea, NATO and around the world in a variety of peace-keeping ventures. They soon began to realize, with pride and satisfaction, that they were equal to or better than most of the soldiers with whom they came in contact. This state of affairs was no fluke. Successive Chiefs of General Staff (Foulkes, Simonds and Graham) must take a great deal of credit for wise policies relating to the Army's roles, its organization and the selection, training and employment of its manpower[147]. Add to these policies good pay, sound administration, vastly improved equipment and a variety of challenging postings, and the end result was a steadily improving, cohesive group of soldiers. The Canadian Provost Corps was cast easily in this mould. Since this was the first ever Canadian Army Military Police organization in peacetime there were no sacred cows or outdated habits to overcome. In other words, the senior Corps officers, warrant officers and NCOs of the day did not, as a conscious policy, define their aim as developing professionalism. They simply accepted, and enthusiastically supported, the concept of soldiering as an interesting, honourable and rewarding career.

The decision taken in 1950 to concentrate service personnel, and their dependents, in large military establishments at home and abroad, had far reaching effects on the requirement for police and security services within the Canadian Army. It resulted in the formation of some 21 camps and stations across the country where servicemen and their dependents resided in self-contained communities. Local municipal officials were not prepared to assume responsibility or find the additional resources which were required to administer the many essential services such as schools, fire, police or safety. Consequently, it was essential that military police be available to carry out basic police functions in the military community. Canadian Provost Corps personnel were also required for several other commitments such as: the two overseas Brigades; three Service Detention Barracks (SDBs); the Canadian Provost Corps School; NDHQ Security Guard: the Emergency Federal Government Command Post (EASE); A and T staff for Militia and the service police elements of infantry battalions and other units and headquarters. It was clear to Army Commanders and staffs by mid 1951 that the Corps must be allocated sufficient manpower resources to enable it to discharge its role in a rapidly expanding Army. A comprehensive review of the Corps manpower requirements was carried out from 1951 through 1954. This review was based on consideration of the following premises:

- service police duties required twenty-four hour daily coverage;
- in many camps and isolated stations the detachment is the Command Post for administrative purposes during silent hours and weekends;
- the local detachment is the only available standby force to deal with emergencies such as fires, serious accidents or blackouts;
- the rotation replacements required for operational Canadian Provost Corps units operating with various United Nations (Peacekeeping) and NATO Forces were drawn from this pool of manpower.

The final review was completed over a three year period, albeit most of the changes were in place by early 1953. It established a Corps organization which remained fairly stable for the next fifteen years. An overview of the structure and deployment of Canadian Provost Corps units and headquarters is given below.

The Provost Marshal's Office was located at 312 Laurier Avenue, East in Ottawa. The position was upgraded from Lieutenant Colonel to Colonel in 1954. The staff consisted of a Deputy (DPM) Lieutenant Colonel; a Major (Plans and Training); a Captain (Operations Officer); a Regimental Sergeant Major (Records and Clerical); a Staff Sergeant (Crime Reader) plus a combined military and civilian clerical staff of six. The Provost Marshal continued to report to the Adjutant General and was responsible for setting policy on provost technical matters. He was responsible to the Adjutant General for the supervision and efficiency of the Canadian Provost

Corps units on all matters related to their duties. He actively assisted and advised the AHQ Staff on the career planning, training, selection, promotions and postings of all Corps personnel. He had a direct channel to Canadian Provost Corps units, headquarters of formations and other units on matters related to provost duties. He provided policy and direction on the day-to-day work of provost through the periodic issue of Provost Marshal Instructions (PMIs) to all Canadian Provost Corps units. His overall status was that of Corps Director.

A Provost Company was established for each of the five Commands. The senior Canadian Provost Corps officer was redesignated the Command Provost Marshal (CPM) as being more descriptive of this position. The strength of these companies varied to reflect the military population and activity. Each Company, as in World War II, had detachments in the areas of troop concentrations. The CPM was also the Officer Commanding the Company and normally delegated responsibilities to Detachment Commanders, who might be an officer or senior NCO depending on local circumstances and conditions. Detachment Commanders reported to the local Commander daily. There was a close relationship between GOCs, Area and Camp Commanders and Provost Officers, at all levels. The Corps established the nature and extent of all provost duties. The local Commander ordered priorities but hopefully never told the responsible provost officer or NCO "how to do it". The Canadian Provost Corps organization for the Commands is shown in the following chart.

Apart from a half-hearted attempt at conscription during 1914–1918 and again in 1939–1945, the Canadian government has always relied on its citizens to VOLUNTEER for military service. There are many pros and cons to this question but the fact remains that the policy of "volunteering" has been moderately successful, albeit very costly and often an unfair method of manning the Canadian forces. For example, the scarcity of front line soldiers in World War II would not have happened had there been universal conscription. Likewise, the enormous delays and problems of recruiting the Korean force arose from "volunteerism" and was greatly aggravated by the political edict to "sign them up" and "ask no questions". Given this somewhat sketchy overview, it is not surprising that the Canadian Armed Forces, particularly the Army, devoted considerable time and effort to screening applicants for military service. As demonstrated in the recent Gulf War, the army of today is an incredibly complex and highly technical machine requiring a great many skilled technicians to start it up and keep it running. The demands placed on the gunner, tank driver and infantry platoon leader are a far cry from those of the bowmen employed by King

Canadian Provost Units as at January 1955

Type of Unit	Comds Establishment	Rank	Location of detachments
Eastern Comd Provost Coy (Halifax)	64 (all ranks)	Major	Halifax, Camp Gagetown, St John's, NFLD
Quebec Comd Provost Coy (Montreal)	96	Major	Montreal, Quebec, Valcartier
Central Comd Provost Coy (Oakville)	130	Lt Col	Toronto, London, Kingston, Petawawa, Camp Borden
*Prairie Comd Provost Coy (Winnipeg)	56	Major	Winnipeg, Regina, Rivers, Shilo, Fort Churchill
*Western Comd Provost Coy (Edmonton)	92	Lt Col	Edmonton, Calgary Wainwright, Victoria, Vancouver, Chilliwack

*Note: Prairie Command was disbanded in 1962 and the Provost Company was absorbed by Western. The CPM was upgraded to Lieutenant-Colonel rank.

Service Detention Barracks			
8, 10 & 14 SDB	75 (25 all ranks ea)	Capt	Gagetown, Borden, Edmonton

Note: New standard design barracks were completed by 1956.

The Canadian Provost School	88 (all ranks) (12 officers (5 WOs (6 S Sgts (23 Sgts (30 Cpls (12 Ptes	Lt Col	Camp Borden, 1946–1953 Camp Shilo, 1953–1961 Camp Borden, 1961–

Note: There were 29 purely administrative positions of which 12 were members of other Corps (RCOC, RCASC and RCEME) ie, storemen, cooks and artificers.

Field Units (1 Div Pro Coy plus NATO Bde)	160 (all ranks) (1 & 2 Pro Pls) (3 Pro Pl (NATO) (1 NCR(A) NATO)	Majors(2)	Gagetown, Petawawa, Borden and Germany
Miscellaneous EASE, A & T Staff, Inf Bns, Korea	212		ESF Bn, NDHQ Sec GD,
TOTAL	973		

Harold at Stamford Bridge. Likewise, the unique demands made on the service policeman of today's Canadian Army require that careful attention be paid to the flow of volunteers into this specialty.

The question is: what are these unique demands, and how can they be satisfied during the <u>selection</u> and training process? Ask any experienced provost officer or, for that matter, any police superintendent and he will mention qualities such as physical fitness, discipline, reliability, honesty and emotional stability.

The majority of these qualities cannot be measured by a scale, a stopwatch or stethoscope. For this reason the Canadian Army, to its everlasting credit, developed a Personnel Selection Branch staffed by skilled and highly qualified officers whose duty it was to develop, administer and follow-up on a battery of tests. These tests were designed to measure the so-called personality traits of all Canadian army personnel, and this they did with much success. The Personnel Selection Service was initially rejected by many senior commanders, however it gained broad acceptance and support, especially in the Canadian Provost Corps, starting about the mid 1950s. The PSOs were remarkably successful in their efforts to stop the practice of trying to put "square pegs in round holes". Lieutenant Colonel M A (Moe) Martin[148], a former Canadian Provost Corps officer and a highly qualified Personnel Selection Officer, gives us this insight on his work in this area.

Personnel Selection Officers (PSOs) had long been assigned to the various Army Personnel Depots. PSOs were either from the professionally trained component of the then General List or were extra regimentally employed officers of the major corps, including the Canadian Provost Corps. Before reaching the assessment stage recruits had to meet various criteria, including education (grade eight for most trades including service police, which alone had a minimum height requirement). The PSO assessment was based on two procedures: a test to determine the applicant's learning ability and an interview to determine behaviourial or emotional suitability. The well known Army M Test, used extensively during the Second World War, was a 211 item test yielding three sub-scores: verbal skills (which, coincidentally, reflect level of education); non-verbal abilities which indicated the learning capacity, for example, of those for whom, in those years, schooling was not readily available; and a score indicating mechanical ability. The average score of young male Canadians was 130, the minimum necessary for entry into most trades and corps including the Canadian Provost Corps. About two thirds of applicants scored between 100 (the minimum for entry) and 160 (the minimum for officer applicants).

The second test was administered to support the interview. The Minnesota Multiphasic Personality Inventory (MMPI) was originally developed to assist in the diagnosis of emotional/mental diseases in clinical psychiatric settings. It was a 373 item test yielding nine diagnostic scores. Four other scores were used to assess the nature of the response "set" and so determine the usefulness of the diagnostic scores – whether the "set" was an attempt to present oneself in the best light rather than accurately, was one of carelessness or of simple lying for whatever reason, and so on. Canadian Army norms (rather than those obtained from clinical settings) and the distribution of scores (which tend to cluster about the average with fewer toward the higher and lower ends of the score range) were based on the test results of 2,772 Canadian males. Thus, scores relevant to the Army applicant context were available reliably identifiable. High scores were not necessarily indicative of some mental illness but provided an indication of the area of an applicant's behaviourial or emotional background to be explored in the interview. So the groundwork was laid for attending to any special concern about the stability of the personality and the maturity of those destined for the Provost Corps. The overall process, testing and interviewing was, obviously, not infallible but a reduction in the numbers of enrollees who could not adjust to the demands made on them was achieved, particularly when the demands were stringent.

The Personnel Selection Service was introduced in September 1941 with the primary purpose of spotting potential officers among the thousands enlisting at Recruiting Centres. This service waned for a period, following World War II, but was revived following the Korean experience in order to assist in ensuring that recruits were allocated to the duty for which they were best suited. This somewhat scientific approach to the selection process did not find favour in the British Army, probably because Winston Churchill, in one of his famous notes to the CIGS, forbade the "quartering of these charlatans on healthy young people". One of our most successful wartime commanders, Major General Chris Vokes, CB, CBE, DSO, CD, was a firm supporter. He said "... they quite often know what they're talking about, and by the end of World War II they had developed tests that were quite remarkable. When they rejected a man they were usually right." One notable example illustrates this point. Somewhere in the mid 1950s a recruit, we will call him "Jones", arrived at the Canadian Provost Corps School. The Command Personnel Selection people were doing one of their periodic "follow-up" checks conducted to validate the results of the MMPI test, described by Moe Martin. It so happened that "Jones" was one of those selected in the random sample for the check. Sure enough, "Jones" was not making it in the Canadian Provost Corps. His training assessment report was full of "not reliable", "untrustworthy", "untruthful" comments by his recruit class officer. It was then determined, in conversation with the PSO, that his MMPI test clearly showed an unacceptable variant under the "LIE" factor. "Jones" was subsequently released. He had been enrolled only because the whole Army was suffering from a shortage of new recruits. So we took a chance. The Corps derived a great deal of benefit from this selection process which saved countless time and much expense by excluding during the intake process those who did not measure up to minimum Corps standards.

In keeping with the theme of this segment (Towards Professionalism) it is now time to mention some measures which, in various ways, contributed to the general well-being of the Canadian Provost Corps. Some of these were innovations which were confined solely to the Corps, others were an extension of common Army practices and, certainly, none of them were instituted contrary to general policies of the day. Without lengthy detail, because most are self explanatory, here are some of those Corps policies.

The Provost Marshal and senior corps officers attended the Annual Canadian Association of Chiefs of Police Convention as full-fledged members.

Officers and NCOs attended courses at the Royal Canadian Mounted Police College for Corps officers and NCO's.

Officers were sent on highly specialized courses in United States universities such as Purdue and Northwestern to keep abreast of latest developments in arson investigation, terrorism, and crowd control.

Officers, warrant officers and NCOs attended the United States Military Police School, Fort Gordon, Georgia on advanced policing and investigation courses.

A total of nine Canadian Provost Corps officers, of captain or major rank, graduated from the one year course at the Canadian Army Staff College in Kingston from 1948 to 1965. These officers were then qualified for Staff employment throughout the Army.

The posting of Canadian Provost Corps officers to junior staff positions at various headquarters throughout the Army was actively promoted. This was referred to as Extra Regimental Employment (ERE). It broadened the officer's horizon and also liberated vacancies for the promotion of Corps officers otherwise denied advancement due to establishment restrictions.

Junior Canadian Provost Corps officers were posted to an infantry battalion for a one year tour as a Platoon Commander. By mutual agreement of both Corps they were treated the same as all infantry platoon commanders, including the completion by the Commanding Officer and Company Commander of his annual Personal Evaluation Report. Direct benefits included qualification as parachutist, tactical knowledge of an infantry battalion, acquisition of the French language when with the R22^{e}R, and gaining an intimate knowledge of the life of a private in the infantry.

Selected Corps officers completed a tour in the United Kingdom as a participant in the British RMP – Canadian Provost Corps Officer Exchange Programme. These tours were of two to three years duration and were of much benefit to both Corps. Commenced in 1952 they are still in effect.

Officers were rotated through a range of Corps positions with a mandatory tour as an Instructor at the Canadian Provost Corps School or in an A and T staff instruction position.

Much attention was devoted by the Provost Marshal and officers of the Corps to the intake of officers. The Army in peacetime adopted a correct policy of commissioning officers from a variety of backgrounds. This precluded the tendency towards inflexible mind sets which inevitably occur when everyone is cast in the same mould. The Corps had, at any given time, officers from sources such as RMC, University COTC, OCP Direct Intake (young recruits who met basic officer standards), transfers from other Corps and commissions from the ranks. In later years many able and experienced NCO's were given so-called Short Service Commissions. They did an excellent job as lieutenants, captains and majors. As mentioned elsewhere in this story, officers who could not or would not qualify for higher ranks were released: lieutenants at age 45, captains at age 47 and majors at 49 years of age.

Promotion in peacetime can be painfully slow, especially for the noncommissioned ranks, unless the matter is kept under active review. Any good soldier worth his salt will aspire to get ahead, if not in his current corps then in another where he sees opportunities for advancement. When he has completed the required training, acquired all qualifications and can see absolutely no outlet ahead for promotion, it is highly unlikely he will stay in that environment. He then exercises his option of transferring to another corps or taking his release. In either event the Corps loses. Measures were initiated in the Canadian Provost Corps to improve efficiency and provide a reasonable career path for the noncommissioned ranks. Ensuring that Standards for Qualification in rank and/or trade were applied strictly but fairly. The normal progression, and average time in each rank before promotion was:

- Pte to L Cpl   6 months   *Gp 1 Svc Pol
- L Cpl to Cpl   4 years   *Gp 2 Svc Pol
                                    *Jr NCO Course
- Cpl to Sgt   5 years   *Gp 3 Pvc Pol or
                                    Gp 3 Discip and
                                    *Sr NCO Course
- Sgt to S Sgt   5 years   Gp 4 Investigator
- S Sgt to Warrant Officer 4 years All above mandatory qualifications

*Denotes mandatory qualification prior to promotion.

The overall rank structure of the Corps provided a balanced ratio of positions for each rank from private to warrant officer. This precluded dead ends for any rank. The approximate ratio was seven privates for each corporal, four corporals for each sergeant, and so on. For this reason the rank of staff sergeant was introduced in the Command Provost Companies, even though it was seldom seen in a Field Provost Company. This provided an outlet for sergeants and was also required where a detachment had two or more sergeants, as frequently happened.

Much emphasis was placed on the development of qualified instructors. Most senior NCOs at the School were required to take the excellent Methods of Instruction course at the School of Infantry. This was an Army-wide course open to all Corps. A high percentage of instructors at the School were qualified Method of Instruction instructors.

All ranks were required to pass Tests of Elementary Training (Ts OET) annually. This was refresher training to ensure all ranks maintained the skills and knowledge in those subjects necessary in war but seldom used in peace, eg, small arms; shooting; nuclear, biological and chemical warfare (NBCW); fieldcraft and the current organization of Canadian Provost Corps field units. This training was taken seriously and was largely responsible for winning the prestigious Cambridge Challenge Bowl[149] in 1955. This trophy was donated to the Canadian Army by the last departing British regiment in 1903.

An annual Personal Evaluation Report was completed for <u>all</u> ranks of the Canadian Provost Corps, including privates and lance corporals. This was introduced in the Corps even though it was not mandatory throughout the Army. It paid huge dividends in ensuring that all were employed to their full potential.

Towards Professionalism 211

Misconduct, poor performance or continued indifference could, and did, lead to release or reallocation to another Corps.

It is sometimes strange how a series of seemingly unrelated events can produce an unexpected and far-reaching result. Such was the case in the early 1950s when the Corps received and infusion of first-class policemen from the London Metropolitan Police (UK). One cannot be sure whether the story begins with Sir Robert Peel, the slow trickle of Canadian Provost Corps recruits or Captain John Dowsett. The account of the Canadian NATO Brigade moving to Hannover is also an ingredient because it was largely due to the sizeable groups of Canadians on leave in London that the decision was made, in early 1951, to install a Canadian Provost Corps detachment in London. John Dowsett[150] was given the task of going to London and organizing this provost element. John has given us this account of some spin-off from this posting.

In many events in life it is often better to be lucky than good, and so it was with the recruitment for the Canadian Provost Corps of a large number of police constables from the London Metropolitan Police Force, in the early 1950s.

I was posted to the Canadian Army Liaison Establishment in London, England in February 1952 to organize a military police detachment in London. The first person hired for the detachment was a Mrs. Ratcliffe to fill the position of clerk / secretary. Mrs. Ratcliffe happened to be married to a Canadian soldier from World War II who was now a member of the London Metropolitan Police. I received authority to enlist Police Constable J C Ratcliffe as a detachment member because it was believed his knowledge of London and the various courts and police stations would be quite useful.

About six months after my arrival in England the Canadian Army decided to launch a recruiting drive in the United Kingdom to fill a serious deficiency in skilled tradesmen, one of these designated shortages was in military policemen. I was placed in charge of the overall recruiting programme which, from the outset, was highly successful for all Corps. The recruitment of J C Ratcliffe, and the appearance of Canadian Provost Corps detachment members in various police stations in London, sparked a high degree of interest amongst the constabulary, the majority of whom were veterans of the British Army. The Metropolitan Police was, at this time, engaged in a somewhat bitter dispute with its members over wages and working conditions. When these policemen learned about Canadian Army salary scales, which were significantly better than their own, and discovered that the Canadian Army would pay for the movement of dependents, furniture and effects from England to Canada, applications for enlistment in the Canadian Provost Corps flooded into my office. Ratcliffe and the other detachment members provided most of the groundwork for the recruiting drive while I was left to process the enrolment into the Canadian Provost Corps of a large number of skilled and experienced police officers who provided many years of valuable service to the Canadian Army.

These former constables from the London Metropolitan Police Force settled into their new positions as members of the Canadian Army, in the Canadian Provost Corps, quickly and smoothly. In a little over one year there were about 55 of these men wearing the Corps badge and a MP armband in units and detachments across Canada. They were absolutely first-class and came at a time when, due to rapid expansion, the Corps was stretched thin. Many of these former London Bobbies went on to higher rank and positions of responsibility in the Corps. Nearly all rose to sergeant rank and at least three became commissioned officers. Sergeant Reg High[151] tells how he came to the Corps.

Having served and fought with a British Army line regiment during World War II, I was imbued with the spirit of regimental pride, that is, pride in one's cap badge. On demobilization I, subsequently, joined The Metropolitan Police, London, England, and, once again, I had a cap badge to be proud of. In 1954 the Canadian Army was recruiting military policemen in England and they made me an offer which, on economic grounds, I couldn't refuse. Having experienced the best of soldiering and police work the job presented no foreseeable challenge, but the monetary side was the real motivation for joining at the time. However, I had not been with the Corps for too long before I realized that, once again, I had a cap badge to be proud of. A pride that has lasted to this very day.

A long standing deficiency was remedied with the publication of a series of Corps manuals during the period 1957 to 1962. These publications contained the doctrine, methods and techniques required for the performance of provost duties in peace and war. The following is a listing of these Canadian Army Manuals of Training (CAMTs), with a brief description of their content:

CAMT 10-1 PROVOST DUTIES, 1957
This manual was designed to provide direction for the efficient performance of provost duties in static environments. It included Chapters on: The Service Policeman; Arrest and Custody; Jurisdiction; Patrols (town, train, foot and mobile); Traffic Check Points; Car Parks; Reports (offence, accident, occurrence, patrol); Books and Records; Evidence (rules, preser-

vation, disposal); Guard and Security Duties. Actual specimen reports, forms and documents relative to provost duties were shown in Appendices.

CAMT 10-2 THE CANADIAN PROVOST CORPS IN WAR, 1960
This manual deals with the provost service in support of an infantry brigade group under conditions of nuclear or conventional war, in the foreseeable future. It includes information on: Role and Organization; Command and Control; Planning; Orders and Deployment; Tactical Movement and Traffic Control; Prisoners of War, Refugees and Stragglers.

CAMT 10-3 TRAFFIC CONTROL, 1962
The aim of this manual was to provide guidance for the control of military traffic. It was written specifically for members of the Canadian Provost Corps, but is also applicable to all personnel concerned with this function. The following detail is covered: Glossary of Terms; Characteristics; Conflicts; Movement Planning; Staff Responsibilities (staff, units and provost); Selection and Reconnaissance of Routes; Systems of Movement (packet, capacity and average speed and density); Time and Space Calculations; Systems of Traffic Control; Methods of Traffic Control (route signing, intersection control, use of wireless communication, mobile route patrols, defile control, route clearance and recovery); Operational Parking of Columns. CAMT 10-3 is well illustrated and contains the relevant NATO Standardization Agreement (STANAG N° 2025) governing Military Road Traffic.

CAMT 10-4 SERVICE PRISONS and DETENTION BARRACKS, 1957
This manual provided direction for officers and men concerned with the care and custody of military personnel committed to a place of detention. Regulations for Service Prisons and Detention Barracks are published as an Appendix to QR (Army) Vol II. Its content includes: Admission Procedure; Custody and Control; Treatment; Restraints; Corrective Measures; Disturbances; Visitors; Escorts; Remission System, Release and Transfers.

CAMT 10-5 INVESTIGATIVE PROCEDURES, 1958
The aim of this manual was to provide special investigators of the Canadian Provost Corps with the basic information required to successfully complete criminal investigations. It includes information on: Sources of Information; Memory and Observation; Physical Descriptions; Evidence; Admissions and Confessions; Interviews; Fingerprints; Surveillance; Casts and Moulds; Identification Parades; Arson; Care and Handling of Real Evidence; Photography and Reports.

The considerable effort required to produce these manuals extended over six years. The scope was set by the Provost Marshal's office and drafts were produced, either at the School or by the Provost Marshal's staff. An editing and quality control committee was established to scrutinize the writing and rewriting. Final approval came from the Adjutant General and General Staff Branches at Army Headquarters. The printed manuals were issued on a generous scale to all Canadian Provost Corps units and certain individuals in command, instructional and supervisory positions. It would have been nice to have had this doctrine during World War II and again in Korea, however, it was in these venues that many of these procedures were born.

Service policemen of the Canadian Provost Corps were required to acquire many skills during the course of their career, none more important than those obtained from Unarmed Combat training. Largely due to an initiative by Major B W E Lee, the first CO of the Canadian Provost Corps School, it was decided in 1947 that the Corps would become one of the few police forces in the world that would not carry weapons. This decision not only ruled out firearms but also the more common truncheon or billy. The Canadian Provost Corps School was given the task of developing a system of unarmed combat with a threefold purpose. First it must enable the service policeman to defend himself against attack by an armed or unarmed attacker, while unarmed himself. It must enable him to subdue an unruly person and, finally, all of this must be accomplished without injury to the policeman, an attacker or any bystander in the vicinity.

The development of a system that would meet this demanding standard required an extensive research effort by Major Lee and his staff over the next three years. Unarmed combat methods currently in use were studied. The techniques of jujitsu, karate, judo defendo and the police holds used by civil police were demonstrated by instructors brought in from commercial firms and police forces. The system which evolved was based on self-defence and quick reaction to any attack. It demanded quick, positive reaction and no flinching or unnecessary retaliation.

Several instructors were qualified and this training became an integral subject in the Service Policeman Group 2 courses conducted at the Canadian Provost School from 1952 onward. The course specifications for unarmed combat skills were placed in the Service Policeman Training Standard, which ensured the continuity of this valuable skill. Major Bill Lee emphasized that unarmed combat, like any physical skill, required constant practice and sound physical condition. As a result, a service policeman must spend time each week maintaining and improving his skills. He may never have to use it but if he does he will have not chance to consult a training manual. There is no question the policy of unarmed service police saved countless inquiries into allegations of improper use of firearms, unnecessary force and harassment against service policemen. This was a measure that greatly enhanced the professionalism of the Corps.

The National Defence Act

The foundation for the organization, administration and discipline of Canada's Armed Forces is the National Defence Act of June 1953. This legislation replaced the outdated, convoluted manual of Military Law adapted from the British for use in Canada during the early 1900s. It had been drafted to meet conditions which existed in Wellington's army with hundreds of amendments designed to keep it abreast of changes and to give it force and effect in Canada. While it listed the purely military offences and provided penalties, it failed to ensure a suitable balance between the offence and punishment; nor did it provide for realistic military tribunals to deal with individual cases, especially under conditions of war. For example, the powers of a commanding officer of lieutenant colonel rank were very limited, which meant that a court martial had to be convened for all except the most minor offences. The result was that serious offences frequently went unpunished. The old manual contained a voluminous index and hundreds of footnotes explaining such things as the elements of offences, rules and requirements of evidence, competent authorities and interpretive clauses. It took a very determined officer, especially if he was young and inexperienced, to face up to the task of conducting a summary trial for a soldier under his command, especially if the accused held a noncommissioned rank[152]. These were but a few of the reasons which made it necessary to update the law governing Canada's military forces.

The initiative to revise military law in Canada was taken by the Judge Advocate Branch of the Defence Department with the approval of the Minister of National Defence. It was a monumental task. It started soon after World War II and was completed, with passage of the Act by Parliament, in June 1953. This comprehensive legislation provided clear, concise and coherent law governing the organization and administration of Canada's Armed Services: Navy, Army and Air Force. The JAG Branch[153] spared no effort to insure the content would be complete and presented in an orderly sequence, under appropriately numbered chapters, parts and sections, for ease of reference. A few of the main headings will suffice to illustrate this point.

Definitions	Terms of Service
DND Organization	Release
Constitution and Command	Disciplinary Jurisdiction
Powers of Command	The Code of Service Discipline
Enrolments	Military Tribunals
Promotions	Punishments
Redress of Grievance	Powers of Arrest

Parts IV and IX of the Act deal with disciplinary jurisdiction. It identifies all persons subject to the Code of Service Discipline and includes, for the first time, all regulars, reserves on training and civilians attached to Canadian Forces when serving outside Canada or on active service. It lists the serious offences which, if committed in Canada, may not be tried by a military tribunal, for example murder, manslaughter or sexual assault. The Code of Service Discipline lists some fifty-six purely military offences ranging from Misconduct in the Presence of the Enemy to Insubordination to Conduct to the Prejudice of Good and Order and Military Discipline (Section 129). The elements of each offence are given together with the punishments which may be awarded upon conviction. The scale of punishments that may be imposed are shown in the following receding (lesser) order:

1. Death
2. Imprisonment for two years or more
3. Dismissal with disgrace
4. Imprisonment for less than two years
5. Dismissal from her Majesty's Service
6. Detention
7. Reduction in rank
8. Forfeiture of seniority
9. Severe reprimand
10. Reprimand
11. Fine
12. Minor punishments (eg, extra guards and drills)

The Act sets out the offences which may be tried by various types of service tribunals such as courts-martial and summary by trial by a senior commander or by a commanding officer. It lists the maximum punishments which may be awarded by a CO and authorizes a CO of lieutenant colonel rank to delegate certain lesser powers of punishment to an officer under his command. Thus, a captain in charge of a platoon on detached duty can be given the powers to enforce the Code of Service Discipline. It also makes provision for a CO of lieutenant colonel rank to preside over a summary trial of an offender who is not under his command, in certain circumstances. A most important feature of the NDA is the increase in powers of punishment given to COs. Punishments awarded under these added powers are subject to approval by higher authority, following a review of the case, thus ensuring fair and consistent awards. The procedures for conducting summary trials also made it mandatory for the presiding officer to ensure certain conditions were met prior to proceeding.

- the CO must conduct a preliminary investigation of the charge to ensure there was evidence to warrant a trial;
- the accused can elect, or the CO may direct, that evidence be given on oath;
- the accused may request an officer to speak on his behalf during the proceeding, or he may request legal counsel at his own expense;
- the accused, if above the rank of private, must agree to accept the CO's award should he be found guilty;
- a CO has no jurisdiction to try an accused person with the rank of warrant officer or officer.

A commanding officer at a summary trial may pass a sentence which includes one or more of the following punishments:

- detention for a period not exceeding ninety days, subject to approval by higher authority (an officer not below the rank of brigadier general) when the sentence is imposed on a noncommissioned member above the rank of private;
- reduction in rank subject to approval by higher authority;
- forfeiture of seniority, severe reprimand, reprimand, a fine not exceeding basic pay for one month and minor punishments.

Delegated officers are authorized to impose the following punishments: detention not exceeding fourteen days; severe reprimand; reprimand; fine not exceeding fifteen days basic pay and minor punishments.

The question of whether special powers of arrest should be given to members of the Canadian Provost Corps was discussed, at some length, with considerable input from the Staff, Commanding Officers, Legal Officers and Corps Officers. The result was that the following broad authority to arrest was included in Part VI, Section 156 of the NDA: "Such officers and noncommissioned members as are appointed under Regulations for the purposes of this section may (**a**) detain or arrest without warrant any person who is subject to the Code of Service Discipline, regardless of the rank or status of that person who has committed, is found committing, is believed on reasonable grounds to have committed a service offence or who is charged with having committed a service offence; (**b**) exercise such other powers for carrying out the Code of Service Discipline as are prescribed in regulations made by the Governor in Council." The persons appointed under Regulations were later defined in Privy Council Order (PC 1986–2131 of 11 September 1986) and promulgated to the Canadian Armed Forces in Chapter 22.02 of Queens Regulations and Orders (QR&O). Under the head Powers of Specially Appointed Personnel they were described as follows:

The following persons are appointed for the purposes of Section 156 of the National Defence Act: (**a**) every officer posted to an established position to be employed on military police duties; and (**b**) every person posted to an established military police position and qualified in the military police trade, provided that such officer or person is in lawful possession of a Military Police Badge and an official Military Police Identification Card.

As previously mentioned, this imposed a responsibility on the Corps, and its successor the Security Branch, to ensure that service policemen were well trained and competent to carry out these considerable responsibilities. The absence of instances of improper arrest or custody of Canadian service personnel has, over the years, spoken volumes for the general efficiency of the Corps.

The National Defence Act provided a comprehensive and sensible guide for the day-to-day administration and control of Canada's Armed Forces. While it served all members, it was especially helpful to the Corps during performance of duties related to the maintenance of discipline.

Previous mention has been made of the employment of officers outside the Corps. The ERE (Extra Regimentally Employed) appointments were designed to fill a large number of staff and specialist positions in most headquarters that were not established for a specific corps. Formal qualification, such as graduation from the Canadian Army Staff College, was required for most staff appointments while others were based on the officer's interest and aptitude for the job. The placement of officers in ERE positions was controlled by a central Directorate of Personnel in the Adjutant General Branch in which each corps had a representative. These appointments were not designed to provide a full career for an officer, however they offered valuable experience during a normal three year tour of duty. Apart from broadening the officer's military education, there was no doubt that this policy benefitted the Army as a whole. The intermingling was instrumental in preventing a tendency towards the parochialism of any one corps, and it provided much needed variety in the sometimes fixed routine of a great many officers.

Successive Provost Marshals actively supported ERE for Corps officers from 1946 onward. At any given time there were up to ten officers filling ERE positions in a variety of appointments such as Grade 2 and 3 Staff Officers, as individuals in peacekeeping contingents and as personnel, administrative, sports and recreation officers throughout the Canadian Army. Major Howard Mansfield relates a somewhat humourous incident which occurred during an ERE tour of duty in New Brunswick.

It was customary for all officers to be given secondary duties over and above their normal functions and, far from being an unwelcome chore, the change of pace this provided was often much appreciated. The duty I recall most fondly was the appointment as aide-de-camp to the Lieutenant Governor of New Brunswick while I was serving as the Camp Provost Marshal at Camp Gagetown.

His Honour Mr J C McNair was in failing health at the time and would ask me to represent him at various ceremonies and events. I was, therefore, privileged to wear the Provost Corps dress uniform where, perhaps, it would not normally be expected to be seen and I became quite familiar with various aspects of protocol, including that of State funerals, and attended that of Governor General Vanier on His Honour's behalf.

My big day, however, was the formal Opening of the Legislature at which, in full dress blues with cape and sword, I accompanied the Lieutenant Governor as he reviewed the Guard of Honour outside the legislative buildings in Fredericton. Inside the chamber my role was to formally present him with the Speech from the Throne and, after he had delivered it, to formally retrieve it from him – a minor but proud role in a historic ceremony.

In the evening a reception was held in the Lieutenant Governor's suite in the Lord Beaverbrook Hotel, across from the legislature. I was required to be in attendance and to escort invited dignitaries from the hotel entrance to the suite. For this occasion the dress was scarlet mess kit adorned with the aide-de-camp's traditional gold aiguilette and, no doubt, I felt I cut a fine military figure. However, I was suitably humbled when an elderly American hotel guest, seeing me near the reception desk, mistook my finery for that of a bellhop and asked if I would take his luggage up to his room. Of course I was happy to do so, but drew the line at accepting his offer of a tip."

Lieutenant Howie Mansfield came to the Corps in 1962 from the Malayan Police Service where he had been a Superintendent. The precise details of his appointment as an aide-de-camp to the Lieutenant Governor are not known, however, it was not just an accident. He was qualified and, like so many of his peers in the Corps, he was fast becoming a professional.

18

Lonely Postings

The Alaska Canada Highway

The presence of Canadian Provost Corps personnel in odd locations around the world was invariably brought about by war or the threat of war. There was one notable example of this when a detachment was installed in Canada's great Northwest immediately following World War II. The story really starts with the Pearl Harbour bombing in December 1941, and the concern of the United States to forestall further Japanese incursions against Alaska via the Aleutian Islands chain. The United States strategists proposed building an overland road through Canadian terrority as a supply route for the several existing airfields in Alaska. Apart from its military value, both Canadian and United States officials realized the importance of such a link for the future economic development of this vast but empty territory. The road, yet to be surveyed, would start at Dawson Creek[154], British Columbia, and wind west and north through British Columbia and Yukon Territory, passing through Whitehorse and ending at Fairbanks, Alaska. With the full cooperation of Canadians this road would be built by the United States Army as a priority project.

It was built by the United States Army Corps of Engineers in what must rate as one of the most notable construction projects of all time. It was started in March 1942 and was opened on 20 November 1942. It went through difficult terrain, over many rivers, large and small, and across five mountain ranges for a distance of 1,442 miles. The road bed was laid on logs in boggy areas and blasted out of rock in the mountains. It had a gravel surface laid on a narrow 12 foot crown. With few exceptions, all bridges were the trestle type made from local timber and often spanning gorges 300 to 400 yards wide. Hundreds of bulldozers, cranes, shovels, earthworms and graders were operated, around the clock, by a workforce of 11,000 United States Army soldiers and another 7,500 mostly Canadian civilian technicians and labourers. Men swinging axes followed surveyors and chopped trees off at shoulder height, then bulldozers would push them over to serve as the road's foundation. It was still very cold in the spring and fall with alternate (−)40 degree cold, and clouds of mosquitoes during the warm but short summer. This Alaska-Canada (ALCAN) Highway was operated and maintained for use by United States and Canadian traffic until April 1946, when it reverted to purely Canadian control by the Canadian Army. An administrative headquarters was located in Whitehorse. Engineer maintenance crews were located at intervals along the road and a Canadian Provost Corps detachment was set-up to police the traffic.

The original provost detachment was located at the headquarters of the NWHS in Whitehorse, Yukon Territory, during the spring of 1947. This six man detachment consisted of Sergeant Terry Foster assisted by Lance Corporals C V Auburn, W J Van Horne, M G Decker, R Oliver and J R McConnery. They faced the formidable task of patrolling the ALCAN Highway from Dawson Creek to the Yukon/Alaska border, a distance of some 1,220 miles. The detachment strength was increased over the next few years to an officer and 23 NCOs. They were deployed at detachments working out of Whitehorse, Fort Nelson and Dawson Creek, British Columbia. A system of interlocking patrols was initiated to deal with some unusual problems caused by the large tractor trailer loads of material required for the extensive resource development then underway in Alaska and Northern Canada. No matter how often the engineer maintenance graders pushed gravel towards the crown these monster trucks, often at high speeds, simply whipped it off again. Drivers, for their own safety, might slow down over the flimsy wooden trestle bridges, but even then the load weight caused considerable damage. Perhaps the most negative aspect was the simple fact that, in the Yukon section of this road, there was no Highway Traffic Act or other law that regulated drivers.

Captain S E (Sammy) Sambrooke[155] was the first Corps officer posted to the NWHS detachment, and it was largely due to his initiative that the legal problem was resolved. A senior magistrate in the Yukon discovered that the Commissioner of the Northwest Territories was empowered to publish laws or ordinances required for the best interest of this vast region. The result was a Yukon Ordinance for the Regulation of Traffic Over the Nothwest Highway, and provost were empowered to enforce it. The provost patrol was then able to deal with excessive speeding, overweight loads and other irregularities. Large signs were posted which listed the speed and load limits and other restrictions. Concrete "snake" road bumps were installed at bridge approaches. Provost patrols carried single-axle portable scales which enabled total load weights to be determined. Drivers were pulled off the road to sit for a day or so until the overload was transferred elsewhere. Speed checks sometimes resulted in an appearance before a magistrate. Once the rules were established there was much improvement in compliance by drivers of the trucking and transport industry. After all, it was in the interest of a Texas, California or Alberta drilling company that its equipment got through to Watson Lake, Whitehorse or Fairbanks.

A patrol might last for several days and cover a round trip distance of up to 1,200 miles. Engineer Road Maintenance camps, spaced about every 300 miles, served as patrol "pit stops" for meals, fuel and communication centres. There was an initial problem in finding a Department of National Defence vehicle that would stand up to the constant pounding over the ever present "washboard" of the gravel roadbed. A standard modification to a commercial van was eventually developed which provided heavy-duty suspension, four-speed transmission, a reliable two-way radio and a spot-light.

Apart from the truck traffic there was an increasing volume of tourist traffic during the summertime. Often these travellers were ill-informed about the distances, lack of tourist or service facilities and, most serious of all, the necessity of traversing 1,200 miles of uncertain gravel road. There were instances of small cars pulling heavy trailers as well as overloaded vans and campers that had no chance of making it to Whitehorse or Fairbanks. It fell to the provost patrol to brief them on what lay ahead and, in extreme cases, to dissuade them from starting up the road in totally unsuitable vehicles and equipment. There were also many instances where these travellers were delayed for days by washouts or bridge and road maintenance. Under these circumstances it was the task of the patrol to render assistance and advice whenever possible, a duty which often required much tact and patience. The provost escort for the Paymaster was a common enough duty but there were some extreme departures from the norm along the NWHS. Here the Paymaster and Provost escort made the long 4 to 5 day trip down the road, stopping to pay people encountered on graders, snowploughs or in maintenance camps. This was a bimonthly function. The control of range horses was another concern. These were packhorses owned by various outfitters who, for a fee, moved the gear of prospectors, geologists, trappers, or anyone desirous of visiting remote areas of Yukon. During slack seasons these hardy animals were simply turned loose to forage for their food. Their search for food frequently led them into camp sites and other cleared areas along the road, often presenting a threat to traffic. Short of organizing a full-scale horse wrangle, there was not much the provost patrol could do apart from driving them away from the area.

A major disruption to the flow of traffic on the ALCAN Highway occurred on 16 October 1957 when the bridge over the Peace River collapsed. Since this was the only road bridge over the Peace for a considerable distance east and west of the ALCAN Highway, there was no alternate route up the highway from Mile 35.3 onward. It would be three years before construction on a new bridge was completed, and two months before an alternate road link was in place. Captain James D (Jim) Lumsden,[156] the last officer to command the Canadian Provost Corps NWHS Detachment, provides a detailed account of this incident.

The first response was the use of a ferry. Control of this crossing method was effected by a section of infantry from 2PPCLI, under the direction of two Provost NCOs. Early in 1958 this section was replaced by members of the Corps. The ferry was replaced in December by the use of an existing bridge of the Pacific Great Eastern Railway (PGER). Reaching this crossing site over the River required travelling a nine mile detour road which had been hastily constructed and was fraught with many hazards in itself. The PGER bridge was 100 feet above the River and 3,330 feet in length. It was modified for vehicle traffic by installing a wider deck (11 feet 3 inches) with a 4 foot guard railing. The defile was a formidable sight for the unsuspecting motorist, however, while a few declined the thrill most, buoyed by the confident assurances of the provost, undertook the crossing.

In April 1958 the PGER commenced its rail service to Fort St John, British Columbia, thus the traffic control became more complex. The provost, controlling traffic across this span, now had to concern themselves with unscheduled rail traffic as well as vehicles crossing in both directions. In spite of the many hazards and adverse environment this provost section operated this defile, without major mishap, until the new bridge was completed in 1960.

The operation and maintenance of the NWHS was transferred from the Canadian Army to the Federal Department of Public Works on 1 April 1964. The provost detachment, which had functioned continuously for eighteen years, was disbanded and its members posted elsewhere. These men had received no special benefits for the difficult and often hazardous duties performed in this remote area of Canada. They gained the respect of citizen and transient alike by their fairness and honesty. An editorial in the Fort Nelson News at this time commented on their departure: "Hell! They may have nicked you now and again and, in doing so, only made it safer for the rest of the pilgrims heading up or down the track. We will miss from the scene, the Provost Corps that have so long rendered a service to all residents and tourists." Nobody could wish for a better tribute.

The United Nations Emergency Force

The next significant sojourn in a far away land arose from Canada's participation in the 1956 peacekeeping effort in the Middle East. Peacekeeping really started with the United nations decision, in November 1956, to use neutral troops from several nations to keep the warring Egyptians and Israelis apart. Although the genesis of the strife between these two peoples is lost in antiquity, it is possible to trace its more recent revival with some degree of accuracy. Troubles started, with renewed vigour, immediately following the United Naions Proclamation of 14 March 1948 creating the state of Israel. This ended the 1920 British mandate for Palestine and the withdrawl from the region of all British forces by 15 May 1948. The following day Israel was invaded by forces from the mostly Arab states of Egypt, Jordan, Syria, Lebanon and Iraq, none of which agreed with the loss of land space in this overcrowded region. Israeli forces not only repulsed these attacks but took over the partitioned area of Palestine, as well as regions along the Sinai border with Egypt. Arab refugees flooded into Jordan and were, eventually, ruthlessly expelled. For the next six years Egyptian forces, from their bases in the Gaza Strip, conducted raids against Israeli settlements. The Gaza Strip was a highly prized corridor which extended along the Mediterranean into the southwest corner of Israel, and contained the towns of Rafah and Gaza.

In September 1956 President Nasser of Egypt closed the Suez Canal to Israeli shipping and prepared for all out war. In what they viewed as a preemptive strike, strong Israeli air and ground forces crossed the Sinai border into Egypt during October 1956. They drove across the Sinai (desert) to the Suez Canal, captured the Gaza Strip and the important town of Sharm El Sheik on the Red Sea. A strong force of British and French paratroops/commandos landed at Port Said, the Mediterranean entrance on the Suez Canal, on 5 November. It was, ostensibly, deployed to protect the Canal but withdrew on 7 November when a general cease-fire was arranged by the United Nations. The Israeli forces also withdrew from the Sinai, but continued to occupy the Gaza Strip and Sharm El Sheik.

On 4 November 1956 the United Nations General Assembly passed a resolution establishing an international force to secure and supervise the cessation of the conflict between Egypt and Israel. This United Nations

Emergency Force (UNEF) was made up of troops from ten countries: Brazil, Canada, Columbia, Denmark, Finland, India, Indonesia, Norway, Sweden and Yugoslavia. A former Canadian Army Corps commander, Lieutenant General E L M Burns, was appointed Force Commander. Canada's initial offer of an infantry battalion was later changed, at the request of the United Nations, to a strong contingent of supply and administrative troops (RCASC, RCOC, Signals, etc.) as well as a provost detachment. These were urgently required to look after a crisis which quickly arose due to the fact that the various national groups had no logistic element in their contingents. The Royal Canadian Service Corps (RCASC) were real professionals and soon set-up a system of rationing, transport and supply for this polyglot force of 5,600 soldiers in a strange land. By 30 Jnauary 1957 the UNEF was deployed along the Sinai border, with the main supply and administrative base located in the Gaza Strip. The Canadian Provost Corps element of the UNEF consisted of one captain, two sergeants, four corporals and ten lance corporals. They provided the nucleus and a major portion of the expertise for an integrated Military Police Company which was to function with this force for the next ten years. Captain Earl Wilson, one of the early Canadian Provost Corps officers with the UNEF, describes some of the events and gives us some insights into this unique military police organization. His report to the Provost Marshal Army, dated 16 August 1960, describes the situation at that time.

UNEF soldiers became international personnel, under the authority of the United Nations, during their period with the Force. All have immunity of jurisdiction from local civilian law enforcement agencies. They remain subject to their own national civil, criminal and military laws and are subject to regulations issued by the UN Secretary-General and the UNEF Commander.

The personnel of the Military Police company were drawn from the MPs of those contingents which brought along its own small detachment. For a time these operated independently with their own troops. When UNEF Headquarters moved from Cairo to El Ballah, in December 1956, an ad hoc arrangement to coordinate military police was set-up by Captain M P Menard, Canadian Provost Corps, with personnel from Brazil, Canada, Columbia, Denmark and Indonesia. The UNEF MP Company carried out normal provost duties such as the physical security of the UNEF Headquarters, route signing, disciplinary patrols, issue and control of identification cards and investigation services.[157] In February 1957 General Burns issued an Organizational Order establishing a Force Provost Marshal and an integrated Military Police Company. This resulted in members from Sweden, Finland

and Norway joining the MP Company, which then brought its total strength to 62 all ranks. The Indian Provost Section also joined the Company in October 1957 for duties, but continued to look after its own living arrangements. Captain Menard was appointed Force Provost Marshal and Commanding Officer of the MP Company, an arrangement which continued in effect throughout the life of this Company.

The Military Police Company Headquarters was located in Gaza, including the Provost Marshal, a Special Investigations Unit and a MP Detachment. Other detachments were located at the UNEF Maintenance Area in Rafah, the UNEF Air Base in El Arish and at the UNEF Leave Centre in Beirut, Lebanon.

The international aspects of the unit was reflected in the unit appointments. The Commanding Officer was Canadian; the Second-in-Command was Indian; the Company Sergeant Major was Danish; the Officer IC Investigation Section was Indian with three senior investigators a Canadian, Dane and Swede. The NCO IC Rafah Detachment was Canadian assisted by a Brazilian. The NCO in charge of the Detachment in Beirut was Danish.

While this was not the first integrated military police unit (as veterans of Korea will recall) it was the first to be formed from many countries, each with different laws, language, religion and cultural backgrounds. The official language of the UNEF was English so that all correspondence and reports were in this language. This presented a difficult problem, probably most difficult for the MP Company. The Canadian Provost Corps system for maintaining records, filing and police procedures was adopted and proved sound and workable. It was surprising how quickly the members from other contingents learned to use it.

The multiplicity of languages, customs, laws, regulations and authorities presented the UNEF Military Policeman with, what would appear to be, an unsurmountable obstacle from a legal point of view. He was called upon to exercise a high degree of tact, understanding, patience and personal integrity in carrying out his daily tasks. The fact that the UNEF Military Police were respected by all members of the UNEF, whether investigating a loss or theft, directing a soldier on leave, or apprehending a night intruder in the Maintenance Area, illustrates their high sense of responsibility and dedication to the job of policing this unique Force.

The UNEF was withdrawn in May 1967 and the Canadian Provost Corps members came home. The now famous "Seven Days War" between Israeli and a coalition of Egyptian and Syrian Forces commenced 3 June 1967. It resulted in the complete destruction of the Egyptian and Syrian Forces and the occupation by Israel of the Golan Heights (Syria) and the West Bank (Jordan). Not exactly a ringing endorsement for peacekeeping.

The Congo

The Congo had been a Belgian colony since 1908 and was governed as an absolute monarchy under successive Belgian regimes. This huge area in equatorial Africa, larger than France and Spain combined, had a population of about 20,000,000 made up of several tribes each with a different language and culture. The country was divided into the five provinces of Equatier, Orientale, Kivu, Katanga and Kasai, each with an appointed governor reporting to the Central Government in Leopoldville. Katanga was the most highly developed and economically advanced of the five and contained rich deposits of cobalt, copper and tin. The capital of Katanga was Elizabethville (later renamed Lumumbashi), located over 1,000 miles from Leopoldville. Kamina was also an important city in Katanga.

The native Congolese had not been brought into the mainstream of life except as labourers and soldiers in the local Belgian Army. Incidents of civil unrest began to occur in the early 1950s during the period when many of the so-called third world states were emerging from colonial to self-governing status. The volatile situation in the Congo was aided and abetted by overt help from the USSR and Red China. Both saw the Congo situation as a golden opportunity to establish a communist surrogate state in Central Africa, under the guise of a popular uprising by the Congolese to secure their freedom from Belgium rule.

Largely due to escalating civil unrest, and the mutiny of Congolese soldiers in the Army, Belgium quickly granted independence to the Congolese in June 1960. A period of almost total anarchy followed during which nearly all Belgian officials, including army units, departed the country. There was one notable exception to the general exodus. The recently installed premier of Katanga, one Moise Tshombe, viewed the removal of every vestige of Belgian rule with some disfavour. He retained a force of 10,000 former Belgian army troops and, on 11 July 1960, announced that Katanga had seceded from the Congo. On 14 July 1960 the United Nations Security Council approved the organization of a Security Force to restore order and assist the Congolese in achieving nationhood. This force, referred to as ONUC, was composed of military and civilian personnel from thirty countries: Argentina, Australia, Burma, Brazil, Canada, Ceylon, Denmark, Ethiopia, Ghana, Guinea, India, Ireland, Italy, Indonesia, Liberia, Mali, Malaya, Morocco, Netherlands, New Zealand, Nigeria, Norway, Pakistan, Sudan, Sweden, Switzerland, Tunisia, United Arab Republic, United States of America and Yugoslavia. The United Nations Headquarters and communication centre was located in Leopoldville.

The Canadian contingent consisted of a strong, fully equipped group of signals personnel (Royal Canadian Corps of Signals (RCCS), and a Canadian Provost Corps detachment of one officer, one warrant officer, one staff sergeant, two sergeants and seven corporals or lance corporals). They were all bilingual (English and French) since French had been the working language of the Belgian regime and was widely spoken in the Congo. These members of the Corps were warned for this duty on 15 August 1960 and nine days later, on 24 August, departed Trenton Air Force Base in an RCAF Northstar bound for Leopoldville. Two days later, following a somewhat turbulent flight, with stops in Gander, the Azores, Dakar and Accra, they arrived at the airport about 15 miles outside Leopoldville.

The scene in Leopoldville resembled a wild west movie following the arrival of a cattle drive at Dodge City. Groups of mutinous Congolese soldiers, under no particular command and with no specific mission beyond harassing incoming United Nations personnel and outgoing Belgians, were everywhere. They took over buildings for barracks, walked off with food and drink wherever they found it, slept throughout the tropical day and became increasingly intoxicated in the evening. They adopted the democratic practice of choosing a new commanding officer every day or so and indulged in wild rides in assorted stolen vehicles, during which they fired their weapons at random. RSM Arthur Heymans, Canadian Provost Corps, who was the Canadian contingent Chief Warrant Officer, had arrived with the first group from Canada on 16 August. They were greeted at the airport by a platoon of these marauding Congolese bandits. They were fired upon, suffered verbal and physical abuse and robbed of their watches and wallets. WO2 Marcel Fortier tells of his concerns when the provost detachment arrived on 26 August.

We arrived at Ndjili Airport at 0830 hours, 26 August. Prior to landing the pilot ordered us to hide our weapons under our jump seats. Being good soldiers we did as ordered. The aircraft landed and stopped mid field, far from the terminal building. On disembarking I noticed a red truck speeding toward us. I had expected white painted United Nations transport. Anxious seconds were spent trying to identify the vehicle which, to our relief, turned out to be a ten-ton United Nations Mercedes truck. We immediately loaded our baggage, retrieved our weapons and got aboard.

The Canadian Provost Corps detachment spent the first few days settling into their quarters in the Athenee Royale and establishing contact with the military police of the contingents from Denmark, India, Indonesia and

Norway. The ONUC Military Policy Company was formed in Leopoldville under the direction of the United Nations Chief of Staff, one Colonel Hajiboy. A military police (MP) headquarters was set up, patrols were organized and contact was made with the few remaining remnants of the cities' civil police as well as MPs of the Congolese army. The men of the Canadian Provost Corps were in much demand partly because they were bilingual but, mainly, due to their knowledge and experience in coping with similar situations. The members of the Corps were soon swamped with requests from United Nations Headquarters for patrols, investigations of all types, preparing reports for the C of S and providing liaison and interpreter function. It became necessary to establish a 24 hour Military Police Information and Control post which, of necessity, was manned by a member of the Canadian Provost Corps. The provost detachment was further weakened with the departure of Captain Bill Fiddes who was despatched to Kamina, in far off Katanga, to assist with organizing and operating a training unit for police and fire fighters. Warrant Officer Marcel Fortier was then in charge of the Canadian Provost Corps element and, in reality, became the defacto commander of the ONUC MP Company for the next six months.

It may be useful at this juncture to list some Congolese officials who played a significant role in this turbulent period together with a brief chronology of events.

PERSONS

Joseph Kasavubu: First President of Congo, 1960.
Patrice Lumumba: Prime Minister, assassinated February 1961.
Moise Tshombe: Premier of Katanga. Ousted by United Nations troops December 1962.
Joseph Mobuto: Chief of Staff Congolese Army and Prime Minister vice Lumumba.
Antoine Gizenga: Lumumba's vice-premier and leader of pro communist faction in Stanleyville until 1962.
Cyrille Adaula: Prime Minister for a short period in 1962.

EVENTS

April 1961: Kasavubu signed United Nations/Congo Agreement authorizing United Nations troops to prevent civil war by use of force.
September 1961: United Nations Secretary General, Dag Hammarskjold, killed in a plane crash at Ndola, near southern border of Katanga.
August–December 1961: United Nations troops retake Elizabethville

Tshombe agrees to reunification of Katanga with the Congo, but retains control of Katanga.
December 1962: Katanga forces defeated by United Nations troops, Tshombe deposed, secession ends.
January 1993: United Nations troops gradually withdrawn.
June 1963: Civil unrest continues.
July 1963: Tshombe returns as Prime Minister of Katanga. White mercenaries, under "Mad" Mike Hoare defeats rebels now backed by Red China.
November 1963: Congolese Army, under Mobuto, recapture Albertville (Kivu Province) from rebels. Tshombe hires Belgian paratroopers to retake Stanleyville (Orientale Province) and freed 1,800 white hostages.
November 1965: Mobuto ousts Tshombe. Mobuto controlled all of the Congo and still remains in power. The country was renamed Zaire in 1971, with the capital at Kinsashi.

Members of the Corps continued to serve in the Congo for the next three years. The six month tour rotations continued, however, the requirement for all members to speak French was gradually relaxed as conditions in the Congo, particularly in the western region, were stabilized. United Nations Headquarters in New York requested, through normal channels, that the Canadian Provost detachment be increased in order to provide more support for the development of police and security training facilities being developed in the Congo. For several reasons, the main one being lack of overall manpower, this was declined. The ONUC peacekeeping/peacemaking force was withdrawn by 1964. By any standard this had been a test of physical endurance, determination and no small measure of courage. It is no exaggeration to say that the leadership and expertise of men like Fortier, Martin and Pitre, and their successors, was a huge factor in maintaining some semblance of law and order in the volatile days of the United Nations Force in the Congo. A detailed account of the unpredictable and often hazardous experiences of this C Pro C Detachment, as written by Warrant Officer Marcel Fortier, is reprinted as Appendix "D" to this history.

Cyprus

The last, and longest, continuous tour of peacekeeping for members of the Canadian Provost Corps started in Cyprus during 1964. As usual, the Island was undergoing much tumult and violence by its inhabitants of

Greek and Turkish origin. Cyprus had been under Turkish rule from 1570 to 1878 when it became a crown colony under British administration. This status was recognized by the Treaty of Lausanne in 1923. Following World War II, in 1950, the Greek patriot Makarious became archbishop of Cyprus and vigorously pursued a movement (ENOSIS) to foster a union with Greece. Another more militant, organization (EOKA), led by one Colonel Grivas, sprang up in 1955. EOKA sought to speed up the departure of the British by such means as murdering off-duty British servicemen and blowing up government buildings. At this stage the strife between Greek and Turkish residents began to cause much unrest and violence. The Greeks were a vast majority so the Turkish government interceded on their behalf.

In February 1959 the London-Zurich Agreement, between Britain, Greece and Turkey, set-up an independent republic with British sovereign base areas in two locations. Tension between the Greeks and Cypriots continued and by 1964 the Island was on the verge of civil war. Makarious was the first president of this new republic and this did nothing to stop the violence between Greeks and Turks. Turkey responded by issuing threats of a take-over in order to protect the Turkish residents. Under these circumstances the United Nations, in March 1964, authorized and soon despatched a peacekeeping force which included troops from Canada, Britain, Denmark, Finland, Sweden and Ireland. Their task was to patrol a marked Demarcation Line (The Green Line) extending across the Island to prevent people from either side from crossing over. Canada sent an infantry battalion, an armoured squadron (recce element) and some support troops. The Canadian Provost Corps element consisted of an officer, to be the force Provost Marshal, another Canadian Provost Corps captain and 21 NCOs. This Force Provost Marshal was a Canadian Provost Corps officer with the rank of Lieutenant Colonel. He was located at UNCICYP HQ in the town of Nicosia, as was the United Nations Headquarters and Force Headquarters. The Force Commander was, and still is, a Canadian Army Brigadier.

The Military Police Company Headquarters was located in Nicosia with detachments at Famagusta, the Leave and Recreation Centre and, on occasions, in Troodos, Lefka and Morphou. As was done in the UNEF and ONUC, the MPs from the six contributing nations of the UNFICYP formed an integrated MP company with a total strength of about 100 all ranks. The CO was Danish and the 2IC was Canadian. They looked after the security of United Nations and Force Headquarters, provided escorts, patrolled roads and carried out investigations into numerous vehicle accidents, theft of military stores and other general provost duties. The most common, or recurring, disciplinary problem arose when soldiers spent too much time and money in the local bars. There was a Special Investigation Section located in Nicosia which functioned under the British Headquarters and carried out investigations into more serious crimes. Finally, there was an Australian civil police section which provided escorts for Cypriots who wished to cross the Line on a visit to friends, relatives or some other legitimate business. Why this was not done by the Military Police Company was never quite clear, however, they did not function under the direction of the Force Provost Marshal. Corporal R G (Bob) Thomas[158], one of the first Canadian Provost Corps members to arrive in Cyprus, gives an account of his experience.

In March of 1964 the United Nations authorized a force to serve on the island of Cyprus. Initially Canada committed a battalion of the Royal 22nd Regiment and a Recce squadron from the RCDs. Shortly after Brigadier James Tedley, Commander of 2 CIBG in Camp Petawawa, was appointed the commander of Nicosia Zone. LSGT Brian Kent, myself (LCPL at the time) from Petawawa, sergeant Dennis Dixon from the School and Sergeant George Gardiner from Calgary were sent over to handle security at the Nicosia Zone Headquarters. On arrival in Nicosia we were escorted by the RCDs to Camp Troodos. After a few days we moved into the Nicosia Golf and Country Club. Sounds very fancy, however, I can assure you that it was in pretty rough condition. We lived in dirt floor tents behind the main building. Our beds were canvas camp cots and we shared a clothes locker with a partner. Shortly after arrival we started forming the Nicosia Zone Provost Unit that eventually had representation from the United Kingdom, Denmark, Finland, Ireland and Canada. The unit headquarters was in Wolsely barracks near the walled city of Nicosia. The first morning I reported for duty I was instructed to take a Land Rover and patrol inside Nicosia with a member of the Royal Military Police. I had never driven a right hand drive vehicle and it was a totally new experience to drive on the left side of the road. As we entered Paphos Gate I misjudged the distance on my left and started climbing the pedestrian stairs. I was able to get the vehicle back under control and managed to escape with a dented wheel rim. It caused some commotion with the people in the area who, no doubt, were wondering who the crazy Canadian driver was. I later worked on a traffic investigation detail and found that many United Nations soldiers were put on the road with little or no driver training. I'm sure this "school of hard knocks" method resulted in many unnecessary vehicle accidents. In July of 1964 we were visited by the then Minister of National Defence, the Honourable Paul Hellyer. He advised us that he was the bearer of some good and some bad news. The bad news was that the United Nations mandate had been extended and we would be there for 3 more months. The good news was that if the mandate was extended again, we would be replaced with fresh troops. It is interesting that 28 years later Canadian service personnel are still serving the United Nations on the island of Cyprus.

As Bob states, this force is still in place after twenty-eight years. This Canadian Provost Corps detachment spent many thousands of man days on duty in this unusual setting. The Minister of National Defence was a bit optimistic about a quick withdrawl, however, apart from the Turkish armed incursion during 1972 this area has remained relatively peaceful. Perhaps this makes it all worthwhile.

19

Brotherhood and Badges

Unification

This narration of the history of the Canadian Provost Corps has now reached the point where something must be said about the Canadian Forces Reorganization Act. Bill C-243 received second reading in the House of Commons in December 1966, having been moved by the Minister of National Defence the Honourable Paul Hellyer. It became law effective 1 February 1968. The end result was the UNIFICATION of the Navy, Army and Air Force into a single service: The Canadian Armed Forces. Previous to this, the Report of the Royal Commission on Government Organization (Glasco Commission), and the government's White Paper on Defence (1964), had both stressed the necessity of reducing the manpower costs of headquarters administration and operating expenses in the Services. The total defence budget of 1962–63 was approximately $1,500,000,000. By far the major portion of this funding was used to pay for the daily upkeep of the military such as pay and allowances, supplies, maintenance of shops, aircraft, buildings and military equipment. These costs were referred to as operating and maintenance costs (O & M) and consumed on average about 90 percent of the total defence budget. The remaining 10 percent was then available for *capital* expenditures such as the purchase of modern armaments, new equipment as well as military construction and development. Furthermore, the giant strides being made in the research and development of military hardware and arms meant that any military force, to remain effective, must renew its arsenal at ever decreasing intervals and at a greatly expanded cost. Failure to do this would inevitably result in a "bow and arrow" Army, Navy and Air Force.

The alternative was a substantial increase in the defence budget, an unlikely event given the traditional reluctance of the Canadian public to put guns ahead of butter in times of relative peace. This point is illustrated by the fact that Canada spends the lowest percentage of its gross national product on national defence of any of the industrialized western nations. The actual figure, which has varied only slightly over the past twenty years, is 1.7 percent of the GDP, notwithstanding that our per capita GDP was the third highest of the NATO countries in 1983. By way of comparison, the United States' defence expenditure for 1983 was the highest in NATO with 7 percent of its GDP. Britain was second highest with 5.5 percent and only tiny Luxembourg spent less than Canadians at 1.2 percent.

The enormously complex task of implementing the unification programme was carried out in three phases over a period of two and one-half years. Phase one was the organization of a single headquarters and staff for the control and administration of the three Services (Navy, Army and Air Force) and henceforth designated the Canadian Forces Headquarters (CFHQ). Bill C-90 of July 1964 provided the Minister with legal authority to proceed with the initial plan. A single Chief of Defence Staff was appointed to replace the former Chief of each Service. Four branch Chiefs, reporting to the CDS, were appointed to replace the existing twelve. This process was then repeated down to the functional level of the Army equivalent of Corps Director. Instead of each Service having its own head of branch or corps there was now one director who was responsible for all of the common functions existing in the three Services. By the end of October 1964 this new command and control structure was in place; appointments were made, personnel slates were drawn up and filled, and all were physically relocated.

The second phase was the reorganization of the field command structure, which was announced in June 1965. The essential difference between the existing field command organization was that the Army commands were based on the principle of one commander being responsible for all aspects of military activity within a designated *geographical* boundary. Thus, there were four major Army headquarters in Canada: Eastern, Quebec, Central and Western. The Navy's main operational (fleet) headquarters was located in Halifax with a sub-headquarters in Esquimalt and a smaller logistic and training headquarters. The Air Force system was termed *functional* in that each of their five command headquarters had responsibilty for a specific function such as supply, training, air defence and transport regardless of location in Canada. The Minister announced, in June 1965, that the new command headquarters structure in Canada would consist of six functional commands to replace the existing eleven. These Commands were to be:

Air Defence Command: air operations (Air Force)
Mobile Command: ground operations (Army)
Maritime Command: naval operations (Navy)
Air Transport Command: based on existing Air Force
Material Command: logistics and supply
Training Command: training policy and coord

A seventh command, The Canadian Forces Communication System was also formed. It was responsible for strategic communications and communications for emergency government. It was not responsible for tactical field communications. Commanders and staffs were appointed and headquarters were developed for each of the six new unified commands, which became operational in late 1965.

The final phase, referred to by a significant portion of the serving military as the "crunch", became effective on 1 February 1968. Henceforth there would be no Army, Navy or Air Force, just the CAF. The nomenclature for staff appointments common to the Army would now be the same as used in the Royal Canadian Air Force. For example, the Brigade Major became the Staff Officer Operations 3 and the Command Provost Marshal would now use the title of Senior Security Officer (SSO). The systems and standards for rank qualification developed and in use by the Army was now changed. Officers and NCOs were no longer obliged to achieve formal qualification prior to promotion, which would now depend on seniority and a personnel evaluation based on the judgement of staff officers. All ranks of the Army and Air Force woudl wear the same uniform, the same rank identification and rank titles. The Navy, after much anguish, were allowed to retain their navy blue uniforms and rank designations. Somehow, it boggled one's mind to refer to "Admiral" Jones as "General" Jones. The trade structures were revised, recruiting was integrarted, pay and allowances standardized. The practical affect was that the service policemen of the former Canadian Provost Corps were initially placed in a lower pay field. Army "camps" became bases, following the Air Force custom. The combat arms of the Army (infantry, armour and artillery) retained their regiment and corps affiliations but were subject to all other fundamental changes relative to conditions and terms of service. The Royal Canadian Engineers were particularly hard hit because no provision was made to maintain their hard earned battlefield skills. Maintenance tasks in bases and married quarters were not a substitute for clearing minefields or erecting bridges over rivers, under fire. Finally, all of the service support corps ceased to exist on 1 February 1968, the Canadian Provost Corps included. Henceforth, the serving members of the Corps would now belong to the Security Branch of the Canadian Armed Forces. This Branch comprised the personnel formerly employed in the following functional groups:

The Canadian Provost Corps
The Air Force Police
The Naval Bosun Trade
The Army Intelligence Corps (C Int C)
The Royal Canadian Air Force Director of Security
The Provost Marshal (Army)
Elements of the Directorate of Intelligence (Army)

Sentiment and semantics notwithstanding, the unification of the Army, Navy and Air Force resulted in some success and a few obvious failures. Most of the failures resulted from process rather than substantive change, however, all would have a long-term detrimental affect on the Services.

- The process for determining the new structure was arbitrary and, in some cases, unnecessarily callous. For example, policy decisions were taken on major organization changes with little or no input from those most affected. Despite the Minister's statement in the house that "a planning group" of senior officers and departmental officials was formed to determine the structure of the Forces, this group was small and was not representative of some important elements of the three services. There was never a plan beyond a terse "take-it-or-leave-it" edict by the Minister. This resulted in the premature retirement of many loyal and efficient officers and men.
- In mid October, 1964, all of the Army Corps Directors were assembled and informed bluntly that there would be no more Corps or Corps Directors. This, after almost a century of loyal and efficient service to Canada by the represented Corps.
- There was no effort to keep the many units and headquarters informed about the unification program and the reasons for it. The result was a major drop in morale and the loss of many well trained men.
- The revised Field Command Structure completely failed to meet the needs of the Army, in particular the Canadian Army Reserves who were left leaderless and forgotten. This was subsequently revised and, more recently, it appears that the Army is now well back to a geographical

command structure. While the functional system is suited to the Air Force, it does not serve the needs of the Army.
- The Army lost most of its tradition, customs and philosophy. It was not permissible to use the word "Army" officially. The practice of giving junior Army leaders complete responsibility for their personnel was abrogated. For example, if a soldier had a problem he now went to the padre, paymaster or medical officer rather than to his officer. This was almost a complete reversal of the Army custom of unit officer leadership in all matters pertaining to the welfare of the troops.
- While there was some justification for reducing the number of trades and specialties and, therefore, enabling a reduction in training manpower, this was carried to extremes. For example, for a period of fifteen years following unification there was no training given to the personnel of the combat Support Branches in the skills required in battle. The Security Branch officers and men received little or no training, for example, in the control of military traffic during war. This failure was finally recognized and has been corrected.

It would be incorrect and unfair not to balance this somewhat negative comment about unification without mentioning the positive results. The logic of the concept must be apparent to any except the most die-hard critics. It made sense to integrate those functions being duplicated and triplicated in the three Services, often at a high cost in dollars and efficiency. For example, why have a triplicate pay, recruiting, rationing, medical, police, security, supply or transport system when each was carrying out the same basic function regardless of the colour of the uniform? Granted there were some areas, notably in the Navy, where the environment dictated a different approach, however the majority of functions performed by service support tradesmen were largely the same for each Service. This was certainly the case in the police, security and intelligence field. There were some notable advantages to unification.

- The organization of the Canadian Forces Headquarters (CFHQ) on a single service basis successfully eliminated scores of inter-service committees. These committees had a common purpose, which was to develop policy on the many issues of common concern to the three services. The most senior was the Chiefs of Staff Committee (COS), made up of the Chiefs of each Service and chaired by a Chairman appointed by the Minister, usually a former Chief. Beneath this there were literally dozens of tri-service committees dealing with matters such as pay and allowances, terms of service, budgets, security, intelligence, accommodation, equipment and on and on. They absorbed the time of countless officers and support staff and rarely made a correct decision. Hundreds of meetings invarialbly resulted in compromise or deferment. By actual count there were 257 committees functioning in National Defence Headquarters prior to unification. The concept of having a single officer making decisions in a specific field eliminated this waste of time and effort and produced workable results.

- The expanded base derived from grouping work functions and duties in the trade fields of support corps/branches not only provided more varied and interesting jobs for the members in that trade, but greatly improved career prospects for promotion and advancement. For example, the Canadian Provost Corps had one colonel position for about 1,000 all ranks. The unified organization of Security/Intelligence had four colonels for about 2,000 all ranks, with an overall chief established in the rank of Major General. Improved rank structures for non-commissioned ranks greatly benefitted the rank and file in the new Security Branch. This point is well illustrated by the fact that since unification no fewer than seven former Canadian Provost Ccorps officers have attained the rank of colonel and one has risen to General rank.
- The unified force provides greater flexibility to meet changing requirements in defence organization, made necessary by advances in military technology and a changing international situation. The nature of modern warfare has compressed the time and distance factor so that decision making and reaction time must be greatly accelerated. A unified force stands the best chance of meeting this demand.
- Considerable cost savings were achieved through economies of scale by bulk-buying, reduced inventories and lower distribution costs for items such as fuel, clothing and uniforms, food, light vehicles, personal kit and equipment and training facilities.
- Recruiting and manpower allocation systems were made more efficient and responsive through single recruiting centres as opposed to the three former systems, each competing against the other.

The overall objective of unifying Canada's three armed services made sense. Here we had a relatively small military establishment forced, by increasing fiscal scarcity, to compete with each other just to survive. The disparity between opertation/maintenance and capital expenditures simply could not be continued if anything resembling an efficient military force was to be sustained. This much was clear and acceptable to the professional soldiers in the Army. What was not logical or necessary was the methods used to achieve unification. Soldiers in the Canadian army have long understood the need to plan, fight and move on. A feature of the army process for policy decisions and planning had always been that those with a stake in an issue were given an opportunity to put forward their views. However, when a final decision was made it was then "shoulder-to-the-wheel". One did not sulk or complain, but got on with it despite personal conviction. The old saying was trite but true: "a soldier receiving an order has two options – obey it or change it". It was most unfortunate that the collaborative process was simply ignored during unification. The failure of the Minister, and his small select group, to communicate his intentions and plans is exemplified by the method previously mentioned, of imforming the Corps Directors of the Army of the demise of their positions and the corps they loved and led. These officers, mainly of colonel rank, were the leaders of the corps of the Canadian Army and symbolized its spirit and professionalism. To be hastily assembled and told that the Army, their Corps and their jobs no longer existed was almost unbearable. Their shock, anger and despair, which was felt by every soldier, was something that hopefully will never happen again.

Associations

During the Provost Marshal's conference of February 1960 it was suggested that the possibility be explored of creating an association for officers of the Canadian Provost Corps. This initiative was started by Regular Officers and was considered timely since there was now a significant number of retired Corps officers across Canada. There was a general consensus that a fraternal association would serve several purposes, including that of keeping in touch with retired members. A pro tempore committee was formed to prepare a draft constitution for ratification by all Canadian Provost Corps serving officers. This committee, consisting of Major J A Dowsett and Captain J M Jacques of the Provost Marshal's staff, completed a draft charter which was circulated to all officers of the Corps during November 1960. Following some minor changes, resulting from comments received by the Pro Tempore committee, the first Constitution was approved by the Adjutant General in December and was forwarded to all officers on 29 December 1960. The first Executive Committee was appointed by the Provost Marshal. It comprised the Chairman, Major C A Breakey, Secretary, Captain L N Henderson, and Treasurer, Lieutenant W E R Chambers, all of the Canadian Provost Corps School, Camp Borden. The stated aim of the Canadian Provost Corps Officers' Association was "to provide an organization which would serve the mutual interests of the serving and retired officers of the Canadian Provost Corps". The association objectives were listed as follows:

a. Assist in maintaining the traditions of the Corps;
b. Provide an employment assistance programme for serving officers on retirement from the Army;
c. Provide the Corps with the means of drawing on the experience of serving and retired members;
d. Provide assistance to other Canadian Provost Corps Associations that may be created from time to time;
e. To disseminate information of interest to members of the Association.

Membership was open to all serving and retired officers of the Corps. The methods of operating were contained in appropriate By-Laws, which covered activities such as Fees, Election of Committees, Voting Procedures, Finances, Membership, Annual Meetings and Reports to Members.

The first Annual General Meeting was held in Camp Borden in conjunction with the January 1961 Provost Marshal Conference, and attended by some 32 officers. The constitution was approved and the decision was taken to meet annually to conduct Association business and hold a formal Mess Dinner. The membership grew from 60 officers in 1961 to 140 in 1966. A membership list of September 1966 shows 78 CA(R), 48 retired and 22 militia officers. A number of projects were initiated during the first five years and the Association grew, both in size and popularity. For example, it was decided at the 1962 meeting to provide a retirement momento to those members retiring during the past year, the value not to exceed $40.00. The retired officer employment assistnce programme created more work for the Secretary, however it was quite successful. The idea was that a list of job opportunities, as notified by members, would be kept by the Secretary and released to the members, from time to time, in a newsletter.

The Association played a major role in a series of events held in 1965 to mark the twenty-fifth anniversary of the Corps. Perhaps the most significant event was the ceremonies held at the Canadian Provost School in Camp Borden to dedicate a Corps Memorial Cairn which had been designed and constructed under the direction of Lieutenant Colonel B W E Lee, the School Commandant and also, fortuitously, the Chairman of the Association. This cairn is located in a pleasant open area in the School lines featuring a neat lawn surrounded by tall cottonwood trees. The cairn was constructed from local field stone on a stepped concrete base. It measures about 15 feet square at the base and slopes upward to a height of about 14 feet. There are four life-size bronzed lions in the "passant guardant" position on the base, one at each corner. A suitable bronze plaque is affixed to the south side of the cairn at about eye level. The area was designated "STEWART SQUARE" as a memorial to the first, and recently deceased, peacetime Provost Marshal – Lieutenant Colonel James Reginald Stewart, MBE, CD. The northwest corner of the square is marked by a suitably inscribed bronze plaque fixed to a large boulder. It is a permanent and fitting memorial to those Corps members who gave their lives in war.

The dedication ceremony took place on Sunday, 13 June 1965. it was attended by over two hundred and fifty serving and retired members including two former Provost Marshals, Colonel Phillipe August Puize, OBE, ED and Colonel Leonard Hanson Nicholson, OC, MBE, GC StJ, LLD. The Secretary of the Association, Captain Jack Rand (former Royal Air Force and Metropolitan London Police), gave us this complete and witty account of the 25th Anniversary celebrations held throughout the Corps during June 1965. Excerpts from his Newsletters of 25 March, 19 May and 28 June 1965 are very revealing.

24 March 1965

The Silver Jubilee is likely to be the biggest thing we do in the Canadian Provost Corps as we know it today. All Regular and Militia Units will be celebrating in their respective locations. The programme at the Canadian Provost Corps School will be a full one. Though the actual day of the Corps birthday is Tuesday, 15 June 1965, the bulk of the celebrations are going to be held on the 13th and 14th, the preceding Sunday and Monday. This is being done so that visitors who cannot stay over until Wednesday may enjoy most functions. Sunday morning will be given over to a Parade, followed at 1400 by a Memorial Service to dedicate the Corps Memorial Cairn.

Lieutenant Colonel Stewart's widow, Mrs Grace Stewart, will unveil the plaque marking Stewart Square, in memory of her husband. Colonel Puize will unveil the Memorial Cairn. The Band of the Royal Canadian Regiment will be in attendance for all functions at the School. On Monday there will be a Sports Day with a midday barbecue (with ale) and in the evening the All Ranks Silver Jubilee Ball will be held in the Buell Building, Camp Borden. The 18 hole Jubilee Golf Tournament, open to all past and present members, will be held on Tuesday.

Corps Medallions and Decals are available from local detachments or the Provost Marshal's Office. A Silver Jubilee Memorial Book is being produced and will be distributed for sale to all members at a cost of $2.50 per copy.

A Special Postage Cancellation Stamp will be used by Post Offices in Halifax, Montreal, Ottawa, Toronto, Camp Borden and Edmonton. If other areas would like to avail themselves of this service the die costs $11.99 and can be ordered through the Director of Security (Provost Marshal) Canadian Forces Headquarters, Ottawa 4, Ontario.

Other news of Association interest is that No 2 Company (Militia) held their final parade before transfer to the new establishment in the Toronto Service Battalion, in the College Street Armoury on 11 February 1965. Major Frank Burrard Creasey, the first OC of No 2 Company (WWII), took time out to send an interesting letter describing 2 Company's early days. He related hazards attached to having a company of 114 souls, 93 motorcycles and six men who could ride them. As a result of the good offices of OPP Staff Superintendent Bill Gilling, Major Creasey is now a member of the Association.

Sam Sambrooke was "wined" out of the Service at a function in Edmonton which included old stalwarts like RCMP Superintendents Chris Forbes and Eric Porter and Ex 5 Provost Company Major Earl Wilson. Sammy asks that his appreciation for the gift of the cigarette box be conveyed to all members.

19 May 1965

In Camp Borden the Dedication Service for the Corps Memorial will begin at 1400 hours on 13 June 1965. Dress has been laid down as No 1 with Sword for the Commander of the Guard, other School officers and ADCs No 1 without sword, visiting officers No 1 without sword, or Tropical Worsted with medals or plain clothes in that order of preference. Civilian gentlemen in plain clothes.

The Silver Jubilee Ball in Ottawa will be held at HMCS Carleton on Friday, 11 June 1965 at 2100 hours. Colonel and Mrs Nicholson and Colonel and Mrs Ritchie will attend. You may obtain more information on this function from Major A F Ritchie, Directorate of Security.

Camp Petawawa members are holding a formal ball to celebrate the Silver Anniversary at Dundonald Hall on 5 June 1965. The admission is $2.00 per couple. Wherever you are, and whatever functions you have arranged around 15 June, here's hoping you have a gay old time.

28 June 1965

Everything went as planned and we think that everyone was impressed. To us "Johnnie-come-latelies" it was a revelation to see so many of the founding members assembled. The naming of Stewart Square was a simple but impressive ceremony and, like all simple affairs when well done, it was extremely moving. Mrs

Stewart felt it keenly, as did many more who knew Colonel Stewart well. There was a biting cold wind blowing and with a piper playing a lament, we might well have been back in Scotland.

The ceremony to Dedicate the Memorial Cairn was colourful and impressive. Colonel Puize was delighted that he had been asked to unveil the memorial, which he has since confirmed in a wonderful letter of appreciation to the Chairman of the Association. Colonel Puize is a wonderful gentleman – they certainly did not do us wrong when he was appointed Provost Marshal. Mrs Puize is a charming lady and a bit of a character.

Anybody who was anybody was there. Colonel and Mrs Nicholson were front and centre at the ceremonies. Colonel Scotti made the longest trip from Paris and probably didn't endear himself around home by missing his daughter's graduation. Director of Security and Mrs Ritchie had to get back to Ottawa the same evening. Superintendent and Mrs "Red" Stevenson represented Commissioner McLellan, who was away in South America. Major Frank Creasey was there as was Major Ed Watts, plus many regulars of the Association.

War stories got a good towsing at the Garden Party and reception afterwards at the Sergeants Mess. You could pick up a wound stripe just by leaning on the bar and listening. The Corps received official congratulations from the Colonel Commandant, Director of Security, the Commander UNEF (Gaza), all ranks in the Gaza Strip and from the APM and all ranks serving in the NATO Brigade Europe. The Minister of National Defence sent his greetings to all ranks of the corps in the following message:

On the occasion of your Silver Jubilee Anniversary I send you my sincere congratulations. Although 25 years is a short period in our military history, in that time your Corps has achieved a distinguished record and won the respect and admiration of all members of the Armed Forces. Through the Second World War and Korea you supported the fighting man. On the Gaza Strip, in the Congo and in Cyprus you formed the base for the United Nations Military Police Organization. You can be proud of your past achievements, which have been a true reflection of your Corps motto "Discipline by Example". I wish you continued success in all your endeavours, in the knowledge that your past achievements will be your guide for the future.

Paul Hellyer
Minister of Defence

Lieutenant Colonel Quentin Earl (Joe) Lawson sends this straight Lawson special from Ottawa: Did you know that we had a race named for us at the Rideau Carleton Raceway on Monday 14 June 1965? Well we did. The 9th was the Canadian Provost Corps Silver Jubilee Pace over a distance of one mile. The hunch players went home smiling. The No 5 horse "Lucky Stone" won handily and paid rather well, so we went away laughing kit-bags. He sent a photo for the museum showing himself with "Lucky Stone" in the winner's circle. "Lucky Stone" is a roan mare and its easy to tell which is which even from the front.

Fun was had in Cyprus. Apart from Church Parades split into three groups (RCs, Prots and Angry Separatists), they had a Bar-B-Que and Skin Diving competition where anyone who failed to surface after 10 minutes was disqualified. A Commemoration Dance was held, including as guests: General Thimaya, the Force Commander, The Canadian High Commissioner, Commanding Officers of major units, some grim visaged student nurses from Dkekalia and wary British school teachers from Limassol. Compliments of Lieutenant Colonel Eric Hill from UNFICYP.

Members of the corps owe a debt to people like Bill Lee, Jack Rand and all of those who gave their time and energy unsparingly to plan and implement the many events that marked this milestone in the life of the Corps. Perhaps the planning, construction and dedication of the Memorial Cairn is the one that will survive for years to come. The Silver Jubilee Book was also most successful. The 2,700 copies printed in the first run were quickly snapped up and, as it is now out of print, it is something of a collector's item. Complimentary copies were mailed to a few libraries and archives. The following senior serving officers were also presented with a copy:

Lt Gen G Walsh	Comm G B McLellan (RCMP)
Lt Gen R W Moncel	Col J R Stone (Ex-PM)
V Adm K L Dyer	Col L H Nicholson (Col Comdt)
Maj Gen W A B Anderson	Col P A Puize (Ex-PM)
Maj Gen R P Rothschild	D Hist J M Hitsman (Army)
Maj Gen J M Rockingham	Editor Cdn Army Journal
Maj Gen F J Fleury	Library CFHQ (Ottawa)
Maj Gen R Rowley	Library RCMI (Toronto)
Maj Gen C B Ware	Director Info Svcs
Maj Gen G A Turcot	The C Pro C Museum

The Association continued to function for the next five years (1965–70) with only minor changes. The constitution was amended in 1966 to provide for the appointment of life members. The Secretary's Newsletter continued to be a popular communication medium, especially since the number of officers leaving the service was steadily increasing. For many this was their only means of keeping in touch. The Newsletter issued by the Secretary, Captain David L Stone, in June 1968 lists the following names in the recent "retiree" column: Lt Col J J Platt 1965, Col A R Ritchie 1967, Col A F Scotti 1968, Lt Col Q E Lawson 1968, Lt Col E M Hills 1966, Lt Col J C Treleaven 1968, Maj C A Breakey 1967, Maj Jim Walsh 1966, Maj T J Quirk 1959, Capt Jack Rand 1968, Capt Terry Downie 1967, Capt Claude Brown 1968, Capt Al Abrams 1968, Maj A S (Art) Bird 1968, Capt H C Reynett 1968, Capt W E R (Ray) Chambers 1967, Capt Laurie Paulhus 1968, Capt Nat Smith 1968, Capt Bill Fiddes 1967, Lt Col George Wilkinson 1968. The retirements listed in the October 1969 newsletter show Lt Col R I (Bob) Luker 1969, and Maj J A (John) Fogg 1969. The May 1969 letter by Captain Murray Wilson conatains a listing of Corps Officers who were posted in July 1969. This list illustrates two points. First it shows the tremendous variety of positions in which corps officers were serving. Secondly it clearly shows the versatility of these former Corps officers.

NAME	FROM	TO
Maj R T Hall	Staff College Toronto	SIU St Hubert
Maj Ross Mooney	CFHQ	CFB Petawawa
Capt J R Gervais	SIU St Hubert	Staff College Toronto
Capt R Desormeaux	4 Svc Bn	CFB Valcartier
Capt H E Hughes	DPCLL/SC	D Secur 5 (Ottawa)
Capt J D Lumsden	CFB Edmonton	DPCLL/SC (Ottawa)
Capt S P Jamieson	CFB Valcartier	CFSIS (Borden)
Capt V McDougall	CFB Soest	CFB (Borden)
Capt R Parker	CFB Soest	CFSIS (Borden)
Capt A B P Robertson	CFSIS	SFB Soest
Capt L Barbeau	Staff College (Kingston)	Francotrain
Capt M C MacDonald	CFB Gagetown	CFB Edmonton
Capt G MacDonald	CFB Borden	4 Svc Bn (Germany)

It did not take long for some of the realities of unification to surface. Even though the stated aim of the Association was to maintain links with previous areas, places and persons, nevertheless there was something incongruous about the Corps officers going off as a separate group to celebrate the past without their workplace associates in the Security Branch. There was also the problem of continuity for the young officers entering the Branch who were often confused on the fundamental question of just where their loyalty should lie. Finally, the membership of the Association was declining, as revealed by the reports of successive Presidents. In 1967 the membership stood at a healthy 132, declining to 106 in 1968 and to a low of 63 in 1969.

The Air Force Police element had no formed fraternal organization. The Intelligence officers had a formal association in the Canadian Military Intelligence Association (CMIA). It was a member of the powerful National Conference of Defence Association (CDA) which has functioned continuously since 1932. The feasibility of broadening the Canadian Provost Corps Association by the inclusion in its membership of the other Security Branch officers (former RCAF and C Int C) was discussed at the September 1968 annual meeting. This proposal received favourable reaction throughout the Association. The Executive Committee, headed by Lt Col Bob Luker, drafted a revised constitution which was circulated to all officers and again it received overwhelming approval. A combined meeting of former Canadian Provost Corps, Air Force Security Officers and former Canadian Intelligence Corps and CMIA officers was held at Camp Borden on 24 June 1969. The new Constitution was approved and, henceforth, the Association would be known as the CANADIAN FORCES SECURITY SERVICES OFFICERS' ASSOCIATION (CFSSOA).

The preamble to the revised Constitution read as follows:

In view of the amalgamation of the Canadian Provost Corps, the Canadian Intelligence Corps and the police and security elements of the Royal Canadian Navy and the Royal Canadian Air Force in the Canadian Forces Security Services, it was decided by overwhelming vote of the members of the Canadian Provost Corps Officers in early 1969 to change its name. Accordingly this Constitution provides for the organization and operation of an association to be known as the Canadian Forces Security Services Officers association.

The aims, objectives and by-laws were amended to include participation by all service and retired officers of the two Corps as well as RCAF and RCN officers formerly employed in police, security and intelligence positions. New membership cards were developed and issued, membership lists were distributed and a handy vest pocket edition of the CFSSOA constitution was prepared and sent to each member. As expected, the membership increased dramatically. However, it must be said that there were a few Corps officers who disagreed with this initiative, and their opinion was respected. New By-Laws were introduced to enlarge the Executive Committee and extend the retirement gift and employment assistance programmes. A new educational assistance programmme and the Academic Awards Programme was established whereby the association would award $150.00 annually to a dependent child of each of three members to assist in defraying the costs of education. This was subsequently revised as a Bursary of $600.00 to one student applicant to be selected by a special panel of the Executives each year. It was also decided to establish the position of Patron of the Association. The officer so selected would wear the official Chain of Office, which was designed and manufactured by Major E Roberts a former RCAF Security Branch Officer. The membership had increased to 137 by the end of 1969 and the Directory published in October 1972 shows, in alpha order, the names of 180 members. For anyone interested in a statistical breakdown, there were 62 regular, 56 retired and 19 militia officers listed in the 1969 directory. Canadian Provost Corps members may be interested to know that no fewer than six former Provost Marshals were also listed in the 1969 directory.

Lt Col Bob Luker was prescient when he concluded his annual President's report at the October 1969 meeting, with this statement:

I believe that the change of name of the Association will bring many new members and that it will continue to prosper. While we may have lost many of the old customs and traditions as a result of integration and unification, the good fellowship, spirit and dedication to duty that made our Corps and our Association so successful can be perpetuated in the new organization. If it is successful it will be because of the example set for it by you.

The newly created CFSSOA was highly successful in terms of increased membership and activities in support of its stated aims. A further boost to the Association occurred in 1972 when the members of the Canadian Military Intelligence Association (CMIA) voted to expand by making all Security Branch officers eligible as members. This entailed amending the CMIA Charter to provide for the necessary changes, including the new title: Canadian Intelligence and Security Association (CISA). A brief explanation of the long established Conference of Defence Associations (CDA) is in order. CDA was established in the fall of 1932 at a meeting in Ottawa, attended by delegates from the Infantry, Artillery and Cavalry Associations of that day. Historically the CDA has provided leadership for the often contentious issues of defence in Canada, and has provided much support in times of trouble for the military Reserves. It was reorganized in the early 1960's to encompass the Naval and Air Reserves, largely as a result of the HENDY and DRAPER Commissions. The CMIA was formed by serving and retired officers of the Canadian Intelligence Corps (C Int C) in 1948. Membership of the CMIA in CDA ensured representation of the functions and organization of military intelligence in the National association. The CDA now comprises several member associations.

Maritime Defence Association
Royal Canadian Armoured Corps Association
Royal Canadian Artillery Association
Military Engineering Association of Canada
Land Ordnance Engineering Branch Association
Canadian Forces Communications and Electrical Association
Canadian Infantry Association
Canadian Forces Logistics Association
Defence Medical Association
Royal Canadian Dental Corps Association
Canadian Intelligence and Security Association
Air Reserve Association
Affiliated with Canadian Institute of Strategic Studies

The CDA meets annually in Ottawa, usually in January, to conduct its business, seek consensus on issues relating to Canada's defence and to submit agreed recommendations to the Minister of National Defence and Chief of the Defence Staff. Its major aims are to coordinate activities of member associations, place National Defence problems before the people of Canada and make recommendations to the Government of Canada. The Chairman of CDA has direct access to the Minister of National Defence and the Conference makes representations to the Government through this channel. The First Annual meeting of CISA was held at the CFSIS at Camp Borden on 15 June 1973. The minutes show 243 names on the membership list, including some 20 former serving and retired officers of the former Canadian Provost Corps. The foregoing action had the practical effect of giving military police a voice in the CDA for the first time in history.

The CFSSOA continued to function with only minor changes in its activity until the end of the decade. However, it was becoming apparent, particularly to senior serving and retired officers of the Security Branch, that the long-term effects of Unification was beginning to reveal some reasons for concern. The President, Lieutenant Colonel R F Bornor, assisted by the Vice-President, Major F A Leigh, and Secretary, Captain D E Clemis, conducted a thorough review of the current situation regarding organization, purpose and activity of the several associations within the Security Branch. The following list illustrates, beyond a doubt, that forming associations had become a growth industry in the Branch:

1. Canadian Military Intelligence Association –   Formed 1948
2. Canadian Provost Corps Officers Association   1961

3. Canadian Forces Security Service Officers Association   1970
4. Canadian Intelligence and Security Association   1973
5. Canadian Provost Corps Association   1974
6. Military Police Association*   1983
*Under consideration from 1979

A comprehensive report was prepared and forwarded to the membership in January 1980. The report pointed out several disadvantages of having two associations (CISA and CFSSOA) operating side by side, with the former finding its members from retired, regular and militia officers with an intelligence background, and the latter from those with a security and police background. The CISA, as a member of the Conference of Defence Associations, has an official avenue for input into policy decisions affecting the Branch. The CFSSOA, a purely fraternal association, had no such opportunity. Each association had between 230 and 250 members. Of these only 30 officers had joint memberships in both associations. There was evidence to suggest that neither was attracting the younger officers so necessary for long-term viability. A comparison of the CFSSOA membership list and the Security Branch list of regular force officers clearly shows that only a small percentage have joined CFSSOA. New officers, commissioned in the "Green" environment did not have the background or tradition to actively support both associations. The common result was they joined neither.

Discussions to amalgamate the two Associations had been taking place for the past five years amongst members and the Executives of both. While there were some differences in wording of the basic objectives of the two, the fundamental purpose of each was the same, that is to say: to support the best interests of the security and/or intelligence service within the Canadian Armed Forces. On the basis of the ongoing informal discussions over the past few years, it was clear that there was overwhelming support for amalgamation which would achieve the following long-term benefits:

- it would be a meaningful step towards greater Branch unity;
- the aims of both associations can be continued;
- increased membership should result in an increase in Government funding and a larger base of support for recommendations to the CDA;
- one officers' association would reduce much of the confusion among junior officers.

The proposal to merge the CFSSOA with CISA was approved by the membership of both at a joint meeting in Base Borden on 25 September 1980. The President of CISA, Captain David Rubin, and Secretary, Major John (Pappy) MacKinnon, undertook the drafting of new By-laws for CISA, providing for the continuation of CFSSOA projects such as:

- officers' retirement recognition;
- academic award programme;
- donations to C F Borden Museum;
- provision for life members;
- publication of a newsletter;
- regional representatives; and
- publication of membership lists.

It was also agreed that the executive committee officers would be drawn from both groups with the presidency alternating, as far as possible, between both.

The merger was remarkably smooth thanks to the thorough preparation and foresight of the two Executive Committees. There is no doubt that this action achieved the aims of improving Branch unity and the inclusion of reserve police and security officers in CISA. The membership increased sharply, although it did not reach the forecast figure of doubling the 1980 CFSSOA figure. The CISA is still an active and progressive organization after more than a decade since the merger with CFSSOA. Before leaving the Canadian Provost Corps Officers and Canadian Forces Security Services Officers Association it is appropriate to record the names of those on the executive committees from 1961 to 1980. The list does not include the names of treasurers or membership secretaries, and are not necessarily listed in order of serving.

Chairman/President	Secretary
Maj J A Dowsett (1961)	Capt L N Henderson (1961)
Maj C A Breakey	Capt D Stone
Maj E M Hills	Maj W P Stoker
Lt Col B W E Lee	Capt M Wilson
Lt Col Q E Lawson	Capt H E Hughes
Maj W P Stoker	Maj J D Lumsden
Lt Col J A Dowsett	Capt P A H Dupille
Maj L N Henderson (Vice-Pres)	Capt H C Reynett
Lt Col R T Grogan	Capt J Rand
Lt Col A J Murtagh	Capt A B Robertson

Lt Col R F Bornor   Capt B Kent
Maj F A Leigh (Vice-Pres 1980)   Capt D E Clemis (1980)

The Canadian Provost Corps Association

A move to form an all-ranks Corps association was started in Ottawa by a group of former Canadian Provost Corps NCOs in the mid 1970's. The matter was discussed at several meetings throughout 1974 and 1975, and on 22 November 1975 an interim committee was formed to pursue this initiative. On 10 April 1976 a "founding" meeting was held at Wallis House, Ottawa attended by about twenty-five former members of the Corps. An executive committee was elected, a constitution was adopted and the Canadian Provost Corps Association was born. The main features of this association, as expressed in the Constitution, were:

- the Headquarters to be located in Ottawa;
- all persons who served in the Corps prior to 1 February 1968 were eligible for membership;
- the Executive Committee was empowered to initiate by-laws for operation of the Association, subject to approval of the members.

The Association was an instant success. By June 1977 the membership had reached one hundred, and by June 1980 the membership listed over two hundred names. The stated purpose of the Association was to provide an organization which would foster and maintain the traditions and comradeship of the Canadian Provost Corps, and to serve and assist members of the Association. A variety of programs and activities were introduced to achieve these goals, such as a Kit Shop which stocked items of Corps dress and insignia. A Benevolent Fund was set up to assist needy members and provide appropriate condolences to families of a deceased member, and other like matters. Up-to-date membership lists were distributed at regular intervals, annual meetings and reunions were held where members and their wives rejoiced in nostalgic memories. By far the most meaningful project was the regular publication of an Association Journal. The WATCHDOG[159] quickly became the voice of the Corps and was invaluable as a means of communicating information to all members. For example, it notified the dates of forthcoming events, published information on members and articles on past Corps activities and events. It was, and is, an absolutely first class effort.

The Constitution was amended from time-to-time to provide for Associate and Honourary members, a Colonel Commandant, Life Members and the issue of membership cards. One of the earlier amendments relative to membership stated: All regular members of the Association will be deemed to have been appointed Permanent Lance Corporals Without Pay (L/Cpl WOP). All regular members shall be addressed as "Lance Corporal". Presumably this was to ensure the Association continued to operate on strictly democratic lines.

The highlight of the Association's activities came in 1990, which was the 50th anniversary of the Corps. The Executive Committee, assisted by some additional members, planned a three day celebration in Ottawa on 14, 15, and 16 of June. The University of Ottawa Convention facility was obtained for the main assemblies and proved ideal. Over 300 members and their wives attended, coming from coast to coast in Canada and several from locations in the United States of America. The first event was a "meet-and-greet" during the evening of the 14th. It was held in the large outdoor patio and featured a bar, ragtime band, food and much renewal of old friendships. On Saturday, 15 June, the ladies were taken on a scenic bus tour of the Ottawa area, culminating with lunch at LaRonde Restaurant atop the Skyline. The members attended the Annual General Meeting in the afternoon, where the ususal Association business was conducted, albeit never before such a large audience of voting members. A formal dinner was held in the evening. The overall ambience of this event was augmented by the attendance of a few guests of honour, including the Chief of Defence Staff General John deChastelain, Deputy Minister of Veterans Affairs Mr David Broadbent and Commissioner of the Royal Canadian Mounted Police Norman Inkster and his wife Mary Anne. The RCMP Band was in attendance throughout the evening.

A Corps Memorial Service was held at the National Cenotaph in Confederation Square on Sunday, at 11:00 o'clock. The service was conducted by the Principal Chaplains General, both Protestant and Roman Catholic. It featured the laying of wreaths by the CDS, DM DVA, Commr RCMP, the Colonel Commandant, Director General of Security, and President Canadian Provost Corps Association. It was a beautiful sunny day and a fitting climax to these three, never to be forgotten, days in Ottawa.

It is appropriate to list the names of those members who have shared the burden of conducting the affairs of the Association. Unfortunately we do not have a complete record except for the President position. While all have given freely of time and energy it is fitting that one person should get special mention. L/Cpl Joe Rivet has been the efficient, hard-working Secretary since 1983 and still serves after ten years of performing these demanding duties. The Presidents, in order of service, were: Ted Genest 1974–1976 (Interim Period); Don Tresham 1976–1978; Marcel Fortier 1978–1979; Vance McDougall 1979–1980; Reid Surrett 1980–1983; Lorne Henderson 1983–1990; James Lumsden 1990–.

This Association has done wonders to cement the bonds of brotherhood among members of the old Corps. One day it will inevitably fade away and the last two surviving members will stand and toast the Canadian Provost Corps from a bottle of fine old brandy. The BOTTLE is now held by the President, in a special case, and is to be passed on to successors until the day arrives when it "shall be decanted". That, as they say, will be the day.

20

A Few Good Men

An effort was made in compiling this history to focus on events rather than individuals because it is not possible to name the countless number of Corps members who contributed to its history. It is appropriate, however, to list the names of a few who were representative of the many. Accordingly, the names of some who served, during varying periods, are listed below.

PROVOST MARSHALS OF THE CANADIAN ARMY

Colonel Gilbert Godson Godson	1917–1920
Colonel Phillipe August Puize	1940–1943
Colonel George Thomas Goad	1943–1945
Colonel Leonard Hanson Nicholson	1945–1946
Lieutenant Colonel James Reginald Stewart	1946–1954
Colonel James Riley Stone	1954–1959
Colonel Allan L Brady	1959–1962
Colonel Anthony Joseph Scotti	1962–1964
Colonel Andrew Reginald Ritchie*	1964–1964

*Director of Security – Canadian Armed Forces 1964 – 1967

DEPUTY (Dpms), ASSISTANT (Apms) and DEPUTY ASSISTANT (Dapms) PROVOST MARSHALS

Canadian Active Service Force – Overseas World War II
(Not necessarily complete)

Abbreviations:
- CMHQ — Canadian Military Headquarters
- HQ CRU — Headquarters Canadian Reinforcement Units
- Cdn — Canadian
- L of C — Lines of Communciation (base areas)
- Inf Div — Infantry Division
- Armd Div — Armoured Division
- OC — Officer Commanding
- Rft — Reinforcements
- Trg — Training

CMHQ (London)	DPM	Colonel A D Cameron
	APM	Major O G Supeene
		Major R R R J Holmes
		Major A J Gillis
HQ CRU (Farnham)	APM	Major F B Creasey
		Major R J Risley
HQ First Cdn Army	DPM	Lieutenant Colonel G W Ball
	APM	Major R J Stewart
	DAPM	Captain J H Platt
HQ First Cdn Army Troops	DAPM	Captain M E Byers
HQ 1 Cdn Corps	APM	Major G W Ball
		Major L H Nicholson
		Major E S W Batty
	DAPM	Captain R Risley
(L of C)	DAPM	Captain H F Law
HQ 2 Cdn Corps	APM	Major L H Nicholson
		Major N Cooper
		DAPM(N / K)
		Captain George Kerr
HQ 1 Cdn Inf Div	APM	Major C Hill
		Major W R Day
		Major J A Stevenson
		Major E S W Batty

		Major G W Mudge
HQ 2 Cdn Inf Div	APM	Major J E B Hallett Major J B Harris Major H C Forbes
HQ 3 Cdn Inf Div	APM	(N/K) Major W G Lloyd Major J R Stewart (CAOF)
HQ 4 Cdn Armd Div	APM	Major H M Baker Major E H Stevenson Major J J Platt Major E S W Batty
HQ 5 Cdn Armd Div	APM	Major L H Nicholson Major J A Stevenson Major A J Scotti

OFFICERS COMMANDING OVERSEAS PROVOST UNITS IN WORLD WAR II

1 Provost Company (1 Cdn Inf Div)	OC	Captain W R Day Captain W G Lloyd Captain C F Wilson Captain E S W Batty Captain G W Mudge Captain (N/K)
2 Provost Company (2 Cdn Inf Div)	OC	Captain F B Creasey Captain J E B Hallett Captain E H Stevenson Captain H C Forbes Captain B W E Lee Captain L W Paige Captain J M Tweddle
3 Provost Company (3 Cdn Corps)	OC	Captain J E Pratt Captain J R Stewart

		Captain W G Lloyd
		Captain H F Law
		Captain E M Hills
		Captain R P Harrison
4 Provost Company (3 Cdn Inf Div)	OC	Captain J Shipp
		Captain N Cooper
		Captain A J Gillis
		Captain H R German
5 Provost Company (5 Cdn Armd Div)	OC	Captain A S Renton
		Captain H M Childerstone
		Captain A J Scotti
		Captain T E Clark
		Captain Q E Lawson
6 Provost Company (CMHQ London)	OC	Captain R H Kidston
		Captain M E Byers
		Captain S Dalton
		Captain J R R Carrier
9 Provost Comapny (Cdn Rft Unit–England)	OC	Captain C W Graham
		Captain R A Ogilvie
		Captain T J Quirk
7 Provost Company (First Cdn Army Troops–UK & NWE)	OC	Captain E F Putnam
8 Provost Company (4 Cdn Armd Div)	OC	Captain S Dalton
		Captain J P Stewart
		Captain C L Ray
		Captain J M Walsh
11 Provost Company (First Cdn Army)	OC	Captain E Porter
13 Provost Company (2 Cdn Corps)	OC	Captain S H G Margetts
		Captain E Porter
		Captain G Kerr
		Captain A R Ritchie

		Captain C M Newman
		Captain T J Quirk
14 Provost Company (Cdn Repat Depots–UK)	C	Captain W Gilling
17 Provost Company (Cdn Repat Depots–UK)	OC	Captain T S Reid
1 L of C Provost Company (1 Cdn Corps Base Area–Italy)	OC	Captain G W Mudge Captain H M Childerstone Captain J Dursch
2 L of C Provost Company (Cdn Army Base Area – NWE)	OC	Captain A F Allendorf Captain C L Ray Captain J B Tweddle
Canadian Provost Corps Depot (Rft and Trg Unit – UK)	OC	Captain C Woods Captain J S Speakman Captain S Dalton Captain J P Stewart
No 1 C Pro C Trg & Rft Depot (Aldershot 1945–46)	CO 21C C1 Coy Comds	Lieutenant Colonel W G Lloyd Major J P Stewart Major A R Ritchie Major H E Matteson Major R L Kyle

REGIMENTAL SERGEANT MAJORS (RSMs) OF THE CANADIAN PROVOST CORPS SHOWING PRINCIPAL UNIT

G W (George) BALL	1 Provost Company
A M (N/K) BENNETT	N/K
A S (Art) BIRD	2 L of C Provost Company
G (Gil) BOUDREAU	Provost Marshal's Office
M E (Pat) BYERS	3 Provost Company
E R (Cappy) CAPPIELLO	8 Provost Company
G E (George) CHRISTIE	C Pro C School
C T E (N/K) COLEMAN	N/K

C W (Charlie) DOUGLAS	C F S I S
G (George) ELLIOTT	C F S I S
R (Ron) FINNIE	C Pro C Depot (Aldershot)
M L (Marcel) FORTIER	C Pro C School
E (Earl) GREY	C Pro C School
T S (N/K) GILES	4 Provost Company
E D (Denny) HARPER	4 Provost Company
H L (Hank) HATCH	12 Service Detention Barracks
D (Danny) ILLINGWORTH	A-32 Provost Training Centre
W B (Bill) KNIGHT	8 Provost Company
J (Jules) KNUYVER	C F S I S
J (Jack) MacDONALD	8 Service Detention Barracks
A (Archie) MacKENZIE	1 Provost Company
E (Ernie) MacNAMARA	7 Provost Company
A (N / K) MANVEILER	2 Provost Company
H (Hughie) McCALLUM	13 Provost Company
J E (Jim) McCARDLE	1 Provost Company
A S (Al) MAYS	11 Provost Company
E S (Squeeky) NEILSEN	2 Provost Company
G W (N / K) OAKES	2 Provost Company
E F (Fred) PUTNAM	3 Provost Company
G J (Prize) PRIESWERCK	C F S I S
A G (George) POWELL	C W O Security Branch
J (Jimmie) RAE	11 Provost Company
J H (Jack) STAUNTON	5 Provost Company
R M (Bob) WALLACE	3 Provost Company
R L (Len) WHITWORTH	9 Provost Company

COMMANDING OFFICERS THE CANADIAN PROVOST CORPS SCHOOL

Major B W E (Bill) LEE	1946–1951
Lt Col J J (Jack) PLATT	1951–1956
Lt Col A R (Andy) RITCHIE	1956–1960
Lt Col W J (Tony) SCOTTI	1960–1962
Lt Col B W E (Bill) LEE	1962–1965
Lt Col R I (Bob) LUKER	1965–1967*

*Redesignated the Canadian School of Intelligence and Security (CFSIS) during 1967. Of the ten Commandants at CFSIS since 1967 six have been former officers of the Corps. They were:

Lt Col R I LUKER	1967–1969
Lt Col J A DOWSETT	1969–1973
Lt Col J S DUNN	1976–1978
Lt Col M WILSON	1978–1981
Lt Col A R WELLS	1984–1987
Lt Col B N WRIGHT	1987–1989

DEPUTY ASSISTANT PROVOST MARSHALS AT DISTRICT AND CAMP HEADQUARTERS IN CANADA as of 31 August 1943

M D 1	Major W S P GOW	London
M D 2	Lieutenant Colonel T DANN	Toronto
	Lieutenant Colonel H C WHITTON	Toronto (Oct 1943)
M D 3	Major E WATTS	Kingston
M D 4	Lieutenant Colonel G D MASSUE	Montreal
	Lieutenant Colonel M C LALONDE	Montreal
M D 5	Major G O BIGAOUETTE	Quebec City
M D 6	Lieutenant Colonel C W CLARKE	Halifax
M D 7	Lieutenant Colonel T E GUY	Saint John
M D 10	Lieutenant Colonel W S JONES	Winnipeg
Pacific Command	Lieutenant Colonel R B LONGRIDGE	Vancouver
M D 12	Major E SCOTT	Regina
M D 13	Major J H KENNEDY	Calgary
	Major T OLDFIELD	Calgary (Nov 1943)
M D 2	Major R B MORRISON	Camp Borden
M D #	Captain J E McCREADY	Camp Petawawa

OFFICERS COMMANDING HOME WAR ESTABLISHMENT PROVOST COMPANIES as at 31 August 1943

30 Provost Company	Major A L MENNIE	London
31 Provost Company	Major H C WHITTUN	Toronto

Provost Company	Major F E McMAHON	Toronto
32 Provost Company	Captain W R LUKE	Camp Borden
33 Provost Company	Major J STOCKS	Ottawa
34 Provost Company	Major W H DRAPER	Montreal
35 Provost Company	Captain W R POULIOTTE	Montreal
36 Provost Company	Major J F HAMEL	Quebec City
37 Provost Company	Major C F LORWAY	Halifax
38 Provost Company	Major R O MATTESON	Halifax
39 Provost Company	Major J G LeBLANC	Saint John
40 Provost Company	Major E K CARTER	Winnipeg
41 Provost Company	Major W S DINGLEY	Vancouver
42 Provost Company	Major F T M LAKE	Prince George
43 Provost Company	Captain J E EREMKO	Regina
44 Provost Company	Major R F C ALLEN	Calgary
45 Provost Company	Captain W O GRIMM	Sydney N S
46 Provost Company	Captain J L St-JEAN	Rimouski
47 Provost Company	Captain J W CALLANDER	Camp Petawawa

COMMANDING OFFICER AND PRINCIPAL STAFF
A-32 PROVOST TRAINING CENTRE August 1943

Commandant	Lieutenant Colonel J H MILLAR
Chief Instructor	Major A E PITCHER
O C Training Company	Captain T CRANSHAW
O C School of Instruction	Captain G W MONGER
Adjutant	Lieutenant P E OETIKER

CANADIAN PROVOST CORPS REGULAR OFFICERS
Showing Rank and Unit as at 1 October 1953

ABRAMS A W	2/Lt	C Pro C School–Camp Borden
AMIRAULT E J	Maj	CPM Quecom (Montreal)
ANDERSON C C	Capt	OC Eascom Pro Coy (Halifax)
BARRE J R	Capt	DAPM East Que Area (Quebec City)
BATEMAN J T	Lt	OC7SDB (Halifax)
BATES C F	Lt	1 & A Cadre Quecom (Montreal)
BEAULNE C	Lt	OC 17 SDB (Montreal)

BIRD A S	Lt	OIC Cdn Leave Centre, Tokyo
BORNOR R F	Lt	Instructor C Pro C School
BREAKEY C A	Capt	1 & A Cadre Cencom (Toronto)
CHAPMAN A B	2/Lt	Quecom Pro Coy (Montreal)
CONROY G J	2/Lt	C Pro C School
DABROS W J	Lt	Quecom Pro Coy (Valcartier)
DOWSETT J A	Capt	C A L E London (UK)
DUNN J S	2/Lt	C Pro C School
EASTAUGH N A	Lt	C A F I B Ottawa
ELLIOTT E F	2/Lt	C Pro C School
FIDDES W	Lt	Quecom Pro Coy (Quebec City)
FOY R A	2/Lt	Quecom Pro Coy (Winnipeg)
GERVAIS J R	2/Lt	C Pro C School
GILLIS A J (X-RCMP)	Maj	C P M Wescom (Edmonton)
GROGAN R T	Lt	1 & A Cadre Pracom (Winnipeg)
HARDY W R	Lt	25 F D B Seoul, Korea
HENDERSON L N	Lt	Instr C Pro C School
HILLS E M	Capt	C P M Cencom (Oakville)
HODGKISS G H	Maj	C P M Pracom (Winnipeg)
HONEY J G H	2/Lt	HQ West Ontario Area (London)
HOOPER J J	Lt	0 C 16 S D B Petawawa
HUFF G W	Lt	C Pro C School
HUGHES H E	Lt	C Pro C School
JACQUES J M	Capt	D Adm AHQ (Ottawa)
JAMIESON S P	2/Lt	1 & A Cadre B C Area (Vancouver)
KELLY H M	Capt	Cdn Army Staff College (Kingston)
KYLE G A	Capt	HQ B C F K, Japan
LAWLOR R W	Capt	DAPM Eascom (Halifax)
LAWSON Q E	Maj	OC 25 Pro Det – Korea
LEE B W E	Maj	OC 27 Pro Det – Germany
LEVESQUE L A	Lt	C Pro C School
LUKER R I	Maj	Chief Instr C Pro C School
LUMSDEN J D	2/Lt	Cencom Pro Coy (Camp Borden)
MARTIN D C	Capt	OC 27 F D B, Germany
MARTIN M A	Lt	1 & A Cadre Eascom (Halifax)
McMANUS J C	Lt	East Ontario Area (Kingston)
McNEILL J B	Capt	0C 27 F D B, Germany
MENARD M P	Lt	C Pro C School
MURPHY R H	Lt	2 IC 27 Pro Det (Germany)
PATERSON D S	Capt	DAPM Pracom (Winnipeg)

PENDOCK F	Lt	CAFIB (Ottawa)
PERRY A G T	Lt	Wescom Pro Coy (Edmonton)
PETE N	Lt	C Pro C School
PETTY E W	Capt	2 IC 27 Pro Det (Germany)
PLATT J J	Lt Col	CO C Pro C School
PROUTEN J L	Lt	HQ B C F K (Japan)
QUIRK T J	Maj	OC 1 Special Trg Coy (Wainwright)
RICHARDSON V H	Capt	OC Pracom Pro Coy (Winnipeg)
RITCHIE A F	Lt	27 F D B Germany
RITCHIE A R	Maj	DPM AHQ (Ottawa)
SAMBROOKE S E	Lt	OC 9 S D B (Winnipeg)
SCOTTI A J	Maj	SHAPE Paris, France
SMEDMOR A H	Maj	APM AHQ (Ottawa)
SMITH W T	Capt	OC 12 S D B (Camp Borden)
SNELGROVE E O	Capt	OC 25 F D B Seoul, Korea
STEWART J R	Lt Col	PM AHQ (Ottawa)
STINSON R J (X-RCMP)	Capt	OC NDHQ Sec Gd (Ottawa)
STOKER W P	Lt	Eascom Pro Coy (Halifax)
STONE D L	2/Lt	Pracom Pro Coy (Regina)
SUTHERLAND J B	2/Lt	Cencom Pro Coy (Toronto)
THOMS E W	2/Lt	HQ N B Area (Fredericton)
THOMSON J A	Capt	DAPM AHQ (Ottawa)
TOMALIN G R	Lt	C Pro C School
TURNER J H	2/Lt	25 Pro Det, Korea
WALLIS J C	Capt	OC Wescom Pro Coy (Edmonton)
WALSH J M	Maj	HQ B C F K, Korea
WATERTON J E	Lt	Wescom Pro Coy (Vancouver)
WATSON W C	Capt	HQ B C Area (Vancouver)
WILKINS C F	Lt	OC 14 S D B (Camp Valcartier)
WILKINSON G	Capt	Adjt C Pro C School
WILSON A E	Capt	OC Cencom Pro Coy (Toronto)
WOODBURN R F	Lt	HQ Calgary Area (Calgary)

CANADIAN PROVOST CORPS RESERVE OFFICERS
Showing Rank And Unit as at 1 October 1953

BELANGER L	Capt	3 Pro Coy (R) Montreal
BELLE E	Maj	OC 3 Pro Coy (r) Montreal
CHEVRETTE P	Lt	3 Pro Coy (R) Montreal

CLARK A N	Lt	13 Pro Coy (R) Winnipeg
DUMAIS D	Maj	OC 4 Pro Coy (R) Winnipeg
FERGUSON J	Lt	13 Pro Coy (R) Winnipeg
FRIESEN E	Lt	13 Pro Coy (R) Winnipeg
GREGOR A	Maj	OC 13 Pro Coy (R) Winnipeg
HODSON J S	Capt	8 Pro Coy (R) Vancouver
HURST N	Maj	OC 5 Pro Coy (R) Halifax
INGEBERG T	Capt	OC 1 Pro Coy (R) London
JARRY M	Lt	3 Pro Coy (R) Montreal
KEIGHTLEY T	Lt	2 Pro Coy (R) Toronto
KELLY H M	Lt	11 Pro Coy (R) Ottawa
LALUMIERE A G	Capt	4 Pro Coy (R) Quebec City
LYTTON B C	Lt	8 Pro Coy (R) Vancouver
MacFARLANE F S P	Capt	2 Pro Coy (R) Toronto
McKEOWN W	Lt	2 Pro Coy (R) Toronto
O'CONNELL J D	Capt	4 Pro Coy (R) Quebec City
OLIVER J S	Maj	OC 2 Pro Coy (R) Toronto
ROBINSON C E	Maj	OC 8 Pro Coy (R) Vancouver
SHEPHERD W J	Lt	13 Pro Coy (R) Winnipeg
STEWART C O	Lt	1 Pro Coy (r) London
STEEDS J R	Capt	OC 11 pro Coy (R) Ottawa

MEMBERSHIP LIST OF THE CANADIAN PROVOST CORPS OFFICERS ASSOCIATION as at July 1966

Legend: CA(R) – Canadian Army Regular
CA(M) – Canadian Army Militia
RETD – Retired C Pro C Officer
Asterisk * – Employed outside the Corps at this time

ABRAMS A W	Captain	CA(R)	CFB Borden
ALLENDORF C J	Captain	Retd	Edmonton
AMIRAULT E J	Major	Retd	Ashbridges Bay, Ontario
ANDREW H J	2nd Lieutenant	CA(R)	CFB Borden
ANDERSON C C	Major	Retd	Alliston, Ontario
BARBEAU J L F	Lieutenant	CA(M)	CFB Petawawa
BATES G L C	Captain	CA(R)	Quebec City
BERGERON D H G	Captain	CA(R)	Laval, Quebec
BIRD A S	Major	CA(R)	St Hubert, Quebec

BOISVERT R	2nd Lieutenant	CA(R)	Ville D'Anjou, Quebec
BOBBIT J R	2nd Lieutenant	CA(R)	London
BORNOR R F	Major	CA(R)	CFB Borden
BRADY A L	Colonel	CA(R)	Regina
BROCKLEBANK W R	Lieutenant	CA(R)	Winnipeg
BROWN C W	Lieutenant	CA(R)	CFB Petawawa
BURRARD-CREASY F	Major	Retd	Etobicoke, Ontario
CAMERON A D	Colonel	Retd	Victoria, British Columbia
CAMERON A G	Lieutenant	CA(M)	Toronto
CHAMBERS W R	Captain	CA(R)	CFB Toronto
CHILDERSTONE M	Captain (X-RCMP)	Retd	London, England
CHISHOLM R W	2nd Lieutenant	CA(M)	Halifax
CLARK C W	Lieut-Colonel	Retd	Halifax
CONROY G J	Captain	CA(R)	Kingston
COWAN C N	Captain	CA(R)	CFB Borden
CULLEN J L	Captain	CA(R)	Calgary
*DABROS W J	Captain	CA(R)	HQ 2 CIBG Petawawa
DESORMEAUX J G	Lieutenant	CA(R)	Soest, Germany
DOWNIE T	Captain	CA(R)	Calgary
DOWSETT J A	Captain	CA(R)	St Hubert, Quebec
DUNN J S	Captain	CA(R)	CFB Borden
DUPILLE P A H	Captain	CA(R)	Ottawa
EASTAUGH N A	Captain	Retd	Pembroke, Ontario
FIDDES W	Major	CA(M)	Montreal
FOGG J A	Major	CA(M)	Toronto
FRECHETTE J L J	Captain	CA(M)	Trois Rivieres, Quebec
FULLERTON J A	Major	CA(M)	Toronto
GAUTHIER A D	Captain	CA(R)	CFB Borden
GERVAIS J R	Captain	CA(R)	Montreal
GILLING W	Captain	Retd	Toronto
GRIFFIN M E	Captain	CA(M)	London
GROGAN R T	Major	CA(R)	Ottawa
HADDOCK C A	Captain	CA(M)	Calgary
HALL R T	Captain	CA(R)	Germany
HARDY J D	Captain	Retd	Trois Rivieres, Quebec
HARRIS J B	Major (X-RCMP)	Retd	Ottawa
HENDERSON L N	Major	CA(R)	Soest, Germany
HILLS E M	Lieut-Colonel	Retd	Deep Brook, Nova Scotia

HODGSON R A	Lieutenant	CA(M)	Edmonton
*HOOPER J J	Major	CA(R)	Winnipeg
HUFF G W	Major	CA(R)	CFB Borden
*HUGHES H E	Captain	CA(R)	Ottawa
JACQUES J M	Major	CA(M)	Quebec City
JAMIESON S P	Captain	CA(R)	CFB Valcartier
JOHNSON J W	Captain	Retd	Edmonton
JONES J E	2nd Lieutenant	CA(R)	Calgary
*JONES J M	2nd Lieutenant	CA(R)	Cyprus (2 RHC)
*KERNAGHAN W R	Captain	CA(R)	CFB Borden
KYLE G A	Major	Retd	London
LALUMIERE A G	Major	CA(M)	Quebec City
LAMBERT J E B	2nd Lieutenant	CA(R)	Montreal
LAW M F	Major (X-RCMP)	Retd	North Bay, Ontario
LAWSON Q E	Lieut-Colonel	CA(R)	Ottawa
LEARY H F	Lieutenant	CA(R)	CFB Borden
*LEE B W E	Lieut-Colonel	CA(R)	Winnipeg
LEIGH F A	Lieutenant	CA(R)	Gaza (UNEF)
LUKER R I	Lieut-Colonel	CA(R)	CFB Borden
LUSSIER G A	Captain	CA(R)	Soest, West Germany
LUMSDEN J D	Captain	CA(R)	Edmonton
MACASKILL A E	Lieutenant	CA(R)	Halifax
MACDIARMID D R	Lieutenant	CA(M)	Moncton, New Brunswick
MAC DONALD G J C	Lieutenant	CA(R)	CFB Borden
MacDONALD J	Captain	CA(R)	CFB Gagetown
MAC DONALD M C	Lieutenant	CA(R)	CFB Gagetown
MANSFIELD H J	Captain	CA(R)	CFB Gagetown
MARION T E	Captain	CA(R)	CFB Gagetown
MARSHALL P F	Lieutenant	CA(M)	Cooksville, Ontario
MARTIN A L D	Major	CA(M)	Winnipeg
MARTIN D C	Major	CA(R)	CFB Borden
*MARTIN M A	Major	CA(R)	Ottawa
MASTERSON A C	Captain	CA(M)	Vancouver
Mc CULLOUGH W J	Lieutenant	CA(R)	Soest, West Germany
Mc DONALD R J	Major	Retd	Scarborough, Ontario
Mc DOUGALL A K	Lieutenant	Retd	Ottawa
Mc NEILL J B	Major	Retd	Toronto
MERCIER A	Lieutenant	CA(M)	Quebec City
*MOONEY R C	Captain	CA(R)	Kingston

*MONTPETIT J P	Captain	CA(R)	CFB Valcartier
MOREY R B	Lieutenant	CA(R)	CFB Moose Jaw
*NICE R L	Lieutenant	CA(R)	St John's, Newfoundland
NICHOLSON L H	Colonel (X-RCMP)	Col Comdt	Woodlawn, Ontario
OLDFIELD T W	Major	Retd	Edmonton
PAINE D M L	Captain	CA(R)	Trenton
PARKER R W	Captain	CA(R)	Soest, West Germany
PATTERSON D S	Captain	Retd	Willowdale, Ontaoi
PAULHUS J L	Lieutenant	CA(R)	Ottawa
PENDOCK F	Captain	Retd	Montreal
PERRY A G T	Captain	CA(R)	CFB Gagetown
PETE N	Captain	Retd	Kingsotn
PETERSON J C	Major	CA(M)	Halifax
PETTY E W	Captain	Retd	London
PIUZE P A	Colonel	Retd	Quebec City
PLATT J J	Lieut-Colonel	Retd	Victoria, British Columbia
QUIRK T J	Major	Retd	Vermilion, Alberta
*RAND J	Captain	CA(R)	North Bay, Ontario
REYNETT H C	Lieutenant	CA(R)	Gaza (UNEF)
RITCHIE A F	Major	CA(R)	Ottawa
RITCHIE A R	Colonel	CA(R)	Ottawa
ROBERTSON A B P	Lieutenant	CA(R)	CFB Borden
ROBBIE I R	Captain	Retd	Burlington, Ontario
*RODGER G A	Captain	CA(R)	Winnipeg
SAILLANT G E	Captain	CA(M)	Neufchatel, Quebec
*SCOTTI A J	Colonel	CA(R)	Paris, France
SMITH P P	Lieutenant	CA(R)	CFB Shilo
SMITH N W	Lieutenant	CA(R)	Toronto
SMITH W T	Captain	Retd	Cooksville, Ontario
SOMERVILLE W I	Captain	CA(M)	Moncton, New Brunswick
STEWART J H	Lieutenant	Retd	Ottawa
ST JOHN T	Lieutenant	CA(R)	CFB Borden
STOKER W P	Major	CA(R)	Gaza (UNEF)
STONE D L	Captain	CA(R)	Calgary
STONE J R	Colonel	Retd	Ottawa
THOMPSON J A	Captain	Retd	Edmundston, New Brunswick
TOMALIN G R	Captain	Retd	Liberia, WEst AFrica
TOWERS G L	Lieutenant	CA(M)	Calgary
TRELEAVEN J C	Leiut-Colonel	CA(R)	Cyprus (UNFICYP)

*WALLIS J C	Captain	CA(R)	Ottawa
WALSH J M	Major	Retd	Halifax
WARE R G	Captain	Retd	Santa Ana, California
WATTS E	Major	Retd	Kingston
WATTS J	Lieutenant	Retd	Vancouver British Columbia
WELLS A R	Lieutenant	CA(R)	CFB Borden
WHITEFORD J G	Major	CA(M)	Calgary
WILKINS C F	Major	Retd	Quebec City
WILKINSON G	Lieut-Colonel	Retd	Cyprus (UNFICYP)
WILSON A E	Major	Retd	Fort Saskatchewan, Alberta
WILSON C F	Major	CA(R)	Calgary
WILSON P W M	2nd Lieutenant	CA(R)	Ottawa
WOODBURN R F	Captain	CA(R)	Vancouver British Columbia
WRIGHT J L	Lieutenant	CA(R)	Ottawa

Colonel Phillipe Auguste PUIZE OBE, ED

Apart from a brief biographic sketch which appears in the book *Silver Jubilee: The Canadian Provost Corps 1940–1965*, very little has been written about the achievements of this outstanding officer. He was born in Frazerville, Quebec on 20 October 1888. Following schooling at Ste Anne de la Pocatiere and St Michael's Colleges, he joined the Militia and rose to the rank of major in the 20th Battery, Canadian Field Artillery. He enrolled in the CEF early in World War I. At 28 years of age he was promoted Lieutenant-Colonel and appointed Commanding Officer of the 189th Infantry Battalion, in February 1916. He continued in command of the 189th, in the Training Division in England, for the last two years of the war. He remained in the Permanent Force of the Canadian Army with the substantive rank of captain and the brevet rank of Lieutenant-Colonel, serving initially with the Royal 22^e Regiment (Van Doos), and later in a senior AQ staff position at headquarters No 5 Military District in Quebec City. He retired from the Army in 1928 after twenty-six years service (Militia, war and PF) to become Director of the St Vincent de Paul Penitentiary near Montreal. He later became Director of the Quebec Provincial Police. He was appointed Provost Marshal of the Army and Officer Administering the Canadian Provost Corps in June 1940 and held that position until forced to retire, due to ill health, in August 1943.

The development of a provost service for the Canadian Army was a task of considerable magnitude. It is one thing to build on an existing organization but quite another to start from scratch. That the Corps was up and running in a short space of time is a testimonial to his genius as an organizer. He had a clear vision of the basic requirements for an effective provost service and he had little time for mediocrity. He established sound working procedures for all units and kept in close touch with commanders and staffs at all levels. He was a firm but fair disciplinarian who took great care to ensure the ordinary soldier was treated fairly. He knew that an ounce of prevention was worth a pound of cure, as evidenced by the development of Information Centres in busy terminals. His training programme for soldiers serving detention was practical and timely. His action, in 1942, to raise the M score for provost recruits illustrates his concern that the Provost service was effectively staffed. He possessed enormous energy, as indicated by his Unit Inspection Schedules. From December 1940 to June 1942 he carried out 64 inspections of Corps units in Canada, often returning after two or three weeks for follow-up action.

His last official function in the Corps occurred in June 1965 when he presided at the dedication of the Memorial Cairn, in Camp Borden. He passed away, in Montreal at 78 years of age, during July 1966. He truly was the architect of the Canadian Provost Corps.

Colonel Leonard Hanson NICHOLSON OC, MBE, GCStJ, LLD

Colonel L H (Nick) Nicholson was born at Mount Middleton, New Brunswick in 1904. He joined the RCMP in 1923 at the height of the prohibition and rum-running era in the Maritimes. Largely due to the many tedious hours spent on surveillance duty related to rum-running, he resigned from the Force in 1926 to join the West Australia State Police. Australia's loss was Canada's gain when he missed his ship out of Vancouver later that year. In 1928 he joined the New Brunswick Provincial Police, serving initially in the ranks but was soon promoted Inspector. He resigned and joined the Nova Scotia Provincial Police in 1930, as an Inspector. In 1932, when the Nova Scotia Police was absorbed by the RCMP, he was once again back in the Force with Inspector rank. From 1932 to 1937 he was officer in charge of criminal investigations in Nova Scotia, and held the same position in Saskatchewan from 1938 to 1941.

Due to an order by the Federal Minister of Justice prohibiting any further members of the Force from leaving to join the CASF, he resigned and enlisted in the Saskatoon Light Infantry (SLI) as a private in May 1941. The fact that he was commissioned, promoted captain and posted to the newly formed 5 Canadian Armoured Division as Assistant Provost Marshal speaks well for the manpower allocation system of the Army. The Division, like its predecessors, was soon in England and undergoing intense unit and formation training. Nick was upgraded to major rank in early 1942. He mastered the intricacies of Army organization and administration in a remarkably short space of time, largely because of his unfailing habit of learning by "seeing" and "doing".

He was appointed APM of the newly formed 2 Canadian Corps, in March 1943. Following a short period in this appointment he was appointed APM of 1 Canadian Corps prior to its departure for Italy in November 1943. This position made him the senior officer of the Canadian Provost Corps in all of the Italian theatre. He left 1 Canadian Corps in Holland and returned to Canada in May 1945. He was appointed Provost Marshal of the Canadian Army in September 1945, and served in this post until April 1946 when he was released from the CASF with the rank of Colonel.

Colonel "Nick" returned to the RCMP in May 1946 and was promoted to the rank of Assistant Commissioner at Headquarters in Ottawa. He served for the next five years as Director of Criminal Investigation and was appointed Commissioner of the Force in May 1951. He was Commissioner for the next eight years and retired to pension on 31 March 1959.

The mere fact that he served so effectively in many senior police appointments for over thirty-four years would be quite enough for most men. However, during and after his police and military career he served his country in the following important positions:

1951–1960: Member of the Northwest Territories Council.
1954: Commanded the Canadian Rifle Team at Bisley, England. He was a Past President and Life Governor of the Dominion of Canada Rifle Association, and a crack shot.
1959: Chairman of the United Nations Narcotic Survey Mission in the Middle East.
1960–1970: Honourary Colonel Commandant of the Canadian Provost Corps.
1960–1964: Deputy and Chief Scout of the Boy Scouts of Canada.
1961–1965: Chief of Protection and Investigation Services, Bank of Nova Scotia.
1964–1968: Chief Commissioner of the St John Ambulance Brigade.
1969–1972: Chancellor of the Priory of Canada of the Most Venerable Order of Saint John of Jerusalem.

1975–1976: Director of the Canadian Wildlife Federation. Presented with the award of "Outdoorsman of the Year" by the Wildlife Federations and the Outdoor Writers of Canada.

He received the following honours and awards throughout his long and distinguished service to Canada:

1945: Member of the British Empire (MBE)
Mentioned in Despatches (MID)
1955: Honourary Degree of LLD from the University of New Brunswick
Made an Honourary Chief of the Blackfoot Confederacy, Alberta
1957: At Fort MacLeod, Alberta, admitted to the Kainal Chieftainship of the Blood Indian Tribe with the tribal name: "Honourary Chief Buffalo Child"
1967: Awarded the Service Medal of the Order of Canada
1971: Invested with the Order of Bailiff Grand Cross of the Most Venerable Order of St John of Jerusalem. he was only the second Canadian to attain this rank, the first being the Right Honourable Vincent Massey.
1972: Admitted to The Order of Canada with Officer Grade (OC).
1975: Three Scout Awards:
 – The Bronze Wolf from the World Scout Conference;
 – The Silver Wolf from the Boy Scouts of Canada;
 – The Vanier Medal from L'Association des Scouts du Canada.

Colonel "Nick", as he was affectionately called, was the fourth Provost Marshal of the Canadian Army. Though his term was short, he served in the highly volatile era following World War II. Like Phillipe Puize before him, he had the task of forming the first ever peacetime provost service. There is absolutely no doubt that his presence on the scene was largely responsible for the decision to include the Canadian Provost Corps in the order of battle of the Canadian Army. Such was his prestige and stature.

This quiet, strong, motivated and intelligent man was an inspiration to all who were privileged to serve with him and for him. It is difficult to find words which adequately describe the sheer nobility of his character. However, the above listing of his achievements speak louder than words. He died in Ottawa on 22 March 1983.

Colonel James Riley STONE DSO, MC, CD

The Peace River District of Northern Alberta was one of the last agricultural regions to be settled in western Canada. Despite its short growing (frost-free) season and severe climate settlers started to arrive in the early 1920s to try their luck at growing cereal grains and raising livestock. Land was cheap, highly fertile and plentiful. Apart from the region's short summers and severe winters, its main drawback was lack of road or rail links to outside markets. Roads were rutted wagon trails and the only railway ran westward to eventual outlets at Vancouver and Prince Rupert. All of this begs the question: What did this remote region have to do with the Canadian Provost Corps? The answer is that it tells us a great deal about the character of a remarkable man who would become the sixth Provost Marshal of the Canadian Army. His name was James Riley Stone, and he came to the Peace River country as a young man in the early 1930s.

He was born in Goucester, England on 2 August 1908. His motivation for moving to the Peace was, undoubtedly, a result of his youth, strength, a passion for adventure and a better than average academic education in England. Why else would he spurn the softer life in a teeming city during this depression wracked decade in Canada? he remained in the Peace River region for the next ten years, during which he farmed, hunted, trapped, worked at odd jobs and, of much significance to his later military career, he enrolled in the local Militia, the (49th) Loyal Edmonton Regiment. He was a Corporal in the "Loyal Eddys" when the regiment was mobilized as part of 1 Canadian Infantry Division in September 1939. He remained with the Loyal Eddys throughout World War II and participated in the countless battles fought by this outstanding body of men throughout Sicily, Italy and Northwest Europe. He held progressively higher leadership positions in the regiment and was, ultimately, appointed the Commanding Officer. During the course of his five hears frontline service, from 1939–1945, he was decorated no fewer than three times, having been awarded the prestigious Distinguished Service Order (DSO) on two occasions, as well as the rare Military Cross (MC), which is awarded for bravery in combat.

On return to civilian life, in 1945, he became involved in the travel and tourist industry as the owner and operator of a tourist resort in the beautiful area of Salmon Arm, British Columbia. As mentioned previously, he was called out of his peacetime pursuits by the Minister of National Defence in August 1950 to take command of an infantry battalion[160] being formed for action in the Korean War. This battalion, under his superb skill as a leader, went on to play a significant role by stopping a major attack by a large Chinese Peoples Army (CPA) designed to penetrate and occupy the entire Korean peninsula. This encounter, know known as the Battle of Kapyong, took place on 23–25 April 1951 and stopped the Chinese forces from over-running the United Nations Forces positions and gained much valuable time. For this stout defence against an overwhelming enemy the PPCLI was awarded a Presidential Citation by the President of the United States of America. A high honour indeed. Colonel "Big Jim" Stone returned to Canada in the Fall of 1951 and was appointed to the important position of Chief Instructor at the Royal Canadian School of Infantry at Camp Borden. He served in this post until August 1954 when he was promoted to the rank of Colonel and appointed Provost Marshal of the Army.

His appointment came at a time when the Corps was settling into the routines of peacetime soldiering. It had come through the volatile post World War II era and was getting it sea legs. Its role was well defined and was being effectively carried out by well trained and suitably deployed working units at home and abroad. The new Provost Marshal fitted the scenario like a well worn glove. Perhaps his most important asset for the job was his complete understanding of the ordinary Canadian soldier. One of his first initiatives was designed to solve the vexing problem of completing the training of younger, inexperienced Corps subaltern officers. It really was a chicken and egg thing in that there were few positions in the Corps where the new officer could gain essential leadership and command experience under the eye of a seasoned Corps officer, since the majority of Canadian Provost Corps Detachments were small and frequently supervised by an experienced senior NCO. The new Provost Marshal solved this problem by arranging with the Director of Infantry for Canadian Provost Corps lieutenants to be attached for all purposes to an infantry battalion where he would serve for one year as a Platoon Commander. The first such attachments were made in the Fall of 1955 and were an immediate success. The Provost officer, by agreement, was treated exactly the same as his peer in the infantry and quickly learned the intricacies and delicacies of infantry organization, tactics, equipment, training and, above all, how to motivate the riflemen in the ranks. The Canadian Provost Corps lieutenant gained the knowledge and experience that would bolster his confidence and equip him to function effectively in almost any position of the Corps. The success of this programme is attested by the fact that many of these officers went on to higher rank and successful careers in the Canadian Forces.

The Canadian Provost Corps Fund for Blind Children resulted from a tragic event in the life of Jim and Esther Stone in 1956. When their daughter Moira was eight years old she died from cancer of the eyes. She had been a pupil at the Brantford (Ontario) School for Blind Children and had related some hearttouching stories to her parents about some schoolmates who did not have the basic "extras" such as toys, party dresses, new shoes or pocket money, all dear to the heart of a child. When Moira died it was suggested that the Corps establish a fund to be used to provide a few comforts and extras not otherwise available to blind children. The response was immediate, generous and sustained, and donations to the Canadian Provost Corps Fund for Blind Children poured in. This outpouring of goodwill and charitable expression continues to this day, some thirty-five years later. In fact, contributions to the Fund have gained momentum over the years, as shown in the following statistics:

1957 –	$2,059.05	1965 –	$ 3,228.99
1958 –	2,372.55	1966 –	3,121.02
1959 –	1,924.42	1967 –	3,119.14 (1st year of unification)
1960 –	2,280.59	1968 –	5,371.92
1961 –	2,255.98	1969 –	8,075.04
1962 –	2,555.85	1972 –	11,186.91 (1st 5 figure total)
1963 –	3,480.09	1991 –	143,130.79 (1st 6 figure total)

The members of the Corps and, following unification, the combined efforts of all components of the Security Branch used some innovative methods for raising funds. The following are a few of the many original ideas.

- A small detachment at CFB London raised $500.00 in 1967 by working at odd jobs on weekends;
- In 1958 the Provost Section at EASE, near Carp, Ontario, raised $97.00 by picking up empty bottles along local roadsides;
- The Soest (Germany) Provettes in 1970 produced $85.00 by a bake sale;
- The MP Detachment a No 1 Wing, 1 Canadian Air Division in Markville, France, raised over $600.00 in 1966 by placing a deposit box on the counter passed by all those returning by aircraft to Canada. The notice read "MP Fund for Blind Children–Leave your funny money here".

The money was distributed annually to four schools across Canada to be expended for the individual and group needs of blind students 13 years of age and under, with the proviso that the school superintendent could assist a needy child of any age. The distribution of funds to the four schools for 1969, based on the number of children under 14 years of age, follows.

Ontario School for the Blind, Brantford 108 Children $2,580.00
Halifax School for the Blind, Halifax 100 Children 2,390.00
Nazareth Institute for the Blind, Montreal 82 Children 1,960.00
Jericho Hill School for Blind Children, Vancouver 49 Children 1,170.00

The Fund continues to be administered by a senior officer in the Directorate of Security. Following unification, in 1967, it was redesignated "The Military Police Fund for Blind Children", in keeping with the much broader base of its support. It has since been established as a registered charity and continues to make an annual distribution to the Schools for Blind Children in Canada. In fact, it now has a significant capital surplus held in trust for this worthwhile charity. The following excerpt from a letter from Dr MacDonald, Superintendent of the Jericho Hill School in Vancouver, was received by the Fund administrators in the Fall of 1966. It illustrates the end result of this effort by members of the Corps, and is a fitting tribute to Moira Stone's memory:

As has become customary with us over the years, part of the donation will go to restocking our "Provost Corps Toy Library" for small Children. A major portion of the remainder will be used to purchase musical instruments for junior band members. We do appreciate the thoughtfulness and generosity of those in the Provost Corps towards our children and, in fact, all blind children of our country.

The foregoing description of one or two initiatives are merely representative of the many contributions he made during his tour as Provost Marshal of the Army. If ever there was a man who was born with good old-fashioned common sense, it was Jim Stone. His enthusiasm and leadership were examples not only to the members of the Canadian Provost Corps but to all in the Army. he gave the Corps identity and stability. He displayed a deep interest in all ranks and made a special effort to visit everyone at their work stations. He spoke with a positive voice for the best interests of the Corps wherever and whenever the occasion demanded. Once again, the Corps "lucked in" when he was the leader from August 1954 to November 1959.

It is again emphasized that the naming of an individual is not intended to confer any special acclaim on that person. In the case of the three former Provost marshals it simply illustrates some of the challenges which faced all who held this position. This is equally true for every rank, from Colonel to Lance Corporal, in the Corps. Since it is impossible to develop a complete biography on each of the thousands who served in the Corps throughout its existence, we select a few who are representative of the many. Accordingly, the following five members are listed as representative of a category who served in the ranks during World War II, were enrolled in the post war Interim Force and were accepted in the first ever peacetime provost Corps, in most cases at a reduced rank. There were many such men who started in October 1946 and went on to a full and rewarding career.

Alan W ABRAMS

Al was born in Sombra Township (Ontario) on 11 October 1923 and spent his boyhood years in and near the town of Wallaceburg on Lake St Clair. He travelled to western Canada in the Summer of 1939 and secured employment as a harvest hand. The next major decision was enlisting in the 77th Battery of the 3rd Field Regiment at Moose Jaw, Saskatchewan on 24 September 1939. He was with the Regiment in 1 Canadian Infantry Division when it desembarked in Scotland on 17 December. Gunner Abrams served with the 3rd Field in the United Kingdom for the next fourteen months, then transferred to the Canadian Provost Corps following an Army-wide appeal made at this time, in February 1941. A review of his posting, promotion and appointments clearly indicate the wide range of his service in the Corps and the Army for the next thirty years.

Chronology

1941 February	Transferred from RCA to C Pro C in the UK. Training at Provost Depot, Aldershot.
1941 April	Posted to 7 Provost Company located at Tweesledown Race Track, near Aldershot. Duties included patrols and traffic duty in the area.
1941 September	Recommended for officer training, leading to a commission in either the Armoured or Infantry Corps. Transferred to RCAC. Training at Pro-OCTU Centre, UK.
1944 January	Posted to Italy with RCAC reinforcement draft. Employed on Orderly Room clerical duties in RCAC Holding and Rft Unit, Italy.
1944 October	Transferred from RCAC to C Pro C and posted for duty (L/Cpl) with No 1 L of C Company, C Pro C in the Avellino area.

1945 February	Moved to Belgium, Northwest Europe with Goldflake, still with 1 L of C Company.
1945 July	Repatriated to Canada (Ontario). Elected to join Interim Force.
1945 September	Following repat leave, was posted to HWE Provost Company in London, Ontario for duty.
1946 October	Enrolled in Canadian Army (Regular) and posted to HQ Central (Army) Command, Oakville, as APM's Chief Clerk with rank of private.
1950 July	Promoted sergeant and posted to No 12 Service Detention Barracks at Camp Borden.
1951 March	Posted to 3 Bn PPCLI in Calgary as NCO IC Bn Provost Section.
1951 September	Promoted to rank of Lieutenant in the C Pro C and posted to C Pro C School as Instructor, and later as Adjutant.
1954 July	Posted to No 1 Provost Company, 1 Canadian Infantry Division as Administrative Officer, Camp Borden and Gagetown, New Brunswick.
1957 May	On course at US Army Military Police School, Fort Gordon, Georgia for Officers Criminal Investigation Course.
1957 July	Posted to the Infantry Bde in Germany as 2 I/C of the MDB at Soest.
1960 August	Returned to Canada and posted to C Pro C Administrative and Training Staff position in Central Ontario Area, Toronto.
1961 September	Posted to HQ Central Ontario Area as Area Provost Marshal.
1961 October	Passed Captain to Major Qualifying Exams, Parts 1 and 2 (common-to-all-arms and special to Corps).
1963 June	Posted to the HQ Staff of Central Ontario Area as Staff Captain (A). Assumed duties of the Command Provost Marshal at Oakville prior to the dissolution of the Command in 1966.
1966 July	Posted to Halifax and appointed to command the Atlantic Detachment of the Special Investigation Unit.
1968 December	Retired from the Canadian Army Regular.

Arthur Byron ROBERTSON

Robbie was born 15 February 1925 in Victoria, British Columbia. He grew up and went to school in Victoria where he was a good student and an above average athlete, good enough to receive an offer for a University Scholarship, but the war intervened. His military career started at age 16 and continued for the next thirty-seven years, all but a few months in the Canadian Provost Corps. It is hard to imagine that Canada ever produced a more talented soldier. A quiet, disciplined and thoughtful man, he excelled in everything he did, and he was employed in almost every duty that was ever carried out by the Corps. He possessed several qualifications. However, he will be remembered for his skill and enthusiasm as a teacher. He was, quite simply, the finest instructor who ever served in the Corps and, possibly, the Army.

Chronology

1941–1943	Served in the Royal Canadian Air Cadets while completing high school, including summer training with the RCAF.
1943 July	Enlisted in the RCAF, allocated to air crew and took pilot training in Edmonton, Saskatoon, Neepawa and London.
1944	Released from the RCAF due to surplus of pilots. Enlisted in Cdn Army and allocated to C Pro C. Trained at A-32 Training Centre and posted to 41 Provost Company, Vancouver.
1945–1946	Served in 41 Company (Vancouver, Victoria and Vernon). Volunteered for Pacific Force and Interim Force.
1946 April	Posted to A-32 Training Centre in Camp Borden on assessment for the Canadian Army Regular, Canadian Provost Corps. Posted to Vancouver Detachment of 6 Provost Company (the first Canadian Provost Corps Regular Army Unit).
1946 October	Enrolled in Canadian Army Regular.
1947 July	Posted to PPCLI Regiment in Calgary as member of the Provost Section.
1949 January	Promoted Corporal and posted to Edmonton Detachment, Western Command Provost Company.
1951 March	Promoted Sergeant and posted to Canadian Provost Corps School as Instructor.

1954 July	Promoted Staff-Sergeant.
1956 August	Posted to Whitehorse (YT) Detachment of Western Command Provost Company and appointed NCO I/C Detachment. The collapse of the Peace River Bridge occurred during his tour in the Yukon.
1959 August	Posted to Vancouver Detachment of Wescom Provost Company.
1961 June	Posted to the UNEF Military Police Company in the Gaza Strip.
1961 October	Promoted Lieutenant while serving in the UNEF, Gaza.
1962 July	Posted to No 2 Personnel Depot, Camp Gagetown, as Administrative Officer and employed as Staff Captain "A" at Headquarters, New Brunswick Area.
1966 October	Promoted Captain and posted to Canadian Provost Corps School, employed as Adjutant.
1969 July	Posted to the Infantry Brigade in Soest, West Germany as APM.
1972 August	Promoted Major and posted to Headquarters Special Investigation Unit in Rockcliffe as Operations Officer.
1973 September	Posted to Headquarters CFB Ottawa as Base Security Officer.
1975 June	Seconded to the Federal Ministry of Transport to assist in upgrading airport security for the 1976 Olympic Games in Montreal.
1977 January	Posted to Directorate of Security at National Defence Headquarters, Ottawa as Police Advisory Officer.
1980 October	Retired from the Canadian Army.

Anthony Edward MacASKILL

Tony was born at East Harve Boucher, Antigonish County, Nova Scotia on 24 September 1924. He enlisted in the Canadian Active Service Force on 18 April 1942 and spent the next sixteen months completing basic training as well as a six months Commercial course. He transferred to the Canadian Provost Corps in the Fall of 1943 and took the three month advanced training course at A-32 Provost Training Centre in Camp Borden. He would serve for over thirty years in the Corps in a variety of locations at home and abroad. He was a capable administrator and a natural leader who always led from the front, and he never left a position where the general efficiency was not improved during his tenure. Perhaps his most notable success was bringing senior Royal Canadian Navy officers on-side during his tour as a Base Security Officer in the volatile mid 60s unification era. The Navy had never felt the need for a full-time service police element to deal with disciplinary problems ashore. During his tour in Halifax Tony MacAskill saw to it that all servicemen were treated fairly, and he maintained close liaison with all commanders. The RCN Base Commander would make the comment that it was the first time in his career that he had an Occurrence Report on his desk every morning telling him exactly what had happened, disciplinary wise, during the past 24 hours. It was the type of attention to all aspects of his job that earned him the respect and goodwill of all ranks.

Chronology

1944 March	Completed Provost training at A-32 and posted to 37 Provost Company, Halifax.
1944 September	Posted to 18 Provost Company, Newfoundland. Attained rank of Warrant Officer Class 2. Enrolled in the Interim Force.
1946 April	Posted to A-32 Training Centre in Camp Borden for training and evaluation for the Regular Army.
1946 October	Accepted in the Regular Army in the rank of Corporal, Canadian Provost Corps. Posted to the Camp Borden Detachment.
1947 January	Posted to Fredericton Detachment as NCO I/C.
1947 June	Posted to Halifax Provost Detachment.
1948 October	Promoted Sergeant.
1951 October	Promoted Staff-Sergeant.
1953 November	Posted to 1 Field Detention Barracks in Germany.
1954 June	Posted to the Provost Platoon with the Brigade, Germany.
1955 November	Posted to the Office of the Provost Marshal, Ottawa as Crime Reader in the Investigation Section.
1960 July	Posted to Fort Churchill Detachment of Prairie Command Provost Company as NCO I/C.
1961 December	Promoted Lieutenant and posted to Instruction and Administrative Staff at Winnipeg.
1964 July	Posted to London, Ontario as Area Provost Marshal.
1966 July	Posted to CFB Halifax as Base Security Officer. Promoted to rank of Captain 1 October 1966.

1968	Posted to Atlantic Detachment, Special Investigation Unit, Halifax, as Detachment Commander.
1971 January	Promoted Major and posted to UNIFICYP, Cyprus as Force Provost Marshal and OC of the MP Company.
1972 February	Posted to the Directorate of Security, Ottawa.
1972 July	Posted to CFB Halifax as Base Security Officer.
1974, 29 August	Retired from the Canadian Army Regular.

William John PATTERSON

Bill was born in Tisdale, Saskatchewan on 9 July 1927, where he grew up and attended schools in the decade preceding World War II. His long association with the Canadian Army began at age 12 when he enrolled in the local army Cadet Corps. At age 15 he joined the local militia unit as a boy soldier at 70 cents a day, the Prince Albert Volunteers. He was one of the few who served in the CASF during the War, was accepted in the Canadian Army Regular (1 October 1946) in the rank of private, and went on to serve another thirty-two years in the Canadian Provost Corps. This remarkable period of service, through good times and bad, provides ample proof of the loyalty, strength of character, intelligence and determination that were the hallmarks of this fine young Canadian. It took courage and fortitude to serve, as he did, in almost every position offered in the Corps and, later, in the unified Security Branch for a period in excess of three decades. Bill will be remembered for his positive approach to life, his sunny disposition and, above all, his sense of responsibility. He made it his business to know every facet of his trade, which led to his skill as a teacher and a highly effective leader. With the exception of the war years and the first three years of service in the Regular Army, he has been active in volunteer community work, as indicated by the following:

Manager of a Bantam Hockey League for three years;
Manager of a girls Little League softball team for two years;
Supervisor of Teens Clubs at CFB Borden and Calgary;
Assistant Director of the Alberta Summer Games at Fort McMurray;
Chairman of Access Control and Accreditation of Alpine teams – Calgary Winter Olympics.

This busy man has continued an active and productive life since his retirement in 1978, in Calgary.

Chronology

1944 January	Joined the Canadian Army as a boy soldier at 70 cents a day. Trained in the Canadian Technical Training Corps, Saskatoon and Saint John, New Brunswick. Qualified Clerk Administrative in march 1945.
1945 March	Advanced infantry training at Utopia, New Brunswick. Transferred to Canadian Provost Corps.
1945 August	Served in 39 Company, Saint John, New Brunswick, 43 to Company in Regina Maple Creek, Saskatchewan, posted 1946 Mayto A-32 for evaluation in the Canadian Army Regular.
1946 October 1	Accepted in CA(R), Canadian Provost Corps, in rank of private. Posted to Camp Borden detachment.
1947 April	Posted to 6 Company Headquarters, Camp Borden as Clerk Administration. Promoted Corporal May 1948. Promoted Sergeant April 1949.
1950 April	Posted to Calgary as Section Sergeant; to Chilliwack, British Columbia in October 1950; to Edmonton March 1951 and to Camp Wainwright (Alberta) in August 1951.
1953 February	Posted to 1 Battalion PPCLI as Provost Sergeant.
1953 July	Promoted Staff Sergeant and posted to 10 SDB Calgary and 1 Special Training Company, Wainwright.
1954 February	Posted to 1 Field Detention Barracks, Soest, Germany as Chief Clerk.
1956 April	Posted to NDHQ Security Guard, Ottawa as NCO IC Kildare Barracks.
1958 September	Posted to UNEF MP Company, Gaza as NCO IC Investigation Section (6 months), to NCO IC Beirut Section, Lebanon (7 months).
1959 December	Posted to Central Command Provost Company, Petawawa Detachment as NCO IC.
1964 March	Promoted Warrant Officer Class 2 and posted to Canadian Provost Corps School as CSM Specialist Training Company.
1966 July	Posted to UNIFICYP MP Company, Nicosia, Cyprus as Company Sergeant Major.
1967 February	Promoted Lieutenant in Canadian Provost Corps and posted to Canadian Provost Corps School, Camp Borden.

1967 May	Posted CFB Moose Jaw, Saskatchewan as Base Security Officer.
1970 February	Promoted Captain.
1971 July	Posted to Headquarters Air Transport Command, CFB Trenton, Ontario as Staff Officer Security 2.
1974 May	Posted to 1 MP Platoon at CFB Calgary as Officer Commanding.
1978 September	Retired from Canadian Armed Forces.

Walter Edward Raymond CHAMBERS

Ray Chambers was born on 13 January 1913 at Woodstock, Ontario. His long career in the Canadian Army started in May 1930 when he joined the Royal Hamilton Light Infantry (Militia), where he served as a part-time soldier for the next ten years. He came to the Canadian Provost Corps early in 1941 and served, with distinction, for the next twenty-six years.

Much has been said in the preceding pages about the key role played by the Section Sergeant of a field provost company. As has been stated, the section was the workhorse of the Canadian Provost Corps and the sergeant was its mainspring. Ray Chambers was arguably one of the very best of a good lot. This self-effacing, quiet man had the policeman's retentive memory along with the God-given ability to retain the relevant and discard the trivial. In the fast moving turmoil of the battlefield there was never a time when he did not know what was going on around him. It was this concentration on the job at hand which allowed him, and his fifteen men, to maintain control of the situation at all times. He was always ready for the next move. Sergeant Chambers was one of a few who landed in Normandy on D-Day, participated in every battle fought by the 3rd Canadian Infantry Division across Northwest Europe, and finished the war at Aurich, Germany one year later. He remained in the Corps for another twenty-three years and continued to serve, with quiet efficiency, in a wide range of posts as an NCO, Warrant and Commissioned Officer. Ray passed away in Thamesford, 18 May 1993.

Chronology

1940 June	Enlisted in the Elgin Regiment, Canadian Active Service Force, at St Thomas, Ontario.
1941 January	Transferred to the Canadian Provost Corps and posted

	to No 4 Provost Company, 3 Canadian Infantry Division.
1941 September	Embarked at Halifax with 4 Provost Company in the main body of 3 Canadian Infantry Division. Disembarked in the United Kingdom and stationed in southern England.
1943 January	Promoted to rank of Sergeant and appointed NCO IC "D" Section, 4 Provost Company.
1944, 6 June	Landed in Normandy on D-Day. Remained Sergeant IC "D" Section throughout the campaign in NWE. Repatriated to Canada in September 1945.
1946 October	Enrolled in Canadian Army Regular, Canadian Provost Corps.
1946 Fall	Attended a ten week police training course at the Provost Marshal General's School at Fort Sam Houston, San Antonio, Texas.
1947 January to 1948 March	Posted to Whitehorse, Yukon on special investigation duties related to losses and thefts from a wartime supply depot.
1953 September to November	Completed the Special Investigator's Course at the PMG School at Fort Gordon, Georgia, United States of America.
1954 August	Promoted to rank of Warrant Officer, Class 2 (WO2) and posted to the Commonwealth Division, Special Investigation Section in Seoul, Korea. NOTE: This was an integrated British, Canadian, Australian and New Zealand unit serving 1 Commonwealth Division.
1955 June	Posted to Canadian Provost Corps School, Camp Shilo, Manitoba as Assistant Instructor and Supervisor of a Canadian Provost Corps Team of Motorcyclists. This team performed in a series of shows across Canada.
1955 October	Posted to the Canadian Armed Forces Identification Bureau (CAFIB) in Ottawa as WO IC Fingerprint Section.
1956 Spring	Graduated from the RCMP Police College, Course No 28, at Regina. This course in investigation techniques was conducted for senior police officers in Canada.
1957 March	Promoted Lieutenant in the Corps.
1961 October	Promoted Captain in the Corps.
1967, 18 May	Retired from the Canadian Armed Forces.

Conclusion

The inclusion of police and security specialists as an integral part of the Canadian military is a relatively recent innovation, even though this element had long been established in European armies. The Roman speculatore, British provost and French gendarmerie all emerged to fill a similar need in their armies. Stated in broad terms, military police were developed because commanders required a trusted, loyal and disciplined body to assist with the control and protection of military resources, both at home and abroad. They were, and continue to be, an extension of the commanders' long arm.

Apart from the fact that Major General Murray had a Provost Marshal in Quebec in 1760, there is no record of a provost service in Canada prior to the Great War of 1914–18. Military police surfaced in 1916 to deal with the volatile issue of conscription in Quebec. The Corps of Military Police functioned in Canada, and to a lesser extent overseas, during the latter stages of that War. It was quickly demobilized in 1919 and emerged, twenty years later in 1940, as the Canadian Provost Corps. The mobilization process for the Canadian Army, which commenced in September 1939, reveals the interesting fact that provost were not authorized for a period of ten months, that is to say from September 1939 to June 1940. Presumably the Army Headquarters planning staff, using British Army organization charts, simply pencilled in a provost company for each division. The immediate need for a provost unit in 1 Canadian Infantry Division was met, most fortunately, by an offer from the Commissioner of the RCMP to provide a company of RCMP volunteers from the Force. One can only conclude that the need for a provost service was not uppermost in the minds of Canadian Army commanders of that era.

There was little change in the organization of the Corps during the war years. The concept of self-contained, fully mobile sections in a field company provided the flexibility required to deploy provost resources under the uncertain and often difficult conditions of war. The 65 detachments across Canada were also well placed to perform the multitude of duties in the home environment. An apparent anomaly concerning the manner in which the Corps was managed during World War II deserves comment. The responsibility for control and supervision was vested in two senior Corps officers, and a third officer who dealt with those Corps units in formations under command First Canadian Army. Each ran his own show. Apart from the provision of reinforcements, there is no evidence of much communication between the Provost Marshal, the Deputy Provost Marshal

CMHQ and the Deputy Provost Marshal First Canadian Army. It may never be known whether closer ties between them would have greatly assisted in dealing with problems such as training, equipment and doctrine that arose from time to time.

Reference is made in Table 1, Chapter 1, to the breakdown of the various corps into Arms and Services. The corps, with the primary function of combat (fighting), were designated Arms and controlled by the Operations or "G" staff. Those concerned with personnel were Services and came under "A" staff, while the supply/logistics corps were managed by the "Q" staff. This neat arrangement worked well for most corps but not so well for provost, because they performed duties, especially during battle, for all three staff branches. This frequently resulted in the provost company being tasked by three masters. The inevitable result was often a severe over commitment of resources and, even worse, conflicting orders. It was in these circumstances that the formation APM came into his own. This tasking problem has been solved in today's Security Branch, which now functions solely under the Operations Branch of the Staff.

The advent of peacetime soldiering was one of the three major milestones in the life of a continuing member of the Army. The other two being the wartime experience and the unification drama of the 1960s. The conversion from war to peacetime conditions of service was, perhaps, more of an eye-opener to provost than to most older corps. With one exception, the Canadian Provost Corps was the only new addition to the Canadian Army Regular on 1 October 1946. There were many changes, but one which was to have the most lasting affect was the introduction of a married establishment and the concept of a family life for all servicemen. This also brought new duties and responsibilities to the Corps in the form of policing communities of men, women and children. Provost became dog catchers, lawn watchers, traffic cops, firemen, truant officers and detectives. They served in far away places such as the Yukon and in the Gaza Strip, the Congo and Cyprus with multinational forces on so-called peacekeeping duties. They performed an extraordinary variety of police and security tasks, not the least of which was establishing the base for an integrated military police unit made up of men from the four corners of the earth. This they did with a minimum of fuss or bother under difficult and often hazardous conditions.

In retrospect, the most important factor in the evolution of the Corps was the attention given to the selection, training and ongoing development of its members. It is trite but true to say that good men, well led and committed to a cause will usually succeed in their ventures. From the beginning it was recognized that a military policeman must be intelligent, honest, decent and highly disciplined. A high standard was gradually achieved by measures such as the introduction of minimum standards for height, health, M test and MMPI scores, together with sound training and good conduct and performance appraisal reports. There were no exceptions made, no matter what rank or position.

Life in the Canadian Provost Corps was never a sinecure for those who served. There were no soft touches. The foundation of the Corps was its human resources and the unfailing commitment of these men to do their duty to the very best of their ability. One of the distinguishing features of the Corps was the cohesion within its ranks. A state of high esprit-de-corps was achieved and maintained throughout its entire existence. It adopted the motto: DISCIPLINE BY EXAMPLE. This simple but effective creed was accepted, without qualification, by all who were worthy of wearing the badge and responding to the challenges. They quietly achieved excellence in an era of unprecedented scientific and technological change. They did not seek acclaim or fret about the possibility of failure. These watchdogs understood the frailties of human nature and saw the world as it was rather than the way it ought to be. They were loyal Canadians who earned a place in the history of Canada; a few good men who made a difference.

References and Notes

Chapter 1: The First Provost

1 The word "Caesar" is the equivalent of King, Czar and Kaiser.
2 A cohort was about 500 men.
3 Michael Grant "The Army of the Caesars", pgs 90 & 91.
4 Justin Wintle "The Dictionary of War", pg 219.
5 Clodes "Articles of War", published 1629.
6 Addingtons "The Life of Wellington", pg 179.
7 A Y Lovell-Knight "History of the Provost Marshal and the Corps of Military Police", unpublished, pg 11.
8 Official Journal of the Gendarmerie "Voici La Gendarmerie", 1954.
9 Colonel R Coulin "Historique et Traditiones de la Gendarmerie Nationale", Annex 19, pg 131. The letter is dated 26 June, 1918 at Kovno, Poland.
10 C P Stacey "Six Years of War", pg 4.
11 Detachments, with an average strength of 60 CMPC, were organized at each of 13 locations, from 15 October 1917 to 1 April 1918 viz: London, Toronto, Kingston, Winnipeg, Halifax, Montreal, Quebec City, Saint John, Regina, Calgary, Victoria. Two detachments (nos 8 and 9) were allocated to the Canadian Corps in France.
12 Colonel Godson Godson's record of service is given, in more detail, in "Silver Jubilee 1940–1965, The Canadian Provost Corps", pg 8.
13 Desmond Morton "A Military History of Canada", pg 136.
14 Ibid, pg 152.
15 C Frank Turner "Across The Medicine Line", pg 16.
16 Ibid, pg 17.
17 Later designated "Royal Northwest Mounted Police" (RNWMP) and later still "Royal Canadian Mounted Police" (RCMP).

References and Notes   291

18 The first Commissioner was Lieutenant Colonel George Arthur French, a Permanent Force Artillery officer.
19 Including the Strathcona Horse and Canadian Mounted Rifles.
20 Not mentioned in the exchange between the Commissioner and the Department, but now a well known fact, is that a large number of RCMP officers and men requested permission to volunteer for service in the CASF, prior to the Commissioners letter of 7 September.
21 Members of the RCMP who served in the Canadian Provost Crops during WWII were, on reengagement with the Force, authorized to count their wartime service towards RCMP pensions.
22 The diarist was Sergeant John Alexander Primrose who joined the Force in 1936. He was commissioned in 1943, returned to Canada and reengaged in the RCMP in 1945. He rose to become the Regimental Sergeant Major of the Force and retired after 29 years combined Canadian Provost Corps and Royal Canadian Mounted Police service. He died at Vernon, British Columbia in 1990.
23 This Depot and Training Centre was, initially, located in Badojoz and later moved to Maida barracks in Aldershot. Its function was to train and hold Canadian Provost Corps reinforcements.
24 Due to a serious manpower shortage in the Royal Canadian Mounted Police, the policy of supplying reinforcement Royal Canadian Mounted Police constables recruited in Canada was discontinued.
25 This "day" would be sometimes in the Fall of 1940, after the disaster at Dunkirk the previous May.

Chapter 2: The Corps is Born

26 Troops were classified in two broad categories: ARMS and SERVICES. The "Arms" were Armour, Artillery and Infantry with Engineers and Signals designated as "Support Arms". The "Services" were the units whose function was to provide the Division with essential administrative and logistic support to enable it to live, move and fight, and included the removal and repair of equipment and evacuation of casualties from the battlefield.
27 A detailed biography of Colonel Phillipe Auguste Puize, OBE,ED is given in the final chapter.
28 Lieutenant Colonel Howard M Baker, MBE,MID, in addition to his early service, went on to be come the APM of 4 Canadian Armoured Division, the DAQMG (Mov) at Headquarters 3 Canadian Corps, DAQMG (Mov) at Headquarters First Canadian Army and Commandant of A-32 Canadian Provost Corps Training Centre in September 1945. He was a prime mover in establish-

ing SOPs as well as a centralized movement control throughout the CASF. He was awarded the MBE, was mentioned in Despatches and received foreign awards from France, Belgium and Holland.

Chapter 3: Early Days in the United Kingdom

29 Motorcycles used in the Canadian Army included, at various times: Indians, Nortons, Harley-Davidson and Triumphs.
30 Corporal Earl Wilson served with distinction for another 25 years. He retired with the rank of Major as the Command Provost Marshal for Western Command, Edmonton.
31 Wearing whitened web by members of the C Pro C was first introduced by one or two units still in Canada. It served the purpose of aiding the visibility of the men on duty. The disadvantage was that it required an enormous effort to maintain. It was taken into general use, throughout the Corps, early in 1943.
32 The following sidearms were issued to Provost personnel at various times: Webley 30 calibre revolver, 6 rounds; Smith Wesson (short and long barrel) revolver, 6 rounds; Inglis 9 mm automatic pistol, 10 round clip.
33 The standard issue notebook of the British RMP was used initially, however its paper cover and frail binding afforded little protection for the pages which soon became frayed and torn.
34 Some of the instructors were: Captain Charlie Woods (OC); Staff Sergeant J B (Hap) Harris (military law); Staff Sergeant Fred Putnam (police procedure); Sergeant Hugh McCallum (map using and anti gas); Sergeant J A (Johnnie) Primrose (physical training); Sergeant Jim Secord (on loan from 48 Highlanders – close order drill); Sergeant Charlie Stanyer (motorcycle riding).
35 James Cramer "The Worlds Police", pgs 132, 133.
36 Major General, The Honourable P J Montague, CB, CMG, DSO, MC, VD was appointed Commander CMHQ on 17 September 1940. He was a World War I veteran (Lord Strathcona Horse) and hailed from Winnipeg.
37 An Intelligence Test, known as the M Test, was introduced in 1941. Other tests such as the Minnesota Multiphase Personality Inventory were adapted after the war.
38 this Division was later reorganized as 4 Canadian Armoured Division.
39 Public House (PUB): The PUB was the social and recreational centre of the community. Soldiers mingled with the locals to sing, play darts, shove-a-penny and gossip. The pubkeeper was a cheerful, friendly soul who always gave you full measure and would loan you ten shillings until payday.
40 Full regimental particulars comprised the Regimental number, Rank, Name and

Unit of the soldier. An outdated "last pay" entry might well lead to a suspicion of absence without leave.

41 Refer to TABLE 1. This was a set drill whereby the various elements of the Headquarters were grouped in numbered serials, moved on a specified route and relocated in a previously reconnoitered and signposted area. Hence the importance of the Provost Section having full knowledge of the entire Headquarters.

42 It was a rule, strictly enforced by both civil and military police, that any vehicle left unattended must be immobilized in some manner so as to prevent theft or misuse. The most common method was to lift the distributor cap and remove the rotor arm.

43 A route-signing system was gradually evolved. In its simpler form it consisted of posting a circular disc-directional at intervals. The broad black arrow on a white background indicated the desired direction.

44 Density: It was essential that vehicle convoys moved in a dispersed mode, having regard to the interference by enemy aircraft. Density was controlled by the Movement Order, which specified the VTM (vehicles per mile) of road space. A normal density would be about 30 VTM, or a gap of 60 yards between each vehicle. this pattern was difficult to maintain so that a large part of training was devoted to practicing march discipline by unit drivers, as well as Provost engaged on traffic duty.

45 See Appendix "F" to Staff Duties In the Field, 1949. All military vehicles were identified by a number on a square, coloured background. These "Tac Signs" denoted unit, corps (RCA, RCASC, RCE, etc) and headquarters. This system of numbering and colour coding was most helpful to Provost on Traffic Control duties. Some examples:
HQ Inf Div: 40 White on Black field
HQ Inf Bde: 81 Black on Red field
Three Bns of Bde: 55, 56, 57 Black on Red
Three Fd Regts: 42, 43, 44 Black on Red and Blue Horizontal
Four Tpt Coys: 70, 71, 72, 73 Black on Blue and Yellow Diagonal.

46 Kim Beattie "Dileas", pg 114. The move of 1 Canadian Infantry Division from Aldershot to north of the Thames after the Dunkirk evacuation in May 1940.

47 Standing provost patrols were instituted at the large railway terminals in London to assist the local authorities with the constant crush of Service personnel travelling to and from London. The train service was fast and efficient, and was really the only method of travel.

48 A C Pro C Special Investigation Unit (SIU) was established at CMHQ, during 1942, to deal with serious crimes such as fraud, robbery and assault. It had an establishment of three officers and 12 NCOs who were invariably men with pre-

vious experience in crime detection. A similar SIU was also formed on the Continent, in 1944, by the DPM, First Canadian Army. This SIU investigated the infamous incident when several Canadian soldiers were summarily shot while held as prisoners-of-war by troops of a German SS Panzer division.

Chapter 4: Bumper, Tiger and Spartan

49 C P Stacey, "The Canadian Army, 1939–1945", pgs 41–48. This proposed organization was changed somewhat. The final result was an ARMY of two CORPS to command and control three infantry and two armoured DIVISIONS, plus two independent armoured BRIGADES.

Chapter 5: The Dieppe Raid

50 C P Stacey, "The Canadian Army, 1939–1945", pgs 51–59 (meetings between Roosevelt, Churchill and their staffs during December 1941 and June 1942).
51 Ibid, pg 553.
52 A Robert Prouse, "Ticket to Hell", pg 8.
53 A NCO in each company was appointed NCO Investigator and assigned investigative duties where expertise and continuity were required.
54 Captain E H "Red" Stevenson was the OC of 2 Provost Company at this time.
55 Assault Landing Craft (LST, LCT, LCP) were designed to carry tanks, guns, vehicles and troops ashore during beach landing operations. The front-end featured a large ramp door that could be lowered to permit rapid unloading. the flat bottom and low draft enabled their use in shallow water but also meant a bumpy ride in rough seas.
56 Field Marshal Von Rundstedt was Commander-in-Chief of German Forces in the West.
57 Robert Prouse, "Ticket to Hell", pg 11.
58 C P Stacey, "The Canadian Army, 1939–1945", pg 80 and "Six Years of War", pg 389.

Chapter 6: Sicily, Italy and Goldflake

59 German troops were encountered here for the first time.
60 This figure includes 12 Canadian nurses from 5 Canadian General Hospital who were wounded by enemy shell fire at Catania.
61 Major General Chris Vokes, CB, CBE, DSO, CD, "My Story", pg 136.

62 This company was formed at the Canadian Provost Corps Depot, Aldershot, in 1943. Its task was to look after the Base Areas of 1 Canadian Corps in and around Naples and Avellino.
63 Located in Avellino, it provided detention facilities for all Canadian units in this theatre. It emphasized sound basic training and discipline, and was said to be the best Junior NCO school in Italy.
64 The provision of RCMP reinforcements was discontinued in 1940. The result was that the RCMP component of 1 Provost Company was gradually reduced until, in late 1944, there was not a single member left.
65 The Abbey of Monte Cassino, a dominant feature on the right, was held by the Germans.
66 Captain A J Scotti, MC, commanded 5 Provost Company in Italy. He was appointed APM of 5 Canadian Armd Division and promoted Major early in 1945. He went on to serve in the Canadian Army Regular and held several command and staff positions in Canada and at HQ SHAPE in Europe. He was appointed Provost Marshal (Army) in October 1961 and served as head of the Corps until July 1964.
67 Lieutenant Colonel Leonard Hanson Nicholson, MBE. A detailed biography of this former Provost Marshal and RCMP Commissioner is given in the final chapter.

Chapter 7: Northwest Europe, June 1944–October 1945

Normandy and Caen

68 Sergeant Ray Chambers was a section sergeant in 4 Provost Company (3 Canadian Infantry Division) throughout this campaign. A detailed biography is given in the last chapter.
69 An important feature of the overall security programme for the Normandy landings was the identification of each unit, during the embarkation process, by a serial number only. Each unit commander was issued with a sealed package containing maps and the location of the landing and assembly area inland. On no account was this to be opened prior to embarkation.
70 RCE units were responsible for the supply of potable water.
71 The six Divisions:
   2 Canadian Infantry Division
   3 Canadian Infantry Division
   59 British Infantry Division
   3 British Infantry Division
   4 Canadian Armd Division
   1 Polish Armd Division

The 7 (British) Armed Division (Desert Rats) also passed through Caen during this period. These Divisions were placed, in varying grouping, under command of HQ 2 Canadian and HQ 1 British Corps during this phase of the campaign.

72 This segregation was designed to forestall an effort by officers to discourage their men from giving us useful information at subsequent interrogations.

Quesnay Woods, Falaise and the Gap

73 "H Hour" was the term used to indicate the exact start time of the attack. It was used to coordinate the fire and movement of all participating troops.
74 C P Stacey, "The Victory Campaign", pg 265.
75 The "Gap" area was located in the Dives River valley between the villages of Trun and Chambois.
76 This was in addition to another 1,270 tanks and vehicles destroyed elsewhere.

The Seine, Channel Ports and Antwerp

77 Jerrican: So-called because this 4 gallon, rectangular metal container was developed by the "Jerries" in North Africa, in 1943. It was adopted by USA, British and Canadian forces.
78 C P Stacey, "The Victory Campaign", pg 178.
79 This vehicle was designed for the recovery of large vehicles and tanks. It was called a "Scammel".
80 A special practice for the Seine crossing was held on the Trent River in Lincolnshire, during March 1944. Exercise Kate involved the Engineers of 2 Canadian Corps, under Brigadier Geoffrey Walsh, the Chief Engineer. An actual pontoon bridge was constructed and "dummy" vehicles from 4 Canadian Infantry Brigade practiced crossing. Sections from 13 and 2 Provost Companies performed traffic control duties.
81 This Armoured Division was part of the Second British Army, which was on the right flank of the Canadian Army.
82 Captain Chris Forbes was a Royal Canadian Mounted Police "original" in 1 Provost Company. He commanded 2 Provost Company through most of the Northwest Europe campaign and was promoted to Major and appointed APM late in 1944. He kept a diary and later wrote his memoirs, which were subsequently published in the Royal Canadian Mounted Police Quarterly, Volume 50 of November 1985.
83 C P Stacey, "The Victory Campaign", pg 301.
84 No sooner had the V-1 "Buzz" Bomb attacks stopped than a new weapon, the V-2 Rocket, was launched by the Germans. It carried a sizeable warhead and was launched in a very high arc so that it came straight down on London. There was no defence.

85 The "BRASCO" (Brigade Supply Officer) notified the Division Headquarter staff of the location (Map reference) for next day's supply point (Sup P). This information was quickly relayed, by signal or DR, to all units. In actual fact, locations were more often than not spread by word of mouth.
86 The ordinary Werhmacht soldier was considered a rather decent chap, as opposed to the SS and paratroopers who were doctrinaire Nazis and treated as an elite by the German High Command and Hitler.
87 This story was the subject of a book entitled "The Execution of Private Slovik" by William B Huie. It was also made into a movie of the same name. Eddie Slovik was a conscientious objector who refused to participate in a battle. His widow lived in Detroit.
88 C P Stacey, "The Victory Campaign", pg 424 and Map 8.
89 The 1st Canadian Parachute Battalion formed part of the British Parachute Division.
90 Warrant Officer A S (Art) Bird came to the Canadian Provost Corps from the Loyal Edmonton Regiment in 1941. He served in the Corps, in peace and war, until his retirement in January 1968, with the rank of major.
91 HQ 2nd Canadian Echelon was an administrative unit responsible for maintaining the service record of each Canadian soldier in the Northwest Europe theatre. This was done from a system, a daily "Casualty and Strength Returns", received from each unit. By September 1944 this unit employed 150 CWAC personnel, of which four were wounded in the V-1 raid on Antwerp during October 1944.
92 Major General Kurt Meyer commanded the 12SS Division in Normandy. He was tried for war crimes after the war. A Canadian Army Court-Martial found him guilty and sentenced him to death, which was subsequently commuted to life imprisonment. Meyer spent five years in Dorchester Penitentiary, in New Brunswick, and was transferred, in 1951, to a British prison in West Germany. His release was approved by the Canadian Government in 1954.
93 Officers and vehicles from the 2 Corps Light Anti-Aircraft Regiment were employed on this project.
94 Captain Eric Porter, RCMP, commanded 11 Provost Company throughout. RSM "Jimmie" Rae was a former militia sergeant from the 48th Highlanders.

Chapter 8: The Reichwald, Hochwald, Groningen and Victory

95 General H D G Crerar was the senior commander of this operation. It was the largest force ever commanded by a Canadian:
First Canadian Army – with under command:
   2 Canadian Corps: 2 Canadian Infantry Division

	3 Canadian Infantry Division
	4 Canadian Armoured Division
	2 Canadian Armoured Brigade
30 British Corps:	15 Infantry Division
	43 Infantry Division
	51 Infantry Division
	53 Infantry Division
	11 Armoured Division

96 Lieutenant John A Dowsett (4 Provost Company, 3 Canadian Infantry Division) and Lieutenant George Wilkinson (8 Provost Company, 4 Canadian Armd Division) both enrolled, in October 1946, in the Canadian Provost Corps as part of the peacetime Canadian Army Regular. Both retired, after many years service, with the rank of Lieutenant Colonel, and both had pre-World War II service in the Permanent Force.

97 These POW were processed through the Divisional and Corps PW cages prior to being evacuated to a large Canadian Base Camp at Le Havre. It was designed to hold up to 17,000 POW and was under the overall command of the O1C 2nd Echelon. The POW were then moved, by sea, to PW Camps in Canada. A second PW Base Camp, with a capacity of 10,000, was later established in Dieppe.

98 Previously used in the ill-fated Arnhem battle.

99 The Commanding Officer of 6 Canadian Parachute Battalion was killed during this operation, on 24 March.

100 C P Stacey, "The Victory Campaign", pg 537.

101 This operation took place on 25 March. The crossing place was about five miles east of Rees, towards Emmerich. The 9 Canadian "Highland" Brigade comprised three battalions: North Nova Scotia Highlanders, Highland Light Infantry and the Stormont Dundas and Glengarry Highlanders, under the command of Major General John Rockingham. Sergeant Ray Chambers and his section were placed "under command" of the Brigade Headquarters, as was frequently done when a brigade was off on its own.

102 Captain B W E (Bill) Lee stayed on in the postwar Canadian Army Regular, Canadian Provost Corps and served many years in various command and staff positions within and outside the Corps. He retired in 1971 with the rank of Lieutenant Colonel.

103 The headquarters of a Field Army is a large organization containing over 1,500 officers and men and about 600 assorted vehicles. Sergeant (later RSM) A S May, BEM, was in charge of the Provost section of 11 Provost company that was permanently allocated to HQ First Canadian Army. It was one of his many responsibilities to move this huge installation from time to time. He recalled

this as a task equalling in complexity the move of a good-sized town from one locality to another. The system developed for such a move was to group the various elements into numbered serials. Ideally the new area was on well-drained ground with a road network, and under cover of trees. The space allotted to each serial was then marked with an appropriate signpost, off the internal route. This ensured smooth dispersal off the road into the new location and quick entry into the site marked for each serial. Corps and Division headquarters also had a Provost Section allocated full-time. The Division headquarters was much smaller (see Table 1) and would relocate frequently. Army headquarters would move once to about every seven moves of a Corps, and a Corps headquarters once for every five moves of a Division, as a rule of thumb.

104 Each armoured division had a "motorized" infantry battalion, in this case the Westminister Regiment from British Columbia. Its counterpart in 4 Canadian Armoured Division was the Lake Superior Regiment from Thunder Bay.

105 C P Stacey, "The Victory Campaign", pg 583.

106 Book, "silver Jubilee, The Canadian Provost Corps, 1940–1965", pg 31.

Chapter 9: Repatriation

107 The Canadian Government had already authorized 6 Canadian Infantry Division for action against the Japanese. It was to be formed by Pacific Command on the west coast and was to be manned by trained volunteers from units in Europe and Canada. Those volunteering from units in Europe would have first priority for repatriation. The collapse of Japan in August rendered this plan redundant.

108 The war establishment provided 17 Canadian Provost Corps officers and 63 Other Ranks comprising a headquarters and three training companies. The RSM was the well-known Ron Finnie of Canadian OCTU fame. This was a completely self-contained unit with its own pay, medical, reception, despatch and record sections.

109 Corporal Christensen served with 6 Provost Company in London and Glasgow. On return to Canada he enrolled in the Toronto Police Force, later the Metropolitan Toronto Police, where he served for the next 37 years. He now resides in Scarborough.

110 Soldiers under sentence (SUS).

Chapter 10: The War in Canada

111 Ration items included: gasoline, meat, butter, tires, liquor, sugar, new cars, nylons and all wages were frozen at 1939 levels.

112 C P Stacey, "The Victory Campaign", pgs 118–120.
113 Desmond Morton, "A Military History of Canada", pgs 184–185.
114 Much of the detail contained in this chapter is taken from the document "Résuméd History of The Canadian Provost Corps And Its Activities For the Period October 1940 to September 1943", by Colonel Phillipe Auguste Puize.
115 30 Coy-London, Ont: Kitchener, Woodstock, Chatham, Windsor, Sarnia

    31 Coy-Toronto, Ont: Niagara, Hamilton

    32 Coy-Toronto, Ont: Capreol, Kirkland Lake, Orillia, Sault Ste Marie, Timmins, Meaford

    33 Coy-Ottawa, Ont: Kingston, Brockville, Cornwall, Carleton Place, Smiths Falls

    34 Coy-Montreal, Que: Sherbrooke, Three Rivers,

    35 Coy-Montreal, Que: St-Anne-de-Bellevue, Val d'Or, Rouyn

    36 Coy-Quebec, Que: Chicoutimi, Roberval, Jonquiere Megantic, St Joseph de Beauce

    37 Coy-Halifax, NS: Mulgrave, Kentville,

    38 Coy-Halifax, NS: Digby, Charlottetown, Dartmouth, New Glasgow, Bridgewater, Amherst, Shelburne

    39 Coy-Saint John, NB: Moncton, Fredricton, St Stephen, Campbellton

    40 Coy-Winnipeg, Man: Port Arthur, Brandon, Portage la Prairie

    41 Coy-Vancouver, BC: Vernon, Kamloops, Chilliwack, Sicamous

    42 Coy-Prince George, BC: Prince Rupert, Terrace, Wainwright, Jasper

    43 Coy-Regina, Sask: Saskatoon, Dundurn, Moose Jaw, Prince Albert, Maple Creek

    44 Coy-Calgary, Alta: Edmonton, Red Deer, Camrose, Grande Prairie, Lethbridge, Medicine Hat, Wetaskiwin, Vermillion

    45 Coy-Sydney, NS: Glace Bay, Sydney Mines, North Sydney, North Waterford

    46 Coy-Rimouski, Que: Matapedia, Riviere-du-Loup, New Carlisle, Gaspe, Ste-Anne, Tadossac

    47 Coy-Camp Petawawa, Ont: Pembroke

    48 Coy-Camp Borden, Ont: Barrie, North Bay, Sudbury

116 This detail is taken from the Colonel Puize History, pg 12.

Chapter 11: The Interim Force

117 Plan "H" was the name given to the proposed overall organization of the post-war Canadian Army Regular which became operative on 1 October 1946.

References and Notes 301

118 Lieutenant Colonel James Reginald Stewart, MBE,CD was appointed Provost Marshal in April 1946.

Chapter 12: Absentees and Deserters

119 Desertion was more serious than absence without leave. It was necessary to prove that the soldier did not "intend" to return. Evidence for this might include a lengthy absence, taking up full-time civilian employment, disguise, name change and so on. It would be rare to charge desertion when the soldier returned of his own volition.
120 A large number of absentees were apprehended by Civil Police, usually as a result of some minor offence.

Chapter 13: Beginning the Resurrection

121 The Bilateral Agreement provided for the acquisition and use, by Canada's three Services (Army, Navy and Air Force), of American equipment, weapons and, when required, tactical doctrine and communications.
122 Regimental police vacancies to be covered by Canadian Provost Corps personnel existed in infantry battalions, armoured regiments and RCASC companies.
123 Each Army Command had an establishment for Regular Army administrative and training staff (A & T Staff) to augment the resources of Reserve units. These officers and NCOs provided much needed continuity in the Reserve.
124 A more complete biography for Major Art Bird is given in note 90 to Chapter 7.
125 This was Claude Brown, a World War II veteran from an armoured regiment. he was employed int he Ministers' Office prior to transferring the Canadian Provost Corps. He served for another 23 years and retired with the rank of captain.
126 This stately, old Ottawa mansion had been a CWAC barracks throughout the war. It housed the Provost Marshal from 1945 to 1964 and is now the National Headquarters of Saint John Ambulance in Canada.
127 The heraldic description of the button: "A lion, crowned couchant guardant and holding, in the dexter paw, a maple leaf".

Chapter 14: Provost in the Militia

128 This detail is taken from the October 1956 issue of The Canadian Army Journal, which was the official organ of the Army from 1948 to 1965.
129 Lieutenant Colonel J J (Jack) Platt enrolled in the Canadian Provost Corps

early in 1940 as a Lieutenant. He was posted to 2 Provost company and went overseas with that unit. He held many command and staff appointments including: OC 2 Provost Company, DAPM First Canadian Army, APM 4 Canadian Armoured Division, APM Western Command, DPM at Army Headquarters (PM's office), CO Canadian Provost Corps School and CPM Central Command. He was an able and efficient officer and an outstanding administrator who was committed to improving standards wherever he served. He retired to Victoria, British Columbia in 1965 where, sadly, he passed away in 1989.

130 Captain J V (Jim) Findlay, CStJ, CD was born in Toronto and joined the Cadets of the 48th Highlanders as a piper. He served with the 48th throughout World War II. He was a Platoon Commander and was wounded during the attack on the Gothic Line during September 1944. On return to Canada he attended the University of Toronto and graduated, with a degree in Engineering, in 1949. He was employed in industry for the next 20 years and served as General Manager (National) of the Industrial Accident Prevention Association (IAPA) from 1976 to 1987. He is now retired and was recently elected President of The Canadian Provost Corps Association.

131 The Service Battalion was designed to administer and command most of the small service and logistic units normally allotted to an independent, all arms brigade. The same policy was carried on in the Reserves and Militia. Hence, the provost platoon functioned as part of this larger unit.

Chapter 15: Korea

132 Joseph C Goulden, "Korea, The Untold Story", pg 19.
133 The establishment called for 38 All Ranks:
   Major   OC and Brigade APM
   Lieutenant   2 IC
   Sergeant   Clerk and Storeman
   Corporal   Cook (RCASC)
   Privates (4) Orderlies 2, Clerk 1, Cook 1
   Two sections each:
   Sergeant   Service Policeman
   Corporals (2) Service Policeman
   L/Cpls (12)   Service Policeman
134 The APM was Major R I (Bob) Luker, MC, CD.
135 The infantry component of this brigade group was formed from the second battalions of the three existing Regular Army Regiments (RCR, PPCLI and R22^{e}R). the remaining units were:
   "A" Squadron 1/2 Armoured Regiment

  2 Canadian Fd Regiment, RCHA
  57 Fd Squadron, RCE
  54 Tpt Company, RCASC
  25 Fd Amb, RCAMC
  25 Fd Workshop, RCEME
  25 Provost Detachment, Canadian Provost Corps
136 Colonel Robert T Grogan served in the Royal Canadian Navy during World War II, first in the North Atlantic aboard a cruiser on the Murmansk run. He was in the Pacific off Okinawa when the Japanese surrendered in August 1945. He joined the Canadian Provost Corps Militia Company in Winnipeg after the war and enrolled in the Canadian Provost Corps as a regular officer in October 1951. He served for the next 35 years in various positions including two peacekeeping tours (Gaza and Cyprus), two tours with the Canadian Brigade in Germany and a tour at NATO Headquarters in the rank of Colonel. He retired as the Director of Security, the head of the Security Branch, at Department of National Defence Headquarters in Ottawa.
137 Joseph C Goulden, "Korea, The Untold Story", pgs 170 – 171.
138 January 1955 Issue, "The Canadian Army Journal".
139 The American troops devised and acronym for almost every unit and formation, most of which were highly descriptive and "catchy". Some examples:
  2½ ton truck – "deuce and a half"
  622 Military Policy Company – "six double deuce"
  55 Replacement Depot – "Double nickel ripple depple"
  "X" Armoured Regiment – "the jolting joes"
  25 Infantry Division – "Big Red".
140 R & R (rest and relaxation) sometimes called "rack and ruin".
141 Corporal E M Butler, Canadian Provost Corps
  Corporal D H Cummings, Royal Military Police
  Corporal J W Wright, RAA, Provost Corps
142 8 United States Army Headquarters was the senior command for all operations in Korea. It was commanded by a four-star United States Army general.
143 The GSOI at this time was Lieutenant Colonel Mike Dare, Canadian Army.

Chapter 16: NATO

144 The CGS (Chief of General Staff) was the senior commander in the Canadian Army. The Chiefs of Staffs Committee was formed to coordinate the activities of the Navy, Army and Air Force. This Committee comprised the CGS and his opposite numbers in the Navy and Air Force. The full-time chairman was a general, or equivalent, appointed by the Minister.

145 New items of equipment included:
    Armoured Personnel Carrier (APC) designed to reduce casualties and move infantry quickly into battle;
    Radio Wireless sets that were lighter, more reliable and with increased range;
    Infantry Anti-Tank weapons that were lighter, highly accurate and with increased range;
    Field cookers, heaters and an array of camp equipment that was lighter, durable and easily portable.
146 Captain André D Gauthier graduated from the University of Ottawa Regular Officer Training Plan in 1955 and enrolled in the Canadian Provost Corps in the rank of Lieutenant. He served with distinction for the next 34 years, culminating in senior appointments such as Director of Security at National Defence Headquarters and Military Attache in Yugoslavia. He retired from the military, with Colonel rank, in 1989, to pursue a career as an artist and sculptor. Now one of Canada's foremost sculptors of military subjects, he has two public monuments and several award winning works to his credit. André will be remembered for the life-like statue of the "POINTSMAN", which he produced and presented to the Corps in the late 1950s. This much revered Corps symbol still appears on special occasions such as mess nights and reunions.

Chapter 17: Towards Professionalism

147 The term "manpower" is used to denote the species and not a gender.
148 Lieutenant Colonel M A (Moe) Martin enlisted in the CASF in September 1944 and saw service in the United Kingdom and Germany in the Canadian Army Occupation Force. He was commissioned through the University of Toronto COTC programme in 1950 and served in the Canadian Provost Corps until 1959. His next 18 years were spent in the Personnel Selection Branch of the Canadian Army where he rose to become the Staff Officer Coordination and Administration in the Directorate of Personnel Applied Research at Army Headquarters. Following his retirement from the Canadian Armed Forces he was employed at RCMP Headquarters in Ottawa, in a senior personnel selection appointment, for several years.
149 The Cambridge Challenge Bowl was donated by officers of the British Army stationed in Halifax, in 1903, "for the encouragement of shooting amongst the several units of the Permanent Force of Canada". It was awarded annually to the unit which attained the highest aggregate score during the Annual Classification Practice for the rifle. The rules and conditions for the competition were contained in Canadian Army Order 57-8 of 1950. It was first presented

in 1907 under rules published in Militia Order 92 of 1906, signed by Colonel H B Vital, Adjutant General.

150 Captain J A (John) Dowsett served on the staff of the Canadian Army Liaison Establishment (CALE) in London from February 1951 to November 1953. He moved across the Channel to assume the appointment of APM 27 Canadian Infantry Brigade at Hannover, Germany. On return to Canada in 1957 he was appointed Chief Instructor at the Canadian Provost Corps School, attended and graduated from the Canadian Army Staff College in 1959 and served in a number of command and staff positions at Army Headquarters. He was Commandant of the Canadian Forces School of Intelligence and Security (CFSIS) from 1969 to 1973, prior to his retirement from the Canadian Armed Forces with Lieutenant Colonel rank. John was one of the very few members of the corps with pre-World War II service in the Permanent Force (RCR), and continuous service in the Canadian Army Active Force (CASF WWII), the Canadian Army Regular (CA(R)) and the Canadian Armed Forces (CAF), the Unified Services.

151 Sergeant Reg High had the rare distinction of organizing "Polar Bear Patrols" while in charge of the Fort Churchill, Manitoba provost detachment.

152 the term "Non-Commissioned Officer" (NCO) was used to refer to anyone above Private but lower than Warrant Officer rank. This has been revised in the National Defence Act to "Non-Commissioned Member" (NCM). The latter term encompasses all those below officer rank, including privates. Thus, the term "Other Ranks" (OR) is no longer used. They are Non-Commissioned Members (NCMs).

153 The Judge Advocate General (JAG) was the senior legal officer for the Department of National Defence. The incumbent at this time was Brigadier Reg Orde, later replaced by Brigadier S Lawson.

Chapter 18: Lonely Postings

154 A town of 12,000 people in northeast British Columbia.

155 Captain S E (Sammy) Sambrooke was a native born Albertan from a town southeast of Edmonton. He came to the Canadian Provost Corps from the Loyal Edmonton Regiment in 1941. He was commissioned in 1943 in the United Kingdom and served in 13 Provost Company until the war ended. Following three years in "civvy street" he enrolled in the Canadian Provost Corps as a Lieutenant in 1951. He served in the Yukon from 1956 to 1960 and retired, with Captain rank, in 1966. He passed away in 1980.

156 Captain J D (Jim) Lumsden was commissioned and came to the Corps in 1952. He was Detachment Commander of the NWHS from 1961 to 1964.

Jim went on to serve in a variety of Corps positions and retired with the rank of Lieutenant Colonel.

157 Vehicle accidents involving UNEF drivers and the "locals" were common. A case where a UNEF vehicle injured a local Bedouin camel required an enormous amount of time and patience by the MP Detachment.

158 Corporal R G (Bob) Thomas was promoted Sergeant while serving in Cyprus. He returned to Canada in 1965 and spent the next three years on Canadian Provost Corps investigative duties in Ottawa. He left the Army in 1968 and continued his career as a police officer with the Belleville Police Force. He took up employment with Sears Canada Incorporated in the early 1980s and is now the National Manager, Resources Protection and Environmental Programme for this large corporation.

Chapter 19: Brotherhood and Badges

159 "WATCHDOG" was the code name for the senior Provost appointment in a specified formation. It was used to disguise identities during wireless transmissions in battle areas. See "Staff Duties In The Field", pg 627.

Chapter 20: A Few Good Men

160 2 Princess Patricia Canadian Light Infantry (2PPCLI).

APPENDIX A

Summary of Subjects Discussed at Provost Conference, Camp Borden, Ont., 16–19 March, 1949

Officers assembled at 1000 hours 16 March 1949 and were officially welcomed by Colonel D K TODD, DSO, Garrison Commander, CAMP BORDEN.

Officers in Attendance

P M (A)	Lt Col J R STEWART, MBE	AHQ	Chairman
D P M	Maj A J GILLIS, MBE	AHQ	D/Chairman
D A A & Q M G	Maj A J SCOTTI, MC	BORDEN	Member
A P M	Maj J J PLATT	West Comd	Member
A P M	Capt R I LUKER, MC	Prairie Comd	Member
A P M	Maj A R RITCHIE	Central Comd	Member
A P M	Maj C O ROCHON	Quebec Comd	Member
Rep A P M	Lt J A THOMSON	Eastern Comd	Member
O C 6 Pro Coy	Maj Q E LAWSON	CAMP BORDEN	Member
O C C Pro C School	Maj B W E LEE	CAMP BORDEN	Member

Note: Major A. J. SCOTTI, MC, Canadian Provost Corps, through the kindly expressed permission of Colonel D. K. TODD, DSO, was permitted to attend the conference in a dual capacity, as a member of the Corps with wide experience and as DAA & QMG, CAMP BORDEN Garrison.

Opening Remarks – PM(A)
1   See precis at Appendix "A".

Outline
2   An outline of subjects on the agenda to be covered was given by the DPM and the conference was then declared open by the PM(A) for discus-

sion of points raised in the PM's address, and the completeness of the agenda (shown at Appendix "B").

Provost Charges
3   The OC The Canadian Provost Corps School raised the point that charges laid by Provost on placing a man in close arrest and confining him in a guardroom, are not the charges dealt with by a CO, but are in fact only holding charges.
4   This point was confirmed and it was emphasized that the CO was free to base the formal charges, on CAFB 264, on the evidence supplied and that the holding charge supplied to the Guard Commander at time of initial incarceration was merely the report of an occurrence to be substantiated by a statement of evidence. Provost do not supply the CAFB 264, quoting contravention of a particular section of the Army Act, etc.
5   Major LEE also raised, in connection with the question of guided reading for Corps personnel, the point that if a Multilith machine could be supplied the School, he was prepared to undertake production of a Corps Paper, which, in addition to supplying Corps news of posting, promotions and results of courses, would permit an excellent medium for keeping Active and RF personnel abreast of new developments which directly concern the Army and the Corps. Training of RF and Supplementary Reserve personnel through extension courses could also be handled and would fulfill the present requirement for material to augment precis and lesson plans.
6   Major LEE was instructed to obtain specifications and forward same to AHQ where the matter would be taken up with DMT.

Establishments – Active Force

7   *No. 6 Provost Company*
Company Headquarters and three Sections – Central Command One Section in each of four Commands

8   *No. 16 Special Investigation Section*
Divided equally, with two Investigators in each of five Commands.

9   *Military and Branch Detention Barracks*
No. 7   MDB   HALIFAX, N. S.
No. 12   MDB   CAMP BORDEN, Ont.
No. 9   MDB   WINNIPEG Man.
10. 10   MDB   CALGARY, Alta.

No. 14   BrDB   QUEBEC CITY, Quebec
No. 15   BrDB   ESQUIMALT, B. C.

10   There was unanimous opinion that the present organization is unwieldy and 6 Provost Company and 16 SIS should be reduced to nil strength, also that the staffs of MDBs should be streamlined, reducing the number of NCOs and increasing the number of Privates.

11   Each APM was instructed to review his Command's requirements and draw up, for submission to Command WECs, a Command Provost Establishment incorporating the present detachments of 6 Company and 16 SIS and reducing, where applicable, NCO ranks in detention barracks in favour of an increase of Privates.

12   APMs were requested to solicit the aid of their commands in having their submission ready for despatch to reach AHQ on 15 May 1949.

13   *The Canadian Provost Corps School*

As the School establishment is not up to strength it was considered no action should be recommended at this time, but after one year's operation the question be again raised.

14   *A and T Staffs*

Opinion was expressed in Prairie and Eastern Commands that one Sergeant and one Driver Mechanic or Vehicle Mechanic is insufficient. In Eastern and Western Commands the question of relocalizing parts of RF Companies is being considered.

15   APMs were instructed to review their requirements and request increases where necessary through Command channels. The OC, The Canadian Provost Corps School, was instructed to ensure that personnel with mechanical qualifications or aptitudes be qualified in appropriate courses.

16   In connection with A & T Staffs the DPM stated he had been approached informally by the RCMP as to the possibility of filling the A & T vacancies at ROCKCLIFFE and REGINA for Physical Training and Drill A/Is and in regard to our intentions for replacement of present A/Is who have been stationed at REGINA for three years.

17   Owing to the present shortage of suitable potential A/Is in the Corps, it is considered this question should be thoroughly reviewed at AHQ, NCOs selected and courses arranged to qualify with a view to replacement at a later date. One Staff Sergeant from the MDB, Eastern Command, is presently undergoing assessment course at the School with a view to filling the present vacancy at REGINA as a PTI.

18 *NDHQ Security Guard*
Morale reported to be low owing to nature of duties performed, lack of suitable accommodation in OTTAWA to quarter and mess the single personnel, hours of duty too long and the establishment is too small to allow adequate short passes and annual leave. Twenty percent of present strength have requested or inquired regarding transfers or Postings. Personnel on HE The Canadian Provost Corps School are parading to the OC and requesting they not be sent to OTTAWA because of the soul-destroying nature of the work and the high cost of living in OTTAWA under present conditions.

19 It was explained that policy at AHQ has been to post selected men from the Security Guard to vacancies in other Commands. Major LEE expressed complete dissatisfaction stating this arrangement would result in transfers from the Corps and felt we should endeavour to fill Security Guard requirements with the type of soldier who would be content with routine.

20 AHQ to investigate the possibility of increasing the Security Guard by 15 Other Ranks and take over from the Corps of Commissionaires duty during working hours as well as silent hours, also attempt to secure the Chapel Street, OTTAWA, portion of Kildare Barracks to accommodate and mess the single men and to establish a most needed guardroom for OTTAWA.

21 A submission to the AG will be prepared.

22 *Service Police on Unit Establishments*
Infantry Regiments appear to be content (RCR; R22eR; PPCLI).
Armoured Regiments undecided (LdSH; RCD).

23 Considered the following policy should apply. If units request Provost as Service Police vice Regimental Police, the Corps should supply but that the Corps should go on record as opposed in principle to the idea of supplying Provost as Service Police to units, and that a unit or school problems, especially a seasonal one, should be dealt with on a Command basis, by application to the APM for a detachment.

24 To be further discussed to D Org and DSD at AHQ for a firm policy ruling.

25 *Guardrooms – Canada*
There is an urgent requirement for guardrooms at:
    VANCOUVER, B.C.
    EDMONTON, Alta.
    REGINA, Sask.

TORONTO, Ont.
LONDON, Ont.
KINGSTON, Ont.
OTTAWA, Ont.
FREDERICTON, N.B.

26 The guardrooms listed in CAO 3-1 at VANCOUVER, EDMONTON and OTTAWA Air Stations are manned only when the RCAF have prisoners of their own. No permanent staff is available and when required guardrooms are staffed by tradesmen withdrawn from their regular duties. This situation is not satisfactory for Army purposes and in VANCOUVER and OTTAWA the RCAF guardrooms are located too far from troop centres. It is considered a properly operated Provost guardroom could handle custody and detention to 168 hours. Convenient guardrooms capable of handling up to 168 hours detention sentences would materially assist command officers with their disciplinary problems.

27 APMs, in their submissions for Command Provost Establishments, are to cover this aspect and recommend sufficient Provost at the points mentioned to cover the operation of a guardroom, when required, at Detachment Headquarters.

28 AHQ to deal with the question of a guardroom at OTTAWA when submission is prepared for an increase in this Security Guard to cover 24-hour duty, providing the Chapel Street Annex to Kildare Barracks can be made available.

29 If and when the new organization is completed and guardrooms are established at Provost detachment, CAO 3–1 to be amended.

Training – Active Force

Corps Training Generally

30 Concensus of opinion that present training in all aspects of Corps work is satisfactory with the exception of driver training, practical traffic control signals, report writing and typing.

31 The OC School to investigate and forward recommendations regarding an increase in length of Service Police Courses to take care of additional training on the subjects mentioned.

Officers

32 *Professional Advancement and Promotion Examinations*
Material available for issue on request from AHQ. Promotion exams to be written in 1951 and governed by rank held on 15 February 1950.

33 *Command and Staff Course*
GSPS 40 applies.

34 *Foreign Courses*
Safety Course at New York University of no value to Provost. Safety Course at Northwestern University, CHICAGO, fulfills all Provost requirements. Arson Course at Purdue University of doubtful value in view of short duration – five days. Delaware State Highway Traffic Department conference considered to be worth while. Courses for all Provost officers to standardize procedures of operation will be held not before 1951.
35 PM(A) to take up with DMT and arrange for vacancies on courses considered valuable.

COTC and Command Contingents
36 APMs agree there is a requirement for a two-hour lecture precis as they are periodically called on to lecture to COTC contingents at various universities. The precis to be divided into four parts which could, if necessary, be delivered at one time or as a series.
37 OC School to prepare lecture as noted and distribute. To include history, organization and employment.
38 The present arrangement for COTC is that the C Pro C School accepts only candidates for third year practical phase. It would be preferable if cadets could take GMT at the Provost School.
39 PM(A) to take up matter and discuss further with DMT. Present reaction of DMT is unfavourable on the grounds that GMT requires a larger class than is allotted presently to Canadian Provost Corps.

Other Ranks
40 *Standards – Weaknesses*
Present requirement of an "M" Score of 150 and Grade X is too high to obtain recruits. Suggested that standards remain but that the question be discussed with the SPOs and dealt with on a common sense basis.
41 PM to discuss with Org and SPO. APMs to discuss with SPOs at their own Headquarters.
42 Drivers IC to be deleted from prerequisites for Service Police Group 1 and inserted in prerequisites for Service Police Group 2 trade.
43 To delete from standards all reference to civilian experience.
44 Delete present requirement for one year's in-job training between trade tests Groups 1 and 2. Insert requirement in Group 2 standards for one year's experience on Provost duties.

45   By PM at AHQ to rewrite standards on receipt of new recommendations from the OC, The Canadian Provost Corps School.

46   *Courses Generally*
Wireless procedure has been dropped from GMT.
47   OC School to include in Group 2 Course 12½ periods on No. 58 Sets.
48   In writing of Group 2 Trade Test, Criminal Code of Canada to be permitted in examination room as a reference.
49   By School and commands as applicable.
50   Hours to be at discretion of OC School who will investigate the possibility of shortening daily hours and reducing night assignments. Courses considered to be highly concentrated now.
51   As deemed necessary by OC, The Canadian Provost Corps School.
52   It is considered there is a requirement for a D & M Course of six weeks to be included in schedule of courses at The C Pro C School, to qualify SP on one 4-wheeled vehicle and motorcycle.
53   OC School to arrange.

54   *Courses–Other Canadian Army Schools*
(a)   *Clerks* – C Pro C School to select candidates and submit to AHQ for concurrence and vacancies on RCASC Courses.
(b)   *GMT Instructors* – Same basis.
(c)   *Medical Orderlies* – School to arrange locally.
(d)   *Parachute Jumping*, and *Air Portability* – Very important. Channels for officers and other ranks to be followed up by PM and APMs.

Other Ranks
55   *Courses – Canadian Civil Establishments*
(a)   *CVTS* – Driver and Vehicle Mechanic and Clerks.
       PM to arrange for vacancies through AHQ.
(b)   *Photography* – PM to investigate through CAFIB and RCMP.

56   *Foreign Service Schools*
No change for the present. Additional vacancies are obtainable. Exchanges with United Kingdom in abeyance.

57   *Courses – Foreign Civil Establishments*
No requirement for other ranks.

58 *Training of Clerks*
Include typing on each course, if necessary increasing duration of present applicable courses by one week. OC The Canadian Provost Corps School to arrange.

59 *Training of QMs*
No problem on a Corps basis.

60 *Training of Investigators*
Specialized courses to be arranged for selected Provost personnel of right type. APMs to recommend to AHQ.

61 *A & T Staff and RCMP Cadre*
Policy to be one of rotation on a two or three year basis.

Training – Reserve Force
62 There was unanimous recommendation of all APMs as to advisability and desirability of having all Reserve Force Provost Companies attend central camp at PETAWAWA with their present A & T Staff. Two courses – one for senior NCOs and one for recruits.
63 PM(A) to take up the DMT in effort to arrange for Summer of 1949. Notify Commands as soon as possible to obtain concurrence.

SP Courses for A & T Staff
64 All A & T Staff require courses as soon as possible. Month of November 1949 suggested, or, if possible, other than Central Command Staff to take course to be arranged at conclusion of Summer Camp.
65 PM to review situation and advise all concerned. Consideration to be given to both Service Police and Techniques of Instruction training.
66 APM Western Command queried the possibility of activating a Corps Company slated for CALGARY and Traffic Control Company at EDMONTON; the APM Quebec Command and Traffic Control Company in MONTREAL.
67 PM to discuss with D Org and advise decision to Commands concerned.

Mobilization Planning
68 PM stated policy was not yet firm enough for general discussion and all subject matter was classified. In the matter of a Corps Tactical Doctrine the PM stated that some time in the future a correspondence study period

would be held to develop, so far as is possible, those points which in the past have proved contentious, and endeavour to fix policy and responsibility.

Personnel – Active Force
69   The DPM outlined the new policy on selection and posting of recruits to the School. Holding establishment not to cover vacancies. Policy on disposing of unsuitable personnel not yet firm and will remain in abeyance in the hope that difficulties encountered will be offset by greater numbers for selection at the School. Transfers must be voluntary in effecting transfers within CAMP BORDEN.

Postings
70   To be effected by AHQ on recommendation from School. The NDHQ Security Guard must be kept at strength. Priorities are laid down from time to time by D Pers.

Training
71   Clerks to be given a low priority on Corps training. Thirty recruits will have completed their Group 1 training and be ready for posting by 1 May 1949. An additional 15 by mid-July.

Rotation
72   To be controlled by PM on recommendations from APMs and the School. To be governed by housing and cost of living as well as availability of new recruits to fill vacancies. French speaking personnel for Quebec Command to rotate in the Command at the discretion of Command. DB staffs must be rotated due to the confining nature of their duties. The question of re-engaging personnel who have failed to pass trade tests and who are incapable of being furthered is a serious one and before making any firm recommendation APMs are requested to study the matter thoroughly.

Promotion
73   On a seniority basis coupled with ability and possession of requisite qualifications.

Recruits and Replacements
74   The situation was outlined by Major LEE and is considered to be satisfactory on the basis of present planning. Calibre of recruits is fair and

morale is high. Morale drops when the prospect of a posting to OTTAWA comes up in interviews.

Rank and Seniority
75 Career planning for officers and warrant officers is presently being studied.

Policy on Returning Personnel From The Corps School to Command of Enlistment
76 No promise is to be made to any recruit that he will be returned to his home command and he is to be given to understand that he may be required for duty in any part of Canada.

Personnel – Reserve Force
Formation, Unit Strength, Location
77

			Officers	OR
2 Corps	No 8 Coy	VANCOUVER	4	48
6 Div	13 Coy	WINNIPEG	4	44
2 Div	2 Coy	TORONTO	3	34
1 Div	1 Coy	LONDON	2	32
1 Corps	11 Coy	OTTAWA	Nil	Nil
3 Div	3 Coy	MONTREAL	4	84
4 Div	4 Coy	QUEBEC CITY	3	38
5 Div	5 Coy	HALIFAX	2	40
			22	320

78 No accommodation or other problems which are not in hand. All personnel shown are effectives.

Administration of Discipline
Standardization of Procedures
79 The only question raised concerned the specifying of a particular section of the Army Act when confining prisoners in a guardroom. Policy must be not to quote section but only offence.

Channels of Communication
80 School APMs' channel is through the PM, except in matters of local

Appendices 317

administration concerning Central Command, where channel is CAMP BORDEN to APM.

CAOs – Application of
81   CAO 63-4 – *Courts of Inquiry* Copy of Police or Provost report forming part of the proceedings. This does not concern CAO 255-4 which deals with confidential enquiries made by military Intelligence. As a general rule the Police or Provost report is not required by the unit but by the HQ concerned where the report is married up with the proceedings of the court by the Reviewing Officer. Police or Provost reports are usually more concerned with recovery whereas the C of I deals with the loss discovered.
82   CAO 121-17 – *Recovery of Reserve Force Kit and Equipment* Policy letter has resulted in prosecutions within Central Command. No reports from any other commands.

Canadian Provost Corps Standing Orders – KR(Can) 1490(b)
83   C Pro C Instructions are issued to clarify contentious points and to standardize methods of operation in all commands.

Part II Orders
84   Distribution by AHQ only.

MDB Regulations and Instructions
85   In the process of being rewritten. Pending issue, present regulations to be used only as a guide. Smoking periods in DBs and number of cigarettes permitted should be standardized. AG Letter of February 1946 ordered six cigarettes except on Punishment Diet No 1. On Punishment Diet 2 cigarettes are issued at commandant's discretion. SUS are sent to Military Detention Barracks as punishment, not *for* punishment.
86   At AHQ to investigate and ascertain where surplus stocks of writing materials which were issued by Auxiliary Services during the War are now located. Writing materials should be available for issue to SUS who cannot provide.
87   While it is apparent that each command in which a DB is located should be actively concerned with the welfare of SUS to the point of ensuring each SUS committed is in possession of sufficient funds to enable him to purchase toiletries, cigarettes, writing materials and postage. From an administrative view point the problem of Navy, Army and Air Force uniformity of provision should be considered as all DBs are tri-service.

88   A submission will be prepared at AHQ for AG decision.

Crime Reporting System – Provost Forms
89   It was agreed the present system should continue on the file key issued by the PM(A). Regarding forms, it was suggested by the APM Western Command that we dispense with one of the two report forms now in use and the PM would submit samples to P & S for printing.
90   The OC, Canadian Provost Corps School, submitted for consideration a detailed form to assist investigators of vehicle accidents (copy of form at Appendix "C"). This form was approved and agreement reached that necessary supplies could be run off at Command Headquarters for Provost in Command.
91   The OC, Canadian Provost Corps School, stated h is requirement for finger print forms was 1,500 per year. DPM to obtain from CAFIB and forward.
92   The OC, C Pro C School, submitted two samples of pocket notebooks for Provost. OC The School to obtain and forward to AHQ an approved sample. PM to approach P & S for printing.
93   The OC, Canadian Provost Corps School, requested that joining instructions to candidates attending courses at the School emphasize the necessity of Bringing notebooks. PM(A) to take up with Pers (Canadian Provost Corps).
94   The OC, Canadian Provost Corps School, submitted for consideration an Offence Report Form which was approved (Form at Appendix "D"). This form to be attached to the formal CAFB 264, or may be used without a statement of evidence as a charge report when confining personnel in a guardroom. PM to submit sample to P & S for printing.

Absentees and Deserters (CARO 6851; CAO 301)
95   Discussion revealed Quebec Command is the only command which has been forced, through lack of detention facilities, to temporarily suspend apprehension of deserters. It was agreed that the reporting system is a command problem and falls down only through lack of cooperation on the part of the units concerned in failing to submit notices and cancellations to APMs. Discussion continued with regard Section 163 Aa:

(a)   AA 163–1 (M)   Certificate of apprehension by or surrender to Civil Police must be signed by the police officer in charge of the detachment.

(b) AA 163–1 (J)   Certificate of surrender to Provost (see also Note 12 thereto).
(c) AA 163–1 (JJ) Certificate of apprehension.

96   Administration Letter 133 dated 15 June 1948 covers the payment of meals of absentees held in custody at civil police stations (copy at Appendix "E").
97   APM Western Command requested extra copies of absentee lists for distribution by Provost detachments. Extra copies to provide one for each Provost detachment will be forwarded by PM as lists are produced. Information to contain regimental number as well as Corps Register Number.

Reporting Loss and Theft of Public Stores (CAO 166–2)
98   The APM Western Command stated that authorized distribution of the Appendix to CAO 166-2 is insufficient to provide the pertinent information to each detachment of Command Provost. It was agreed that additional copies or extracts would be prepared by the APM concerned to fulfill his own requirements.
99   The PM stated the RCMP have queried the number and type of investigations referred to that Force for action and suggested maximum discretion be exercised in forwarding requests for action in cases which should be referred for information only. RCMP have advised that, while they are prepared to assist the Army to the fullest extent possible, they are hampered by a shortage of trained investigators and heavy pressure of other duties. The Director of Criminal Investigation has asked that, where possible, all requests for the assistance of RCMP be channelled through the APM or Provost officer in the RCMP Division to Divisional Headquarters.

Provost Monthly Reports
100   In future all criticisms and suggestions made by APMs in Monthly Reports will be dealt with by the PM through Provost Instructions, and not in the general notes forming part of the consolidated report distributed to the APMs months.

Liaison with Civil Police and Other Bodies
101   Discussion of this subject disclosed no problems as all reports indicated liaison is excellent. It was suggested however that possibly we are not making the fullest use of the facilities and information available to the CNR and CPR Investigation Departments.

Special Investigation Sections – Personnel, Clothing and Warrants
102   Discussion of this subject revealed the necessity for a plain clothes allowance to selected NCOs employed on investigations. PM to investigate this question at AHQ.
103   On the question of a Warrant Card for Provost Officers and Investigators agreement was reached that such a card is required to identify Provost out of uniform. The identity card is not sufficient for this purpose.
104   PM(A) will ascertain what information is required from APMs and cover this subject in a Provost Instruction.

Contingent Account for APMs
105   The question was raised that a small contingent account is required by APMs in covering the work of investigators – advances for casual meals, recovering stolen articles from check rooms, bus, train and taxi fares, etc. By PM after consultation with D Pay at AHQ.

Traffic Signing – Standardization of Pattern, Colours, Etc.
106   Agreement was reached that traffic signs in camps and at schools should be of standard sizes, with black letters on a yellow background. These colours have been found to show up well either in Summer or against snow in Winter.
107   Future demand to Ord for Discs-directional, either for training or operations will reflect black on yellow to replace black on white.
108   PM(A) will query through Military Adviser to the British High Commissioner for Canada to obtain the British reaction to this suggestion. In the meantime APMs will follow this procedure and ensure that each Provost sign erected will carry the words "C Pro C Sign" in yellow letters on a black bar at the lower left corner of the sign.

Soldiers Under Sentence
109   The guarding of a SUS removed from a DB to hospital to remain a command responsibility as Provost resources would be quickly depleted if required to guard patients in hospital.

Wearing of Sidearms by Provost
110   Paymaster escorts and NDHQ Security Guard only. Beyond this, at discretion of APMs, under *exceptional* circumstances.

Dress Generally – White Web by Other than Provost
111   While bandsmen and PPCLI are affecting white web belts, it is not

considered this matter should be taken up and the CARO rewritten as a CAO. Provost practice to be – white web for duty and khaki web for instructors and A & T Staff.

Traffic Control – Wrls Net, Field Formations
112   It is envisaged, in light of war experience, that Sigs personnel will be required to operate Provost wireless nets at Division, Corps and Army. In the meantime provision action in the case of Reserve Force Provost Companies will not be taken until training has advanced considerably.
113   Training at The Canadian Provost Corps School to continue on netting and procedure using the six No 58 Sets on issue.

SIS Equipment – Photographic and Sound Recorders
114   In abeyance pending the desired standard of training being reached.

Newfoundland Establishments
115   PM stated as no clearance for discussion of this subject has been received, the question is held in abeyance.

General Discussion–Minor Problems
116   The Canadian Provost Corps School is to advise Commands ETA of personnel from courses as far as possible in advance of despatch.

Provost Officers as Members of Courts Martial and Courts of Inquiry
117   At discretion of APMs. As these courts have a high training value, they should not be avoided except in cases where the opinion of the officers concerned is strongly biased by knowledge of the Provost investigation.

Regimental March – Canadian Provost Corps
118   All APMs are requested to review this question and submit suggestions as to lyrics to AHQ. WO II Nelson, of No 16 SIS, has expressed his willingness to write the music if agreement is reached on lyrics.
119   On the question of a trumpet or bugle call, it is considered this might remain in abeyance pending adoption of a march.

Corps Buttons, Badges, Tie and Lanyard
120   A design for buttons has been submitted for approval and issue.
121   PM(A) to contract Colonel FOOTE, OTTAWA, and obtain tie samples for circulation to APMs as well as Lanyard, as per sealed pattern already approved.

122   On the subject of a Corps badge and also Corps title flashes, a further review of this question will be undertaken by the PM at AHQ as this question is contingent on the Corps request for Royal assent to be given our application for the title "Royal". This application is in abeyance by direction of the Minister, but will be put forward again at a later date.

Officers' Mess Regulations – The Canadian Provost Corps School
123   Agreement was reached that the Corps Mess would be located at The Canadian Provost Corps School and operated by the present committee. Financial statement to be issued to all members at least once each year.

Provost Conferences
124   The PM stated that any future conferences would be held in the latter part of January each year and firm dates would be notified to APMs well in advance in order that their suggestions for the agenda might receive careful consideration at AHQ.

Standard Christmas Cards for Canadian Provost Corps
125   It was generally considered, after discussion, that the Corps should produce a Corps card as the policy on Corps cards varies with each command. It was agreed that distribution and sale should be handled from CAMP BORDEN in the early Autumn and that the price should not exceed 10¢ per card in quantity lots.
126   Major LAWSON to obtain samples and forward to AHQ for approval before placing orders.

Closing Remarks by the Provost Marshal
127   The PM expressed his complete satisfaction with progress made during the conference. It is apparent that the standard methods of operating in all commands is due to Wartime experience and, as we develop and gain further experience with peacetime problems we will more clearly see our strengths and weaknesses and adjust our training more accordingly. Morale in the Corps is high and a fine spirit of cooperation with other Corps exists. This spirit of cooperation must be fostered to the point where our Corps motto, "Discipline by Example", is fully recognized and accepted. By using tact and diplomacy, as well as by setting the highest possible example for the troops in the Armed Services, we can do a great deal towards making man management a minor, instead of a major, problem.
128   Captain LUKER moved a vote of thanks to three Provost officers at

CAMP BORDEN who had, by their attention to detail and constant efforts towards adjusting routine to the needs of the officers assembled, contributed so much to the success of the conference. Unanimous approval was expressed and the conference adjourned.

APPENDIX B

The Hochwald Forest Battle, 25–26 February 1945

An account by Lieutenant George Wilkinson, No 8 Provost Company, 4 Canadian Armoured Division, of his activities during the Hochwald Forest battle on 25 and 26 February 1945.

Although the war in Europe was chronicled by historians, with meticulous detail, I have yet to read anything on the incident which resulted in a confrontation between 4 Canadian Armoured Division and 3rd Canadian Infantry Division on a 60 foot railway embankment in Balderberger Wood on the edge of the Hochwald Forest.

This is how it happened. 4 Armoured Division had passed through the Reichwald Forest and was moving south of Cleve, on the Bedberg/Loisendorf road. It was decided 4 Armoured Brigade should advance cross-country, over farmers' fields, at night using white tapes to guide the tanks over three separate routes. The move started around 2200 hours in cold, wet weather but, from frequent rains, the ground had become so soft that only two or three tanks could follow each other without bellying. As each tank stuck the following tank would bypass it, then stick. By the early hours of the morning only a handful of the brigade's tanks had made it to the start point, while the rest floundered about in a sea of mud, spinning their tracks and belching smoke.

It was a mad scene and, at this point, it was decided to switch the advance to the road. Sergeant Harris and I set off to recce the route south of Udem. We had stopped on the edge of a small stream to check our map when, suddenly, an infantryman came out of the woods waving his rifle to attract our attention. He was a company commander from the Algonquin Regiment and wanted a ride to a farmhouse, which we could see about 500 yards to our front. We agreed, and he hopped on the engine bonnet for the short ride. As I drove into the farmyard he jumped off and tore into the house. The next thing we know he was herding a bunch of terrified German civilians out of the house hollering "Rouse" at the top of his voice. He told us he had been watching the house for some time and was pretty sure there were no German soldiers in it. He asked us to stop where we picked him up to tell his CSM to move the company forward. Sure enough, back at the stream, we could see his company deployed along the bank. The CSM came over to us and, when we told him what had happened, he just rolled his eyes and said, "That's 'Dagger Dan' for you." Sergeant Harris, never one to pass up a good billet, decided to move his section forward into the house as he figured the Algonquins would not stay there very long. "Besides", he asked, "Did you notice the steaks cooking on the kitchen stove?" I also decided to move in with the section for the night. It was a most welcome respite after the cold, wet night we had just experienced. After our steak dinner I piled into my sleeping bag. (Three of the best things that happened to me during the war was that sleeping bag, which I had bought in Normandy from "Deceased Officers Kit Stores", a pair of flannel pyjamas, courtesy of the Red Cross, and my tank suit.) My OC said he could always find me in one of the three.

About midnight I was rudely awakened by my OC with a change of plans. The axis was to be switched from the road, which was breaking down, to the railway track leading through the Hochwald Forest. I was ordered to take two men and recce the track and lay assault telephone wire as we progressed. The plan was to move the armoured brigade up the track and attack at first light. The telephone control was necessary as the embankment was about 60 feet high and there would be a requirement to stop upcoming tanks, and transport wounded back down the line. Armed with our rolls of telephone cable we started up the track, leaving one man at the start point. It was pitch black and deathly still at this time, although earlier in the evening heavy shell and mortar fire had been encountered. About 0300 hours we had traversed about a mile or so when, suddenly, out of the darkness came a whispered challenge, "Halt, who goes there?" "Provost", I answered. "Provost!" came back the astonished reply, "What the hell are you doing up here?" and "Get your bloody heads down." In the dim light I could see two infantrymen in a slit trench. We slid in beside them and were astonished to learn they were a forward platoon of the 2nd Infantry Division's Black Watch. Apparently we had been, literally, walking along a front line. Shortly after that a line crosser was shot as he bumped into an adjoining section's position.

We explained our assignment and decided to hole up with the Black Watch and wait for 4 Division to start their move. Everything was set. Not quite! By first light nothing had happened because 10 Infantry Brigade said they could not move their carriers and half-tracks up the rail line, to support the armoured brigade, unless the track rails were removed. The 8th and 9th Field Squadrons commenced stripping the tracks from the rail line. This was accomplished by rolling out two complete rolls of cordtex, one along each rail. Single 4 ounce cartridges of 808 charges were split, placed on the cordtex and rammed down between the rail and tiebolt over each tie. The resulting demolition stripped the 90 pound rails from the track leaving the steel ties to be pushed off by hand. Unfortunately, this played havoc with my telephone cables causing numerous breaks in the line. I had to repeatedly walk back down the track tracing the wire and repairing the breaks. Trouble was, the further I moved back down the line, the more I encountered other phone cables from adjoining units moving up into our area. Before splicing a break I hooked up my phone to check with my two pointsmen. At a particularly bad break I encountered several lines and, inadvertently, tied into a wrong line. The next thing I heard was someone saying "7 Brigade Headquarters". "7 Brigade Headquarters", I asked? Answer, "Yeah, who's this?" "Never mind" said I, desperately trying to disconnect my phone, but the irate 7 Brigade operator was now vigorously cranking his field phones sending shocks down the line with each crank. I think he thought the Fifth Column was tapping his line.

On reaching the starting point I learned, from the engineers, that the operation would be delayed until the tracks were cleared. So, my two pointsmen and I moved into a house below the railroad track, with Sergeant Buttimer's section, to spend the night. It was uneventful, apart from the fact that the engineers blew a 6 foot length of ties and steel tracks, which demolished Buttimer's section truck. Fortunately the driver, who normally slept in it, had elected to sleep in the house.

At first light Buttimer awakened me and said, "Get a load of this". There, 60 feet above us silhouetted on the skyline, were the tanks and half-tracks of the 4th Armoured Division facing east and facing them, heading west, were Bren Gun Carriers and trucks of the 3rd Infantry Division. Nothing was moving except the drivers, who were arguing over whose route it was. What a schimozzle! If the Germans in the Hochwald could see this, they must have thought we had all gone nuts. I got up on the track to try to sort things out but just then a group of very clean, nattily attired staff officers from Corps Headquarters arrived on the scene, to complete my nightmare. I recall being summoned before this august group to explain this SNAFU. My brigade major was very supportive of me, particularly when one of the staff officers turned out to be an Assistant Provost Marshal from Corps Headquarters who, on realizing that the dirty, unshaven and bedraggled officer well camouflaged in a tank suit, was a provost officer, was being less than charitable. My opposite number from 3rd Division Provost, Lt John Dowsett who had arrived on the scene, didn't fare much better. After much discussion it was decided that the route would remain Green Route Up (4th Division) and 3rd Division would use the Sonsbeck/Udem road as their axis.

My troubles were not completely over however, as my OC then advised me that Sergeant Harris' section, which had remained warm and dry in the farmhouse we had "captured", had been attacked by Germans hiding in the next farm after the Algonquins moved out. Corporal Tuna, coming down to join the section, had missed the farm entrance and stopped at the next house to turn around when a German soldier threw a hand grenade at him and blew the right front tire off his jeep, wounding him in the wrist and neck. He wheeled the jeep around and tore off back to the farmhouse on which the Germans opened fire, wounding two more men in Harris' section. Fortunately another company of Algonquins moved in to secure the situation. All this happened on the 25/26th February 1945 (my 26th birthday). Not one of my good days in the war, I guess.

APPENDIX C

Provost are Watchdogs for Canadians in Europe

Captain W J Dabros, Canadian Provost Corps

The twenty-first anniversary of the Canadian Provost Corps (21 June 1961) marked the completion of almost a decade of service for its members in Europe. These services include military operations as well as normal detachment police work, and demand that the Service Policeman performs the tasks of traffic expert, driving examiner, soldier, diplomat, police official, and even nursemaid, among others.

The Primary Role

Nestled in the picturesque Province of North Rhine-Westphalia of the industrial Ruhr valley, 4 Canadian Infantry Brigade Group maintains its vigil against aggression as part of the NATO Shield. Within this framework, 4 Provost Platoon provides the necessary provost resources to enable this highly mobile striking force to perform its task.

To maintain its fighting efficiency, training within the Brigade Group is continual. Commencing with individual sub-unit and unit training, and culminating in three complete Brigade Group or NATO concentrations and exercices in the late summer and early fall each year, the soldiers of 4 Provost Platoon are constantly called upon to perform their functions. These tasks include routine reconnaissance, signing and manning, all in cooperation with the other military and civilian police forces in the areas of operations.

This is the primary role – Operations.

The Secondary but Major Role

Stretching about 30 miles throughout the land of "Dambuster" fame is what the German population affectionaly refer to as "Klein Canada" or

"Little Canada". Herein lies the secondary, but major, task of 4 Provost Platoon – law enforcement.

It is appreciated that law observance is far better than law enforcement. Law observance is the exercise of a desire and willingness from within to comply with established rules, whereas law enforcement is the exercise of a power from without, and generally against the will of the individual. There can be true law observance only if all citizens of "Little Canada" are awake to their responsibilities to fulfil their obligations to Canada of good soldiers and citizens.

There are approximately 15,400 soldiers, dependents and sponsored civilians living in this area in Canadian permanent married quarters and German housing, located in the three towns of Soest, Werl and Hemer. These soldiers and civilians operate more than 3,000 privately owned motor vehicles. They are provided with all the facilities found in a comparable community in Canada. From their arrival until departure from Germany they depend on the capable Service Policemen for the provision of all police services, for the Provost Platoon bears full responsiblity for maintaining law and order in each community of "Little Canada".

The provision of police services in the communities of "Little Canada" is a constant requirement since all soldiers and Canadian civilians do not accompany the Brigade Group on training exercises. To this end 4 Provost Platoon has been augmented with an additional 26 Service Policemen and 32 interpreters, typists and others who remain in "home locations" to provide this essential service. Conversely, when members of the Platoon are not required for military operations they are dispersed among rthe detachments in each community and Platoon Headquarters to assist in "municipal" police work.

The coordination of all provost resources is done at Fort Henry, Brandholz, in the office of Major J M Walsh, CD, the Assistant Provost Marshal and Commanding Officer. With a policy of "enforcement, with assistance and cooperation" major strides have been made in the past year to improve the services and efficiency of the local Canadian Police force. This is borne out by the fact that local German authorities have never exercised their right to demand primary jurisdiction in cases involving Canadians. The keynote to these successes is devotion to duty and excellent cooperations with the German Civilian Police. Some of the problems, accomplishments and endeavours of 4 Provost Platoon in this theatre are discussed below.

Registration of Vehicles

On 1 March 1959 4 Canadian Infantry Brigade Group, by agreement with the British Army On The Rhine, assumed the responsibilty for the registration of privately owned vehicles of all Canadian military personnel, dependents, sponsored civilians and organizations in the Federal Republic of Germany. The supervision, operation and control of this registry office, known as the British Forces Germany (Canadian) Licence Office, was subsequently made the responsibility of 4 Provost Platoon. Vehicles had to be certified roadworthy and be insured for third party risks before registration; approved Canadian-type licence plates were issued; and persons were issued with driving permits if in possession of valid Canadian permits.

As the number of vehicles increased, so did traffic offences and accidents. It soon became apparent that Canadian drivers were not familiar with international traffic signs, rules of the road, and driving on narrow, cobblestone roads. A better system was required whereby drivers would be tested before being issued with a permit, and potential "road-killers" would be removed from the wheel and educated before they become involved in serious accidents.

Thus began a period of eight months' trials, frustrations, errors, recommendations and conferences, culminating in the production of regulations detailing everything that a Canadian driver or car owner need know for the operation of his car in the European theatre. Regulations are printed in booklet form and issued to all individual driver and car owners. The job of producing this booklet was given to Captain Dabros, the author of this article, in conjunction with legal officers.

Some innovations of interest in the new "book of rules" are the adoption of a 12–point demerit system similar to that in Ontario; practical and written tests for driver applicants at a Central Testing Bureau; a Safety Council to review individual cases and recommend action; and a Traffic Offender's Clinic to teach and assess those drivers who have had a licence suspended, or who have been advised by the Safety Council to attend the clinic.

The inauguration of the "new system" was acclaimed by Canadian and German police and press as "the greatest single step towards saving life on our highways".

Driver Testing and Education

"The greatest single step towards saving life on our highways" is only as good as its enforcement. This "step" was, therefore, supplemented with the establishment of a Traffic Section within 4 Provost Platoon under the direction of Captain J G Conroy. Their immediate tasks were the establishment of the Central Testing Bureau and Traffic Offender's Clinic. In preparation for their tasks, personnel were trained at the United States Military Police Traffic School at Oberammergau in Southern Germany.

Within a short time written and practical tests were established to examine potential drivers on rules of the road, common sense application of basic driving principles, recognition of international traffic signs, sight, depth perception, field of vision, colour, coordination and reaction time.

Provided with the most modern equipment and training aids, a course in driving techniques, rules of the road, driver courtesy and attitude was designed for the traffic offender. The aim, of course, is to educate and return the worthy driver to the road, and to permanently "ground" the incorrigibles.

Now the programme had acquired depth. As the Central Testing Bureau swung into operation the results were staggering. Sixty percent of all applicants failed to qualify as drivers! The news spread quickly throughout the area – 4 Provost Platoon will not allow an unsafe driver on the road. Senior German police officials from the surrounding counties, and the Safety Committee of the Soest County Council flocked to the Platoon to examine this latest venture of the Canadian Service Police. Their verdicts were summed up by Polizeihauptkommissar Hackbarth of Soest – "Excellent!"

With the adult driving problems seemingly in check, Canada's future drivers were next to receive attention. Armed with bicycles, tricycles and scooters thousands of Canadian school children are daily exposed to the hazards of traffic. They, too, require knowledge of traffic signs, rules of the road, police and mechanical signals. Can this be done in such a way so that they will absorb the knowledge?

The solution came unexpectedly. While visiting the Iserlohn Chief of Police Captain Dabros was informed of a mobile "Traffic Garden" consisting of pedal-cars, scooters, bicycles and traffic signs, designed for the instruction of children and owned by Iserlohn County Police. A request – an agreement – and another example of cooperation came to pass as the Iserlohn Traffic Garden rumbled towards the Canadian schools at Soest, Werl and Hemer.

After a short lecture to each class students moved out into the schoolyard where a miniature "downtown" area had been laid out complete with roads, traffic signs and lights. Under Provost supervision students applied their classroom knowledge to practice. Groups of students moved around the course in vehicles provided while others, employed as policemen, directed traffic and issued "tickets" to erring drivers.

Was it a success? This question is best answered by a quotation from a

German newspaper, the Westfalenpost: "The question whether the boys and girls absorbed and enjoyed the traffic school can be spared . . . It would be appreciated very much if the Iserlohn Traffic Garden would give a 'performance' at the German schools in Soest in the near future."

Enforcing the Law

Although German law provides that a vehicle must be certified roadworthy, and be insured for third party risks prior to registration, and these prerequisites are, in fact, met by Canadians who receive a safety sticker at time of registration, there are always some irresponsible individuals who, shortly after registration, allow their vehicles to deteriorate into hazards or cancel insurance. In addition, easily accessible German beer along the highways increases the driving problem.

An obvious remedy is preventive police action and, once again, the Traffic Section swung into action. The German police admitted that they had similar problems with their civilians and agreed to venture with 4 Provost Platoon into this new project – traffic check points. In very little time the project was in operation. Code words were allotted acceptable points throughout "Little Canada" and lighting plants, as required, were obtained through Brigade resources. Now, a 'phoned code word' by either police force would cause a check point to be established within hours, consisting of two Service policemen and two German policemen.

News spreads quickly in this community and it became apparent that check points have a psychological effect on drivers. "Crocks" disappeared, insurance policies were renewed, registration documents were put in order and, most important, the incidence of impaired driving dropped very noticeably. It is difficult to estimate how many accidents are prevented through the establishment of check points, but statistics show that they are having a good effect. By the combined efforts of 4 Provost Platoon and the German police potential "killers" cannot develop.

Safe Driving Week

"Little Canada" now boasted one of the lowest accident rates, of comparable communities under similar circumstances, and it appeared that the Provost Platoon was employing all conceivable means to keep it that way. However, Major Walsh was not satisfied. "There are still too many foolish accidents being caused by poor driving habits", he stated. "Although driver examinations make every reasonable attempt to determine driver qualifications, they do not make any prediction as to what the driver will do after he gets his licence. Some drivers are irresponsible and will not drive safely. Others will deteriorate in ability with advanced age, or for other reasons. Therefore, there is a need to deal with the driver who cannot, or will not, drive safely."

As a result April 23–29 was proclaimed Safe Driving Week, by Brigadier Cameron B Ware, for all privately-owned motor vehicles within the Brigade. In his remarks, to officially open the programme, Brigadier Ware defined the aim: "to demonstrate to ourselves and others that we can prevent unnecessary accidents".

Once again 4 Provost Platoon "took to the road" to enforce the programme and, once again, the German police offered their assistance. The strength of the Traffic Section was greatly increased to ensure constant coverage of all roads by patrols.

Various leaflets were printed and distributed daily to all Canadian drivers as reminders of their responsibility.

Each day a driver was selected from each community (Soest, Werl, Hemer) and awarded DM 50 as "Driver of the Day". Selections were made by Provost and German police through the use of a standard check list. Drivers who attained high marks, and were likely to win awards, were stopped and their cars were examined for safety and roadworthiness. All drivers were stopped and warned of their shortcomings.

At the end of the week the results spoke for the success of the programme. Decreases in traffic accidents included 9% in major accidents, 18% in minor accidents, 36% in impaired driving and 40% in minor offences. How did the public react? Acclaimed throughout the German press as "The Canadian's Relentless Battle Against Apathy", they summed up the week's activities with: "It is hoped that the indifference towards death and destruction was broken down, and an awareness developed of the individual responsibility each has in the prevention of highway accidents."

Encouraged by what was accomplished by providing incentive and reminders to citizens, a permanent Safe Driving Programme was instituted by 4 Provost Platoon. A Safe Driving mascot, "Fritzi Fox", was adopted and has become synonymous with safe driving. Through messages by Fritzi Fox and the unit news column, The Watchdog Beat, which appear in the Brigade newspaper The Beaver, citizens are constantly reminded of their responsibilities in traffic. Safe driving days have been named throughout the year and plans are now being made to provide trophies, pennants and pins monthly to units and individuals for accident-free driving in an effort to keep the roads of "Little Canada" safe.

Investigations

Despite the efficiency, preventative policing and cooperation of police forces, and the efforts and cooperation of citizens, every community has a degree of crime. Although the crime rate in "Little Canada" is especially low, crime does exist.

To cope with all criminal cases of a special or technical nature, a Special Investigation Detachment is organized at Platoon Headquarters. This compares to a "Detective Branch" within a civilian police organization. The case load in Europe is very diversified and varies from those triable under the National Defence Act to those under the Criminal Code of Canada. In addition, the conduct of crime prevention surveys is the responsibility of the SID.

Since most cases involve German nationals as well as Canadians, cooperation with German police must be of the highest order. SID personnel work very closely with their opposite numbers in the KRIPO, which is the German Special Investigation Branch. Scientific aids to investigations, which are not available at 4 Provost Platoon, and expert opinions, ie, paint analysis, etc, are obtained through the USMP Crime Laboratory at Frankfurt, who give freely of their time and personnel when assistance is requested.

SID personnel work in teams, each with their own highly qualified interpreters. Through a policy of cooperation, and a theme of "5% inspiration, 95% perspiration" in investigative work, they are frequently acclaimed in the German press for the successful completion of their cases.

Liaison With Other Police Forces

If it would be necessary to select one factor that contributes most to the successful completion of tasks of 4 Provost Platoon, it would be liaison with other police forces. Whether the tasks entail military or "municipal" police work, this spirit of cooperation and friendship prevails.

Contrary to some beliefs, liaison is done at all levels and the friendship that it fosters is not restricted to duty. A recent example of this fact is provided by Lance Corporal G R Henderson prior to his departure from 4 Provost Platoon to Canada. Honoured at a party organized by the German police "rank and file", this Service policeman was presented with a handmade souvenir shield for "wunderbare Kameradschaft" (wonderful comradeship) and "gute Zusammmenarbeit" (good cooperation) while enforcing law and order in the area of Soest. The fifteen-inch shield bearing a hand-wrought key, which is the town crest, and a German policeman's hat badge mounted in a mahogany base, was presented by two German police constables who blistered their hands filing the key crests out of sheet metal. The remarks at the presentation are significant: "You symbolize the close fraternity which has developed between our two forces".

Community Activities

The unheralded undertakings of any police force are generally its contributions to the welfare of the community. From locating lost children to organizing youth activities, policemen give unselfishly of their time and effort. Their aim is to provide facilities for the youth to expend their energies, and to foster good relations between the youth of the community and the police force. Their only reward is a feeling of accomplishment for the welfare of the community.

Such is the case in "Little Canada". Members of 4 Provost Platoon volunteer their spare time to organize and supervise such pursuits as Little League Hockey, baseball, scouts, Cubs, swimming classes, etc. Contribution to three major projects are discussed below.

Scouting: Shortly after his arrival, as a member of 4 Provost Platoon, Sergeant J R Wilson became Regional Commissioner of Boy Scouts for the Brigade in Europe. He is the highest qualified Scouter in the Brigade and is responsible for the training of leaders and Group Committees. One of his first tasks was to reorganize the Brigade area into a region of three districts, thus improving liaison between the Scout Organization in Europe and the National Council in Canada. The Organization now boasts a membership of 550 Cubs, 220 Scouts and 77 Scouters.

Little League Hockey: The 1960–61 season saw 183 potential hockey "greats" in action in the Soest area. Between 8 to 14 years of age, these mighty mites entertained both German and Canadian spectators alike with their prowess and knowledge of the world's fastest game. Teaching these youngsters is the voluntary task of Lance Sergeant H D MacKenzie, 4 Provost Platoon, who is head coach of the circuit.

Swimming Classes: As applications for membership to the various youth organizations were received, it became quite obvious that a large majority of the children could not swim. Volunteering to rectify this situation, Sergeant Bill Woolley and Lance Corporal Henderson organized weekly swimming classes at the Soest City Pool during the early evening hours. Attendance varied between 40 to 50 boys at each class, ranging in age from 8 to 10 years. All boys were non-swimmers when they started training, and some of them had an absolute fear of the water. To date, 15 boys have "graduated", being able to swim the length of the Olympic-type pool in various ways. "Graduates" usually remain with classes to assist in teaching other boys.

Inter-Unit Activities

Although the major efforts of 4 Provost Platoon were directed to providing the most efficient services possible for the Brigade and its communities, internal unit activities during this period were not left dormant. On the contrary, Service Policemen of 4 Provost Platoon were frequently called upon to fulfil their primary functions as soldiers, in the forms of parades, inspections and training, and it was necessary to keep the internal organization abreast of new developments and techniques in the maintenance of law and order.

A basic requirement for prevention policing is a police force which is conspicuous by its presence throughout the community. This acts as a deterrent to the commission of crime and encourages citizens to report incidents that may come to their attention. To this end the Provost Platoon succeeded in obtaining specially painted and marked vehicles, two-way radios and blue flasher lights installed on vehicles for emergency use. This enables the Platoon to provide constant police coverage and to communicate rapidly between communities and with German police as required.

During a liaison visit late last year, Colonel A L Brady, DSO, CD, Provost Marshal of the Canadian Forces, toured the Brigade and inspected 4 Provost Platoon Detachments at Soest, Werl and Hemer. After dealing with the police aspects of the unit, and meeting German police officials, Colonel Brady spent several days observing Provost operations in the field during a NATO exercise, prior to returning to Canada.

For the first time in the history of the Canadian Provost Corps, Service Police Group 3 Trades and Tests were authorized to provisionally qualify personnel for the higher trade until they could attend and pass the qualifying course in Canada. In January 1961, 31 Service policemen of 4 Provost Platoon underwent six days of written and practical examinations, following a two-week preparatory course, with high trades pay as an incentive for success. The fact that only nine candidates were successful speaks well for the high degree of military, technical and police ability and skill expected of a Service policeman.

In conjunction with its primary role of maintaining its fighting efficiency, not only must the unit be trained for war but its stores, weapons and equipment must be of the highest standard. To this end, and in order to meet the members of the various units, a series of inspections are conducted by the Brigade Commander, Brigadier Ware. In a brief address, Brigadier Ware expressed his pride "in having such a unit as 4 Provost Platoon under my command".

Conclusion

Such are the tasks and accomplishments of 4 Provost Platoon in Europe. Theirs is a dual role – soldiers first, and policemen second. As soldiers they stand ready with 4 Canadian Infantry Brigade Group as guardians of the peace, prepared to move this force into battle and to fight if necessary. As policemen they are exposed to a panorama of human troubles, worries and sufferings through which they feel the pulse of the community, and the men who devote their lives to this duty must necessarily be as human as those with whom they deal. They are truly the "Watchdogs" for Canadians and Canada's NATO Brigade in Europe.

APPENDIX D

Military Police in the Congo

A report of military police duties in the Congo by Warrant Officer Marcel Fortier, Canadian Provost Corps.

During the first week of August, 1960 WO1 Arthur Heymans, RSM Valcartier Detention Barracks, was ordered to report to Barriefield Camp, Kingston, Ontario where he subsequently was appointed RSM Canadian Contingent. While digesting this information over drinks with friends, my telephone rang at 2200 hours. It was my Detachment Commander, Captain W (Bill) Fiddes, Quebec Provost Detachment. He asked if I was sitting down, after assuring him I was he informed me to be ready to leave for Trenton in two days as he and I were going to the Congo, soonest.

At midnight August 15, 1960 Captain Fiddes and I departed Quebec City, by train, arriving in Kingston the following morning. Members of Kingston Provost Detachment met and transported us to Barriefield Camp for the necessary documentation, medicals, needles, etc, etc. I was assigned room 35, which had just been vacated by RSM Heymans who left that morning for the Congo. The next few days were spent being introduced to new equipment, such as snake-bite kits, and the first new issue of Stirling sub-machine guns, a much improved weapon over the pipe-fitter's dream (Sten) of World War II fame. Time was found in getting to know the component parts of this new weapon and to fire it on the nearby ranges. It is safe to say that the first draft of Canadian Provost Corps were qualified on the Stirling sub-machine gun and Browning 9 mm Pistol before leaving for the Congo.

A few days after RMS Heyman's draft left for the Congo, we were advised to expect trouble on landing in Leopoldville. It appeared that after disembarking at Ndjili airport, some 15 miles from Leopoldville, Heymans' group was attacked by Congolese soldiers who beat some Canadians with rifle butts and stole watches and wallets. As a result, our departure was delayed until August 23, 1960 when Captain Fiddes and I reported to Ottawa for a briefing – the word was "Go". Wednesday, August 24, dawned sunny and cool. After rising at 0530 hours, breakfast at 0600, pay parade at 0630, we left for Trenton at 0730, arriving at 1000, just in time to greet the Provost Marshal, Colonel Brady, who arrived at 1030.

Our flight aboard a RCAF North Star departed Trenton at 1230 hours August 24, 1960. On board were the cockpit crew of 3, the flight engineer and the Loadmaster. The nominal roll of the Canadian Provost Corps personnel attached to United Nations Headquarters, to form a part of ONUC Military Police Company, consisted of: Captain W Fiddes (who, in early October, left to join a United Nations training cadre in Kamina), WO2 Fortier, ML, Ssgt Pitre, JPE, Sgt Martin, EL (involved in the investigation of Lumumba's death, the first Premier of Independent Congo, assassinated in February, 1961), Sgt Pentland, DD, Cpl Lauson, JDA (much in demand by Colonel Mobutu, as unofficial liaison between Mobutu and United Nations Headquarters and unofficial bodyguard), LCpl Glaude, GJ, LCpl Huot, JGB, LCpl Labelle, MOM, Pte Schink, RJJE, LCpl Soucy, JCR, LCpl St Amant, HJ, no other troops were aboard. The remaining space was used to carry one Jeep loaded with K-rations and ammo; two very large generators and a variety of other material essential to the Canadian Contingent. In today's jet age our flight from Trenton, Ontario, via Gander, The Azores, Dakar, Accra to Ndjili airport, Leopoldville, reads like a horror story. For that particular flight the North Star was a freighter; therefore, it was not pressurized for altitudes above 9,500 feet, and travelled a leisurely 230 mph. The West Edmonton Mall's famous ride, "Drop of Doom" cannot compare or match the thrill of flying through "Thunderbolt Alley" (Senegal to the Congo) in thunderstorms, at 9,500 feet! We arrived at Ndjili Airport at 0830 hours, August 26, 1960. Preparing to land the pilot ordered us to hide our weapons under our jump seats. Our protests on being deprived of our personal weapons fell on deaf ears. Being good soldiers we did as we were ordered. The aircraft landed and stopped mid-field, far from the Terminal Building. On disembarking I noticed a red truck speeding towards us; I had expected white painted United Nations transport. Anxious seconds were spent trying to identify the vehicle which, to our relief, turned out to be a United Nations 10 ton Mercedes truck. We immediately loaded our baggage, retrieved our weapons and got ourselves on board. By this time the Congolese Army was running towards us, but no shots were fired. As we departed from the aircraft it left for parts unknown (its propellers had never stopped idling!). Driving across the airfield we noticed other troops racing to intercept the Congolese. No further interference was encountered on our way to Leopoldville. Authorities there ordered us to report to Canadian Headquarters located in the Athénee Royale. *Note 1.* The soldiers intercepting the Congolese Army at Ndjili turned out to be members of the United Nations Ghana Brigade. *Note 2.* Athénee Royale was a boarding school until white teachers (mostly Belgians) had left the country. United Nations took possession and turned it over to the Canadian Contingent.

After being fed, assigned quarters and allowed to sleep a few hours, we were ordered by Canadian Headquarters to conduct disciplinary patrols of the City. However, United Nations Headquarters informed me that our stay with the Canadian Contingent was temporary as the Canadian Provost Corps came under United Nations responsibility and we should take our orders from Colonel Hajiboy, United Nations Chief of Staff, Administration Officer and Acting Provost Marshal. The remainder of the weekend, 28–29 August 1960, was spent setting up an Orderly Room, familiarizing ourselves with the City and organizing patrols in conjunction with the other members of ONUC Military Police Company.

Reconnaissance Patrols began on August 29, 1960, less than three days after arrival. Our patrols established contact with Mobutu's MPs and what was left of the City's Police Force. Contact was also made with MPs of other Contingents. For the record, on August 29, 1960 Canadian Provost Corps made its first arrest; a Canadian soldier was arrested for stealing a car and assaulting the owner. He was immediately arraigned before the Canadian Contingent Commander, ordered to pay damages of $181.70, awarded a fine of $75 plus 21 days CB. The efficient and fair manner in which the case was disposed of was a first class example to other foreign troops, and was the subject of much favourable comment at United Nations Headquarters. The Canadian Provost Corps had good reason to be proud of its first accomplishment, not only was it good for morale but we knew we had the confidence of our superiors and their support.

During our 6 month tour as United Nations Peace Keepers in the Congo, Provost were very much in demand since, not only were we blessed with qualified and experienced Military Policemen eg, 3 qualified special group 4; 1 qualified group 3 clerk/group 3 Administration; 4 qualified group 3 SP; 3 qualified SP2, and all were bilingual, so necessary in a country whose functional language is French. At the outset Canadian Provost personnel conducted all patrols, conducted investigations, prepared reports of United Nations Headquarters, provided and manned an information service, and provided assistance in the form of liaison personnel. Other Military Police were left with little or nothing to do. It was soon obvious Provost personnel were overworked, something had to change. Since we had established good relations with the other members of ONUC Military Police Company, arrangements were made to have patrols consist of any number of unilingual MPs with, always, a member of the Canadian Provost Corps present to provide linguistic (French/English) support. An interesting incident occurred when the Indian Contingent would not accept assistance from the Canadian Military Police. Two Indian Sergeants (one a cook) went out on some mission without information on the local situation and without contacting the Provost on duty in the Orderly Room. Later the Officer in Charge Indian Contingent reported to me that two of his Sergeants were captured and he did not know where they were being held, would the Canadians help. The "captured Indian Sergeants" were found in a police compound, locked up in a steel room with no windows. The temperature at the time was over 100 degrees F and humidity 92 degrees!

The impressions gained at the outset gave rise to much serious trouble ahead for United Nations troops and for some leaders trying to create order out of anarchy. Since some form of government had been formed, only two and half months earlier, by ill-prepared and unqualified people, ie, President Kasavubu had experience as a grade 2 clerk in the postal business, Patrice Lumumba, the first Premier had some training in Moscow (he was assassinated in February, 1961. The investigation was conducted with the assistance of the late Sergeant Ernest Martin, Canadian Provost Corps). Mobutu had recently promoted himself to Colonel from the rank of Warrant Officer, 2nd class. It was also learned that, in a population of 20 million, only 22 were known to have University education. The main language spoken, of course, is French, with over 200 dialects scattered around the country. A thumb-nail sketch of Zaire's tense history appeared in the Ottawa Citizen, Sunday, April 19, 1992, authored by Alan Cowell, of the New York Times. He is presently in Kinshasa (formerly Leopoldville) and is worth repeating: "1960 – As independence movements sweep Africa, Belgium, with little warning, grants the country independence. Its first Premier is Patrice Lumumba. Within two weeks of independence police and army mutiny. Katanga Province – now Shaba – tries to secede, South Kasai follows. Belgium sends in Paratroopers, the United Nations flies in Peacekeepers; these stay until 1964. Power struggles continue. Lumumba is murdered." This is what faced the Canadian Provost Detachment, the ONUC Military Police Company and the remainder of the Peacekeeping troops on arrival in August, 1960. What passed as a government, in

Leopoldville, could not hope to exercise control over the five provinces that made up the "Belgian Congo"; therefore, in the absence of police, troops to aid civil power, a so-called Government, held together by the United Nations presence, confusion, chaos, disorder and, finally, anarchy, reared its ugly head. Looting, raping, vicious incidents occurring in the native quarters, large demonstrations against United Nations Headquarters, threats of attack by armoured columns, theft (over 50 vehicles stolen from the United Nations in a two week period – most were recovered by good police work). The appearance of French Mirage jets over the City quickly put an end to the tank threat and helped immeasurably put down the Congolese military threat. United Nations Headquarters responded by putting on a "show of force" and establishing curfews. When a fire-fight developed one night, near United Nations Headquarters, it was the ONUC Military Police who were ordered out to patrol the City and stop the shooting. All Military Police from Canada, Indonesia, India, Denmark and Norway mounted a fighting patrol and were successful in stopping the shooting in one area and continued their patrol until quiet returned to the City. We were successful in stopping Congolese "policemen" from administering their brand of law and order to a group of civilians, at a bus stop. In their view, striking unarmed civilians with their rifle butts was a good way to instill discipline and break up small gatherings, regardless of the fact the people were waiting for a bus. Before going out on this patrol Sergeant Martin and I proceeded to General Van Horne's office to get written orders regarding the return of incoming fire, thus exposing the men to criminal charges and putting the United Nations in an unfavourable light. The General ordered the Irish C of S to "come up with something that will authorize United Nations troops to return fire when fired upon". This document was sent to National Defence Headquarters, Ottawa, and it eventually found its way to the Military Police Museum in Camp Borden, Ontario. It was the first, and last, time Military Police were ordered to provide a fighting patrol, a task normally assigned to Infantry or Armour. There was, at the time, a Duty Company of Infantry at United Nations Headquarters plus some 10,000 troops scattered about the City. Perhaps the purse carrying officer who ordered the patrol was more comfortable dealing with disciplined troops! In any event, everything went well, the job was done to everyone's satisfaction, no shots were fired by our side, and the Canadian Provosts earned more kudos!

During our first tour members of the Canadian Provost Corps were employed on various tasks including; escort to VIPs; bodyguards; investigations; patrols; liaison; general police duties; eg, traffic control, parking, security at VIP meetings, parties, banquets, conferences, etc. They were, also, employed as instructors in the City and elsewhere, ie, Captain Fiddes was employed in Kamina at the Firefighters and Police school. Because of our expertise in police sciences, coupled with our being bilingual, we were privileged to participate in many high level meetings. We provided assistance wherever and whenever it was needed. Since Captain Fiddes had left in early October, 1960, arrangements were made, with the approval of the representatives of other Military Police Contingents, whereby orders from United Nations Headquarters for Military Police assistance were, for the most part, channelled through the Orderly Room for action. This worked very well and improved not only communications, but working conditions for all concerned.

To make everything a real joy, insofar as life in the Congo was concerned, we assisted United Nations Headquarters in finding suitable quarters for all Military Police, including offices and cooking facilities, on Major Ruwet Street, not too far from United Nations Headquarters and the Canadian Officers Mess. General Van Horne occupied a beautiful estate overlooking the Congo River, as did Brigadier Rhykkie, only a short distance from our quarters. A company of infantry, from the Tunisia Battalion, surrounded the General's grounds. At the other end of Major Ruwet Street is Boulevard Albert (renamed Boulevard du 30 Juin, a reference to Independence) and where was located a marvellous, small French restaurant named "Le Petit Pont". A Senior Noncommissioned Officers' Mess (Canadian) located behind the large grounds at the rear of Canadian Contingent Headquarters, between the Ghanaian Ambassador's Residence and Tunisian Infantry grounds. (Later the Officers' Mess found itself in the direct line of fire between Tunisian forces and Congolese Army troops trying to arrest the Ghanaian Ambassador. Several rounds of machine gun fire were exchanged through the screened windows of the Officers' Mess, and a 2 pdr HE shell exploded just above the door leading to the bar of the Officers' Mess. The barman was slightly injured when he jumped over the bar, striking his mouth on his watch as he "hit the dirt". Colonel Kokolo, Congolese Army, was killed during this incident.) While in the Mess, awaiting a quiet period, I learned that Colonel Mobutu had requested the services of Corporal Lauzon, Canadian Provost Corps, to escort him during his visit to the hospital to view the body of Colonel Kokolo – another function performed by Canadian Provost Corps which had a calming effect on a very tense situation. It might be of interest to some that the only time I was required to carry a side arm or SMG was on our initial fighting patrol. The Noncommissioned Officers on patrol carried side arms but never had to draw them. The point here is that I believe it was the cool-headedness of the men that calmed explosive situations; certainly it was confidence in themselves, and in their training, that commanded respect. It was a pleasure, indeed it was an honour, to serve with such men.

As feared, the workload, coupled with the heat and humidity, began taking their toll. Flu-like illnesses, high temperatures and skin infections began showing up. Bouts of depression, lasting for short periods, appeared and were quickly dealt with. Large sores appeared on men who perspired heavily and did not towel-off properly. The most serious infection experienced was caused by a small, thread-like, white parasite (worm) found in vegetables, fruit, meat and water. Having received excellent advice and training from the medical staff in Trenton, and constantly being reminded to take precautions, we were able to protect ourselves to some extent; however, we did lose one man. He eventually died in Canada of an illness contacted in the Congo.

In conclusion, after serving six months in Equatorial Africa, with temperatures between 85 and 120 degrees F, humidity between 85 and 100 percent, almost daily thunderstorms, experiencing food shortages at the beginning of our tour (who can forget the beans, beans and more beans!), the constant exposure to infections, the continuous patrols and travel under very trying conditions, investigations of all kinds (a request from a foreign soldier for advice on inducing an abortion – weird!), rescue missions, etc., etc, – we would not miss this part of the Tour! What we would miss would be the camaraderie of comrades, the quiet conversations over a quart of excellent Belgian beer, the haggling over paintings and sculptures on the Ivory Market, travel around the countryside, the daily swim in the pool at the Athénee Royale, or the tennis games with my old pal, Ernie Martin. I almost forgot something else we would not miss, the horrible, old, old movies sent to us by concerned folks! Therefore, it was with mixed feelings that we left Leopoldville for Ndjili Airport. How comforting it was to see the 'big' North Star, motors idling, just outside the terminal and to see the smiling faces on our replacements, WO2 Don Watts and Sergeant Réne Boisvert – (I thought to myself, little do they know!). The experience gained in a peacekeeping roll made us appreciate what diplomats were exposed to. We had provided a safe haven for the American Ambassador and his family during one serious incident when some 2,000 angry Congolese wanted to kill him. Looking back, I'm glad National Defence Headquarters sent me, the experience helped immeasurably determine the course and direction I would take after my service in the Army was completed.